T0339429

ECONOMETRIC MODELLING AND FORECASTING OF TOURISM DEMAND

This insightful and timely volume provides a succinct, expert-led introduction to the latest developments in advanced econometric methodologies in the context of tourism demand modelling and forecasting.

Written by a plethora of worldwide experts on this topic, this book offers a comprehensive approach to tourism econometrics. Accurate demand forecasts are crucial to decision-making in the tourism industry and this book provides real-life tourism applications and the corresponding R code alongside theoretical foundations, in order to enhance understanding and practice amongst its readers. The methodologies introduced include the autoregressive distributed lag model, vector autoregression, time-varying parameter modelling, spatiotemporal econometric models, mixed-frequency forecasting, hybrid forecasting models, density forecasting, forecast combination techniques, judgemental forecasting, scenario forecasting under crises, and web-based tourism forecasting.

Embellished with insightful figures and tables throughout, this book is an invaluable resource for those using advanced econometric methodologies in their studies and research, including both undergraduate and postgraduate students, researchers, and practitioners.

Doris Chenguang Wu, Ph.D., is a Professor in the School of Business at Sun Yat-sen University, China. Her research interests include tourism demand forecasting and tourism big data analytics.

Gang Li, Ph.D., is a Professor of Tourism Economics in the School of Hospitality and Tourism Management at the University of Surrey, UK. His research interests include economic analysis and forecasting of tourism demand.

Haiyan Song, Ph.D., is Chan Chak Fu Professor of International Tourism in the School of Hotel and Tourism Management at the Hong Kong Polytechnic University. His research interests are in tourism demand modelling and forecasting, tourism supply chain management, and wine economics.

ECONOMETRIC MODELLING AND FORECASTING OF TOURISM DEMAND

Methods and Applications

Edited by
Doris Chenguang Wu, Gang Li
and Haiyan Song

Routledge
Taylor & Francis Group

LONDON AND NEW YORK

Cover image: Getty Images

First published 2023
by Routledge
4 Park Square, Milton Park, Abingdon, Oxon OX14 4RN

and by Routledge
605 Third Avenue, New York, NY 10158

Routledge is an imprint of the Taylor & Francis Group, an informa business

British Library Cataloguing-in-Publication Data
A catalogue record for this book is available from the British Library

ISBN: 978-1-032-21642-3 (hbk)
ISBN: 978-1-032-21641-6 (pbk)
ISBN: 978-1-003-26936-6 (ebk)

DOI: 10.4324/9781003269366

Typeset in Times New Roman
by codeMantra

Contents

Figures

Tables

Contributors

Chenyu Cao is a Ph.D. student in the School of Business at Sun Yat-sen University, China. His research interests include tourism demand modelling and forecasting and tourism data mining.

Zheng Chris Cao, Ph.D., is a Lecturer in Economics in the Aston Business School at Aston University, UK. His research interests are in tourism economics, economic development, globalisation, and applied macroeconometrics.

Jason Li Chen, Ph.D., is a Senior Lecturer in the School of Hospitality and Tourism Management at the University of Surrey, UK. His research interests include tourism economics and applications of quantitative research methods.

Mingming Hu, Ph.D., is an Associate Professor in the School of Business at Guangxi University, China. His research interests include tourism demand forecasting, tourism big data, and smart tourism.

Xiaoying Jiao, Ph.D., is a Research Assistant Professor in the School of Hotel and Tourism Management at the Hong Kong Polytechnic University, Hong Kong, China. Her research interests include tourism demand forecasting and spatial econometrics.

Gang Li, Ph.D., is a Professor of Tourism Economics in the School of Hospitality and Tourism Management at the University of Surrey, UK. His research interests include economic analysis and forecasting of tourism demand.

Mei Li is a postgraduate student in the School of Economics at Guangxi University, China. Her research interest is tourism demand forecasting with big data.

Vera Shanshan Lin, Ph.D, is an Associate Professor in the School of Management at Zhejiang University, China. Her research interests include tourism forecasting, big data analysis in tourism, and Chinese tourist behaviour.

Anyu Liu, Ph.D., is an Assistant Professor in the School of Hotel and Tourism Management at the Hong Kong Polytechnic University, Hong Kong, China. His research interests are in tourism demand modelling and forecasting, tourism's economic impact, and big data analytics.

Han Liu, Ph.D., is a Professor in the Center for Quantitative Economics and School of Business and Management at Jilin University, China. His research interests include applied econometrics related to tourism demand modelling and forecasting.

Xinyang Liu is a Ph.D. research student in the School of Hospitality and Tourism Management at the University of Surrey, UK. His research interests include tourism demand modelling and forecasting with a focus on the application and development of time series forecasting techniques.

Ying Liu is a Ph.D. student in the School of Business and Management at Jilin University, China. Her research interests include tourism demand modelling and forecasting, and macro-econometric analysis.

Yuan Qin is a Ph.D. student in the School of Management at Zhejiang University, China. Her research interests include tourism demand modelling and forecasting, tourist behaviour, smart tourism, and big data.

Richard T. R. Qiu, Ph.D., is an Assistant Professor in the School of Hotel and Tourism Management at the Hong Kong Polytechnic University, Hong Kong, China. His research interests are tourism economics and demand analysis, tourist choice modelling, and tourist behaviour analysis.

Shujie Shen, Ph.D., is a Senior Lecturer in the School of Organisations, Economy and Society at the University of Westminster, UK. Her research interests include applied econometrics and tourism demand forecasting.

Haiyan Song, Ph.D., is Chan Chak Fu Professor of International Tourism in the School of Hotel and Tourism Management at the Hong Kong Polytechnic University, Hong Kong, China. His research interests are in tourism demand modelling and forecasting, tourism supply chain management, and wine economics.

Long Wen, Ph.D., is an Assistant Professor in the School of Economics at the University of Nottingham Ningbo China, China. His main research interests are tourism economics, and tourism demand modelling and forecasting.

Doris Chenguang Wu, Ph.D., is a Professor in the School of Business at Sun Yat-sen University, China. Her research interests include tourism demand forecasting and tourism big data analytics.

Hongrun Wu, M.Sc., is a research assistant in the School of Hotel and Tourism Management at the Hong Kong Polytechnic University, Hong Kong, China. Her research interests include behavioural economics and tourism forecasting.

Peihuang Wu is a postgraduate student in the School of Business and Management at Jilin University, China. Her research interests focus on tourism demand modelling and forecasting.

Xinyan Zhang, Ph.D., is a Lecturer in the College of Professional and Continuing Education at the Hong Kong Polytechnic University, Hong Kong, China. Her research interests include information and communication systems, tourism management, tourism supply chain management, and tourism demand forecasting.

Xinyi Zhang is a Ph.D. student in the School of Management at Zhejiang University, China. Her research interests include tourist behaviour and service robots in tourism.

Xin Zhao is a postgraduate student in the School of Economics at Guangxi University, China. His research interest is tourism demand forecasting.

PREFACE

Accurate demand forecasts are crucial to decision-making in the tourism industry. They help tourism-related businesses make short-term pricing and operations management decisions and formulate long-term strategies. They also help governments decide on infrastructure investments and tourism-related policies. In recent years, tourism forecasting has received increasing attention from both scholars and industry practitioners for three main reasons. First, the tourism industry has changed considerably over the last few decades. It has not only grown significantly but also become increasingly volatile because of the disruptions and uncertainties brought by crises such as the 9/11 attacks, the 2007–2008 global financial crisis, and the COVID-19 pandemic. Therefore, more accurate, timely, and comprehensive demand forecasts are needed to help industry practitioners understand the market and predict future trends. Second, in recent years, increasing numbers of decision-makers have recognised the value of quantitative evidence and sought to leverage it, increasingly relying on or referring to such data in their strategy and policy formulations. Third, internet technology has enabled the development of big data, and thus the industry has more data on tourist behaviour and can more accurately forecast future trends.

In light of these factors, the purpose of this book is to introduce both undergraduate and postgraduate students, researchers, and practitioners to the latest advanced econometric methodologies in tourism demand modelling and forecasting. Along with theoretical foundations, the book presents real-life applications in the tourism context and the corresponding R code to enhance understanding and practice of tourism demand modelling and forecasting. The principles and computation methods of advanced econometric models are introduced at a level accessible to non-specialists.

However, the book aims at readers who have taken an introductory course in statistics that included multiple regression analysis and who have some knowledge of the tourism industry. The methodologies introduced in the book include the autoregressive distributed lag model, the time-varying parameter model, vector autoregressive models, spatiotemporal econometric models, mixed-frequency forecasting, hybrid forecasting models, density forecasting, forecast combination techniques, judgemental forecasting, scenario forecasting under crises, and a web-based tourism forecasting system. The book's contributors are experienced tourism forecasters who have contributed extensively to both academic research and consultancies.

The editors would like to acknowledge the financial support of Mr. and Mrs. Chan Chak Fu Endowed Professorship fund.

Doris Chenguang Wu
Gang Li
Haiyan Song
May 2022

1

OVERVIEW OF ECONOMETRIC TOURISM DEMAND MODELLING AND FORECASTING

Haiyan Song and Hongrun Wu

1.1 Tourism demand forecasting studies using econometric methods

1.1.1 Literature description

Since the pioneering work of Guthrie (1961), many studies have been published on tourism demand modelling and forecasting using econometric methods. Relevant papers have been published in a wide range of journals on tourism, such as *Tourism Management, Tourism Economics, Journal of Travel Research, International Journal of Tourism Research*, and *Annals of Tourism Research*; on economics and business, such as *International Journal of Forecasting and Applied Economics*; and on computer science, such as *Expert Systems with Applications* and *Mathematics and Computers in Simulation*. A summary of 131 key studies is presented in Table 1.1. This review identifies emerging trends in tourism demand modelling and forecasting, complementing and expanding on the earlier reviews of Song and Li (2008), Goh and Law (2011), Wu, Song, and Shen (2017), and Song, Qiu, and Park (2019).

1.1.2 Econometric models in tourism demand modelling and forecasting

Quantitative approaches to tourism demand forecasting can be divided into three main types: time-series models, econometric models, and artificial intelligence (AI)-based models. This chapter focuses on econometric models that have played distinctive roles in tourism demand forecasting research and practice.

DOI: 10.4324/9781003269366-1

TABLE 1.1 Summary of econometric studies on tourism demand modelling and forecasting.

Study (year)	Destinations/origins	Data frequency	Dependent variable(s)	Ex post data	Aggregate data	International tourism demand	Modelling or forecasting model(s)	Sub-categories
1960s								
Keintz (1968)	To and from the US	/	TA	1	1	1	SR	SS
Laber (1969)	From the US to Canada	A	TE	1	1	1	SR	SS
1970s								
Artus (1972)	To Western Europe and North America	A	TE	1		1	DL	SD
Barry & O'Hagan (1972)	From the UK	A	TE	1	1	1	SR	SS
Cesario & Knetsch (1976)	To parks in the US	Q	TA	1	1	0	SR	SS
1980s								
Fotheringham (1983)	US	A	Airline passengers	1	1	0	SR	SS
O'Hagan & Harrison (1984)	European countries	A	Share of TE	1	1	1	AIDS	MS
Uysal & Crompton (1984)	Turkey	A	TA & TE	1	1	1	SR	SS
Martin & Witt (1987)	US, Canada, and Europe	A	TA	1	1	1	SR	SS
Witt & Martin (1987)	From Germany and the UK	A	TA	1	1 & 0	1	ARX	SD
Martin & Witt (1988)	European countries	A	TA	1	1	1	SR	SS
Martin & Witt (1989)	France and Germany	A	TA	1	1	1	SR	SS
1990s								
Morley (1992)	/	/	/	/	1	1	SR	SS
Crouch, Schultz, & Valerio (1992)	Australia	A	TA	1	1	1	SR	SS

Study	Destination	Freq	Dependent variable				Econometric model	Design
Smeral, Witt, & Witt (1992)	European countries	A	Tourism imports	0	1	1	System of SR	MS
Chan (1993)	Singapore	M	TA	1	1	1	SR	SS
Di Matteo & Di Matteo (1993)	From Canada to the US	Q	TE	1	1	1	DL	SD
Sheldon (1993)	To the US	A	TA & TE	1	1	1	SR	SS
Syriopoulos & Sinclair (1993)	From the US and European countries to the Mediterranean	A	Share of TE	1	1	1	AIDS	MS
Gonzalez & Moral (1995)	Spain	M	TA	1	1	1	STSM; ECM; TFM	SD
Syriopoulos (1995)	From European countries and the US to the Mediterranean	A	TE	1	1	1	ECM	SD
Kulendran (1996)	To Australia	Q	TA	1	1	1	ECM	SD
Qu & Lam (1997)	From mainland China to Hong Kong	A	TA	1	1	1	SR	SS
Aki (1998)	Turkey	A	TA	1	1	1	SR	SS
Kim & Song (1998)	To South Korea	A	TA	1	1	1	ECM; VAR	SD & MD
Law & Au (1999)	From Japan to Hong Kong	A	TA	1	1	1	SR	SS
Uysal & El Roubi (1999)	From Canada to the US	Q	TE	1	1	1	ARX	SD
Papatheodorou (1999)	To the Mediterranean	A	Share of TE	1	1	1	AIDS	MS
2000s								
Garin-Munoz & Amaral (2000)	To Spain	A	TA	1	1	1	PDR	MD
Law (2000)	To Taiwan and Hong Kong	A	TA	1	0	1	SR	SS
Song, Romilly, & Liu (2000)	From the UK	A	TA	1	1	1	ECM; VAR	SD; MD

(Continued)

Study (year)	Destinations/origins	Data frequency	Dependent variable(s)	Ex post	Aggregate data	International tourism demand	Modelling or forecasting model(s)	Sub-categories
Vanegas & Croes (2000)	From the US to Aruba	A	TA	1 & 0	1	1	ARX	SD
Burger, Dohnal, Kathrada, & Law (2001)	From the US to South Africa	M	TA	1 & 0	1	1	SR	SS
Greenidge (2001)	To Barbados	Q	TA	1	1	1	STSM	SD
Kulendran & Witt (2001)	From the UK	Q	TA	1	1	1	ECM	SD
Lim & McAleer (2001)	From Hong Kong and Singapore to Australia	Q	TA	1	1	1	VECM	MD
Ledesma-Rodríguez, Navarro-Ibáñez, & Pérez-Rodríguez (2001)	To Tenerife	A	TA	1	1	1	PDR	MD
Weatherford, Kimes, & Scott (2001)	/	W	TA	1	1 & 0	/	SR	SS
Webber (2001)	Australia	Q	TA; TE	1	1	1	VECM	MD
Mello, Pack, & Sinclair (2002)	From the UK	A	Share of TE	1	1	1	AIDS	MS
Divisekera (2003)	To Australia	A	Share of TE	1	1	1	AIDS	MS
Durbarry & Sinclair (2003)	From France	A	Share of TE	1	1	1	ECM-AIDS	MD
Kulendran & Witt (2003a)	To Australia	A	TA	1	1	1	ECM; STSM	SD
Kulendran & Witt (2003b)	From the UK	Q	TA	1	1	1	TFM; ECM	SD
Lanza, Temple, & Urga (2003)	13 OECD economies	A	Share of TE	1	1	1	AIDS	MS

Study	Location	Frequency	Measure			Model	Category
Song & Wong (2003)	To Hong Kong	A	TA	1	1	TVP	SS
Song, Wong, & Chon (2003)	To Hong Kong	A	TA	0	1	ADLM	MS
Song & Witt (2003)	To Korea	A	TA	1	1	ADLM (GETS); ECM; ARX	MS
Song, Witt, & Jensen (2003)	To Denmark	A	TE	1	1	SR; ECM; VAR; ADLM; TVP	SS; SD; MD
Song, Witt, & Li (2003)	To Thailand	A	TA	0	1	ADLM; ECM; ARX	SM
Weatherford & Kimes (2003)	/	D	TA	1	/	SR	SS
Akal (2004)	To Turkey	A	TA	0	1	ARMAX; SR	SS; SD
Chu (2004)	To Singapore	M	TA	1	1	SR	SS
Dritsakis (2004)	From Germany and the UK to Greece	A	TA	1	1	VECM	MD
Li, Song, & Witt (2004)	From the UK	A	Share of TE	1	1	ECM-AIDS; AIDS	MS; MD
Lim (2004)	Australia	Q	TA	1	1	ARX	SD
Nadal, Font, & Rosselló (2004)	Balearic Islands	M	TA	1	1	ECM	SD
Narayan (2004)	To Fiji	A	TA	1	1	ADLM	SD
Naudé & Saayman (2005)	To Africa countries	A	TA	1	1	PDR	MD
Blake et al. (2006)	Scotland	Q	TA	1	1	STSM	SD
Blunk, Clark, & McGibany (2006)	UK	M	Revenue passenger miles	1	0	ADLM; VAR	SD; MD

(Continued)

Study (year)	Destinations/origins	Data frequency	Dependent variable(s)	Ex post	Aggregate data	International tourism demand	Modelling or forecasting model(s)	Sub-categories
Bonham, Edmonds, & Mak (2006)	Hawaii	M	TA	1	1	0	VECM	MD
Garin-Munoz (2006)	To Canary Islands	A	TA	1	1	1	PDR	MD
Han, Durbarry, & Sinclair (2006)	From the US to European countries	A	Share of TE	1	1	1	AIDS	SD
Li, Song, & Witt (2006)	From the UK	A	TE	1	1	1	TVP; ECM-AIDS; TVP-ECM-AIDS	SD; MD
Li, Wong, Song, & Witt (2006)	From the UK	A	TE	1	1	1	SR; ADLM; VAR; ECM; TVP; TVP-ECM;	SS; SD; MD
Song & Witt (2006)	To Macau	Q	TA	1	1	1	VAR	MD
Wong, Song, & Chon (2006)	To Hong Kong	A	TA	1	1	1	BVAR; VAR; AR	MD
Garin-Munoz (2007)	From Germany to Spain	A	TA; Duration of stay	1	1&0	1	PDR	MD
Garin-Munoz & Montero-Martín (2007)	To Balearic Island	A	TA	1	1	1	PDR	MD
Wong, Song, Witt, & Wu (2007)	To Hong Kong	A	TA	1	1	1	VAR; ECM; ADLM; Combined	SD; MD
Zhang & Jensen (2007)	13 countries	A	TA; TE	1	1	1	SR	SS

Study	Country/region	Freq.	Variable				Method	Type
Khadaroo & Seetanah (2008)	28 countries	A	TA	1	0	1	PDR	MD
Ouerfelli (2008)	To Tunisia	Q	TA	1	1	1	ECM	SD
Bonham, Gangnes, & Zhou (2009)	Hawaii	Q	TA	1	1	1	VEC; VARX	MD
Smeral (2009)	From European countries	A	Tourism imports	1	1	1	ECM	SD
Wang (2009)	To Taiwan	Q	TA	1	1	1	ADLM	SD
2010s								
Díaz & Nadal (2010)	From the UK to Balearic Island	M	TA	1	1	1	TFM	SD
Guizzardi & Mazzocchi (2010)	Italy	Q	Overnight stays	1	1	1&0	STSM	SD
Moore (2010)	To the Caribbean	M	TA	1	1	1	ECM	SD
Smeral (2010)	Australia, Canada, the US, Japan, and the EU: 15 countries	A	Tourism imports	0	1	1	ADLM; ECM	SD
Song, Lin, Zhang, & Gao (2010)	To Hong Kong	M	TA&TE	1	1	1	ADLM	SD
Song & Lin (2010)	Asia	A	TA&TE	0	1	1	ECM	SD
Athanasopoulos, Hyndman, Song, & Wu (2011)	/	M; Q; A	TA	1&0	1	1	SR; ADLM; VAR; TVP	SS; SD; MD
Carson, Cenesizoglu, & Parker (2011)	US	A	TA	1	1	1	ADLM	SD
Fildes, Wei, & Ismail (2011)	UK	A	International passenger traffic	1	1	1	ADLM; TVP-ADLM; VAR	SD; MD

(Continued)

Study (year)	Destinations/origins	Data frequency	Dependent variable(s)	Ex post	Aggregate data	International tourism demand	Modelling or forecasting model(s)	Sub-categories
Song, Li, Witt, & Athanasopoulos (2011)	Hong Kong	Q	TA	1&0	1	1	STSM; ADLM; TVP; TVP-STSM	SD
Song, Lin, Witt, & Zhang (2011)	Hong Kong	Q	Hotel rooms	0	1	/	ADLM-ECM	SD
Choi & Varian (2012)	Hong Kong	M	TA	0	1	1	ARX	SD
Goh (2012)	Hong Kong	M	TA	1	1	1	ECM	SD
Page, Song, & Wu (2012)	UK	A	TA&TE	1	1	1	SR-TVP	SD
Pan, Wu, & Song (2012)	US	W	Hotel rooms	1	1	/	ARX; ARMAX; ARIMAX; ADLM; TVP; VAR	SD; MD
Smeral (2012)	US	A	Tourism imports	1	1	1	ADLM	SD
Marrocu & Paci (2013)	Italy	A	TA and nights	1	0	0	SAR	SD
Song, Gao, & Lin (2013)	Hong Kong	Q	TA; TE; Hotel rooms	1&0	1&0	/	ADLM; Combined (ADLM, Delphi)	SD
Morley, Rosselló, & Santana-Gallego (2014)	/	/	TA	/	1	/	SR	SD
Ridderstaat, Oduber, Croes, Nijkamp, & Martens (2014)	US and Venezuela to Aruba	M	TA	1	1	1	PDR	MD

Study	Location	Freq.			Dependent variable			Modelling technique	MD/SD
Saha & Yap (2014)	139 countries	A	1	1	TA; TE	1	1	PDR	MD
Tsui, Ozer Balli, Gilbey, & Gow (2014)	Hong Kong	M	0	1	Air passenger traffic	1	1	ARIMAX	SD
Yang, Pan, & Song (2014)	Charleston	W	0	1	Hotel rooms	1	/	ARMAX	SD
Bangwayo-Skeete & Skeete (2015)	Jamaica	Mixed	1	1	TA	1	1	MIDAS; Combined (AR, SARIMA, MIDAS)	SD
Guizzardi & Stacchini (2015)	Rimini	M	1	1	TA	1	0	DL; STSM	SD
Gunter & Önder (2015)	Paris	M	1	1	TA	1	1	ADLM-ECM; VAR; BVAR; TVP	MD
Lin, Liu, & Song (2015)	Mainland China	A	0	1	TA	1	1	ADLM	SD
Yang, Pan, Evans, & Lv (2015)	Mainland China	M	1	1	TA	1	0	ARMAX	SD
Balli, Balli, & Louis (2016)	OECD countries	A	1	1	TA	1	1	PDR	MD
Gunter & Önder (2016)	To Vienna	M	1	1	TA	1	1	VAR; BVAR; Combined	MD
Önder & Gunter (2016)	To Vienna	M	1	1	TA	1	1	ADLM	SD
Pan & Yang (2016)	Charleston area	W	1	1	Hotel occupancy rate	1	/	ARMAX	SD
Dogru, Sirakaya-Turk, & Crouch (2017)	To Turkey	Q	1	1	TA	1	1	PDR	MD

(Continued)

Study (year)	Destinations/origins	Data frequency	Dependent variable(s)	Ex post	Aggregate data	International tourism demand	Modelling or forecasting model(s)	Sub-categories
Li, Pan, Law, & Huang (2017)	To Beijing	M	TA	1	1	/	ARMAX	SD
Park, Lee, & Song (2017)	From Japan to South Korea	M	TA	1	1	1	SARIMAX	SD
Rodríguez (2017)	From Germany and the UK to Balearic Islands	M	TA	1	1	1	ARMAX	SD
Assaf, Li, Song, & Tsionas (2018)	Southeast Asia	Q	TA	0	1	1	VAR; BVAR; GVAR; BGVAR	MD
Dergiades, Mavragani, & Pan (2018)	To Cyprus	M	TA	1	1	1	VAR	MD
Li, Goh, Hung, & Chen (2018)	Hong Kong	Q	TA	1	1	0	ARX	SD
Li, Chen, Wang, & Ming (2018)	To Beijing	M	TA	1	1	1	VAR	MD
Liu, Tseng, & Tseng (2018)	Mainland China	D	TA	1	1	0	VAR	MD
Wen, Liu, & Song (2019)	Mainland China	M	TA	1	1	0	SR; PDR	SS; MD
Hu & Song (2019)	From Hong Kong to Macau	M	TA	1	1	0	ADLM	SD
Li, Wu, Zhou, & Liu (2019)	To Hong Kong	Q	TA	1	1	1	STSM; VAR; ADLM; ECM; TVP	SD; MD
2020s								
Kulshrestha, Krishnaswamy, & Sharma (2020)	Singapore	Q	TA	1	1	1	ADLM	SD

Study	Region	Data frequency	Dependent variable			Models	Subcategories
Liu, Lin, Li, & Song (2020)	Asia-Pacific	A	TA	0	1	ADLM-ECM	SD
Wu, Cao, Wen, & Song (2020)	25 countries	Q	Tourism imports	1	1	TVP-PVAR	MD
Gunter & Zekan (2021)	Asia-Pacific and Latin America/the Caribbean	Q	Air passenger numbers	0	1	GVAR	MD
Jiao, Li, & Chen (2020)	Europe	Q	TA	1	1	GNST	SD
Ouchen & Montargot (2021)	43 countries	A	TA	1	1	PDR; SAR	MD
Qiu et al. (2021)	20 countries	Q	TA	1 & 0	1	ADLM; TVP	SD
Tsui, Chow, Lin, & Chen (2021)	From China to New Zealand	M	TA	1	1	SARIMAX	SD
Wen, Liu, Song, & Liu (2021)	From mainland China to Hong Kong	Mixed	TA	1	0	SARIMAX; Combined (SARIMA, MIDAS)	SD
Zhang, Song, Wen, & Liu (2021)	Hong Kong	Q	TA	0	1	ADLM-ECM	SD

Note: **Data frequency:** A = annual, Q = quarterly; M = monthly; W = weekly; D = daily; **Dependent variable:** TA = tourist arrivals, TE = tourist expenditure; For ex post, **Aggregate data, International demand:** 1 = yes, 0 = no; **Models:** ARX: autoregressive exogenous model; TFM: transfer function model; TVP-STSM: the time-varying parameter structural time-series model; TVP-PVAR: the time-varying parameter panel vector autoregressive; BGVAR: the Bayesian global vector autoregressive; other models are as defined in the text; **Subcategories:** SS = single-equation static model, SD = single-equation dynamic model, MS = multi-equation static model, MD = multi-equation dynamic model

Over the last six decades, there has been continuous interest in the use of econometric forecasting models to explore the causal relationships between economic factors and tourism demand under various empirical settings. The main advantage of an econometric model over the time-series model is its ability to capture the causal relationship between tourism demand and its influencing factors, enabling one to explain and forecast the movement in tourism demand. An econometric model is not only a tool for generating forecasts; it is also useful for explaining the reasons why changes occur in tourism demand so that policy recommendations and evaluations could be made (Goh & Law, 2011; Li, Song, & Witt, 2005; Song & Li, 2008).

Tourism demand studies have shown increasing sophistication in the application of econometric methods. The progress of econometric models applied in such studies is closely related to methodological developments in the field, with later models resolving certain problems associated with earlier models (Song et al., 2019). Most early econometric tourism studies used single-equation regression (SR) models. Although these studies reported high levels of explanatory power and prediction accuracy, most of the results that they obtained were spurious, as they did not account for unit roots (Witt & Witt, 1995). Other statistical limitations in these early studies included multicollinearity and serial correlations (Crouch, 1994; Goh & Law, 2011; Lim, 1997). More sophisticated econometric approaches have since been developed to overcome these shortcomings. The features of these newer models provide for better performance, either separately or in conjunction with other individual models. The panel data approach of pooling cross-sectional data across time series has also become increasingly popular.

This section provides a brief summary of these econometric approaches and their applications in the tourism demand literature. Subsequent chapters provide technical illustrations and specific examples of some of these models.

1.1.2.1 Single-equation static models

As shown in Table 1.1, until the 1990s, most econometric tourism studies concentrated on strategic rationale models, which are the most basic econometric forecasting models and are used to determine the influence of various factors on current values. The methodologies for specifying these models vary both in methods of estimation and in functional forms. Most of these SR models adopt ordinary least squares (OLS) estimation, either alone or in conjunction with other estimation methods. The log-linear (multiplicative) functional form is most popular in these studies because the estimated coefficients of the log-linear model can be regarded as demand elasticities (Crouch, 1994; Uysal & El Roubi, 1999; Witt & Witt, 1995). Until the early 1990s, econometric tourism demand modelling was restricted to static models. However, numerous problems are associated with the constant elasticity structure of these models, such as spurious regression and even absurd results when the values of the independent variables extend well beyond their original ranges (Kanafani, 1983; Li, Song, & Witt, 2005; Song & Li, 2008; Vanegas & Croes, 2000). In more recent years, SR has been adopted as a benchmark for evaluations of tourism demand forecasting (Athanasopoulos, Hyndman, Song, & Wu, 2011; Song et al., 2019).

1.1.2.2 Single-equation dynamic models

To avoid the spurious regression that often characterises SR analysis based on OLS and to account for the intertemporal relationships between tourism demand and assorted independent variables, great effort has been made to improve the econometric approach to modelling and forecasting tourism demand. Since the mid-1990s, dynamic models have appeared in the tourism demand literature, such as the distributed lag (DL) model; its advanced counterpart, the autoregressive distributed lag model (ADLM); and the error correction model (ECM).

The ADLM, proposed by Sargan (1964), is one of the most popular single-equation dynamic models, as it can reduce the possibility of excessive data mining associated with the traditional specific-to-general modelling approach. Early studies adopting the ADLM focused on either partial adjustment models (Kulendran & Witt, 2001; Ledesma-Rodríguez, Navarro-Ibáñez, & Pérez-Rodríguez, 2001; Morley, 1997; Uysal & El Roubi, 1999; Vanegas & Croes, 2000) or finite DL models (Crouch, Schultz, & Valerio, 1992; Di Matteo & Di Matteo, 1993). In addition to assessing the influence of lagged independent variables, more recent studies using the ADLM have integrated lagged demand variables to indicate the influence of habit persistence and time lags in supply adjustments (Li, Song, & Witt, 2006; Song & Witt, 2003; Song, Witt, & Jensen, 2003). The ADLM has been shown to perform well in forecasting turning points (Nadal, 2001), but a possible problem is that the structure of the selected final model relies heavily on the data that are used, even though economic theory plays an important role in the initial specification of the general model (Song & Witt, 2003).

Building on the foundation of the ADLM, the ECM (also called the cointegration model) inherits the ADLM's advantage of overcoming the spurious regression problem by differencing the variables and its reduction of data mining during estimation. The ECM further considers both the long-run equilibrium relationship between tourism demand and its determinants, and the short-run error correction mechanism in explaining tourism demand (Choyakh, 2008; Dritsakis, 2004; Halicioglu, 2010; Song, Witt, Wong, & Wu, 2009). The ADLM and the ECM show excellent performance in tourism demand modelling and forecasting, and both play significant roles in tourism demand studies.

Traditionally, the ECM and many other tourism demand models have been estimated using OLS, with the assumption that the coefficients of the model are constant over time. This assumption may not always hold, however, given that systemic changes may occur. To avoid the unrealistic assumption of constant coefficients, which represent the demand elasticities in log-linear regression, Song and Witt (2000) introduced the time-varying parameter (TVP) technique to tourism demand studies. TVP models consider the parameter evolutions over time caused by external shocks, including policy and regime shifts, economic reforms, and political uncertainties to overcome the problems of structural instability in the tourism demand system. Furthermore, TVP models perform well in capturing external influences of a gradual and diffuse nature, such as changes in consumer tastes and other social–psychological trends (Song & Witt, 2003), as they give insights into how coefficient estimates are to be revised for the rational economic agency of tourists. This approach rewrites the regression in the state space form (SSF) and estimates the variation in tourism demand by means of the Kalman filter technique (1960) through a recursive procedure using the maximum likelihood estimation method. The TVP technique has been popular since Song and Witt (2003) because of its good performance in short-run tourism forecasting.

To improve forecasting accuracy, researchers have also combined the ADLM and the ECM with the TVP technique, such as the TVP-ADLM and the TVP-ECM (Fildes, Wei, & Ismail, 2011; Song, Li, Witt, & Athanasopoulos, 2011). The flexibility of the ADLM permits its use with other features that represent parameter assumptions or data utilisation. The TVP technique has been found to work well with both the ADLM and the ECM in capturing gradual structural changes (Li, Song, & Witt 2006; Song, Witt, & Jensen, 2003). Bangwayo-Skeete and Skeete (2015) integrated mixed-data sampling (MIDAS) with a reduced form of the ADLM (a partial adjustment model) to use mixed-frequency data to forecast tourist arrivals. Taking advantage of the effectiveness of the ECM in overcoming spurious regression problems and capturing short-term dynamics, and the ability of the TVP model to capture structural instability, Li, Song, and Witt (2006) combined the two models and found that this new model outperformed the individual models.

Whereas the ADLM and the ECM extend the static single-equation models by introducing time dynamics, similar extensions have been made by adding exogenous variables to the time-series models already used in tourism demand forecasting. Two examples of this approach are the structural time-series model (STSM), which adds explanatory variables to the basic structural model (BSM), and the AR(I)MAX model, which is built on the autoregressive (integrated) moving average (AR(I)MA) model. The STSM can capture the trends, seasonal patterns, and cycles in demand variables. Like TVP models, the STSM is written in the SSF and estimated by the Kalman filter, which is useful for seasonal data. The AR(I)MAX model has been shown to outperform some of the original time-series models, including the AR(I)MA and seasonal AR(I)MA (SAR(I)MA) models, in many tourism demand forecasting studies (Bangwayo-Skeete & Skeete, 2015; Pan & Yang, 2016; Park, Lee, & Song, 2017; Tsui, Ozer Balli, Gilbey, & Gow, 2014). The AR(I)MAX model and STSM share with time-series models a strong focus on discerning the dynamics of tourism demand rather than measuring causal relationships between tourism demand and its influencing factors. Furthermore, like the ADLM and the ECM, AR(I)MAX-type models also perform well when combined with the TVP technique and MIDAS features for tourism demand modelling and forecasting (Bangwayo-Skeete & Skeete, 2015; Pan & Yang, 2016).

1.1.2.3 Multi-equation static models

Unlike single-equation models, multi-equation models reveal bidirectional causality and can account for any interdependencies between the independent variables and the possible correlation of disturbances among the equations.

The system of demand equations model used in tourism demand studies was derived from Stone (1954). Deaton and Muelbauer (1980) then developed the almost ideal demand system (AIDS) model, which assumes a multi-stage decision process and the feature of separability that allows consumers' preferences within different groups of products to be described independently of quantities in other groups. The AIDS model was first adopted in tourism studies by O'Hagan and Harrison (1984) as a system of equations approach. The AIDS model normally takes tourism expenditure shares as dependent variables to capture the tourism demand for certain products or services. Its stronger underpinnings in economic theory make it more powerful for tourism demand elasticity analysis than its single-equation counterparts.

Although the classical AIDS model is estimated within a static system, it can easily be combined with the TVP technique and the ECM to devise extended dynamic AIDS models (e.g., ECM-AIDS, TVP-ECM-AIDS), which perform well in tourism demand forecasting (Durbarry & Sinclair, 2003; Li, Song, & Witt, 2004; 2006). For instance, Li, Song, and Witt (2006) incorporated the TVP technique into a system of demand equations in both long-run (static) and short-run (dynamic) error correction forms (TVP-LR-AIDS and TVP-ECM-AIDS, respectively), the forecasts of which were found to outperform the fixed-parameter AIDS.

Another type of multi-equation static model applied to tourism demand analysis is the simultaneous equations model, also known as the structural equations model (SEM), which examines the structure of causal relationships among a set of exogenous and endogenous variables (Dwyer, 1983;

Turner and Witt, 2001; Zamparini, Vergori & Arima, 2017). However, the theoretical restrictions imposed on the parameters of the SEM have been challenged, and many researchers have viewed the SEM as an infeasible approach (Sims, 1980).

1.1.2.4 Multi-equation dynamic models

The vector autoregressive (VAR) model and vector error correction model (VECM) are extensions of single static equation models. In addition to avoiding spurious regression, these extended models can capture the interdependency of multiple time series.

To fulfil the need for structural modelling, the VAR model was developed for forecasting interrelated time-series without imposing a priori restrictions and for analysing random shocks on the system of variables (Sims, 1980). In contrast with econometric models that include influencing factors as exogenous variables, the VAR model treats all independent variables as endogenous and specifies all variables as being in a linear relationship with the others. The VAR model can generate forecasts of the dependent variables without an implicit theoretical framework for the construction and estimation of the independent variables or advance forecasts of their values. The use of the VAR model in tourism demand forecasting can be traced back to the late 1990s, and the VAR model can produce accurate medium- to long-term tourism demand forecasts (Song & Witt, 2006). Nonetheless, many comparative studies of tourism demand forecasting models have found that the classical VAR model is outperformed by other modern econometric models (e.g., Assaf, Li, Song, & Tsionas, 2018; Song & Li, 2008). To improve the forecasting accuracy of the classical VAR model, Wong, Song, and Chon (2006) developed a Bayesian VAR (BVAR) model that outperforms its non-Bayesian counterpart by imposing Bayesian priors on the model estimation. To capture the global interactions among tourist destinations, Cao, Li, and Song (2017) initially applied a global vector autoregressive (GVAR) model in tourism. The GVAR model is to divide the global tourism demand system into several subsystems, which can be estimated individually before restacking them to form a relatively complete system, thus avoiding the simultaneous estimation of a large set of parameters within a global model (Dees, Mauro, Pesaran, & Smith, 2007; Pesaran, Schuermann, & Weiner; 2004). Assaf et al. (2018) combined BVAR and GVAR models to further improve the efficiency and forecasting accuracy of the VAR approach.

Some of the variables used in the system demand models might not be cointegrated. To avoid model misspecification and the identification of spurious relationships between the variables in the model, the VECM was developed by introducing an error correction term to the VAR model. Studies adopting the VECM have suggested that there are cointegration relationships (long-run relationships) between the independent variables normally used in tourism demand models, such as tourism demand, income, and exchange rate (Bonham, Edmonds, & Mak, 2006; Dritsakis, 2004; Lim & McAleer, 2001).

Other multi-equation dynamic models used in tourism demand studies are the aforementioned combined models, such as the ECM-AIDS, incorporating the AIDS model and the ECM; and the TVP-ECM-AIDS, incorporating the TVP technique into the ECM-AIDS (Durbarry & Sinclair, 2003; Li, Song, & Witt, 2004; 2006).

1.1.2.5 Panel data regression

Panel data regression (PDR), which incorporates information from time-series (intertemporal movement) and cross-sectional (heterogeneity) data, has a number of advantages over the aforementioned time-series econometric models, which emphasise functional form and parameterisation. PDR can reduce the multicollinearity problem and provide more degrees of freedom in estimation; it has been used in forecasting tourism demand when the time series of the variables are shorter but the cross-sectional data of these variables are available. Indeed, PDR analysis can be used in many of the models discussed above (Dogru, Sirakaya-Turk, & Crouch, 2017; Ledesma-Rodríguez, Navarro-Ibáñez, & Pérez-Rodríguez, 2001; Li, Song, & Li, 2016; Naudé & Saayman, 2005; Roget & González, 2006; Saha & Yap, 2014; Sakai, Brown, & Mak, 2000; Wen, Liu, & Song, 2018).

For example, Saha and Yap (2014) used PDR to analyse the effects of political instability on tourism demand, and Dogru et al. (2017) used a fully modified ordinary least squares (FMOLS) panel data model to estimate Turkey's inbound tourism demand.

However, whether a panel data model is appropriate or not depends heavily on the homogeneity of the intercept and coefficients of the explanatory variables, and on any individual cross-sectional effects correlated with the explanatory variables (Romilly, Liu, & Song, 1998). Furthermore, the required panel data are unavailable for many destinations.

1.1.2.6 Spatial econometric models

Spatial econometrics can explain spatial interactions between geographically related regions and has therefore received much attention in tourism demand studies. According to Jiao, Chen, and Li (2021), Jiao, Li, and Chen (2020), and Yang and Zhang (2019), spatial models outperform their non-spatial counterparts in tourism demand forecasting.

Spatial econometric models incorporate the weighted average of neighbouring values of a location as a spatial lag (Kelejian & Prucha, 1998), and they vary in the way that they incorporate this information. Although most spatial models were initially designed to handle cross-sectional data, researchers have recently started to integrate both cross-sectional and time-series data to examine the spillover effects in tourism demand among regions/countries and over time The most popular of such models is the spatial autoregressive (SAR) model (Lee & Yu, 2010), which integrates the spatial lag into the dependent variable only. The SAR model can be expanded into a spatial autoregressive combined (SAC) model by incorporating spatial lags not only into the dependent variable but also into error terms, thus accounting for spatial interaction effects in unobserved factors. The general nesting spatial (GNS) model further incorporates the spatial lags into independent variables as well as dependent variables and error terms; it thus considers all spatial interaction effects, including endogenous and exogenous interactions and interaction effects between error terms (Elhorst, 2017).

Whereas spatial models for cross-sectional data are limited to single-equation models, spatial models for panel data, which have recently gained more scholarly attention, extend the modelling possibilities to multi-equation models. Elhorst (2014) introduced static and dynamic spatial panel data models by integrating temporal panel data with time variants. Like spatial models for cross-sectional data, static spatial panel data models introduce observations over time for the same set of cross-sectional observations, and dynamic spatial panel data models include time lags in the dependent variable and the spatial lagged dependent variable. Furthermore, by extending the GNS model into a spatiotemporal form, Jiao, Li, and Chen (2020) proposed a general nesting spatiotemporal (GNST) model considering the spatial and temporal effects of the dependent and independent variables, as well as unobserved factors, to improve the accuracy of tourism demand forecasts.

1.1.2.7 Forecast combinations

As mentioned above, combined forecasts based on different methods or data have emerged as an important way to improve forecasting performance. Although the first study of forecast combinations in the tourism field appeared in the 1980s (Fritz, Brandon, & Xander, 1984), research on this topic has increased since 2010 (Song et al., 2019).

The forecasts from individual models can be combined in different ways in terms of assigning weights to individual models. These include average-based, forecast error-based, and regression-based approaches. Average-based methods use Pythagorean (arithmetic, geometric, or harmonic) means to combine individual forecasts and are easy to apply, but they do not involve relative weighting of individual forecasts (Wong, Song, Witt, & Wu, 2007). Forecasting error-based methods give more weight to better-performing models (Bates & Granger, 1969; Fritz et al.,

1984; Coshall, 2009). Regression-based methods, which consider individual forecasts as input variables, fit linear or non-linear models to the actual values (Shen, Li & Song, 2011).

Forecast combinations can also be carried out hierarchically by making adjustments after an initial forecast. A notable example of this approach is combining quantitative models with human judgement obtained through qualitative methods (Song, Gao, & Lin, 2013; Zhang, Song, Wen, & Liu, 2021). The judgement approach aims to provide a complete and definitive description of future developments by drawing on the accumulated experience and insight of individual experts or groups of people; it works well in long-term demand forecasting and ex ante tourism demand forecasting in crises (Lin & Song, 2014; Uysal & Crompton, 1984; Vanhove, 1980). However, qualitative methods have generally been criticised for introducing human bias. Given that quantitative and qualitative forecasting methods are complementary, the forecasts generated by integrating these two approaches are likely to be more accurate than those generated by either of these two methods in isolation. Song et al. (2013) proposed a tourism demand forecasting system that adjusted the quantitative forecasts of the ADLM with the judgements of a panel of experts using scenario analyses and dynamic Delphi surveys. In a recent study, to forecast possible paths to post-COVID-19 tourism recovery, Zhang et al. (2021) combined the baseline forecasts of the ADLM-ECM with Delphi adjustments based on different recovery scenarios reflecting different levels of severity of the pandemic's influence.

1.2 Performance of forecasting models

Over the last six decades, numerous studies have focused not only on tourism demand modelling and forecasting with econometric models but also on model construction and performance evaluation to identify the most accurate models and identify pathways to improved forecast performance. There is a broad consensus that no single forecasting model outperforms all others for every situation, as environment-specific conditions determine which method is most suitable for each forecasting task (Kim & Schwartz, 2013; Song & Li, 2008). Inconsistencies in forecasting performance can be attributed to variations in conditions and types of data. A review by Peng, Song, and Crouch (2014) of 65 studies published between 1980 and 2011 indicated that tourist origin, destination, time period, modelling method, data frequency, number of variables, variable measures, and sample size all had a significant influence on the accuracy of forecasting models.

The last six decades have witnessed the development of econometric models for tourism demand modelling and forecasting with increasing accuracy, from the simplest single-equation static model to more complex multi-equation dynamic models. As mentioned above, combined models (incorporating more than one individual econometric model) normally perform better in tourism demand forecasts than their constituent models. Although combining forecasts from the same model family can increase the stability of the variable and the lag selection process, many researchers are working on combining models from different model families (Song et al., 2019). Some combinations perform better than others; for example, the combination of econometric models and judgement techniques works well for long-term demand forecasting and for forecasts involving the influence of financial or other crises (Song & Lin, 2010; Zhang et al., 2021).

More recently, models using AI algorithms have gained increasing popularity, as their extraordinary ability to handle big data can provide superior accuracy in tourism demand forecasting (Goh & Law, 2011; Li, Chen, Wang, & Ming, 2018; Song et al., 2019). However, these models cannot identify causal relationships because they lack a theoretical foundation in economics and human behaviour. The future integration of econometric models and AI-based models has the potential to improve the accuracy of tourism demand forecasting.

1.3 General observations

1.3.1 Estimation and general-to-specific modelling

Econometric models vary not only in their functional forms but also in their estimation methods. The traditional approach to the econometric forecasting of tourism demand is based on the specific-to-general modelling approach, which starts by specifying a relatively parsimonious regression model with OLS estimation. This simple model is then tested and respecified repeatedly by introducing additional explanatory variables into the model estimations (Gray, 1966; Loeb, 1982), but this approach has been criticised for excessive data mining. An alternative approach known as the general-to-specific (GETS) approach overcomes this problem by eliminating insignificant or wrongly signed variables from a general multi-variable model. For example, the ADLM is usually combined with the GETS approach (Önder & Gunter, 2016; Song, Witt & Li, 2003). The more recent bootstrap aggregation GETS models appear to achieve a stable model reduction process that generates more reliable forecasts than the original GETS models (Athanasopoulos, Song, & Sun, 2017).

1.3.2 Variables and measures

The measures of tourism demand used today are largely unchanged from those used in pre-1990 studies. The most popular measure in tourism demand studies is still tourist arrivals, followed by tourist expenditure. Furthermore, researchers have mostly concentrated on international tourist flows because their characteristics are more amenable to statistical analysis than those of domestic tourism (Athanasopoulos & Hyndman, 2008; Blunk, Clark, & McGibany, 2006; Chen, Bloomfield, & Fu, 2003; Dogru et al., 2017; Ellis & Doren, 1966; Koo, Lim, & Dobruszkes, 2017; Li et al., 2016). Tourist arrivals and expenditure are generally analysed using aggregated data at the country or regional level, which are normally affected by different types of internal or external shocks, such as government policies, natural or man-made disasters, and business cycles. As the use of aggregated data may cause model misspecification in depicting tourism decision-making (Masiero, 2016; Vu & Turner, 2005), some studies have attempted to discern the indicators of tourism demand through disaggregated data.

Before 1990, econometric studies of tourism demand focused on identifying its determinants. Drawing on the findings of these studies, most later forecasting studies selected the categories of tourists' income, relative prices (tourism prices in the destinations relative to prices in the origins), substitute prices (tourism prices in competing destinations), and exchange rates as the most important determinants in their econometric tourism demand models (Li et al., 2005; Song & Li, 2008). Climate change (Goh, 2012; Li et al., 2016; Moore, 2010), political instability (Saha & Yap, 2014), terrorist attacks (Bonham, Edmonds & Mak, 2006), infectious diseases (Zhang et al., 2021), and other non-economic factors (Song, Gartner & Tasci, 2012; Tang, Yuan, Ramos & Sriboonchitta, 2019) have also been found to significantly influence tourism demand.

1.3.3 Ex ante forecasts and forecasts during crises

Over the last six decades, tourism demand forecasting studies have been mainly focused on ex post forecasts using actual values of independent variables. Ex post forecasts work well in assessing the performance of a particular forecasting model because the errors from predicting the explanatory variables are not mixed with the forecasting errors of the dependent variable. In contrast, little attention has been paid to ex ante forecasts using the predicted values of independent variables (Liu, Lin, Li, & Song, 2020). Because ex ante forecasts do not rely on prior information about any independent variable over the forecasting period, they have more direct implications for real-world forecasting, especially during sudden and volatile crises such as the COVID-19 pandemic (Liu et al., 2020; Zhang et al., 2021).

Most studies of tourism demand forecasting in the context of crises have examined the effects of such crises (such as SARS in 2003 and the global financial crisis of 2007–2008) on ex post forecasts by introducing dummy variables into their statistical models. Few studies (Page, Yeoman, Munro, Connell, & Walker, 2006; Yeoman, Galt, & McMahon-Beattie, 2005) have considered the effects of crises on ex ante forecasts in ways that are more attractive to tourism practitioners. However, these statistical methods may not be effective in forecasting the recovery of tourism demand during a sudden and volatile crisis (e.g., a disease, natural disaster, or financial crisis). As mentioned in Section 1.1.2.7, statistical forecasts can be adjusted and improved through judgemental approaches. Tourism demand studies have commonly used scenario analyses and the Delphi technique as a more systematic and reliable combined method for volatile periods such as the COVID-19 pandemic. For example, Zhang et al. (2021) integrated qualitative (scenario-based Delphi adjustments) and quantitative (ADLM-ECM) methods to forecast tourism demand in Hong Kong and predict tourism income losses due to COVID-19 under different impact scenarios. The results indicated that the combination of the econometric model and the judgemental method was effective in reflecting different levels of severity of the pandemic's impact and in forecasting possible paths to the recovery of tourism demand.

1.4 Conclusion

This chapter reviews the published studies on econometric modelling and forecasting tourism demand during the period 1961−2021. The last six decades have witnessed the development of econometric methods for tourism demand forecasting from the simplest single-equation static regression models to more sophisticated multi-equation and dynamic models to achieve better forecasting accuracy.

During the 1960s and 1970s, the SR approach was dominant in tourism demand studies, which focused on the determinants of tourism demand. In the 1980s, researchers continued to use SR models in their studies, but dynamic models such as the ADLM increased in popularity. Multi-equation models, such as the STSM, the VAR, and AIDS models, emerged in the 1990s. This trend continued in the 2000s, as the development of econometric models and relevant combined or hybrid methods flourished. Since 2010, multi-equation dynamic models have been dominant in tourism demand studies.

These trends have been primarily related to changes in the functional forms of individual models for tourism demand forecasting. Advanced parameterisation (e.g., the TVP technique), model combination (e.g., TVP-ECM-AIDS, ARIMAX, and econometric models combined with AI or judgement approaches), and diverse approaches to data utilisation (e.g., MIDAS) and estimation (e.g., BVAR and bootstrap aggregation GETS) are possible pathways for improved forecasting performance in future tourism demand studies.

Self-Study Questions

1 List and discuss the main econometric models used for tourism demand forecasting.

2   How has the application of econometric methods to tourism demand forecasting evolved since the 1960s?
3   How have various econometric models been integrated over the past few decades?
4   Do any econometric models perform better than others in practice?

References

Akal, M. (2004). Forecasting Turkey's tourism revenues by ARMAX model. *Tourism Management, 25*(5), 565–580. https://doi.org/10.1016/j.tourman.2003.08.001

Aki, S. (1998). A compact econometric model of tourism demand for Turkey. *Tourism Management, 19*(1), 99–102. https://doi.org/10.1016/S0261-5177(97)00097-6

Artus, J. R. (1972). An econometric analysis of international travel. *Staff Papers, 19*(3), 579–614. https://doi.org/10.2307/3866418

Assaf, A. G., Li, G., Song, H., & Tsionas, M. G. (2018). Modeling and forecasting regional tourism demand using the Bayesian global vector autoregressive (BGVAR) model. *Journal of Travel Research, 58*(3), 383–397. https://doi.org/10.1177/0047287518759226

Athanasopoulos, G., & Hyndman, R. J. (2008). Modelling and forecasting Australian domestic tourism. *Tourism Management, 29*(1), 19–31. https://doi.org/10.1016/j.tourman.2007.04.009

Athanasopoulos, G., Hyndman, R. J., Song, H., & Wu, D. C. (2011). The tourism forecasting competition. *International Journal of Forecasting, 27*(3), 822–844. https://doi.org/10.1016/j.ijforecast.2010.04.009

Athanasopoulos, G., Song, H., & Sun, J. A. (2017). Bagging in tourism demand modeling and forecasting. *Journal of Travel Research, 57*(1), 52–68. https://doi.org/10.1177/0047287516682871

Balli, F., Balli, H. O., & Louis, R. J. (2016). The impacts of immigrants and institutions on bilateral tourism flows. *Tourism Management, 52*, 221–229. https://doi.org/10.1016/j.tourman.2015.06.021

Bangwayo-Skeete, P. F., & Skeete, R. W. (2015). Can Google data improve the forecasting performance of tourist arrivals? Mixed-data sampling approach. *Tourism Management, 46*, 454–464. https://doi.org/10.1016/j.tourman.2014.07.014

Barry, K., & O'Hagan, J. (1972). An econometric study of British tourist expenditure in Ireland. *Economic and Social Review, 3*(2), 143.

Bates, J. M., & Granger, C. W. (1969). The combination of forecasts. *Journal of the Operational Research Society, 20*(4), 451–468. https://doi.org/10.1057/jors.1969.103

Blake, A., Durbarry, R., Eugenio-Martin, J. L., Gooroochurn, N., Hay, B., Lennon, J., Sinclair, M. T., Sugiyarto, G., Yeoman, I. (2006). Integrating forecasting and CGE models: The case of tourism in Scotland. *Tourism Management, 27*(2), 292–305. https://doi.org/10.1016/j.tourman.2004.11.005

Blunk, S. S., Clark, D. E., & McGibany, J. M. (2006). Evaluating the long-run impacts of the 9/11 terrorist attacks on US domestic airline travel. *Applied Economics, 38*(4), 363–370. https://doi.org/10.1080/00036840500367930

Bonham, C., Edmonds, C., & Mak, J. (2006). The impact of 9/11 and other terrible global events on tourism in the United States and Hawaii. *Journal of Travel Research, 45*(1), 99–110. https://doi.org/ 0.1177/0047287506288812

Bonham, C., Gangnes, B., & Zhou, T. (2009). Modeling tourism: A fully identified VECM approach. *International Journal of Forecasting, 25*(3), 531–549. https://doi.org/10.1016/j.ijforecast.2008.11.014

Burger, C., Dohnal, M., Kathrada, M., & Law, R. (2001). A practitioner's guide to time-series methods for tourism demand forecasting—A case study of Durban, South Africa. *Tourism Management, 22*(4), 403–409. https://doi.org/10.1016/S0261-5177(00)00068-6

Cao, Z., Li, G., & Song, H. (2017). Modeling the interdependence of tourism demand: The global vector autoregressive approach. *Annals of Tourism Research, 67,* 1–13. https://doi.org/10.1016/j.annals.2017.07.019

Carson, R. T., Cenesizoglu, T., & Parker, R. (2011). Forecasting (aggregate) demand for US commercial air travel. *International Journal of Forecasting, 27*(3), 923–941. https://doi.org/10.1016/j.ijforecast.2010.02.010

Cesario, F. J., & Knetsch, J. L. (1976). A recreation site demand and benefit estimation model. *Regional Studies, 10*(1), 97–104. https://doi.org/10.1080/09595237600185101

Chan, Y. M. (1993). Forecasting tourism: A sine wave time series regression approach. *Journal of Travel Research, 32*(2), 58–60. https://doi.org/10.1177/004728759303200209

Chen, R. J., Bloomfield, P., & Fu, J. S. (2003). An evaluation of alternative forecasting methods to recreation visitation. *Journal of Leisure Research, 35*(4), 441–454. https://doi.org/10.1080/00222216.2003.11950005

Choi, H., & Varian, H. (2012). Predicting the present with Google Trends. *Economic Record, 88,* 2–9. https://doi.org/10.1111/j.1475-4932.2012.00809.x

Choyakh, H. (2008). A model of tourism demand for Tunisia: Inclusion of the tourism investment variable. *Tourism Economics, 14*(4), 819–838. https://doi.org/10.5367/000000008786440238

Chu, F. L. (2004). Forecasting tourism demand: A cubic polynomial approach. *Tourism Management, 25*(2), 209–218. https://doi.org/10.1016/S0261-5177(03)00086-4

Coshall, J. T. (2009). Combining volatility and smoothing forecasts of UK demand for international tourism. *Tourism Management, 30*(4), 495–511. https://doi.org/10.1016/j.tourman.2008.10.010

Crouch, G. I. (1994). The study of international tourism demand: A survey of practice. *Journal of Travel Research, 32*(4), 41–55. https://doi.org/10.1177/004728759403200408

Crouch, G. I., Schultz, L., & Valerio, P. (1992). Marketing international tourism to Australia: A regression analysis. *Tourism Management, 13*(2), 196–208. https://doi.org/10.1016/0261-5177(92)90061-B

Deaton, A., & Muelbauer, J. (1980). An almost ideal demand system. *American Economic Review, 70*(3), 312–326.

Dees, S., Mauro, F. D., Pesaran, M. H., & Smith, L. V. (2007). Exploring the international linkages of the euro area: A global VAR analysis. *Journal of Applied Econometrics, 22*(1), 1–38. https://doi.org/10.1002/jae.932

Dergiades, T., Mavragani, E., & Pan, B. (2018). Google Trends and tourists' arrivals: Emerging biases and proposed corrections. *Tourism Management, 66,* 108–120. https://doi.org/10.1016/j.tourman.2017.10.014

Di Matteo, L., & Di Matteo, R. (1993). The determinants of expenditures by Canadian visitors to the United States. *Journal of Travel Research, 31*(4), 34–42. https://doi.org/10.1177/004728759303100406

Díaz, M.Á., & Nadal, J. R. (2010). Forecasting British tourist arrivals in the Balearic Islands using meteorological variables. *Tourism Economics, 16*(1), 153–168. https://doi.org/10.5367/000000010790872079

Divisekera, S. (2003). A model of demand for international tourism. *Annals of Tourism Research, 30*(1), 31–49. https://doi.org/10.1016/S0160-7383(02)00029-4

Dogru, T., Sirakaya-Turk, E., & Crouch, G. I. (2017). Remodeling international tourism demand: Old theory and new evidence. *Tourism Management, 60*, 47–55. https://doi.org/10.1016/j.tourman.2016.11.010

Dritsakis, N. (2004). Cointegration analysis of German and British tourism demand for Greece. *Tourism Management, 25*(1), 111–119. https://doi.org/10.1016/s0261-5177(03)00061-x

Durbarry, R., & Sinclair, M. T. (2003). Market shares analysis. *Annals of Tourism Research, 30*(4), 927–941. https://doi.org/10.1016/s0160-7383(03)00058-6

Dwyer, J. H. (1983). *Statistical models for the social and behavioral sciences*. Oxford University Press.

Elhorst, J. P. (2014). Dynamic spatial panels: Models, methods and inferences. In *Spatial Econometrics* (pp. 95–119). Springer.

Elhorst, J. P. (2017). Spatial panel data analysis. *Encyclopedia of GIS, 2*, 2050–2058.

Ellis, J. B., & Doren, C. S. (1966). A comparative evaluation of gravity and system theory models for statewide recreational traffic flows. *Journal of Regional Science, 6*(2), 57–70. https://doi.org/10.1111/j.1467-9787.1966.tb01316.x

Fildes, R., Wei, Y., & Ismail, S. (2011). Evaluating the forecasting performance of econometric models of air passenger traffic flows using multiple error measures. *International Journal of Forecasting, 27*(3), 902–922. https://doi.org/10.1016/j.ijforecast.2009.06.002

Fotheringham, A. S. (1983). A new set of spatial-interaction models: The theory of competing destinations. *Environment and Planning A: Economy and Space, 15*(1), 15–36. https://doi.org/10.1177/0308518X8301500103

Fritz, R. G., Brandon, C., & Xander, J. (1984). Combining time-series and econometric forecast of tourism activity. *Annals of Tourism Research, 11*(2), 219–229. https://doi.org/10.1016/0160-7383(84)90071-9

Garin-Munoz, T. (2006). Inbound international tourism to Canary Islands: A dynamic panel data model. *Tourism Management, 27*(2), 281–291. https://doi.org/10.1016/j.tourman.2004.10.002

Garin-Munoz, T. (2007). German demand for tourism in Spain. *Tourism Management, 28*(1), 12–22. https://doi.org/10.1016/j.tourman.2005.07.020

Garin-Munoz, T., & Amaral, T. P. (2000). An econometric model for international tourism flows to Spain. *Applied Economics Letters, 7*(8), 525–529. https://doi.org/10.1080/13504850050033319

Garin-Munoz, T., & Montero-Martín, L. F. (2007). Tourism in the Balearic Islands: A dynamic model for international demand using panel data. *Tourism Management, 28*(5), 1224–1235. https://doi.org/10.1016/j.tourman.2006.09.024

Goh, C. (2012). Exploring impact of climate on tourism demand. *Annals of Tourism Research, 39*(4), 1859–1883. https://doi.org/10.1016/j.annals.2012.05.027

Goh, C., & Law, R. (2011). The methodological progress of tourism demand forecasting: A review of related literature. *Journal of Travel & Tourism Marketing, 28*(3), 296–317. https://doi.org/10.1080/10548408.2011.562856

Gonzalez, P., & Moral, P. (1995). An analysis of the international tourism demand in Spain. *International Journal of Forecasting, 11*(2), 233–251. https://doi.org/10.1016/0169-2070(94)00570-3

Gray, H. P. (1966). The demand for international travel by the United States and Canada. *International Economic Review, 7*(1), 83–92. https://doi.org/10.2307/2525372

Greenidge, K. (2001). Forecasting tourism demand: An STM approach. *Annals of Tourism Research, 28*(1), 98–112. https://doi.org/10.1016/S0160-7383(00)00010-4

Guizzardi, A., & Mazzocchi, M. (2010). Tourism demand for Italy and the business cycle. *Tourism Management, 31*(3), 367–377. https://doi.org/10.1016/j.tourman.2009.03.017

Gunter, U., & Önder, I. (2015). Forecasting international city tourism demand for Paris: Accuracy of uni- and multivariate models employing monthly data. *Tourism Management, 46*, 123–135. https://doi.org/10.1016/j.tourman.2014.06.017

Guizzardi, & Stacchini, A. (2015). Real-time forecasting regional tourism with business sentiment surveys. *Tourism Management* (1982), *47*, 213–223. https://doi.org/10.1016/j.tourman.2014.09.022

Guthrie, H. W. (1961). Demand for tourists' goods and services in a world market. *Papers in Regional Science, 7*(1), 159–175. https://doi.org/10.1007/BF01969078

Gunter, U., & Önder, I. (2016). Forecasting city arrivals with Google Analytics. *Annals of Tourism Research, 61*, 199–212. https://doi.org/10.1016/j.annals.2016.10.007

Gunter, U., & Zekan, B. (2021). Forecasting air passenger numbers with a GVAR model. *Annals of Tourism Research, 89*. https://doi.org/10.1016/j.annals.2021.103252

Halicioglu, F. (2010). An econometric analysis of the aggregate outbound tourism demand of Turkey. *Tourism Economics, 16*(1), 83–97. https://doi.org/10.5367/000000010790872196

Han, Z., Durbarry, R., & Sinclair, M. T. (2006). Modelling US tourism demand for European destinations. *Tourism Management, 27*(1), 1–10. https://doi.org/10.1016/j.tourman.2004.06.015

Hu, M., & Song, H. (2019). Data source combination for tourism demand forecasting. *Tourism Economics, 26*(7), 1248–1265. https://doi.org/10.1177/1354816619872592

Jiao, X., Chen, J. L., & Li, G. (2021). Forecasting tourism demand: Developing a general nesting spatiotemporal model. *Annals of Tourism Research, 90*. https://doi.org/10.1016/j.annals.2021.103277

Jiao, X., Li, G., & Chen, J. L. (2020). Forecasting international tourism demand: A local spatiotemporal model. *Annals of Tourism Research, 83*. https://doi.org/10.1016/j.annals.2020.102937

Kalman, R. E. (1960). A new approach to linear filtering and prediction problems. *Journal of Basic Engineering, 82*(1), 35–45. https://doi.org/10.1109/9780470544334.ch9

Kanafani, A. (1983). *Transportation demand analysis*. New York: McGraw-Hill.

Keintz, R. M. (1968). A study of the demand for international travel to and from the United States. *Travel Research Bulletin, 7*(1), 6–10.

Kelejian, H. H., & Prucha, I. R. (1998). A generalized spatial two-stage least squares procedure for estimating a spatial autoregressive model with autoregressive disturbances. *The Journal of Real Estate Finance and Economics, 17*(1), 99–121.

Khadaroo, J., & Seetanah, B. (2008). The role of transport infrastructure in international tourism development: A gravity model approach. *Tourism Management, 29*(5), 831–840. https://doi.org/10.1016/j.tourman.2007.09.005

Kim, N., & Schwartz, Z. (2013). The accuracy of tourism forecasting and data characteristics: A meta-analytical approach. *Journal of Hospitality Marketing & Management, 22*(4), 349–374. https://doi.org/10.1080/19368623.2011.651196

Kim, S., & Song, H. (1998). Analysis of inbound tourism demand in South Korea: A cointegration and error correction approach. *Tourism Analysis, 3*(1), 25–41.

Koo, T. T. R., Lim, C., & Dobruszkes, F. (2017). Causality in direct air services and tourism demand. *Annals of Tourism Research, 67,* 67–77. https://doi.org/10.1016/j.annals.2017.08.004

Kulendran, N. (1996). Modelling quarterly tourist flows to Australia using cointegration analysis. *Tourism Economics, 2*(3), 203–222. https://doi.org/10.1177/135481669600200301

Kulendran, N., & Witt, S. F. (2001). Cointegration versus least squares regression. *Annals of Tourism Research, 28*(2), 291–311. https://doi.org/10.1016/S0160-7383(00)00031-1

Kulendran, N., & Witt, S. F. (2003a). Forecasting the demand for international business tourism. *Journal of Travel Research, 41*(3), 265–271. https://doi.org/10.1177/0047287502239034

Kulendran, N., & Witt, S. F. (2003b). Leading indicator tourism forecasts. *Tourism Management, 24*(5), 503–510. https://doi.org/10.1016/S0261-5177(03)00010-4

Kulshrestha, A., Krishnaswamy, V., & Sharma, M. (2020). Bayesian BILSTM approach for tourism demand forecasting. *Annals of Tourism Research, 83.* https://doi.org/10.1016/j.annals.2020.102925

Laber, G. (1969). Determinants of international travel between Canada and the United States. *Geographical Analysis, 1*(4), 329–336. https://doi.org/10.1111/j.1538-4632.1969.tb00628.x

Lanza, A., Temple, P., & Urga, G. (2003). The implications of tourism specialisation in the long run: An econometric analysis for 13 OECD economies. *Tourism Management, 24*(3), 315–321. https://doi.org/10.1016/S0261-5177(02)00065-1

Law, R. (2000). Back-propagation learning in improving the accuracy of neural network-based tourism demand forecasting. *Tourism Management, 21*(4), 331–340. https://doi.org/10.1016/S0261-5177(99)00067-9

Law, R., & Au, N. (1999). A neural network model to forecast Japanese demand for travel to Hong Kong. *Tourism Management, 20*(1), 89–97. https://doi.org/10.1016/S0261-5177(98)00094-6

Ledesma-Rodríguez, F. J., Navarro-Ibáñez, M., & Pérez-Rodríguez, J. V. (2001). Panel data and tourism: A case study of Tenerife. *Tourism Economics, 7*(1), 75–88. https://doi.org/10.5367/000000001101297748

Lee, L., & Yu, J. (2010). Some recent developments in spatial panel data models. *Regional Science and Urban Economics, 40*(5), 255–271. https://doi.org/10.1016/j.regsciurbeco.2009.09.002

Li, G., Song, H., & Witt, S. F. (2004). Modeling tourism demand: A dynamic linear AIDS approach. *Journal of Travel Research, 43*(2), 141–150. https://doi.org/10.1177/0047287504268235

Li, G., Song, H., & Witt, S. F. (2005). Recent developments in econometric modeling and forecasting. *Journal of Travel Research, 44*(1), 82–99. https://doi.org/10.1177/0047287505276594

Li, G., Song, H., & Witt, S. F. (2006). Time varying parameter and fixed parameter linear AIDS: An application to tourism demand forecasting.

International Journal of Forecasting, 22(1), 57–71. https://doi.org/10.1016/j. ijforecast.2005.03.006

Li, G., Wong, K. K. F., Song, H., & Witt, S. F. (2006). Tourism demand forecasting: A time varying parameter error correction model. *Journal of Travel Research, 45*(2), 175–185. https://doi.org/10.1177/0047287506291596

Li, G., Wu, D. C., Zhou, M., & Liu, A. (2019). The combination of interval forecasts in tourism. *Annals of Tourism Research, 75,* 363–378. https://doi.org/10.1016/j. annals.2019.01.010

Li, H., Goh, C., Hung, K., & Chen, J. L. (2018). Relative climate index and its effect on seasonal tourism demand. *Journal of Travel Research, 57*(2), 178–192. https:// doi.org/10.1177/0047287516687409

Li, H., Song, H., & Li, L. (2016). A dynamic panel data analysis of climate and tourism demand. *Journal of Travel Research, 56*(2), 158–171. https://doi. org/10.1177/0047287515626304

Li, S., Chen, T., Wang, L., & Ming, C. (2018). Effective tourist volume forecasting supported by PCA and improved BPNN using Baidu index. *Tourism Management, 68,* 116–126. https://doi.org/10.1016/j.tourman.2018.03.006

Li, X., Pan, B., Law, R., & Huang, X. (2017). Forecasting tourism demand with composite search index. *Tourism Management, 59,* 57–66. https://doi. org/10.1016/j.tourman.2016.07.005

Lim, C. (1997). Review of international tourism demand models. *Annals of Tourism Research, 24*(4), 835–849. https://doi.org/10.1016/S0160-7383(97)00049-2

Lim. (2004). The major determinants of Korean outbound travel to Australia. *Mathematics and Computers in Simulation, 64*(3), 477–485. https://doi.org/10. 1016/S0378-4754(03)00113-7

Lim, C., & McAleer, M. (2001). Cointegration analysis of quarterly tourism demand by Hong Kong and Singapore for Australia. *Applied Economics, 33*(12), 1599–1619. https://doi.org/10.1080/00036840010014012

Lin, V. S., Liu, A., & Song, H. (2015). Modeling and forecasting Chinese outbound tourism: An econometric approach. *Journal of Travel & Tourism Marketing, 32*(1–2), 34–49. https://doi.org/10.1080/10548408.2014.986011

Lin, V. S., & Song, H. (2014). A review of Delphi forecasting research in tourism. *Current Issues in Tourism, 18*(12), 1099–1131. https://doi.org/10.1080/13683500. 2014.967187

Liu, A., Lin, V. S., Li, G., & Song, H. (2020). *Ex ante* tourism forecasting assessment. *Journal of Travel Research, 61*(1), 64–75. https://doi.org/10.1177/ 0047287520974456

Liu, Y. Y., Tseng, F. M., & Tseng, Y. H. (2018). Big data analytics for forecasting tourism destination arrivals with the applied vector autoregression model. *Technological Forecasting and Social Change, 130,* 123–134. https://doi. org/10.1016/j.techfore.2018.01.018

Loeb, P. D. (1982). International travel to the United States: An econometric evaluation. *Annals of Tourism Research, 9*(1), 7–20. https://doi.org/10.1016/ 0160-7383(82)90031-7

Marrocu, E., & Paci, R. (2013). Different tourists to different destinations: Evidence from spatial interaction models. *Tourism Management, 39,* 71–83. https://doi.org/10.1016/j.tourman.2012.10.009

Martin, C. A., & Witt, S. F. (1987). Tourism demand forecasting models: Choice of appropriate variable to represent tourists' cost of living. *Tourism Management, 8*(3), 233–246. https://doi.org/10.1016/0261-5177(87)90055-0

Martin, C. A., & Witt, S. F. (1988). Substitute prices in models of tourism demand. *Annals of Tourism Research, 15*(2), 255–268. https://doi.org/10.1016/0160-7383(88)90086-2

Martin, C. A., & Witt, S. F. (1989). Forecasting tourism demand: A comparison of the accuracy of several quantitative methods. *International Journal of Forecasting, 5*(1), 7–19. https://doi.org/10.1016/0169-2070(89)90059-9

Masiero, L. (2016). International tourism statistics—UNWTO benchmark and cross-country comparison of definitions and sampling issues. UNWTO (United Nations World Tourism Organization). https://www.unwto.org/

Mello, M. D., Pack, A., & Sinclair, M. T. (2002). A system of equations model of UK tourism demand in neighbouring countries. *Applied Economics, 34*(4), 509–521. https://doi.org/10.1080/00036840110049310

Moore, W. R. (2010). The impact of climate change on Caribbean tourism demand. *Current Issues in Tourism, 13*(5), 495–505. https://doi.org/10.1080/13683500903576045

Morley, C. L. (1992). A microeconomic theory of international tourism demand. *Annals of Tourism Research, 19*(2), 250–267. https://doi.org/10.1016/0160-7383(92)90080-9

Morley, C. L. (1997). An evaluation of the use of ordinary least squares for estimating tourism demand models. *Journal of Travel Research, 35*(4), 69–73. https://doi.org/10.1177/004728759703500411

Morley, C. L., Rosselló, J., & Santana-Gallego, M. (2014). Gravity models for tourism demand: Theory and use. *Annals of Tourism Research, 48*, 1–10. https://doi.org/10.1016/j.annals.2014.05.008

Nadal, J.R. (2001). Forecasting turning points in International Visitor Arrivals in the Balearic Islands. *Tourism Economics, 7*(4), 365–380. https://doi.org/10.5367/000000001101297928

Nadal, J. R., Font, A. R., & Rosselló, A. S. (2004). The economic determinants of seasonal patterns. *Annals of Tourism Research, 31*(3), 697–711. https://doi.org/10.1016/j.annals.2004.02.001

Narayan, P. K. (2004). Fiji's tourism demand: The ARDL approach to cointegration. *Tourism Economics, 10*(2), 193–206. https://doi.org/10.5367/000000004323142425

Naudé, W. A., & Saayman, A. (2005). Determinants of tourist arrivals in Africa: A panel data regression analysis. *Tourism Economics, 11*(3), 365–391. https://doi.org/10.5367/000000005774352962

O'Hagan, J. W., & Harrison, M. J. (1984). Market shares of US tourist expenditure in Europe: An econometric analysis. *Applied Economics, 16*(6), 919–931. https://doi.org/10.1080/00036848400000060

Önder, I., & Gunter, U. (2016). Forecasting tourism demand with Google Trends for a major European city destination. *Tourism Analysis, 21*(2), 203–220. https://doi.org/10.3727/108354216x14559233984773

Ouchen, A., & Montargot, N. (2021). Non-spatial and spatial econometric analysis of tourism demand in a panel of countries around the world. *Spatial Economic Analysis*, 1–22. https://doi.org/10.1080/17421772.2021.1940256

Ouerfelli, C. (2008). Co-integration analysis of quarterly European tourism demand in Tunisia. *Tourism Management, 29*(1), 127–137. https://doi.org/10.1016/j.tourman.2007.03.022

Page, S., Song, H., & Wu, D. C. (2012). Assessing the impacts of the global economic crisis and swine flu on inbound tourism demand in the United Kingdom. *Journal of Travel Research, 51*(2), 142–153. https://doi.org/10.1177/0047287511400754

Page, S., Yeoman, I., Munro, C., Connell, J., & Walker, L. (2006). A case study of best practice—Visit Scotland's prepared response to an influenza pandemic. *Tourism Management, 27*(3), 361–393. https://doi.org/10.1016/j.tourman.2006.01.001

Pan, B., Wu, D. C., & Song, H. (2012). Forecasting hotel room demand using search engine data. *Journal of Hospitality and Tourism Technology, 3*(3), 196–210. https://doi.org/10.1108/17579881211264486

Pan, B., & Yang, Y. (2016). Forecasting destination weekly hotel occupancy with big data. *Journal of Travel Research, 56*(7), 957–970. https://doi.org/10.1177/0047287516669050

Papatheodorou, A. (1999). The demand for international tourism in the Mediterranean region. *Applied Economics, 31*(5), 619–630. https://doi.org/10.1080/000368499324066

Park, S., Lee, J., & Song, W. (2017). Short-term forecasting of Japanese tourist inflow to South Korea using Google trends data. *Journal of Travel & Tourism Marketing, 34*(3), 357–368. https://doi.org/10.1080/10548408.2016.1170651

Pesaran, M. H., Schuermann, T., & Weiner, S. M. (2004). Modeling regional interdependencies using a global error-correcting macroeconometric model. *Journal of Business and Economic Statistics, 22*(2), 129–162. https://doi.org/10.1198/073500104000000019

Peng, B., Song, H., & Crouch, G. I. (2014). A meta-analysis of international tourism demand forecasting and implications for practice. *Tourism Management, 45,* 181–193. https://doi.org/10.1016/j.tourman.2014.04.005

Qiu, R. T. R., Wu, D. C., Dropsy, V., Petit, S., Pratt, S., & Ohe, Y. (2021). Visitor arrivals forecasts amid COVID-19: A perspective from the Asia and Pacific team. *Annals of Tourism Research, 88.* https://doi.org/10.1016/j.annals.2021.103155

Qu, H., & Lam, S. (1997). A travel demand model for mainland Chinese tourists to Hong Kong. *Tourism Management, 18*(8), 593–597. https://doi.org/10.1016/S0261-5177(97)00084-8

Ridderstaat, J., Oduber, M., Croes, R., Nijkamp, P., & Martens, P. (2014). Impacts of seasonal patterns of climate on recurrent fluctuations in tourism demand: Evidence from Aruba. *Tourism Management, 41,* 245–256. https://doi.org/10.1016/j.tourman.2013.09.005

Rodríguez, Ó. G. (2017). Forecasting tourism arrivals with an online search engine data: A study of the Balearic Islands. *Pasos. Revista de Turismo y Patrimonio Cultural, 15*(4), 943–958.

Roget, F. M., & González, X. A. R. (2006). Rural tourism demand in Galicia, Spain. *Tourism Economics, 12*(1), 21–31. https://doi.org/10.5367/000000006776387178

Romilly, P., Liu, X., & Song, H. (1998). Economic and social determinants of international tourism spending: A panel data analysis. *Tourism Analysis, 16*(3), 3–16.

Saha, S., & Yap, G. (2014). The moderation effects of political instability and terrorism on tourism development. *Journal of Travel Research, 53*(4), 509–521. https://doi.org/10.1177/0047287513496447

Sakai, M., Brown, J., & Mak, J. (2000). Population aging and Japanese international travel in the 21st century. *Journal of Travel Research, 38*(3), 212–220. https://doi.org/10.1177/004728750003800302

Sargan, J. D. (1964). Wages and Prices in the UK: A study in Econometric Methodology. In P.E. Hart, et al. (Eds.). *Econometric analysis for national economic planning.* Butterworth Scientific Publishers.

Sheldon, P. J. (1993). Forecasting tourism: Expenditures versus arrivals. *Journal of Travel Research, 32*(1), 13–20. https://doi.org/10.1177/004728759303200103

Shen, S., Li, G., & Song, H. (2011). Combination forecasts of international tourism demand. *Annals of Tourism Research, 38*(1), 72–89. https://doi.org/10.1016/j.annals.2010.05.003

Sims, C. A. (1980). Macroeconomics and reality. *Econometrica, 48*(1), 1–48. https://doi.org/10.2307/1912017

Smeral, E. (2009). The Impact of the Financial and Economic Crisis on European Tourism. *Journal of Travel Research, 48*(1), 3–13. https://doi.org/10.1177/0047287509336332

Smeral, E. (2010). Impacts of the world recession and economic crisis on tourism: Forecasts and potential risks. *Journal of Travel Research, 49*(1), 31–38. https://doi.org/10.1177/0047287509353192

Smeral, E. (2012). International tourism demand and the business cycle. *Annals of Tourism Research, 39*(1), 379–400. https://doi.org/10.1016/j.annals.2011.07.015

Smeral, E., Witt, S. F., & Witt, C. A. (1992). Econometric forecasts: Tourism trends to 2000. *Annals of Tourism Research, 19*(3), 450–466. https://doi.org/10.1016/0160-7383(92)90130-H

Song, H., Gao, B. Z., & Lin, V. S. (2013). Combining statistical and judgmental forecasts via a web-based tourism demand forecasting system. *International Journal of Forecasting, 29*(2), 295–310. https://doi.org/10.1016/j.ijforecast.2011.12.003

Song, H., Gartner, W. C., & Tasci, A. D. A. (2012). Visa restrictions and their adverse economic and marketing implications – Evidence from China. *Tourism Management, 33*(2), 397–412. https://doi.org/10.1016/j.tourman.2011.05.001

Song, H., & Li, G. (2008). Tourism demand modelling and forecasting—A review of recent research. *Tourism Management, 29*(2), 203–220. https://doi.org/10.1016/j.tourman.2007.07.016

Song, H., Li, G., Witt, S. F., & Athanasopoulos, G. (2011). Forecasting tourist arrivals using time-varying parameter structural time series models. *International Journal of Forecasting, 27*(3), 855–869. https://doi.org/10.1016/j.ijforecast.2010.06.001

Song, H., & Lin, S. (2010). Impacts of the financial and economic crisis on tourism in Asia. *Journal of Travel Research, 49*(1), 16–30. https://doi.org/10.1177/0047287509353190

Song, H., Lin, S., Witt, S. F., & Zhang, X. (2011). Impact of financial/economic crisis on demand for hotel rooms in Hong Kong. *Tourism Management, 32*(1), 172–186. https://doi.org/10.1016/j.tourman.2010.05.006

Song, H., Lin, S., Zhang, X., & Gao, Z. (2010). Global financial/economic crisis and tourist arrival forecasts for Hong Kong. *Asia Pacific Journal of Tourism Research, 15*(2), 223–242. https://doi.org/10.1080/10941661003687431

Song, H., Qiu, R. T. R., & Park, J. (2019). A review of research on tourism demand forecasting: Launching the *Annals of Tourism Research* curated collection on tourism demand forecasting. *Annals of Tourism Research, 75,* 338–362. https://doi.org/10.1016/j.annals.2018.12.001

Song, H., Romilly, P., & Liu, X. (2000). An empirical study of outbound tourism demand in the UK. *Applied Economics, 32*(5), 611–624. https://doi.org/10.1080/000368400322516

Song, H., & Witt, S. F. (2000). *Tourism demand modeling and forecasting: Modern econometric approach* (1st ed.). Pergamon.

Song, H., & Witt, S. F. (2003). Tourism forecasting: The general-to-specific approach. *Journal of Travel Research, 42*(1), 65–74. https://doi.org/10.1177/0047287503253939

Song, H., & Witt, S. F. (2006). Forecasting international tourist flows to Macau. *Tourism Management, 27*(2), 214–224. https://doi.org/10.1016/j.tourman.2004.09.004

Song, H., Witt, S. F., & Jensen, T. C. (2003). Tourism forecasting: Accuracy of alternative econometric models. *International Journal of Forecasting, 19*(1), 123–141. https://doi.org/10.1016/S0169-2070(01)00134-0

Song, H., Witt, S. F., & Li, G. (2003). Modelling and forecasting the demand for Thai tourism. *Tourism Economics, 9*(4), 363–387. https://doi.org/10.5367/000000003322663186

Song, H., Witt, S. F., Wong, K. K. F., & Wu, D. C. (2009). An empirical study of forecast combination in tourism. *Journal of Hospitality and Tourism Research, 33*(1), 3–29. https://doi.org/10.1177/1096348008321366

Song, H., & Wong, K. K. (2003). Tourism demand modeling: A time-varying parameter approach. *Journal of Travel Research, 42*(1), 57–64. https://doi.org/10.1177/0047287503253908

Song, H., Wong, K. K. F., & Chon, K. K. S. (2003). Modelling and forecasting the demand for Hong Kong tourism. *International Journal of Hospitality Management, 22*(4), 435–451. https://doi.org/10.1016/s0278-4319(03)00047-1

Stone, J. R. N. (1954). Linear expenditure systems and demand analysis: An application to the pattern of British demand. *The Economic Journal, 64*(255), 511–527. https://doi.org/10.2307/2227743

Syriopoulos, T. C. (1995). A dynamic model of demand for Mediterranean tourism. *International Review of Applied Economics, 9*(3), 318–336. https://doi.org/10.1080/758537633

Syriopoulos, T. C., & Sinclair, M. T. (1993). An econometric study of tourism demand: The AIDS model of US and European tourism in Mediterranean countries. *Applied Economics, 25*(12), 1541–1552. https://doi.org/10.1080/00036849300000158

Tang, J., Yuan, X., Ramos, V., & Sriboonchitta, S. (2019). Does air pollution decrease inbound tourist arrivals? The case of Beijing. *Asia Pacific Journal of Tourism Research, 24*(6), 597–605. https://doi.org/10.1080/10941665.2019.1610004

Tsui, W. H. K., Chow, C. K. W., Lin, Y.-H., & Chen, P.-L. (2021). Econometric analysis of factors influencing Chinese tourist visits to New Zealand. *Tourism Management Perspectives, 39*. https://doi.org/10.1016/j.tmp.2021.100861

Tsui, W. H. K., Ozer Balli, H., Gilbey, A., & Gow, H. (2014). Forecasting of Hong Kong airport's passenger throughput. *Tourism Management, 42*, 62–76. https://doi.org/10.1016/j.tourman.2013.10.008

Turner, L. W., & Witt, S. F. (2001). Factors influencing demand for international tourism: tourism demand analysis using structural equation modelling, revisited. *Tourism Economics, 7*(1), 21–39. https://doi.org/10.5367/000000001101297711

Uysal, M., & Crompton, J. L. (1984). Determinants of demand for international tourist flows to Turkey. *Tourism Management, 5*(4), 288–297. https://doi.org/10.1016/0261-5177(84)90025-6

Uysal, M., & El Roubi, M. S. (1999). Artificial neural networks versus multiple regression in tourism demand analysis. *Journal of Travel Research, 38*(2), 111–118. https://doi.org/10.1177/004728759903800203

Vanegas, M., Sr, & Croes, R. R. (2000). Evaluation of demand: US tourists to Aruba. *Annals of Tourism Research, 27*(4), 946–963. https://doi.org/10.1016/S0160-7383(99)00114-0

Vanhove. (1980). Forecasting in tourism. *Revue de Tourisme = The Tourist Review = Zeitschrift Für Fremdenverkehr, 35*(3), 2–7. https://doi.org/10.1108/eb057814

Vu, C. J., & Turner, L. (2005). Data disaggregation in demand forecasting. *Tourism & Hospitality Research, 6*(1), 38–52. https://doi.org/10.1057/palgrave.thr.6040043

Wang, Y-S. (2009). The impact of crisis events and macroeconomic activity on Taiwan's international inbound tourism demand. *Tourism Management (1982), 30*(1), 75–82. https://doi.org/10.1016/j.tourman.2008.04.010

Weatherford, L. R., & Kimes, S. E. (2003). A comparison of forecasting methods for hotel revenue management. *International Journal of Forecasting, 19*(3), 401–415. https://doi.org/10.1016/S0169-2070(02)00011-0

Weatherford, L. R., Kimes, S. E., & Scott, D. A. (2001). Forecasting for hotel revenue management: Testing aggregation against disaggregation. *Cornell Hotel and Restaurant Administration Quarterly, 42*(4), 53–64.

Webber, A. G. (2001). Exchange rate volatility and cointegration in tourism demand. *Journal of Travel Research, 39*(4), 398–405. https://doi.org/10.1177/004728750103900406

Wen, L., Liu, C., & Song, H. (2018). Pooling in tourism demand forecasting. *Journal of Travel Research, 58*(7), 1161–1174. https://doi.org/10.1177/0047287518800390

Wen, L., Liu, C., & Song, H. (2019). Forecasting tourism demand using search query data: A hybrid modelling approach. *Tourism Economics, 25*(3), 309–329. https://doi.org/10.1177/1354816618768317

Wen, L., Liu, C., Song, H., & Liu, H. (2021). Forecasting tourism demand with an improved mixed data sampling model. *Journal of Travel Research, 60*(2), 336–353. https://doi.org/10.1177/0047287520906220

Witt, S. F., & Martin, C. A. (1987). Econometric models for forecasting international tourism demand. *Journal of Travel Research, 25*(3), 23–30. https://doi.org/10.1177/004728758702500306

Witt, S. F., & Witt, C. A. (1995). Forecasting tourism demand: A review of empirical research. *International Journal of Forecasting, 11*(3), 447–475. https://doi.org/10.1016/0169-2070(95)00591-7

Wong, K. K. F., Song, H., & Chon, K. S. (2006). Bayesian models for tourism demand forecasting. *Tourism Management, 27*(5), 773–780. https://doi.org/10.1016/j.tourman.2005.05.017

Wong, K. K. F., Song, H., Witt, S. F., & Wu, D. C. (2007). Tourism forecasting: To combine or not to combine? *Tourism Management, 28*(4), 1068–1078. https://doi.org/10.1016/j.tourman.2006.08.003

Wu, D. C., Cao, Z., Wen, L., & Song, H. (2020). Scenario forecasting for global tourism. *Journal of Hospitality & Tourism Research, 45*(1), 28–51. https://doi.org/10.1177/1096348020919990

Wu, D. C., Song, H., & Shen, S. (2017). New developments in tourism and hotel demand modeling and forecasting. *International Journal of Contemporary Hospitality Management, 29*(1), 507–529. https://doi.org/https://doi.org/10.1108/IJCHM-05-2015-0249

Yang, X., Pan, B., Evans, J. A., & Lv, B. (2015). Forecasting Chinese tourist volume with search engine data. *Tourism Management, 46*, 386–397. https://doi.org/10.1016/j.tourman.2014.07.019

Yang, Y., Pan, B., & Song, H. (2014). Predicting hotel demand using destination marketing organization's web traffic data. *Journal of Travel Research, 53*(4), 433–447. https://doi.org/10.1177/0047287513500391

Yang, Y., & Zhang, H. (2019). Spatial-temporal forecasting of tourism demand. *Annals of Tourism Research, 75*, 106–119. https://doi.org/10.1016/j.annals.2018.12.024

Yeoman, I., Galt, M., & McMahon-Beattie, U. (2005). A case study of how Visit Scotland prepared for war. *Journal of Travel Research, 44*(1), 6–20. https://doi.org/10.1177/0047287505276587

Zamparini, L., Vergori, A. S., & Arima, S. (2017). Assessing the determinants of local tourism demand: A simultaneous equations model for the Italian provinces. *Tourism Economics*, 23(5), 981–992. https://doi.org/10.1177/1354816616656423

Zhang, H., Song, H., Wen, L., & Liu, C. (2021). Forecasting tourism recovery amid COVID-19. *Annals of Tourism Research, 87*. https://doi.org/10.1016/j.annals.2021.103149

Zhang, J., & Jensen, C. (2007). Comparative advantage: Explaining tourism flows. *Annals of Tourism Research, 34*(1), 223–243. https://doi.org/10.1016/j.annals.2006.08.004

2

THEORETICAL FOUNDATIONS, KEY CONCEPTS, AND DATA DESCRIPTION

Vera Shanshan Lin, Xinyi Zhang, and Richard T. R. Qiu

2.1 Economic theory of tourism demand

Tourism demand analysis is rooted in the economic theory of demand, whereby researchers attempt to ascertain the willingness and ability of tourists to explore destinations (Song, Witt, & Li, 2009). Tourists visit destinations for a variety of reasons, such as leisure, business, visiting friends and relatives (VFR), education and training, medical and health care, and religious pilgrimages (Song & Witt, 2000). Of the many types of travellers, leisure tourists account for the vast majority of global tourism demand (UNWTO, 2020). As a result, leisure tourists are regularly targeted in tourism and hospitality campaigns (Lockwood, 2007). Unlike other types of tourists whose destinations are predetermined by the reasons for their visit (i.e., the location of a business meeting or their family's city of residence), leisure tourists undertake a complex decision-making process involving the trade-offs associated with their desired destinations, in terms of the quality of the tourism product and other constraints related to price, time, and income (Masiero & Qiu, 2018). Given these complexities and the popularity of leisure tourism, we focus our attention on these travellers.

2.1.1 Tourism demand and its determinants

2.1.1.1 Tourism demand – Dependent variables

Tourism demand can be measured in a variety of ways. In terms of the flow of tourists, tourism demand can be classified into three types: domestic, inbound, and outbound (UNWTO, 2010). Domestic tourism describes the tourism activities of travellers within their region or country of residence,

DOI: 10.4324/9781003269366-2

whereas inbound and outbound tourism refer to tourists entering and leaving their country/region, respectively (UNWTO, 2010). Transit tourists and near-cation/staycation tourists are specifically identified and analysed for their distinct characteristics and preferences relative to other types of tourists. Transit tourists are defined as individuals who make a brief stop at a destination during a long trip, while near-cation/staycation tourists take part in tourism activities within their residential area.

While the terms 'visitor' and 'tourist' are clearly defined (UNWTO, 2010), statistical recording of these data are not easy. Tourism demand analysis normally relies on frontier counts (tourist/visitor arrivals), representing the most common source of tourism demand data (UNWTO, 2020). Ideally, immigration officials will sort arriving passengers' data based on nationality and purpose of visit, thereby providing an accurate picture of tourism demand at the relevant destination (UNWTO, 2020). Relying on frontier count data, however, presents three major problems (UNWTO, 2020). First, there are jurisdictions in which the availability of frontier count data is limited. For example, the European Union's Schengen travel zone allows for border-free travel between member countries, eliminating the possibility of obtaining frontier count data. The same problem exists for domestic tourism. Second, frontier count data may include a substantial number of transit passengers. While such visitors do occasionally enter the location through which they are transiting, their engagement in tourism activities in these places is limited. Third, frontier count data provide more detailed information on incoming flows (inbound tourism) than on outgoing flows (outbound tourism). As such, to obtain a holistic view of outbound tourism flows using frontier counts, researchers would need to engage in the tedious process of consulting the databases of all of the potential destinations of outbound travellers in a particular source market. Given these limitations, frontier count data are often supplemented by other data, including aviation data (arrivals by air) (Fildes, Wei, & Ismail, 2011), accommodation data (records from accommodation establishments) (Zhou-Grundy & Turner, 2014), and, in some small regions such as San Marino and Vatican City, changes in water consumption levels and waste amounts (Gössling et al., 2012). As such, researchers should exercise caution when comparing tourist/visitor arrivals across different countries/regions, given the use of varying data recording methods.

Another measure of tourism demand is tourist expenditure, which places greater emphasis on the consumption process. Unlike arrival data, tourist expenditure data provide a direct indication as to the amount of income generated through the provision of products and services for tourists, thereby assisting researchers seeking to assess the economic effects of tourism. Tourist expenditure data can be collected from banks, by procuring tourist transaction data and assessing the demand for currency in the foreign exchange market. However, with the widespread use of e-payment methods and cyber currencies, data from banks are not always entirely accurate.

Tourist expenditure data may also be determined by way of ascertaining the amount of tax paid by tourism firms, although this method does have its drawbacks. These data do not distinguish between inbound and domestic tourism and may be inaccurate as a result of the potential of these firms to misreport their earnings. In practice, self-reporting through sample surveys can provide reliable data on tourist expenditure. Nonetheless, the sample size of such surveys is often small due to their voluntary nature and the potential high costs associated with their implementation (Song et al., 2009).

2.1.1.2 Demand determinants – Explanatory variables

As with demand theory in economics, many factors influence tourism demand. For example, tourists' income has an important effect on tourism demand. Following the law of demand, an increase in an individual's income will lead to an overall increase in the demand for all of the products in their consumption bundle. In practice, income usually enters the demand function in per capita form and is proxied by gross domestic product (GDP) per capita. When researchers seek to investigate the flow of leisure or VFR tourism, household disposable income is a more appropriate variable when it is available.

Product price is another key factor in classic demand theory, where lower prices should encourage an increase in demand. Price fluctuations in trips to relevant destinations (either substitute or complementary) may also alter tourists' consumption bundles. Unfortunately, the tourism price index is not readily available at most destinations. Instead, the consumer price index (CPI) is usually adopted as a proxy for measuring fluctuations in the costs associated with tourism at a particular destination. The relative fluctuations of an exchange rate-adjusted CPI between the origin market and the destination market further demonstrate tourism price trends in terms of tourists' purchasing power.

A similar strategy can be applied to the approximation of cross prices at the respective destinations. In most cases, multiple tourism destinations within a region are endowed with similar resources and cultural offerings and therefore compete with one another in the marketplace. A price drop at one destination will divert tourists' attention away from other destinations, likely increasing demand for the destination offering a lower price. Some destinations may be presented as a bundle in the international tourism market. A price change associated with one destination in the bundle may hurt the market performance of the other destinations. In practice, instead of including multiple price indices in the demand model, practitioners should consider the weighted average of the various price indices. The exchange rate-adjusted CPI of relevant destinations can be weighted by their market shares in the origin market. In practice, we shall distinguish between the characteristics of the relevant destinations (i.e., substitute or complementary) in our investigation design.

In addition to prices at travel destinations, travel costs emerge as an important factor that affect tourism flows, especially in long-haul tourism. This variable is typically determined using representative airfares from origin to destination, the physical distance between origin and destination, and fluctuations in fuel prices. Despite its reliability, this variable is often omitted in empirical studies due to low data availability and potential multicollinearity with other tourism prices (Song et al., 2009).

Tourist destination preference is also determined by tourists' taste (Song et al., 2009). Taste is affected by tourists' demographic characteristics, including gender, age, education level, marital status, family status, and cultural background, and their understanding of the destination, influenced by previous travel experiences (primary information) and word of mouth and advertising (secondary information). While taste is central in understanding tourists' destination choices, the variable rarely features in tourism demand models at the macro level (Song et al., 2009). Taste is often excluded from such analyses because of the relative stability of tourists' taste over time. Statistical models may fail to identify the significance of the taste variable due to a lack of variation. In studies with longer time horizons, changes in demographic characteristics and flight frequencies may be used as proxies to capture the dynamics of tourist tastes (Song et al., 2009). However, these proxies may have an ambiguous effect, as they often correlate with income and travel costs. As such, further attempts to integrate the taste variable into macro tourism demand analysis are still needed. Dynamic stochastic general equilibrium models and agent-based models, which link macro analyses with micro specifications, may facilitate such explorations.

The above variables (income, price, and tourist taste) are demand-side variables that play key roles in tourism demand analysis. Some situational factors, such as weather and climate conditions, may also temporarily affect the quality of the tourism experience at the destination. In addition, due to the complex, variable, and intangible nature of tourism products, tourists are unable to assess the quality of a product prior to consumption. Tourism suppliers' marketing and promotional efforts are therefore critical in establishing the perceived quality of these products. The number and results of online reviews may also serve as a useful reference for tourists seeking to assess the quality of tourism products. It is important to note that the channels through which supply-side variables influence tourism demand are fundamentally different from those that relate to demand-side variables. As such, we suggest that the underlying mechanism of tourism demand should be carefully specified and clearly elaborated in tourism demand analysis.

When investigating the time series of tourism demand, researchers have often identified an autoregressive process. That is, the lagged values of tourism demand may exhibit some explanatory power for future trends

(Song et al., 2009). The inclusion of lagged values in tourism research has several theoretical justifications. Tourists may make repeated visits to a destination as a result of status quo bias and habit persistence (Song et al., 2009). Given the uncertainty associated with product quality at unknown destinations, tourists often visit the same destination repeatedly to avoid the risk of an unpleasant trip. Furthermore, past volumes of tourism demand send a positive quality signal to first time visitors, as a popular destination is likely to feature high-quality experiences.

Another set of important variables in tourism demand analysis relates to the effects of shocks and major events. For example, social and political instability, natural disasters, and pandemics all discourage individuals from travelling. A significant reduction in international tourist arrivals to Hong Kong was observed after the 9/11 attacks in the USA in 2001 and the Severe Acute Respiratory Syndrome (SARS) outbreak in Hong Kong in 2003 (Song, Lin, Witt, & Zhang, 2011). In addition, the ongoing COVID-19 pandemic has resulted in widespread travel disruptions since 2020. During such periods, tourists hesitate to travel because of travel restrictions and for safety concerns. Moreover, economic or financial crises often lead to a significant drop in tourist income, which may result in the use of tourism budgets for the purchase of essential goods and services, rather than for travel. For example, the total number of international arrivals dropped by 3.6% during the 2008 global financial crisis, from 1.751 billion in 2008 to 1.687 billion in 2009 (United Nations, 2010). At the same time, some events or shocks can increase tourism demand (Song et al., 2009). Sporting events, like the Olympic Games and the World Cup, attract millions of fans from all over the world and boost tourism revenue in the host countries (Pedauga, Pardo-Fanjul, Redondo, & Izquierdo, 2020).

2.1.2 Demand function specification

In a typical economic setting, the demand function of a specific product is derived from maximising its utility function, subject to budget constraints. This system becomes complex and nonlinear when multiple products and intertemporal decisions are considered, resulting in empirical analyses that often use reduced form equations for model estimations. In tourism demand studies, researchers have often adopted two types of relationships: the linear relationship and the log-log model (Song et al., 2009).

In linear relationships, the simpler of the two types of relationships, tourism demand is expressed as the weighted sum of its K influencing factors:

$$y_t = \alpha_0 + \prod_{k=1}^{K} \alpha_k x_{kt} + \xi_t \qquad (2.1)$$

where y_t represents the measure of tourism demand between a specific origin-destination pair at time t; α_0 is a constant level intercept; x_{kt} is a set of influential factors described in the previous section; α_k is a set of model parameters describing the impact of each factor x_{kt} on tourism demand y_t; and ξ_t is the disturbance term. The linear relationship model is easy to estimate and has been shown to be effective in approximating relationships between tourism demand and its influencing factors (Edwards, 1985; Smeral, Witt, & Witt, 1992). At the same time, this model cannot capture nonlinear features, which are frequently observed in tourism demand systems.

The log-log model can approximate nonlinear relationships between variables while keeping the functional form linear for easier estimation. Both the dependent variable and the independent variables enter the model after a logarithmic transformation:

$$\ln y_t = \beta_0 + \prod_{k=1}^{K} \beta_k \ln x_{kt} + \varepsilon_t \tag{2.2}$$

where y_t and x_{kt} are the same as in Equation (2.1); β_0 and β_k are coefficients to be estimated; and ε_t is the disturbance term. Compared with the linear relationship, the log-log model is more flexible in terms of its specifications. Indeed, several scholars have noted the log-log model's superior performance in tourism demand analysis (Lee, Var, & Blaine, 1996; Witt & Witt, 1992). In addition, with the logarithmic transformation of the variables, the model parameters can be directly interpreted as the demand elasticity of the corresponding factors. Given these advantages, the log-log model is one of the most commonly used functional forms in tourism demand analysis (Song et al., 2009).

2.2 Tourism demand elasticity

Tourism demand elasticity is a concept from economics that is used to measure the change in the aggregate quantity of tourism demand in relation to the change in the factors that affect tourism demand, such as visitor income and travel costs (Song et al., 2009). Tourism demand elasticity data provide useful information and guidelines for policymakers and business practitioners. For example, tourism demand elasticity data can assist hoteliers in devising appropriate profit-boosting pricing strategies. Tourism demand is mainly influenced by visitor income and pricing levels at the target destination, which we refer to as 'income' and 'own price'.

Using the econometric method, we can derive elasticities from Equation (2.2). Once the model is well specified, with a long-term relationship being confirmed and all of the diagnostic tests passed, the income and own price elasticities can be found through the model parameters. It is worth noting that in some model specifications, in which the lagged value of tourism demand, tourist income, and tourism prices are considered, the calculation of income and own price elasticities involves integrating multiple model parameters. Based on demand theory, income elasticity is expected to be positive, indicating that an increase in visitor income will lead to an increase in tourism demand, holding other variables constant. A negative own price elasticity result is often observed and would suggest that an increase in the destination price will result in a decrease in tourism demand, holding other variables constant. Considering the absolute value of price elasticity, the following are the three elasticity conditions:

1   If the absolute elasticity is greater than 1 (the change in tourism demand is the result of high responsiveness to price changes expressed as a percentage), tourism demand is price elastic;
2   If the absolute elasticity equals 1 (the change in tourism demand represents a proportional response to price changes expressed as a percentage), tourism demand is price unitary;
3   If the absolute elasticity is less than 1 (the change in tourism demand is the result of low responsiveness to price changes expressed as a percentage), tourism demand is price inelastic.

2.3 Key concepts and terms in tourism demand forecasting

2.3.1 Data frequency

Anything that is observed sequentially over time is a time series. Data frequency refers to regular intervals of time (e.g., daily, weekly, monthly, quarterly, and annual) between pairs of observations in a time series. Researchers generally rely on an existing data set and their specific forecasting purpose when selecting a data set with the appropriate frequency.

Annual data are used most frequently in forecasting, followed by quarterly data and monthly data (Song et al., 2009). As tourism demand shows strong seasonality, monthly and quarterly data are more reliable in terms of reflecting the seasonality of tourism demand than annual data. Weekly data present challenges because the number of weeks in a year is both large and non-integer (the average number of weeks in a year is 52.18) and therefore cannot meet the requirements of most forecasting methods (Hyndman & Athanasopoulos, 2021). Finally, daily and sub-daily data often involve multiple seasonal patterns, making them inappropriate for tourism demand analysis.

The problems associated with a short time series that only exhibits one type of seasonality can be remedied using a single-seasonal method (e.g., a seasonal autoregressive integrated moving average model). However, when the time series is long enough to include multiple seasonality types, re-searchers will need to use more sophisticated statistical forecasting meth-ods, such as seasonal trend decomposition, dynamic harmonic regression, or Prophet (Hyndman & Athanasopoulos, 2021). It is important to note that these methods allow for only regular seasonality. A time series that features irregular seasonality (e.g., with the added complication of holidays such as Chinese New Year) will present additional challenges. Researchers often deal with irregular seasonality caused by moving events by incorpo-rating dummy variables into the forecasting model. Researchers may also use other statistical and artificial intelligence (AI)-based techniques, such as hierarchical pattern recognition (Hu, Qiu, Wu, & Song, 2021).

2.3.2 Missing values and outliers

A missing value refers to the absence of an observation in the existing data set, which may be the result of a variety of factors, such as a defect in the data collection process, data entry errors, or human error (Hyndman & Athanasopoulos, 2021). The missing values in a data set need to be care-fully considered and handled to avoid introducing bias in the forecasting model. Missing values are especially problematic in time-series analyses, as time-series models usually require complete and continuous series. Researchers conventionally use two approaches to address the problem of missing values. The first approach involves simply partitioning the data set, which is only possible when the series of observations after the last missing value is long enough to produce reasonable forecasts. This approach allows researchers to use a complete time series after the last missing value in their forecasting. The second approach, which research-ers may use when partition is not feasible, involves imputation, a process that involves identifying patterns in the existing data set and filling in any missing observations using statistical methods.

Outliers are observations that differ greatly from most of the observa-tions in a time series (Hyndman & Athanasopoulos, 2021). Boxplots pro-vide a visual representation of a data set and are commonly used to detect outliers (Field, 2017). In a regression analysis, outliers are observations with large residuals that could be errors or simply unusual observations. For example, given the severe impact of the COVID-19 pandemic, the number of inbound visitors to any destination in 2020 may be considered an outlier when compared with historical data. In most cases, extreme outliers can greatly influence the performance of forecasting models. However, it would be unreliable to simply replace outliers without considering the reasons for their occurrence. Indeed, outliers sometimes provide researchers with useful information that should be considered when building a forecasting model. Given the unpredictable nature of outliers, no single rule can be universally applied with regard to their treatment. Researchers must rely on the fact that it is substantively reasonable. Any observations that have a score greater (less) than the upper (lower) quartile plus (minus) 1.5 times the interquartile range (IQR) can be considered outliers and any case greater (less) than the upper (lower) quartile plus (minus) 3 times the IQR is an extreme case (Field, 2017). As such, researchers should carefully consider the specific requirements and context of their chosen forecasting practice to select the appropriate methods for identifying and handling outliers.

2.3.3 Ex ante and ex post forecasts

Ex ante forecasting and ex post forecasting are additional key concepts. Figure 2.1 presents the key difference between these two concepts. In this figure, y and t denote the demand series and time index, with historical data available from period 1 to N. If a tourism forecasting model is estimated using sample data from t_1 to t_n, and to produce forecasts from t_{n+1} to t_N, these forecasts (y_{n+1} to y_N) are defined as ex post forecasts. In this case, the actual data of the independent variables are available over the forecasting period, from t_{n+1} to t_N. This practice allows us to compare ex post forecasts across different models and evaluate which model performs the best, irrespective of the data quality of the explanatory variables.

Nonetheless, tourism practitioners and stakeholders are often more interested in forecasts beyond time t_N (Hyndman & Athanasopoulos, 2021), known as ex ante forecasts. In ex ante forecasting, the data of the independent variables are not known after time t_N and must therefore be forecast before generating ex ante forecasts. As information on both the dependent and independent variables is unavailable in the situation described above, it is impossible to evaluate the accuracy of ex ante forecasts until the data after time t_N become available. Forecast errors in ex ante forecasting come from two sources: errors generated from the forecasting model and errors that arise when estimating the independent variables.

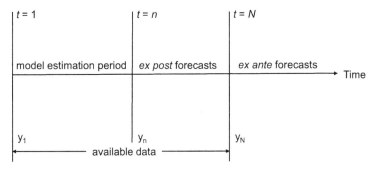

FIGURE 2.1 Time horizon of forecasts
Source: Song, Witt, and Li (2009, p. 183).

2.3.4 Training and testing sets

In forecasting, the size of the residuals after model estimation cannot reflect the magnitude of the forecast errors. The accuracy of a forecasting model should instead be tested by examining the performance of the model on a set of data that were not used in the model's construction.

When building models, researchers usually divide the data available into two parts: a training set and a testing set. Training sets are data sets used to estimate the parameters of a forecasting model, while testing sets are used to evaluate the accuracy of an established model. As testing sets are composed of real data and are not used in model construction, they can provide a reliable indication of how well the forecasting models are likely to work in practice.

In a time-series data set, data from the preceding period is often used as the training set, while data from the subsequent period is utilised as the testing set. For example, in a time-series data set spanning the years 2010 to 2020, we would typically use 2010 to a predefined point before 2020 as the training set and data from that point to the end of the time series as the testing set. Although the widths of the two sets depend on the length of the sample and the intended forecasting horizon, it is common practice to use around 20% of the total sample as the testing set (Hyndman & Athanasopoulos, 2021). Ideally, the testing set should be at least as long as the required maximum forecasting horizon.

It is important to note that a model that fits the training set well may not provide reliable testing set forecasts. Indeed, researchers can always orchestrate a perfect fit by using enough parameters in the model. Overfitting can be as problematic as failing to identify the pattern in the data.

2.3.5 Expanding and rolling windows

Using only one testing set to evaluate model performance may lead to misleading results owing to randomness in the data. To remedy this potential problem, researchers can use time-series cross-validation to provide more robust evaluations. In particular, researchers can rely on expanding or rolling window forecasts to conduct robust evaluations and comparisons of forecasting models. As discussed in Section 2.3.4, researchers should construct their models based on a training set (period t_1 to t_n) and test its performance using a testing set (period t_{n+1} to t_N). Researchers can then transfer the first observation in the testing set (t_{n+1}) to the training set and construct a new training set (period t_1 to t_{n+1}). Next, researchers can generate and evaluate a new set of forecasts on the remaining testing set (periods t_{n+2} to t_N). The process can continue until no data point remains in the testing set. In this way, researchers can generate multiple forecasts and evaluate the model's performance using the average of these multiple forecasts. Given the expanding nature of the training set in this approach, this type of time-series cross-validation is also referred to as an 'expanding window' (Hyndman & Athanasopoulos, 2021). Figure 2.2 illustrates this approach with the training set denoted in black and the testing set denoted in white.

The rolling window approach is another type of time-series cross-validation that researchers can utilise. With this method, a new training set is constructed by appending the first observation of the testing set (t_{n+1}) to the end of training set and dropping the first observation of the training set (t_1). That is, the new training set includes observations from the period between t_2 and t_{n+1}. This iterating process generates multiple training sets and can continue until no data point remains in the testing set. In contrast to the expanding window approach, the sample size is kept constant throughout all training sets under the rolling window method. Figure 2.3 illustrates the rolling window approach with the training set denoted in black, the testing set denoted in white, and the dropped information denoted in grey.

Furthermore, with regard to forecast generation in multiple training sets in expanding or rolling windows, researchers can estimate their model with the first training set and use the estimated parameters and functional form to generate forecasts for all subsequent training sets. Evaluating the forecasts in this way allows researchers to consider only the performance of a model with a fixed functional form and parameter value. Alternatively, researchers may consider maintaining the functional form (e.g., the number of lags of independent variables) and estimating parameters using the new training set. Using this strategy allows researchers to evaluate forecasts using a model with a fixed functional form but flexible parameter

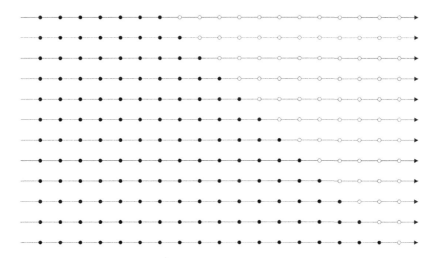

FIGURE 2.2 Expanding window forecasts
Source: Hyndman and Athanasopoulos (2021).

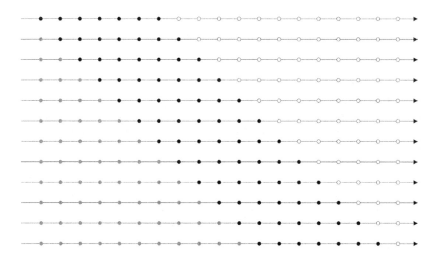

FIGURE 2.3 Rolling window forecasts
Source: Hyndman and Athanasopoulos (2021).

values. Ultimately, researchers can re-estimate both the functional form and parameters with the new training set by evaluating forecasts using the family of models with flexibility in terms of both functional forms and parameter values. Researchers should consider their own forecasting needs when selecting the appropriate approach. In this book, we utilise rolling windows for time-series cross-validation in all chapters to ensure consistency in result comparison.

2.4 Forecast accuracy evaluation

The accuracy of a forecasting model depends on how close the forecasts are to the corresponding actual values. The difference between an actual value and a forecast is defined as a forecast error. The 'error' in this case does not refer to a mistake but to the unpredictable aspect of an observation. The forecast error can be expressed as

$$\varepsilon_{N+h} = y_{N+h} - \hat{y}_{N+h|N} \tag{2.3}$$

where the training set is $\{y_1, y_2, ..., y_N\}$ and the testing set is $\{y_{N+1}, y_{N+2}, ..., y_{N+h}\}$. The forecast of time $N+h$ ($\hat{y}_{N+h|N}$) is a predicted value of y_{N+h} based on the information available at time N. It should be noted that forecast errors differ from residuals in two ways. First, residuals are calculated using training sets, while forecasts errors are measured using testing sets. Second, residuals are normally based on one-step forecasts, while forecasts errors can involve multi-step forecasts (Hyndman & Athanasopoulos, 2021). Forecast accuracy can be measured by forecast errors in a variety of ways. Scale-dependent errors, percentage errors, and scaled errors are introduced in the next three subsections.

2.4.1 Scale-dependent errors

Forecast errors feature the same scale as the data. As such, accuracy measures that are based only on ε_t are referred to as scale dependent (Hyndman & Athanasopoulos, 2021). Mean absolute error (MAE) and root mean square error (RMSE) are two widely used scale-dependent measures. They are expressed as follows:

$$MAE = \text{mean}\left(|\varepsilon_t|\right) \qquad (2.4)$$

$$RMSE = \sqrt{\text{mean}\left(\varepsilon_t^2\right)} \qquad (2.5)$$

Given that MAE is easy to understand and compute, the measure is frequently used when comparing forecasting methods applied to a single time series or to several time series with the same units (Hyndman & Athanasopoulos, 2021). RMSE is also widely used, despite being more difficult to interpret. Median forecasts can be achieved by adopting a forecasting method that minimises MAE, while researchers can determine mean forecasts by minimising RMSE. It should be noted that as scale-dependent errors have the same scale as the data, these measures are not suitable for comparing forecasts of series that feature different scales.

2.4.2 Percentage errors

A percentage error can be generally written as $\delta_t = 100 \times (\varepsilon_t / y_t)$. As percentage errors provide 'unit-free' advantages, these errors are often used to compare the forecasting performance of different data sets. The most frequently used measure of a percentage error in tourism is the mean absolute percentage error (MAPE) (Lin, Goodwin, & Song, 2014), which can be expressed as

$$MAPE = \text{mean}\left(|\delta_t|\right) \qquad (2.6)$$

Measurements based on percentage errors have several disadvantages. First, if $y_t = 0$ exists in the data for any t in the relevant period, the percentage error will be infinite or undefined. Similarly, the percentage error will be extremely high if any y_t is close to 0. Second, percentage errors assume a significant zero in the unit of measure. As such, using percentage errors to estimate the accuracy of temperature forecasts, for example, will provide little benefit as temperature has an arbitrary zero point. The performance of temperature forecasts will change simply by converting the data from Celsius to Fahrenheit.

MAPE's feature of placing a heavier penalty on negative errors than positive errors also represents a disadvantage. This weakness can be overcome by using a 'symmetric' MAPE (sMAPE) measure (Armstrong, 2001), which is defined as

$$\text{sMAPE} = \text{mean}\left(200|y_t - \hat{y}_t| / (y_t + \hat{y}_t)\right) \tag{2.7}$$

While sMAPE overcomes the asymmetry disadvantage of MAPE, two key issues remain. If y_t is close to 0, $\hat{y}_t$ will also be close to 0, leading to division by a number close to 0, making the value unstable. In addition, the value of sMAPE can be negative, deviating from its definition of 'absolute percentage errors'.

2.4.3 Scaled errors

Scaled errors are adopted as an alternative to percentage errors when comparing forecast accuracy across series with different units (Hyndman & Koehler, 2006). Scaled errors suggest scaling the errors by the training MAE from a simple forecasting method. For a non-seasonal time series, a scaled error can be defined by using naïve forecasts:

$$q_t = \frac{\varepsilon_t}{\dfrac{1}{n-1}\displaystyle\sum_{j=2}^{n}|y_j - y_{j-1}|} \tag{2.8}$$

In Equation (2.8), both the numerator and the denominator involve values on the scale of the original data, resulting in q_t becoming scale independent. If the scaled error is less than 1, the forecast performs better than the average one-step naïve forecast. Conversely, a scaled error greater than 1 indicates a worse-performing forecast than the average one-step naïve forecast. For a seasonal time series, a scaled error can be written by using seasonal naïve forecasts:

$$q_t = \frac{\varepsilon_t}{\dfrac{1}{n-m}\displaystyle\sum_{j=m+1}^{n}|y_j - y_{j-m}|} \tag{2.9}$$

with m being the number of seasons per annum (e.g., $m = 4$ for quarterly data and $m = 12$ for monthly data).

Based on the idea of scaled error, the mean absolute scaled error (MASE) is defined as

$$\text{MASE} = \text{mean}\left(|q_t|\right) \tag{2.10}$$

Similarly, the root mean squared scaled error (RMSSE) can be expressed as

$$\text{RMSSE} = \sqrt{\text{mean}\left(q_t^2\right)} \tag{2.11}$$

where

$$q_t^2 = \frac{\varepsilon_t^2}{\frac{1}{n-m}\sum_{j=m+1}^{n}\left(y_j - y_{j-m}\right)^2} \tag{2.12}$$

The error measures discussed in this section have distinct properties and convey different information. Researchers should consider multiple measures to derive comprehensive understanding of their forecasting results. Common error measures in each category, such as MAPE, RMSE, and MASE, are referenced in subsequent chapters when evaluating forecast accuracy.

2.5 Data and variables used in subsequent chapters

The data set used in the subsequent chapters (apart from the chapters on vector autoregressive and spatiotemporal models) relates to tourism demand for travel to Thailand from four source markets, including its two largest short-haul markets, mainland China and Malaysia, and its two top long-haul source markets, the Russian Federation (Russia) and the USA. The time series of international tourist arrivals are used as the measure of tourism demand in this book. We obtain quarterly arrivals (Arr) data from the four markets starting from the first quarter of 2000 to the fourth quarter of 2019 from the official website of the Thai Ministry of Tourism and Sports (https://www.mots.go.th/mots_en/Index.php). Independent variables include the tourists' income and relative tourism price in Thailand, which are proxied by real GDP index of the source markets and the exchange rate-adjusted CPI ratio between the source market and Thailand, respectively. Real GDP index (2010 = 100), CPI (2010 = 100), and exchange rates of both the source market and Thailand are collected from the International Finance Statistics of the International Monetary Fund. The relative tourism price of Thailand tourism ($price_t$) can be calculated as

$$price_t = \left(\frac{CPI\_D_t}{EX\_D_t}\right) \Big/ \left(\frac{CPI\_O_t}{EX\_O_t}\right) \tag{2.13}$$

where CPI_D_t and CPI_O_t are the CPI of Thailand and the source market, respectively; EX_D_t and EX_O_t are the exchange rate indices (2010 = 100) calculated by the period average of domestic currency per US dollar in Thailand and the source market, respectively.

In addition, we include three seasonal dummy variables (Q1, Q2, and Q3) to capture the impact of quarterly seasonality. To capture the impacts of events, a few one-off event dummy variables are introduced. Table 2.1 summaries these one-off event dummy variables. Following Hardy (1993), we assign the dummy variables a value of 1 at the specific time when one-off events have an effect, and 0 otherwise. It should be noted that the setting of an event dummy variable may vary across individual source markets where the effect took place over different periods of time. In this book, the ex post forecasts cover the period from 2017Q1 to 2019Q4, and the sample data begin from 2000Q1 for our model estimation. An example of the data file is shown in Table 2.2.

2.6 Conclusion

This chapter begins with a brief discussion of the theoretical foundation of tourism demand analysis from an economic perspective. We introduce and discuss frequently used variables and functional forms. We then elaborate on some of the key concepts and terms in modelling and forecasting tourism demand, including data frequency and the treatment of missing and extreme values, the concepts of ex ante and ex post forecasts, training

TABLE 2.1 One-off event dummy variables

Code	Affected origin	Affected period	Note
SARS	Mainland China, Malaysia, Russia, USA	2003Q2	The SARS epidemic
SARS1	Malaysia	2003Q3	An extended period affected by SARS epidemic due to cases in Singapore and other Southeast Asian countries
FC_08	Mainland China, Russia, USA	2008Q4 2008Q4–2009Q1 2008Q4–2009Q1	The global financial crisis
PC_05	Mainland China	2005Q1	A series of political events in Thailand at the beginning of 2005
PC_10	Mainland China	2010Q2	Thai political protests from March to May 2010
PC_13	Mainland China	2013Q4–2014Q2	2013–2014 Thai political crisis
PC_14	Malaysia	2014Q1	2013–2014 Thai political crisis
PC_16	Mainland China	2016Q1	Ease of entry visa for Chinese tourists
SC_10	USA	2010Q2–2010Q3	The aftermath of Thai political protests from March to May 2010
SC_14	USA	2014Q3	The aftermath of 2013–2014 Thai political crisis

TABLE 2.2 Data sample (Russia)

Date	Arr	GDP	CPI_O	CPI_D	EX_O	EX_D	Q1	Q2	Q3	SARS	FC_08
...	...	...	...	...	...	...	...	...	...	...	...
2003Q1	41,205	51.78	47.48	80.16	104.24	134.94	1	0	0	0	0
2003Q2	4,389	54.26	48.95	80.53	101.66	133.12	0	1	0	1	0
2003Q3	6,571	62.83	49.61	80.69	100.22	130.24	0	0	1	0	0
2003Q4	37,164	62.31	50.66	80.94	98.15	125.40	0	0	0	0	0
...	...	...	...	...	...	...	...	...	...	...	...
2008Q3	34,680	118.60	84.99	99.46	79.87	106.77	0	0	1	0	0
2008Q4	90,060	107.12	87.00	96.04	89.78	109.82	0	0	0	0	1
2009Q1	107,854	78.89	91.10	95.29	111.85	111.38	1	0	0	0	1
2009Q2	43,130	86.05	93.57	96.85	106.08	109.44	0	1	0	0	0
...	...	...	...	...	...	...	...	...	...	...	...

and testing sets, and time-series cross-validation in forecasting. We then describe the most commonly used forecast error measures in tourism forecasting. Finally, we explain the data used in the subsequent chapters of this book.

Self-study questions

1. What are the most commonly used dependent and independent variables in tourism demand models?
2. How do researchers deal with missing values and outliers?
3. What is the key difference between ex ante and ex post forecasts?
4. List and discuss the main methods used to evaluate forecast accuracy in tourism demand forecasting.

References

Armstrong, S. J. (Ed.). (2001). *Principles of forecasting: A handbook for researchers and practitioners*. Boston: Kluwer.

Edwards, A. (1985). *International tourism forecasts to 1995: EIU special report No.188*. London: Economist Publications.

Field, A. (2017). *Discovering statistics using IBM SPSS statistics* (5th ed.). London: Sage.

Fildes, R., Wei, Y., & Ismail, S. (2011). Evaluating the forecasting performance of econometric models of air passenger traffic flows using multiple error measures. *International Journal of Forecasting, 27*(3), 902–922. https://doi.org/10.1016/j.ijforecast.2009.06.002

Gössling, S., Peeters, P., Hall, M., Ceron, J.-P., Dubois, G., Lehmann, L. V., & Scott, D. (2012). Tourism and water use: Supply, demand, and security. An international review. *Tourism Management, 33*(1), 1–15. https://doi.org/10.1016/j.tourman.2011.03.015

Hardy, A. M. (1993). *Regression with dummy variables (Sage University paper series on quantitative applications in the social sciences, series No. 07–093).* Newbury Park: Sage.

Hu, M., Qiu, R. T. R., Wu, D. C., & Song, H. (2021). Hierarchical pattern recognition for tourism demand forecasting. *Tourism Management, 84*(8), 104263. https://doi.org/10.1016/j.tourman.2020.104263

Hyndman, R. J., & Athanasopoulos, G. (2021). *Forecasting: Principles and practice* (3rd ed.). Melbourne, Australia: OTexts.

Hyndman, R. J., & Koehler, A. B. (2006). Another look at measures of forecast accuracy. *International Journal of Forecasting, 22*(4), 679–688. https://doi.org/10.1016/j.ijforecast.2006.03.001

Lee, K. C., Var, T., & Blaine, W. T. (1996). Determinants of inbound tourism expenditure. *Annals of Tourism Research, 3,* 69–81. https://doi.org/10.1016/0160-7383(95)00073-9

Lin, V. S., Goodwin, P., & Song, H. (2014). Accuracy and bias of experts' adjusted forecasts. *Annals of Tourism Research, 48,* 156–174. https://doi.org/10.1016/j.annals.2014.06.005

Lockwood, A. (Ed.). (2007). *Tourism and hospitality in the 21st century.* Abingdon: Routledge.

Masiero, L., & Qiu, R. T. R. (2018). Modeling reference experience in destination choice. *Annals of Tourism Research, 72,* 58–74. https://doi.org/10.1016/j.annals.2018.06.004

Pedauga, L. E., Pardo-Fanjul, A., Redondo, J. C., & Izquierdo, J. M. (2020). Assessing the economic contribution of sports tourism events: A regional social accounting matrix analysis approach. *Tourism Economics.* https://doi.org/10.1177/1354816620975656.

Smeral, E., Witt, F. S., & Witt, A. C. (1992). Econometric forecasts: Tourism trends to 2000. *Annals of Tourism Research, 19,* 450–466. https://doi.org/10.1016/0160-7383(92)90130-H.

Song, H., Lin, S., Witt, S. F., & Zhang, X. (2011). Impact of financial/economic crisis on demand for hotel rooms in Hong Kong. *Tourism Management, 32*(1), 172–186. https://doi.org/10.1016/j.tourman.2010.05.006.

Song, H., & Witt, S. F. (2000). *Tourism demand modelling and forecasting: Modern econometric approaches.* Cambridge: Pergamon.

Song, H., Witt, S. F., & Li, G. (2009). *The advanced econometrics of tourism demand.* New York: Routledge.

United Nations. (2010). *International recommendations for tourism statistics 2008.* United Nations.

UNWTO. (2010). *Glossary of tourism terms.* Retrieved April 3, 2022, from https://www.unwto.org/glossary-tourism-terms

UNWTO. (2020). International tourism highlights, 2020 Edition. Retrieved March 9, 2022. Retrieved from https://doi.org/10.18111/9789284422456

Witt, F. S., & Witt, A. C. (1992). *Modelling and forecasting demand in tourism.* London: Academic Press.

Zhou-Grundy, Y., & Turner, L. W. (2014). The challenge of regional tourism demand forecasting: The case of China. *Journal of Travel Research, 53*(6), 747–759. https://doi.org/10.1177/0047287513516197.

3

THE AUTOREGRESSIVE DISTRIBUTED LAG MODEL

Anyu Liu and Xinyang Liu

3.1 Introduction

Tourism demand forecasting has been a popular research topic for approximately five decades. The rapid development of tourism forecasting research has motivated recent review articles, such as that of Song, Qiu, and Park (2019), which uses 211 studies published between 1968 and 2018 to comprehensively summarise the new trends and developments in this area. Tourism demand forecasting models are generally divided into three types: time series, econometrics, and artificial intelligence.

In this chapter, we focus on the econometric modelling approach. The greatest advantage in using econometric models among these three categories is the ability to include the information about the explanatory variables in forecasting tourism demand. With a strong foundation in economics, econometrics can offer clear-cut practical implications (Song & Li, 2008). Econometric models are generally classified into single-equation and system demand models. Traditionally, single-equation models include the static regression model, the ADLM (Huang, Zhang, & Ding, 2017; Song & Lin, 2010; Song, Witt, & Li, 2003), the error correction model (ECM) (Goh, 2012; Lee, 2011; Vanegas, 2013), and the time-varying parameter (TVP) model (Page, Song, & Wu, 2012; Song, Li, Witt, & Athanasopoulos, 2011; Song & Wong, 2003). Widely used system models include the vector autoregressive (VAR) model (Song & Witt, 2006; Wong, Song, & Chon, 2006) and the almost ideal demand system (AIDS) model (Li, Song, & Witt, 2004).

Tourism demand is normally regarded as a dynamic process in which tourists' decisions about destinations are affected by time. There are many reasons to capture the temporal behaviour of tourists, as they tend to revisit

DOI: 10.4324/9781003269366-3

destinations at which they have had a pleasant experience because there is less uncertainty associated with returning to a familiar destination than with travelling to an unfamiliar one. Word of mouth is also an important influencing factor of tourism demand. People often share their travel experiences with their friends and relatives after a holiday, and word-of-mouth recommendations can significantly influence a potential visitor's selection of destinations for future holidays. In addition, because people are generally risk-averse and prefer outcomes with low uncertainty to those with high uncertainty, tourists often consider a destination's popularity when making their choice. Therefore, sought-after destinations are likely to continue to receive large numbers of tourists in the future.

The ADLM is the most widely used econometric method, and early studies such as those of Hendry (1995) and Pesaran and Shin (1995) applied it to capture the dynamic pattern in economic variables (Liu, Lin, Li, & Song, 2022). Since being introduced into tourism demand forecasting by Song and Witt (2003), the ADLM has been shown to have powerful analytical and predictive capabilities. Including the current values of independent variables and the lagged dependent and independent variables in the model specification, the ADLM is more accurate to capture the relationship between tourism demand and its determinants compared to the static regression models and can help to reveal how certain economic factors affect others.

The ADLM views the time dynamics in demand variables as accounting for the intertemporal relationships between tourism demand and various explanatory variables. However, the introduction of more independent variables leads to a challenge of model specification and selection. Song et al. (2003) introduced the general-to-specific (GETS) modelling specification approach into the tourism literature. It starts from a general ADLM and removes insignificant variables sequentially according to certain criteria such as the Akaike information criterion (AIC), corrected Akaike information criterion (AICc), and Schwarz Bayesian information criterion (BIC). Song et al. (2003) found that the specified ADLM selected by GETS performed well according to both economic and statistical criteria. The ADLM incorporated with GETS has also been applied in studies of tourism in various destinations, such as Thailand (Song et al., 2003), Fiji (Narayan, 2004), and mainland China (Song & Fei, 2007). In addition, Song and Lin (2010) and Lin, Liu, and Song (2015) further demonstrated that the error correction form of the ADLM can consider not only the long-term relationship between tourism demand and its determinants but also the short-term error correction mechanism in modelled estimates.

The ADLM has been further developed for incorporation into other methods of tourism demand forecasting. Athanasopoulos, Song, and Sun (2018) incorporated the bootstrap aggregation method into the ADLM to forecast tourism demand in six source markets for Australia, and their results showed the superior forecasting performance of bootstrap aggregation in improving the robustness of the ADLM. Song, Liu, Li, and Liu (2021) confirmed the forecasting performance of the ADLM with Bayesian bootstrap aggregation, which showed lower variance in forecasting results compared to its ordinary bootstrap aggregation counterpart. In addition, incorporating spatial dependence and spatial heterogeneity is an effective way to improve the ADLM, as suggested by Jiao, Chen, and Li (2021). By fully reflecting the spatial heterogeneity of European tourism demand forecasting models, the proposed general nesting spatiotemporal model outperformed the benchmark models. An alternative approach to improving the forecasting performance of the ADLM is to use judgemental adjustment. Song, Gao, and Lin (2013) utilised expert adjustments as inputs to combine statistical results with reliable consensus, and they demonstrated improved forecasting results for Hong Kong tourism.

This chapter introduces the ADLM with the incorporation of the GETS procedure and its application in forecasting tourism demand for Thailand from four source markets, with R code included. To showcase how the model can be applied, the key procedures and forecasting practices are also provided.

3.2 Methods

3.2.1 The ADLM specification

From the perspective of neoclassical economic theory, tourism demand is usually related to potential consumers' income, the price of visiting the destination, and the comparable price for competing destinations. Following Chapter 2, a tourism demand function of a specific destination can be written as

$$\ln y_{i,t} = \beta_{0,i} + \ln income_{i,t} + \beta_{3,i,n}\ln price_{i,t} + \varepsilon_{i,t} \tag{3.1}$$

where $\beta_{0,i}$ and $\varepsilon_{i,t}$ are the constant and disturbance terms, respectively. $\beta_{2,i}$ and $\beta_{3,i}$ represent the income and the destination's own price elasticities, respectively. To measure the dynamic features of tourism demand, the static model in Equation (3.1) can be written in an ADLM as

$$\ln y_{i,t} = \beta_0 + \sum_{j=1}^{J}\beta_{1,i,j}\ln y_{i,t-j} + \sum_{k=0}^{K}\beta_{2,i,k}\ln income_{i,t-k}$$
$$+ \sum_{n=0}^{N}\beta_{3,i,n}\ln price_{i,t-n} + Dummies + \varepsilon_{i,t} \tag{3.2}$$

Considering the time lag of tourists' decision-making progress, the ADLM offers more explanatory power, as tourism demand is affected by both the current value of its determinants and the lagged terms of itself and the determinants. The lag length of the time series may vary depending on data frequency. In common practice, 1 lag is frequently used for annual data, 4 lags for quarterly data, and 12 lags for monthly data (Song & Witt, 2003). The dummy variables in Equation (3.2) are used to capture the seasonal effect and offset the impact of one-off events such as the severe acute respiratory syndrome (SARS) outbreak in 2003.

3.2.2 Stationarity and cointegration tests

The concept of cointegration is used to test the existence of a long-run equilibrium among non-stationary variables in the same economic system, such as tourism demand and its determinants (Engle & Granger, 1987).

To prepare for the cointegration test, we begin with unit root tests for all of input variables to identify their stationarity. A stationary time series is a series that has constant mean, variance, and covariance over time, and is denoted by $I(0)$. A non-stationary time series contains unit roots. The number of unit roots contained in the series equals the times that the series must be differenced before a stationary process is reached. The simplest autoregressive model AR(1) is

$$y_t = \lambda_0 + \lambda_1 y_{t-1} + e_t \tag{3.3}$$

where λ_0 is the intercept, e_t is the white noise, and λ_1 is the parameters of the model. If y_t has one unit root, denoted by $I(1)$, then $\lambda_1 = 1$. Moreover, when the constant intercept $\lambda_0 = 0$, the process is termed a random walk; when the constant intercept $\lambda_0 \neq 0$, the process is termed a random walk with drift.

To determine objectively whether a series contains a unit root, in most unit root tests, the null hypothesis $H_0 : \lambda_1 = 1$ is tested against the alternative hypothesis, $H_1 : \lambda_1 < 1$, based on Equation (3.3). In empirical work, the Dickey–Fuller (DF) test, the augmented Dickey–Fuller (ADF) test, and the Phillips–Perron (PP) test are frequently applied.

The DF test assumes that the time series can be modelled by an AR(1) process. Instead of testing $\lambda_1 = 1$ directly, Dickey and Fuller (1979) transformed Equation (3.3) by subtracting y_{t-1} from both sides:

$$\Delta y_t = \psi y_{t-1} + e_t \tag{3.4}$$
$$\Delta y_t = \pi_0 + \pi_1 t + \psi y_{t-1} + e_t \tag{3.5}$$

where Δ is the first difference operator and t represents the time trend variable. Equation (3.4) is used to test a random walk process and Equation

(3.5) for a random walk with drift process. Note that the null hypothesis changes to $H_0 : \psi = 0$, against the alternative hypothesis $H_1 : \psi < 0$.

$$t = \frac{\hat{\psi}}{SE(\hat{\psi})} \tag{3.6}$$

The t value, which is computed by Equation (3.6), can be compared to the critical value for the one-tailed test because $H_1 : \psi < 0$ indicates that the rejection region is on the left.

However, an AR(1) process may not suit every time series; in these cases, the errors of the AR(1) process may be serially correlated. To avoid the problem of autocorrelation in the residuals, the ADF test includes lagged dependent variables in the model specifications. Two variants of the ADF models are based on the following equations:

$$\Delta y_t = \psi y_{t-1} + \sum_{i=1}^{n} \omega_i \Delta y_{t-i} + e_t \tag{3.7}$$

$$\Delta y_t = \pi_0 + \pi_1 t + \psi y_{t-1} + \sum_{i=1}^{n} \omega_i \Delta y_{t-i} + e_t \tag{3.8}$$

where the n lagged first differences approximate the autoregressive moving average dynamics of the time series. Equation (3.7) is used to test a random walk process and Equation (3.8) for a random walk with drift process. The unit root test is then carried out under the null hypothesis $H_0 : \psi = 0$, against the alternative hypothesis $H_1 : \psi < 0$. Therefore, a one-tailed t-test is conducted to examine whether we need to reject the null hypothesis when the t value is less than the critical value.

Both the DF and ADF tests assume that the residuals in the regressions are identically and independently distributed, and they thus are fairly restrictive. Phillips and Perron (1988) generalised the DF test and developed the PP test. However, the model specification of the PP test is rather complex and outside the scope of this book. Many econometric software suites provide functions to conduct a PP test.

For the cointegration test, a conditional error correction form of the ADLM is used to test the existence of long-term relationships between tourism demand and the explanatory variables:

$$\Delta \ln y_{i,t} = \alpha_0 + \sum_{j=1}^{J} \varphi_{1,i,j} \Delta \ln y_{i,t-j} + \sum_{k=0}^{K} \varphi_{2,i,k} \Delta \ln income_{i,t-k} + \sum_{l=0}^{L} \varphi_{3,i,l} \Delta \ln price_{i,t-l}$$
$$+ \theta_{1,i} \ln y_{i,t-1} + \theta_{2,i} \ln income_{i,t-1} + \theta_{3,i} \ln price_{i,t-1} + Dummies + e_{i,t} \tag{3.9}$$

where φ is the short-run parameter that captures short-run deviations from the equilibrium, θ is the long-run parameter that gives the long-run equilibrium and the cointegrating relationships, and α_0 is an intercept. To eliminate insignificant terms and reach the optimal lag structure, the lag orders J, K, and L are determined by a number of criteria, such as AIC, AICc, and BIC. The mathematical details of the ADL-EC model can be found in Song and Turner (2006).

The bounds test is an advanced method proposed by Pesaran, Shin, and Smith (2001) that has been widely used in tourism demand forecasting to examine the long-term relationships between tourism demand and explanatory variables (Song & Lin, 2010). Compared to the traditional cointegration test, the bounds test provides two flexibilities: (1) it is applicable irrespective of the integration order, which means that the variables can be a mixture of $I(0)$ and $I(1)$, and (2) variables considered in the ADLM can have different lag terms.

The bounds test is an F-test with the null hypothesis that no cointegration relationships exist between the variables ($H_0 : \theta_{1,i} = \theta_{2,i} = \delta\theta_{3,i} = 0$ in Equation (3.9)) against the alternative hypothesis that cointegration exists. Based on the situation in which the variables are an arbitrary mix of $I(0)$ and $I(1)$ series the lower bound assumes that all of the variables are $I(0)$, and the assumption of the upper bound is that all of the variables are $I(1)$. By definition, if the computed F-statistic is less than the critical value of the lower bound, we cannot reject the null hypothesis. If the F-statistic exceeds the upper bound, cointegration may exist. If the F-statistic falls between the two boundaries, the test result is inconclusive. The critical values of the lower and upper bounds are provided by Pesaran et al. (2001) in Tables CI (pp. 300–301) and CII (pp. 303–304) in their study.

For further checking, a t-test should also be conducted to identify the existence of cointegration (Pesaran et al., 2001). The t-test considers the null hypothesis $H_0 : \theta_{1,i} = 0$, which means that there is no cointegration relationship in the lagged tourism demand. Therefore, the t-test would confirm the existence of cointegration by rejecting the null hypothesis if the computed t-statistic is greater than the upper critical value, and it would indicate that all of the variables are stationary if the computed t-statistic is less than the lower critical value.

3.2.3 Diagnostic tests

Before we generate a forecast, the estimated model must be checked with numerous statistical tests to ensure that it is properly specified. For the final model, the regression residuals are expected to be normally distributed with a mean of zero and a constant variance, and they should not to contain autocorrelation or heteroscedasticity. In addition, the model functional form should be correctly selected. Here we list the most-used diagnostic tests.

3.2.3.1 Autocorrelation test

The Durbin–Watson statistic is a standard test to determine the existence of autocorrelation (Durbin & Watson, 1950). The statistic is

$$d = \frac{\sum_{i=2}^{n} (\varepsilon_i - \varepsilon_{i-1})^2}{\sum_{i=1}^{n} \varepsilon_i^2} \tag{3.10}$$

where ε_i represents the residuals and n is the sample size.

The statistic d ranges from 0 to 4, where a value of 0 means that the data are perfectly positively autocorrelated and a value of 4 means that the data are perfectly negatively autocorrelated. If the value is around 2, there is no autocorrelation in the regression residuals. However, the Durbin-Watson statistic, constructed by Equation (3.10), is only able to detect first-order autocorrelation. The advanced method known as the Breusch–Godfrey (BG) test is a more general test, as it does allow higher-order autocorrelations, and it includes the lagged dependent variables.

3.2.3.2 Heteroscedasticity test

Heteroscedasticity, which occurs when the errors of the regression do not have a constant variance, is a major concern in the modelling exercise, as it can result in biased standard errors. To make it simple but without the loss of universality, a White test (White, 1980) posits two explanatory variables consisting of a multiple regression model as follows:

$$y_t = \rho_1 + \rho_2 x_{1t} + \rho_3 x_{2t} + \tau_t \tag{3.11}$$

Then, the following auxiliary equation is used to test whether the error term τ_t is homoscedastic or heteroscedastic:

$$\hat{\tau}_t^2 = \gamma_1 + \gamma_2 x_{1t} + \gamma_3 x_{2t} + \gamma_4 x_{1t}^2 + \gamma_5 x_{2t}^2 + \gamma_6 x_{1t} x_{2t} + \varepsilon_t \tag{3.12}$$

where $\hat{\tau}_t$ is the estimated residual from Equation (3.11). The equations can also be expanded to test for heteroscedasticity when the regression model has more than two explanatory variables. The null hypothesis of the White test is that the variances of the error terms are equal, and the alternative hypothesis is that the variances are not equal. The test statistic nR^2, where R^2 is from the auxiliary regression in Equation (3.12), has a χ^2 distribution with degrees of freedom equal to the number of regressors. If the calculated statistic is greater than the critical χ^2 value at the specific level of significance, the null hypothesis is rejected. In the econometric modelling practice, the Breusch–Pagan (BP) test is an effective method for testing heteroscedasticity. Derived from the Lagrange multiplier test, the BP test was developed by Breusch and Pagan in 1979, and subsequent studies further proved its theoretical validity.

3.2.3.3 Testing for normality

The normality test is whether the data is normally distributed or not. In terms of model selection, the normality test is useful in measuring the goodness of fit of a model to the data. Developed by Shapiro and Wilk (1965), the Shapiro–Wilk normality test is

$$W = \frac{\left(\sum_{i=1}^{n} a_i r_{(i)} \right)^2}{\sum_{i=1}^{n} (r_i - \bar{r})^2} \tag{3.13}$$

where r_i is the ordered random samples or the model's residuals. For $r_{(i)}$, the subscript indices within parentheses represent the ith smallest number in the sample. a_i s are the constants computed from the variance, covariance, and means of the sample from a normal distribution. The null hypothesis of the Shapiro–Wilk normality test is that the tested sample is normally distributed. If the small value of W rejects the null hypothesis, the sample is not normally distributed.

3.2.3.4 Test for misspecification

The Ramsey Regression Equation Specification Error Test (RESET) is used to examine whether the nonlinear form of an equation could cause model misspecification (Ramsey, 1969). Taking Equation (3.11) as the example again, the fitted values of y_t are:

$$\hat{y}_t = \hat{\rho}_1 + \hat{\rho}_2 x_{1t} + \hat{\rho}_3 x_{2t} \tag{3.14}$$

The second step is to test whether higher-powered dependent variables have explanatory power for y_t:

$$y_t = \mu_1 + \mu_2 X_{1t} + \mu_3 X_{2t} + \vartheta_1 \hat{Y}_t^2 + \vartheta_2 \hat{Y}_t^3 + \vartheta_3 \hat{Y}_t^4 + \xi_t \tag{3.15}$$

Finally, the Wald test is used to identify the significance of ϑ_1 through ϑ_3. The null hypothesis is that the model is correctly specified and that all ϑ coefficients are zero. If the null hypothesis is rejected because at least one variable with powered value can further explain the dependent variable, then the model suffers from misspecification. However, the RESET test is a general misspecification test, which means that rejection of the null hypothesis only identifies the model is misspecified but not how the model is misspecified.

Once the model passed the cointegration and diagnostic tests, the income and own price elasticities in Equation (3.2) can be derived as

$\dfrac{\sum_{k=0}^{K}\beta_{2,i,k}}{1-\sum_{j=1}^{J}\beta_{1,i,j}}$ and $\dfrac{\sum_{n=0}^{N}\beta_{3,i,n}}{1-\sum_{j=1}^{J}\beta_{1,i,j}}$, respectively. The model can then be used to

predict tourism demand and the forecasting results should be evaluated by forecasting accuracy measures such as MAPE, RMSE, and mean absolute scaled error (MASE) introduced in Chapter 2.

3.3 Application

In this chapter, the ADLM with the incorporation of GETS procedure is used to generate ex ante forecasts of visitor arrivals from mainland China, Malaysia, Russia, and the USA to Thailand.

3.3.1 Unit root test results

Before modelling and forecasting, unit root tests are conducted for all of the log-transformed variables to avoid spurious regressions. Table 3.1 demonstrates the stationarity status of all variables based on the results of the ADF, PP, and Kwiatkowski–Phillips–Schmidt–Shin (KPSS) tests. The null hypotheses of ADF and PP tests are that there is a unit root present in the tested series, and the null hypothesis of the KPSS test is that no such unit root is present.

An identified integration order is set depending on the majority result of the three unit root tests. In the Malaysian model, the ADF and PP tests show that the null hypothesis of a unit root is rejected for the log-transformed visitor arrivals variable. Taking the first differences, all of the variables are stationary in the three unit root tests except for the income variable in the Chinese mainland model. The results of the ADF and KPSS tests suggest that a higher order of integration exists. The above results show that most of the variables in the models are either $I(0)$ or $I(1)$, which justifies the use of the following bounds test.

3.3.2 Bounds test results

After the model specification and selection by GETS procedure, we conduct the bounds test to check whether there is cointegration between the remaining independent variables and visitor arrivals. With the null hypothesis that there is no cointegration between the variables, the bounds test generates the F-statistic and t-statistic together. These are then compared with the threshold interval at the 0.1 and 0.01 significance levels (see Table 3.2). Because the final model for each source country has different

TABLE 3.1 Unit root test results using the ADF, PP, and KPSS tests

		Level			First difference			Integration order
		ADF	PP	KPSS	ADF	PP	KPSS	
Mainland China	lny	−2.218	−19.773*	1.860***	−5.817***	−97.661***	0.141	I(1)
	lnincome	0.465	1.711	2.087***	−2.673	−61.249***	1.074***	higher order
	lnprice	−2.364	−8.554	0.403*	−4.298***	−62.419***	0.095	I(1)
Malaysia	lny	−4.366***	−53.668***	2.062***	−6.585***	−75.967***	0.052	I(0)
	lnincome	−2.786	−16.182	2.045***	−5.489***	−57.582***	0.086	I(1)
	lnprice	−2.612	−21.982**	1.848***	−5.830***	−74.142***	0.266	I(1)
Russia	lny	−1.331	−45.007***	1.951***	−3.388*	−42.207***	0.191	I(1)
	lnincome	−1.822	−18.126*	1.860***	−3.462*	−63.076***	0.215	I(1)
	lnprice	−1.825	−7.316	0.503**	−4.580***	−93.88***	0.641**	I(1)
USA	lny	−2.233	−49.092***	1.817***	−5.267***	−49.299***	0.212	I(1)
	lnincome	−1.561	−3.393	1.991***	−3.058	−62.368***	0.206	I(1)
	lnprice	−1.579	−7.271	1.478***	−4.606***	−49.616***	0.127	I(1)

Note: *, **, and *** denote a rejection of the null hypothesis at the 0.1, 0.05, and 0.01 significance levels, respectively.

numbers of independent variables, the corresponding threshold intervals are also provided as reference.

The results in Table 3.2 show the F-statistics all lie on the right side of the upper bound at the 0.1 significance level. The computed t-statistic supports the existence of a long-run relationship between tourism demand and its determinants in Malaysia and the USA but fails to reject the null hypothesis with the bounds test for mainland China and Russia, which may be due to the fact that those two markets are largely influenced by domestic polices and international politics. The fluctuating outbound tourism series and the limited sample size also provide relatively weak confirmation of cointegration. Therefore, we need to interpret the results with caution for the two destinations. As the results show that the variables have long-term relationships across these tourism demand models, the demand elasticities can be reasonably obtained.

3.3.3 Diagnostic test results

The estimation results and diagnostic tests are included in Tables 3.3 and 3.4, respectively. All four models fit the data very well according to the goodness of fit measure − the adjusted R^2, which exceeds 0.95 for mainland China, Russia, and the USA. These results show that most of the variations in visitor arrivals from the relevant markets over the 2000Q1−2016Q4

TABLE 3.2 Bounds test results

	k	F-statistic	t-statistic
Mainland China	9	13.121***	−3.871
Malaysia	5	8.753***	−3.948*
Russia	7	8.073***	−0.119
USA	9	99.838***	−9.726***

	F-statistic		t-statistic	
Bounds test interval	Lower bound $I(0)$	Upper bound $I(1)$	Lower bound $I(0)$	Upper bound $I(1)$
	0.1 Significance level		0.1 Significance level	
$k = 5$	2.26	3.35	−2.57	−3.86
$k = 7$	2.03	3.13	−2.57	−4.23
$k = 9$	1.88	2.99	−2.57	−4.56
	0.01 Significance level		0.01 Significance level	
$k = 5$	3.41	4.68	−3.43	−4.79
$k = 7$	2.96	4.26	−3.43	−5.19
$k = 9$	2.65	3.97	−3.42	−5.54

Note: k is the number of variables left in the estimated model; *, **, and *** denote a rejection of the null hypothesis at the 0.1, 0.05, and 0.01 significance levels, respectively.

period can be explained well by the estimated models. In addition, all of the F-statistics are significant at the 0.01 significance level.

The diagnostic statistics in Table 3.4 show that the models are generally well constructed, and have passed most diagnostic tests with only a few exceptions. Three models fail the test, which may imply the existence of nonlinear relationships. The Chinese mainland model fails the BG test because of the substantial volatility in the Chinese arrival data over the sample period. The Chinese mainland and Malaysia models fail the Shapiro–Wilk test marginally. The relatively short data period is likely to be a common reason for the above failed tests. Overall, the diagnostic testing results indicate that these four models are reasonably valid and reliable for forecasting.

3.3.4 Demand elasticities

The signs of the coefficients for the income variables are positive for all four markets, which is consistent with theory (Table 3.4). The income elasticities for all four models are greater than one, which suggests that demand

TABLE 3.3 ADLM estimates in the final state and diagnostics

	Mainland China	Malaysia	Russia	USA
$\ln y(-1)$	0.493***	0.586***	0.840***	0.237***
$\ln y(-2)$	0.022		−0.478***	
$\ln y(-3)$	0.161*		0.629***	
ln *income*	0.539***	0.483**	1.778***	1.699***
ln *income* (−1)			−1.893***	
ln *price*	−0.827	0.007	−1.149***	−0.199***
ln *price* (−1)	0.241		0.885**	
ln *price* (−2)	0.911			
ln *price* (−3)	−1.954*			
Q1	0.297***	−0.219***	0.095	−0.061**
Q2	0.037	−0.166***	−0.982***	−0.267***
Q3	0.195**	−0.131***	−0.899***	−0.285***
SARS	−1.496***		−0.882***	−0.383***
PC_05	−0.791***			
FC_08	−0.758***		0.010	−0.125***
PC_10	−0.857***			
SC_10				−0.174***
SC_14				−0.154***
Intercept	1.624***	3.385***	1.179	1.525**

Note: *, **, and *** denote significance at the 0.1, 0.05, and 0.01 levels, respectively.

TABLE 3.4 Demand elasticities and diagnostic test results

	Mainland China	Malaysia	Russia	USA
Income elasticity	1.66	1.17	2.93	2.23
Own price elasticity	−5.02	−	−4.16	−0.26
R^2	0.963	0.893	0.981	0.960
Adjusted R^2	0.952	0.882	0.976	0.953
F-statistic	85.86***	83.37***	181***	135.9***
Diagnostic test				
BG test	6.881***	0.0560	2.182	0.087
BP test	13.617	3.921	8.123	9.8
RESET test	7.282***	4.905**	4.92***	2.961
Shapiro–Wilk test	0.957**	0.958**	0.963	0.98

Note: ** and *** denote a rejection of the null hypothesis at the 0.05, and 0.01 significance levels, respectively.

for tourism in Thailand from these source markets is income elastic. These results imply that visitors to Thailand are sensitive to changes in their income, hence visiting Thailand can be regarded as a luxury travel product. In addition, the magnitudes of the estimated elasticities vary across markets. It is notable that the income elasticities of mainland China and Malaysia are smaller than those of Russia and the USA, perhaps due to the relatively short travel distances. Income is found to be a less significant factor affecting the demand for Thai tourism by tourists from mainland China and Malaysia.

According to the law of demand, all price elasticities are normally expected to be negative. The computed price elasticity for the USA is less than one, revealing that American visitors are relatively less sensitive to changes in the prices of tourism products and services in Thailand. Visitors from mainland China and Russia are more sensitive to price changes, which suggests that price campaigns would be an effective way to attract visitors from these two source markets. The sign of the price elasticity for the Malaysian model is positive but insignificant.

3.3.5 Tourism demand forecasts

The quarterly forecasts of visitor arrivals in Thailand from the selected short- and long-haul markets are generated based on the above estimated models. One- to 12-step-ahead forecasts are generated in a rolling window from 2017Q1 to 2019Q4. To eliminate potential forecasting outliers, we consider the performance of only one- to eight-step-ahead forecasts because they contain adequate forecast points. For example, the forecasting period from 2017Q1 to 2019Q4 allows five eight-step-ahead forecasts using the rolling window. The forecasting performance is compared with the three most-used time-series models: the seasonal autoregressive integrated moving average (ARIMA), exponential smoothing (ETS), and seasonal naïve (SNAIVE) models.

In general, the ADLM performs well across most forecasting horizons in terms of the rankings of MAPE, RMSE, and MASE (details of the forecasting performance can be found in Tables 3.5–3.7). When the forecasting horizon is extended, the forecast accuracy of the benchmark models deteriorates, but the ADLM outperforms the benchmark models. The empirical results suggest that the ADLM is highly consistent and accurate in forecasting tourism demand.

TABLE 3.5 Forecasting performance evaluation measured by MAPE (%)

| | *Forecasting horizon* | | | | |
	1	*2*	*3*	*4*	*8*
Mainland China					
SNAIVE	13.194	13.683	15.039	15.606	14.882
ETS	12.201	16.127	15.163	13.312	15.984
SARIMA	14.753	13.945	16.658	17.642	21.033
ADLM	7.166	11.400	11.122	10.900	7.383
Malaysia					
SNAIVE	7.859	7.559	7.349	8.114	18.818
ETS	7.973	8.113	8.193	8.448	5.081
SARIMA	8.339	8.032	8.422	7.148	8.964
ADLM	8.401	8.743	8.318	7.099	12.550
Russia					
SNAIVE	9.800	8.259	7.474	7.783	13.722
ETS	9.956	12.781	16.648	13.287	26.609
SARIMA	12.221	16.511	15.800	19.900	46.633
ADLM	12.307	12.278	12.900	10.960	11.817
USA					
SNAIVE	5.703	5.563	5.098	4.839	9.991
ETS	3.956	3.919	4.345	6.008	11.263
SARIMA	4.553	7.014	8.247	9.483	14.186
ADLM	5.268	5.935	5.854	6.102	5.379

TABLE 3.6 Forecasting performance evaluation measured by RMSE

	Forecasting horizon				
	1	*2*	*3*	*4*	*8*
Mainland China					
SNAIVE	435,305	451,019	473,032	490,637	465,626
ETS	361,836	454,310	454,610	469,960	496,274
SARIMA	431,710	440,885	532,880	515,603	596,629
ADLM	239,047	346,058	342,582	332,689	233,116
Malaysia					
SNAIVE	114,911	117,014	119,366	125,817	227,894
ETS	86,084	96,150	108,836	92,312	64,159
SARIMA	98,563	100,908	116,794	107,835	131,294
ADLM	96,799	111,594	111,151	107,898	156,260
Russia					
SNAIVE	60,723	49,666	50,755	53,441	72,672
ETS	40,284	35,219	69,387	61,388	92,175
SARIMA	44,255	51,003	58,842	75,123	150,857
ADLM	78,401	53,962	76,022	55,736	65,652
USA					
SNAIVE	17,100	16,758	15,602	15,539	32,290
ETS	12,734	13,027	16,326	19,637	36,930
SARIMA	17,164	22,540	26,103	30,561	45,171
ADLM	16,907	18,062	18,546	19,978	20,142

TABLE 3.7 Forecasting performance evaluation measured by MASE

	Forecasting horizon				
	1	*2*	*3*	*4*	*8*
Mainland China					
SNAIVE	1.624	1.691	1.858	1.926	1.790
ETS	1.472	1.916	1.885	1.678	2.002
SARIMA	1.777	1.631	1.963	2.117	2.503
ADLM	0.902	1.410	1.418	1.398	0.940
Malaysia					
SNAIVE	1.033	1.024	1.010	1.117	2.720
ETS	0.974	1.016	1.069	1.076	0.727
SARIMA	1.052	1.049	1.121	0.983	1.326
ADLM	1.056	1.115	1.103	0.977	1.833

(Continued)

	Forecasting horizon				
	1	*2*	*3*	*4*	*8*
Russia					
SNAIVE	0.830	0.656	0.644	0.698	1.239
ETS	0.657	0.633	1.191	0.912	1.725
SARIMA	0.802	0.959	0.968	1.237	3.059
ADLM	1.044	0.836	1.081	0.895	0.943
USA					
SNAIVE	0.962	0.936	0.875	0.863	1.862
ETS	0.646	0.652	0.768	1.078	2.110
SARIMA	0.773	1.144	1.409	1.684	2.624
ADLM	0.873	0.977	0.989	1.065	0.955

3.4 Conclusion and future directions

This chapter introduces the ADLM with the incorporation of GETS procedure and its application to forecasting demand for tourism in Thailand. The advantage of the ADLM lies in its ability in capturing the dynamics of the dependent and independent variables that contribute to the accurate prediction of future demand, particularly over the longer term. The empirical application in this chapter illustrates the model's superior forecasting performance in most cases and the performance is generally highly stable over different forecasting horizons and with different forecast error measures.

Based on the general form of the ADLM, this method can be further improved for incorporation into other techniques for forecasting tourism demand. Research has shown the forecasting performance of the ADLM could be further improved through bootstrap aggregations (Athanasopoulos et al., 2018; Song & Lin, 2010; Song et al., 2021). Integrating the ADLM with other advanced forecasting approaches such as boosting, staking, and mixed-data sampling methods may also be a possible future research direction.

Self-study questions

1   What are the advantages of the ADLM?
2   What are the limitations of the ADLM?
3   What are the practical implications if the absolute values of income/price elasticities are larger than one (or smaller than one)?

References

Athanasopoulos, G., Song, H., & Sun, J. A. (2018). Bagging in tourism demand modeling and forecasting. *Journal of Travel Research, 57*(1), 52–68. https://doi.org/10.1177/0047287516682871

Durbin, J., & Watson, G. S. (1950). Testing for serial correlation in least squares regression: I. *Biometrika, 37*(3/4), 409–428. https://doi.org/10.2307/2332391

Engle, R. F., & Granger, C. W. (1987). Co-integration and error correction: Representation, estimation, and testing. *Econometrica: Journal of the Econometric Society*, 251–276. https://doi.org/1913236

Goh, C. (2012). Exploring impact of climate on tourism demand. *Annals of Tourism Research, 39*(4), 1859–1883. https://doi.org/10.1016/j.annals.2012.05.027

Hendry, D. F. (1995). *Dynamic econometrics*. Oxford University Press.

Huang, X., Zhang, L., & Ding, Y. (2017). The Baidu Index: Uses in predicting tourism flows–A case study of the Forbidden City. *Tourism Management, 58*, 301–306. https://doi.org/10.1016/j.tourman.2016.03.015

Jiao, X., Chen, J. L., & Li, G. (2021). Forecasting tourism demand: Developing a general nesting spatiotemporal model. *Annals of Tourism Research*, 90. https://doi.org/10.1016/j.annals.2021.103277.

Lee, K. N. (2011). Forecasting long-haul tourism demand for Hong Kong using error correction models. *Applied Economics, 43*(5), 527–549. https://doi.org/10.1080/00036840802599743

Li, G., Song, H., & Witt, S. F. (2004). Modeling tourism demand: A dynamic linear AIDS approach. *Journal of Travel Research, 43*(2), 141–150. https://doi.org/10.1177/0047287504268235

Lin, V. S., Liu, A., & Song, H. (2015). Modeling and forecasting Chinese outbound tourism: An econometric approach. *Journal of Travel and Tourism Marketing, 32*(1–2), 34–49. https://doi.org/10.1080/10548408.2014.986011

Liu, A., Lin, V. S., Li, G., & Song, H. (2022). Ex ante tourism forecasting assessment. *Journal of Travel Research, 61*(1), 64–75. https://doi.org/10.1177/0047287520974456

Narayan, P. (2004). *Reformulating critical values for the bounds F-statistics approach to cointegration: An application to the tourism demand model for Fiji* (Vol. 2, No. 04). Australia Monash University.

Page, S., Song, H., & Wu, D. C. (2012). Assessing the impacts of the global economic crisis and swine flu on inbound tourism demand in the United Kingdom. *Journal of Travel Research, 51*(2), 142–153. https://doi.org/10.1177/0047287511400754

Pesaran, M. H., & Shin, Y. (1995). An autoregressive distributed lag modelling approach to cointegration analysis. *University of Cambridge, working paper, 9514* (9514). https://doi.org/10.1017/CCOL0521633230.011

Pesaran, M. H., Shin, Y., & Smith, R. J. (2001). Bounds testing approaches to the analysis of level relationships. *Journal of Applied Econometrics, 16*(3), 289–326. https://doi.org/10.1002/jae.616

Phillips, P. C., & Perron, P. (1988). Testing for a unit root in time series regression. *Biometrika, 75*(2), 335–346. https://doi.org/10.1093/biomet/75.2.335

Ramsey, J. B. (1969). Tests for specification errors in classical linear least-squares regression analysis. *Journal of the Royal Statistical Society: Series B (Methodological), 31*(2), 350–371. https://doi.org/10.1111/j.2517-6161.1969.tb00796.x

Shapiro, S. S., & Wilk, M. B. (1965). An analysis of variance test for normality (complete samples). *Biometrika, 52*(3/4), 591–611. https://doi.org/10.2307/2333709

Song, H., & Fei, B. (2007). Modelling and forecasting international tourist arrivals to mainland China. *China Tourism Research, 3*(1), 3–40.

Song, H., Gao, B. Z., & Lin, V. S. (2013). Combining statistical and judgmental forecasts via a web-based tourism demand forecasting system. *International Journal of Forecasting, 29*(2), 295–310. https://doi.org/10.1016/j.ijforecast.2011.12.003

Song, H., & Li, G. (2008). Tourism demand modelling and forecasting—A review of recent research. *Tourism Management, 29*(2), 203–220. https://doi.org/10.1016/j.tourman.2007.07.016

Song, H., Li, G., Witt, S. F., & Athanasopoulos, G. (2011). Forecasting tourist arrivals using time-varying parameter structural time series models. *International Journal of Forecasting, 27*(3), 855–869. https://doi.org/10.1016/j.ijforecast.2010.06.001

Song, H., & Lin, S. (2010). Impacts of the financial and economic crisis on tourism in Asia. *Journal of Travel Research, 49*(1), 16–30. https://doi.org/10.1177%2F0047287509353190

Song, H., Liu, A., Li, G., & Liu, X. (2021). Bayesian bootstrap aggregation for tourism demand forecasting. *International Journal of Tourism Research, 23*(5), 914–927. https://doi.org/10.1002/jtr.2453

Song, H., Qiu, R. T., & Park, J. (2019). A review of research on tourism demand forecasting: Launching the Annals of Tourism Research Curated Collection on tourism demand forecasting. *Annals of Tourism Research, 75*, 338–362. https://doi.org/10.1016/j.annals.2018.12.001

Song, H., & Turner, L. (2006). Tourism demand forecasting. *International Handbook on the Economics of Tourism*, 89–114.

Song, H., & Witt, S. F. (2003). Tourism forecasting: The general-to-specific approach. *Journal of Travel Research, 42*(1), 65–74. https://doi.org/10.1177%2F0047287503253939

Song, H., & Witt, S. F. (2006). Forecasting international tourist flows to Macau. *Tourism Management, 27*(2), 214–224. https://doi.org/10.1016/j.tourman.2004.09.004

Song, H., Witt, S. F., & Li, G. (2003). Modelling and forecasting the demand for Thai tourism. *Tourism Economics, 9*(4), 363–387. https://doi.org/10.5367%2F000000003322663186

Song, H., & Wong, K. K. (2003). Tourism demand modeling: A time-varying parameter approach. *Journal of Travel Research, 42*(1), 57–64. https://doi.org/10.1177%2F0047287503253908

Vanegas Sr, M. (2013). Co-integration and error correction estimation to forecast tourism. *Journal of Travel & Tourism Marketing, 30*(6), 523–537. https://doi.org/10.1080/10548408.2013.810992

White, H. (1980). A heteroskedasticity-consistent covariance matrix estimator and a direct test for heteroskedasticity. *Econometrica: Journal of the Econometric Society*, 817–838. https://doi.org/10.2307/1912934

Wong, K. K., Song, H., & Chon, K. S. (2006). Bayesian models for tourism demand forecasting. *Tourism Management, 27*(5), 773–780. https://doi.org/10.1016/j.tourman.2005.05.017

APPENDIX

R CODE

```
### The following codes shows how to estimate an ADLM by GETS
and generate the tourism demand forecast
  ### with the package ARDL in R.
  ### Author: Dr. Anyu Liu and Mr. Xinyang Liu
  ### Last updated: 12-04-2022
  ### R version: R 4.0.5

  ### Clear memory
  rm(list=ls())
  ### install and load ARDL package
  #install.packages("ARDL")
  #install.packages("dynlm")
  #install.packages("aod")
  #install.packages("tseries")
  #install.packages("lmtest")
  #install.packages("forecast")
  library(ARDL)
  library(dynlm)
  library(aod)
  library(tseries)
  library(lmtest)
  library(forecast)
  library(Metrics)

  ###Set the path that the data and function file is stored
  setwd("~")
  source('ardl _ forecast _ function.R')
```

```
###Input the raw data
data<-read.csv("THA _ MAL.csv")

###Generate the relative price and take natural log to non-
dummy variables
#data$RP=(data$CPI _ D/data$EX _ D)/(data$CPI _ O/data$EX _ O)
data$RP=(data$CPI _ D/data$EX _ D)/(data$CPI _ O/data$EX _ O)
data$lnarr=log(data$Arr)
data$lngdp=log(data$GDP)
data$lnrp=log(data$RP)
data1=data[c('lnarr','lngdp','lnrp','Q1','Q2','Q3')]###Modify
and specify the dummy variable names based on the data
data1<-ts(data1,start=c(2000,1),end=c(2019,4),frequency=4)
###Unit root tests
###Level
adf.test(data$lnarr)
adf.test(data$lngdp)
adf.test(data$lnrp)
pp.test(data$lnarr)
pp.test(data$lngdp)
pp.test(data$lnrp)
kpss.test(data$lnarr)
kpss.test(data$lngdp)
kpss.test(data$lnrp)
###1st order difference
adf.test(diff(ts(data$lnarr),differences=1))
adf.test(diff(ts(data$lngdp),differences=1))
adf.test(diff(ts(data$lnrp),differences=1))
pp.test(diff(ts(data$lnarr),differences=1))
pp.test(diff(ts(data$lngdp),differences=1))
pp.test(diff(ts(data$lnrp),differences=1))
kpss.test(diff(ts(data$lnarr),differences=1))
kpss.test(diff(ts(data$lngdp),differences=1))
kpss.test(diff(ts(data$lnrp),differences=1))

###Generate the training data set
datam<-ts(data1[1:68,],start=c(2000,1),end=c(2016,4),
frequency=4)
###Find the best ADLM specification based on AIC by GETS
models<-auto _ ardl(lnarr ~ lngdp + lnrp + Q1 + Q2 + Q3,
data = datam,
                    max _ order = 4, fixed _ order = c(-1,-
1,-1,0,0,0)) ###Modify the formula based on the inclusion of
```

dummy variables, the number of "0" in brakets equals to 3+ number of dummies

```
models$top _ orders
ardl _ fitted=models$best _ model
summary(models$best _ model)
###Estimate the error correction form of ADLM with the best
model specification
model _ l<-models$best _ model
model _ ecm<-uecm(model _ l)
summary(model _ ecm)

###Bounds test
fbd<-bounds _ f _ test(model _ l, case = 2)
tbd<- bounds _ t _ test(model _ l, case = 3, alpha = 0.01)

###Diagnostic tests
res<-model _ l$residuals #save the residual
bgtest(model _ l)#performs the Breusch–Godfrey test for
higher-order serial correlation
bptest(model _ l)#Performs the Breusch–Pagan test against
heteroskedasticity
resettest(model _ l)#Ramsey's RESET test for functional form
shapiro.test(res)#Shaprio test for normality
###Calculate Elasticities
EL<-multipliers(model _ l)

###Forecast Generation
###Generate the testing data set
#  datat  <-ts(data1[69:80,],start=c(2017,1),end=c(2019,4),fre-
quency = 4)
N = nrow(data)
forecasts.matrix = matrix(NA, 12, 8)
LnY0.matrix = matrix(NA, 12, 8)
colnames(forecasts.matrix) = paste0("h=", 1:8)
rownames(forecasts.matrix) = paste0(rep(2017:2019, each = 4),
paste0("Q", 1:4))

# ADLM
# Rolling window: sampling period ending from N-12 to N-1
for (i in 12:1) {
  endi = N - i
  mat = tail(head(data1, endi),68)
  # Fitting ADLM
```

```
    fit.adl <- auto_ardl(lnarr ~ lngdp + lnrp + Q1 + Q2 +
Q3, data = mat,
                                        max_order=4,
fixed_order=c(-1,-1,-1,0,0,0))$best_model
    # Forecasting h=i
    fc.adl <- ardl_forecast(fit.adl, data1, i)
    # Arranging forecasts and original values into 2 matrices
with the same format
    for (j in 1:8) {
       if ((12 - i + j) > 12)
         break
       forecasts.matrix[(12 - i + j), j] = fc.adl[j]
       LnY0.matrix[(12 - i + j), j] = data1[(endi + j), 1]
    }
  }

  # Computing residuals matrix in original scale
  residuals.matrix = exp(forecasts.matrix) - exp(LnY0.matrix)

  # Computing MAPE
  MAPE = colMeans(abs(residuals.matrix) * 100 / exp(LnY0.ma-
trix), na.rm = TRUE)

  # Computing RMSE
  RMSE = sqrt(colMeans((residuals.matrix) ^ 2, na.rm = TRUE))

  # Computing MASE
  MASE.denominator = mean(abs(diff(exp(data1[,1]), 4)))
  MASE = colMeans(abs(residuals.matrix) / MASE.denominator,
na.rm = TRUE)

  #ardl forecasts function
  ardl_forecast = function(model, data_full, horizon) {
    data_train <- model$data
    nrow <- dim(data_full)[1]
    ncol <- dim(data_full)[2]
    outro <- data_full[(nrow - horizon + 1): nrow, 2: ncol]
    #construct forecast matrix
    fore_array <- rep(0, horizon)
    for (i in 1: horizon) {
       if (i == 1) {
          updated_matrix <- rbind(data_train, c(fore_ar-
ray[1:i], matrix(outro, horizon,)[1:i,]))
       } else {
```

```
        updated _ matrix <- rbind(data _ train, cbind(fore _ ar-
ray[1:i], outro[1:i,]))
        }
        #with the help of ARDL fitting function, a complete
forecast (both current value and lag value are included) ma-
trix is construct
        data _ structure <- ardl(as.formula(paste(model$parsed _
formula$y _ part$var,   paste(model$parsed _ formula$x _ part$-
var, collapse = "+"), sep = "~")),
                                data = updated _ matrix, order
= model$order)$model

        nrow _ structure <- dim(data _ structure)[1]
        ncol _ structure <- dim(data _ structure)[2]
            outro _ input  <-  data _ structure[nrow _ structure,
2:ncol _ structure]
        coef <- model$coefficients[2: ncol _ structure]
        coef[is.na(coef)] <- 0

        fore <- as.matrix(outro _ input) %*% coef +
model$coefficients[1]
        fore _ array[i] <- fore
    }
    return(fore _ array)
  }
```

4

THE TIME-VARYING PARAMETER MODEL

Gang Li, Jason Li Chen, and Xiaoying Jiao

4.1 Introduction

Tourism trends and tourists' preferences change over time. These factors and other external shocks affect the structural stability of a tourism demand system. In the general forecasting literature, structural instability has been identified as a key reason for forecasting failure (Song, Smeral, Li, & Chen, 2008). Structural instability can be understood as structural change in the data-generating process, which further causes coefficient changes and predictive failure for standard fixed-parameter econometric models. The fixed-parameter estimation of a tourism demand model, often specified in double logarithm transformation, leads to constant estimates of demand elasticities. It assumes that tourists' preferences or responsiveness to income or price variations remain unchanged over time. This assumption seems to be very restrictive and unrealistic. To overcome the limitation of econometric forecasting models based on fixed-parameter estimation, time-varying parameter (TVP) regression has been developed and applied in tourism demand forecasting (e.g., Gunter & Önder, 2015; Li, Wong, Song, & Witt, 2006; Song, Witt, & Jensen, 2003). To address the structural instability issue, TVP regression relaxes the aforementioned restricted assumptions about constant coefficients of the explanatory variables and allows for stochastic parameters to better reflect the evolution of demand elasticity over time. Fluctuations in the economic structure generating the time series are allowed in TVP specifications, and this approach is more consistent with real-world situations than fixed-parameter methods because a changing environment can affect tourists' behaviour and the tourism industry both quantitatively and qualitatively. The TVP technique is more adaptable when structural instability occurs in econometric

DOI: 10.4324/9781003269366-4

modelling. It thus provides useful insights into the dynamics and evolution of tourism demand, and models implementing the technique tend to perform well in tourism demand forecasting.

The TVP model was introduced into the tourism context in the 1990s, and methodological advancements in TVP specifications and modelling procedures followed. Traditional econometric models with fixed parameters can be combined with TVP by allowing for varying coefficients over time. The most commonly applied TVP model in tourism demand forecasting is the single static regression (SR) with the TVP technique. Empirical applications of this TVP model have found that it provides superior forecasting accuracy to fixed-parameter benchmark models in the short term (e.g., Gunter & Önder, 2015; Song, Witt, & Jensen, 2003).

The TVP approach has been incorporated into other models in tourism demand forecasting. Li, Wong, Song and Witt (2006) combined the TVP model with error correction models (ECM) to forecast tourism spending per capita by UK residents for five major European destinations. They found that TVP-ECM provides superior forecasting performance, particularly in predicting the growth rate of tourism demand. Another model that works well with TVP specifications is the linear almost ideal demand system (LAIDS). Li, Song, and Witt (2006) developed TVP-LAIDS models in both long-run SR and short-run EC forms, and these models showed superior forecasting performance than their fixed-parameter counterparts. More recently, Song, Li, Witt, and Athanasopoulos (2011) combined the structural time series model (STSM) and the TVP approach to forecast quarterly tourist arrivals to Hong Kong from key source markets, and this combined model provided superior forecasting results than benchmark models.

This chapter introduces the general TVP model and its application in forecasting tourism demand for Thailand from four source markets. The R code is included. Further adjustments can be made to the modelling procedure depending on the data characteristics and forecasting objectives.

4.2 Methods

As noted in the previous section, the TVP approach allows for structure instability, and it is thus able to reflect the varying parameters (i.e., demand elasticities) of tourism demand (Song & Wong, 2003). The TVP technique can simulate fluctuating and gradual external shocks to the tourism demand system, which can improve forecasting accuracy when structure instability occurs or tourists' preferences and tourism trends change over time.

The TVP models are typically specified in state–space form (SSF), including measurement and state equations, and use a recursive estimation process that allocates different weights to information from different time periods. Specifically, recent information is given a heavier weight than information obtained in the distant past. SSF representation allows for the estimation of both observed and unobserved components in a time series (Li et al., 2006). The linear SSF of the TVP approach can be written as shown in Equations (4.1)–(4.3):

$$Y_t = \alpha_t + X_t\beta_t + Z_t\gamma + \varepsilon_t \qquad (4.1)$$
$$\alpha_t = \theta\alpha_{t-1} + \omega_t^\alpha \qquad (4.2)$$
$$\beta_t = \varphi\beta_{t-1} + \omega_t^\beta \qquad (4.3)$$

Equation (4.1) is the measurement or observation equation, and Equations (4.2) and (4.3) are the state equations or transition equations. The transition equations are normally pre-calibrated. In this application, Y_t is the log-transformed arrivals from each source market (i.e., $\ln y_t$), X_t is a vector containing five explanatory variables (including $\ln income_t$, $\ln price_t$ and three seasonal dummies) with time-variant parameters β_t, z_t is a vector containing one-off dummies with invariant parameters γ, α_t is a time-variant intercept state vector, ε_t is a vector of temporary disturbances, ω_t^α and ω_t^β refer to the permanent disturbances, and θ and φ are normally pre-determined in the transition equations. Seasonal dummies with time-variant parameters are specified in this application to capture varying seasonal patterns. Other specifications of seasonality can also be considered (Song et al., 2011).

The transition equations can be specified in many different ways. One approach, the random walk (RW) process, has proven sufficient to capture structural changes in tourism demand systems (e.g., Greenslade & Hall, 1996; Kim, 1993). If θ equals one and the components of φ equal unity, the evolutions of α_t and β_t in Equations (4.2) and (4.3) follow a multivariate RW process as specified in Equations (4.4) and (4.5):

$$\alpha_t = \alpha_{t-1} + \omega_t^\alpha \qquad (4.4)$$
$$\beta_t = \beta_{t-1} + \omega_t^\beta \qquad (4.5)$$

The transition equations are normally determined by experimentation based on two criteria: the goodness of fit and the predictive accuracy of the model using transition equations in particular forms. In this application, the RW processes specified in Equations (4.4) and (4.5) are selected as transition equations.

Once the form of the transition equations is determined, the parameters can be estimated using the maximum likelihood method. The Kalman filter (KF) can then be applied to compute the states (details in Harvey, 1990). Essentially, the KF algorithm represents a recursive process in which the initial condition (i.e., the initial values of the parameters and the covariances) is first determined from diffusion priors or ordinary least squares (OLS) estimates. As a new observation becomes available, the KF will update the optimal estimator of the state variable until all of the observations are included in the system. The final estimators returned by the KF process are then used to generate further elasticities and forecasts.

4.3 Application

The TVP model specified in Equations (4.1), (4.4), and (4.5) is applied to the empirical case of demand for international tourism to Thailand from four key source markets: mainland China, Malaysia, Russia and the USA.

4.3.1 Estimation

The model estimation results are presented in Table 4.1. Note that the estimates reported in Table 4.1 reflect the final state of the data at 2016Q4. The values and statistical significance of the state variable estimates are likely to vary across the sample period. The results suggest that at the final state, income elasticities of demand are significant in three source markets: mainland China, Russia and the USA. The income elasticity values for Russia and the US markets are well above one, which suggests that in these long-haul markets Thailand is regarded as a luxury tourism destination. The price elasticity of demand is significant for Russia in the final state. As its absolute value is smaller than 1 (−0.587), Russian tourists' demand for tourism in Thailand is price-inelastic.

Using Russia and the USA as examples, Figures 4.1 and 4.2 further illustrate the evolution of demand elasticities and stochastic seasonality. The fluctuations of the KF estimators at the beginning of the sample period reflect the initial turning process of recursive KF estimation, not necessarily the actual evolution of the elasticities, and should therefore be ignored. The two markets show distinctive income and price elasticities, reflecting different stages of market maturity and different tourist preferences. As a more mature market, the USA displays relatively stable income and price elasticities of demand for tourism in Thailand, with a slightly upward trend in recent years. The less mature Russian market has seen continuously declining income elasticity and fluctuating price elasticity of demand for tourism in Thailand. Both markets show varying seasonal patterns, although the trends are inconsistent.

4.3.2 Forecasting

Using the estimated TVP models featuring data up to 2016Q4, ex post forecasts of one to eight quarters ahead are generated for the period 2017Q1−2019Q4 based on the rolling window method. Country-level performance and overall performance are evaluated against the benchmark models: the seasonal naïve (SNAIVE), seasonal autoregressive integrated moving average (SARIMA) and exponential smoothing (ETS) models.

TABLE 4.1 TVP estimates in the final state and diagnostics

Final state	Mainland China	Malaysia	Russia	USA
Intercept	9.225***	11.094***	7.299***	1.876
	[3.020]	[1.655]	[1.621]	[2.083]
ln income	1.003*	0.526	1.182***	2.243***
	[0.596]	[0.339]	[0.338]	[0.439]
ln price	0.352	0.640	−0.587**	−0.216
	[0.818]	[0.491]	[0.260]	[0.165]
Q1	0.178***	−0.114***	0.356***	0.01
	[0.049]	[0.032]	[0.068]	[0.015]
Q2	0.011	−0.135***	−0.575***	−0.198***
	[0.054]	[0.029]	[0.126]	[0.016]
Q3	0.108	−0.151***	−0.916***	−0.271***
	[0.082]	[0.026]	[0.104]	[0.016]
Invariant coefficient				
SARS	−1.392***	−0.571***	−0.570***	−0.374***
	[0.150]	[0.094]	[0.150]	[0.050]
SARS_1		0.000		
		[0.094]		
PC_05	−0.729***			
	[0.155]			
FC_08	−0.445***		−0.218*	−0.107***
	[0.160]		[0.127]	[0.040]
PC_10	−0.751***			
	[0.162]			
SC_10				−0.173***
				[0.039]
PC_13	−0.335**			
	[0.155]			
PC_14		−0.257***		
		[0.089]		
SC_14				−0.144***
				[0.050]
PC_16	0.082			
	[0.173]			
Diagnostics				
AIC	88.187	−42.854	4.390	−101.203
BIC	120.509	−12.761	33.548	−70.285

Note: *, ** and *** denote significance at the 0.1, 0.05 and 0.01 levels, respectively; values in brackets are standard errors; the sample period for estimation is 2000Q1–2016Q4.

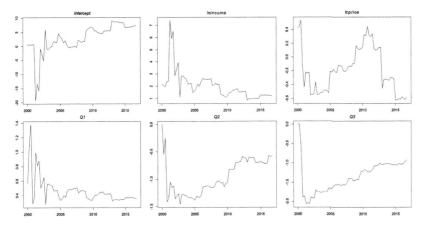

FIGURE 4.1 Evolution of states – Russia

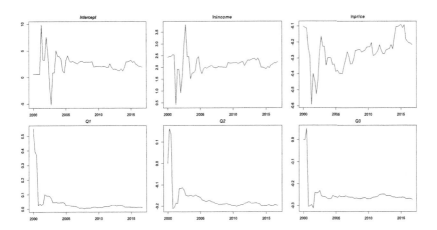

FIGURE 4.2 Evolution of states – USA

The TVP model outperforms the three benchmark models for short-term (one- and two-quarter-ahead) forecasting horizons in the cases of mainland China and the USA across all forecast accuracy measures (see Tables 4.2–4.4). This finding is consistent with most of the literature (e.g., Li et al., 2006, Song et al., 2003). As the forecasting horizon extends, the TVP model still performs relatively well except in the case of Malaysia for eight-quarter-ahead forecasts.

Overall, the TVP model outperforms all the benchmarks in 35%, 50% and 45% of cases, according to MAPE, RMSE and mean absolute scaled error (MASE), respectively. In 60–70% cases across the three forecast accuracy measures, the TVP model is able to beat at least two out of three benchmark models. The empirical results indicate that, overall, the TVP model provides good forecasting performance.

TABLE 4.2 Forecasting performance evaluation measured by MAPE (%)

	Forecasting horizon				
	1	2	3	4	8
Mainland China					
SNAIVE	13.194	13.683	15.039	15.606	14.882
ETS	12.201	16.127	15.163	13.312	15.984
SARIMA	14.753	13.945	16.658	17.642	21.033
TVP	9.418	12.565	15.305	17.507	9.398
Malaysia					
SNAIVE	7.859	7.559	7.349	8.114	18.818
ETS	7.973	8.113	8.193	8.448	5.081
SARIMA	8.339	8.032	8.422	7.148	8.964
TVP	8.306	10.180	7.960	6.685	11.003
Russia					
SNAIVE	9.800	8.259	7.474	7.783	13.722
ETS	9.956	12.781	16.648	13.287	26.609
SARIMA	12.221	16.511	15.800	19.900	46.633
TVP	11.454	12.707	10.371	11.746	15.000
USA					
SNAIVE	5.703	5.563	5.098	4.839	9.991
ETS	3.956	3.919	4.345	6.008	11.263
SARIMA	4.553	7.014	8.247	9.483	14.186
TVP	3.535	3.740	4.556	6.078	7.886

TABLE 4.3 Forecasting performance evaluation measured by RMSE

	Forecasting horizon				
	1	2	3	4	8
Mainland China					
SNAIVE	435305	451019	473032	490637	465626
ETS	361836	454310	454610	469960	496274
SARIMA	431710	440885	532880	515603	596629
TVP	306137	387623	473355	487537	254365
Malaysia					
SNAIVE	114911	117014	119366	125817	227894
ETS	86084	96150	108836	92312	64159

SARIMA	98563	100908	116794	107835	131294
TVP	96819	113998	110378	98758	140996

Russia

SNAIVE	60723	49666	50755	53441	72672
ETS	40284	35219	69387	61388	92175
SARIMA	44255	51003	58842	75123	150857
TVP	52129	50634	45894	64620	52183

USA

SNAIVE	17100	16758	15602	15539	32290
ETS	12734	13027	16326	19637	36930
SARIMA	17164	22540	26103	30561	45171
TVP	12345	12583	15643	19383	23668

TABLE 4.4 Forecasting performance evaluation measured by MASE

	Forecasting horizon				
	1	2	3	4	8
Mainland China					
SNAIVE	1.624	1.691	1.858	1.926	1.790
ETS	1.472	1.916	1.885	1.678	2.002
SARIMA	1.777	1.631	1.963	2.117	2.503
TVP	1.124	1.443	1.896	2.141	1.122
Malaysia					
SNAIVE	1.033	1.024	1.010	1.117	2.720
ETS	0.974	1.016	1.069	1.076	0.727
SARIMA	1.052	1.049	1.121	0.983	1.326
TVP	1.023	1.305	1.074	0.907	1.611
Russia					
SNAIVE	0.830	0.656	0.644	0.698	1.239
ETS	0.657	0.633	1.191	0.912	1.725
SARIMA	0.802	0.959	0.968	1.237	3.059
TVP	0.876	0.832	0.749	0.996	1.025
USA					
SNAIVE	0.962	0.936	0.875	0.863	1.862
ETS	0.646	0.652	0.768	1.078	2.110
SARIMA	0.773	1.144	1.409	1.684	2.624
TVP	0.582	0.609	0.767	1.058	1.377

4.4 Conclusion and future directions

This chapter introduces a general form of the TVP model and its application in tourism demand forecasting. The advantage of the TVP model lies in its ability to capture the evolution of the parameters in a demand model. These parameters are interpreted as demand elasticities in a double-log-transformed specification. Capturing the dynamics in a demand system enables more accurate prediction of future demand, particularly for short-term forecasting. The empirical application in this chapter demonstrates the overall satisfactory forecasting performance of the TVP model in terms of average accuracy measures.

Future research could combine TVP with other econometric models in tourism demand forecasting. Several attempts to date (e.g., TVP-ECM and TVP-STSM), although limited, have achieved improved performance in tourism demand forecasting (e.g., Li et al., 2006; Song et al., 2011). Future research should consider broader applications of these integrated models in different contexts and assess their general applicability in tourism demand forecasting. In addition, researchers could explore further integration of the TVP approach with recently developed, more advanced econometric techniques such as the global vector autoregressive (GVAR) models, the mixed-data sampling (MIDAS) models and the spatiotemporal econometric models. Given the technical merits of these advanced econometric techniques, further integration with the TVP approach will likely enable greater forecasting accuracy.

Self-study questions

1 What are the key advantages of the TVP model over fixed-parameter econometric models?
2 What is a measurement equation and what is a transition equation in state–space form in the TVP model?
3 Why is the TVP model able to capture the evolution of tourism demand elasticities?

References

Greenslade, J. V., & Hall, S. G. (1996). Modelling economies subject to structural change: The case of Germany. *Economic Modelling, 13*(4), 545–559. https://doi.org/10.1016/0264-9993(96)01023-1

Gunter, U., & Önder, I. (2015). Forecasting international city tourism demand for Paris: Accuracy of uni- and multivariate models employing monthly data. *Tourism Management, 46*, 123–135. https://doi.org/10.1016/j.tourman.2014.06.017

Harvey, A. C. (1990). *Forecasting, structural time series models and the Kalman filter.* Cambridge: Cambridge University Press.

Kim, C.-J. (1993). Sources of monetary growth uncertainty and economic activity: The time-varying-parameter model with heteroskedastic disturbances.

The Review of Economics and Statistics, 75(3), 483–492. https://doi.org/10.2307/2109462

Li, G., Song, H., & Witt, S. F. (2006). Time varying parameter and fixed parameter linear AIDS: An application to tourism demand forecasting. *International Journal of Forecasting, 22*(1), 57–71. https://doi.org/10.1016/j.ijforecast.2005.03.006

Li, G., Wong, K. K. F., Song, H., & Witt, S. F. (2006). Tourism demand forecasting: A time varying parameter error correction model. *Journal of Travel Research, 45*(2), 175–185. https://doi.org/10.1177/0047287506291596

Song, H., Li, G., Witt, S. F., & Athanasopoulos, G. (2011). Forecasting tourist arrivals using time-varying parameter structural time series models. *International Journal of Forecasting, 27*(3), 855–869. https://doi.org/10.1016/j.ijforecast.2010.06.001

Song, H., Smeral, E., Li, G., & Chen, J. L. (2008). *Tourism forecasting: Accuracy of alternative econometric models revisited* (Working Paper No. 326). WIFO Working Papers. https://www.econstor.eu/handle/10419/128885

Song, H., Witt, S. F., & Jensen, T. C. (2003). Tourism forecasting: Accuracy of alternative econometric models. *International Journal of Forecasting, 19*(1), 123–141. https://doi.org/10.1016/S0169-2070(01)00134-0

Song, H., & Wong, K. K. F. (2003). Tourism demand modeling: A time-varying parameter approach. *Journal of Travel Research, 42*(1), 57–64. https://doi.org/10.1177/0047287503253908

APPENDIX

R CODE

```
# TVP model for Chapter 4
  library(dlm)
  library(forecast)

  # Function to build a Time Varying Parameter state space
model
  buildTVP = function(parm, x.mat) {
    parm = exp(parm)
    mod = dlmModReg(X = x.mat, addInt = T, dV = parm[1])
    diag(W(mod))[1:3] = c(parm[2:4])
    diag(W(mod))[4:6] = c(parm[5:7])
    return(mod)
  }

  countries = c("CHN", MAL", "RUS", "USA")
  table.MAPE.all.countries=NULL
  table.RMSE.all.countries=NULL
  table.MASE.all.countries=NULL

  for (country in countries) {
    datafile = paste0("data/THA _ ", country, ".csv")
    dat = read.csv(datafile)

    # Generating variables
    N = nrow(dat)
    ln _ arrivals = log(dat$Arr)
    ln _ income = log(dat$GDP)
```

```
    ln _ price = log((dat$CPI _ D / dat$EX _ D) / (dat$CPI _ O /
dat$EX _ O))
    dummies = dat[, 11:ncol(dat)]
    X = cbind(ln _ income, ln _ price, dat$Q1, dat$Q2, dat$Q3,
dummies)
    colnames(X)[1:5] = c("Ln _ Income", "Ln _ Price", "Q1", "Q2",
"Q3")
    X = ts(X, freq = 4, start = c(2000, 1))
    Y = ts(ln _ arrivals, freq = 4, start = c(2000, 1))

    forecasts.snaive=matrix(NA,12,8)
    forecasts.ets=matrix(NA,12,8)
    forecasts.arima=matrix(NA,12,8)
    forecasts.tvp=matrix(NA,  12,8)
    Y0.h=matrix(NA,12,8)

    colnames(forecasts.snaive)=paste0("h=",1:8)
    colnames(forecasts.ets)=paste0("h=",1:8)
    colnames(forecasts.arima)=paste0("h=",1:8)
    colnames(forecasts.tvp)=paste0("h=",1:8)

    rownames(forecasts.snaive)=paste(rep(2017:2019,each=4),
paste0("Q",1:4))
    rownames(forecasts.ets)=paste(rep(2017:2019,each=4),
paste0("Q",1:4))
    rownames(forecasts.arima)=paste(rep(2017:2019,each=4),
paste0("Q",1:4))
    rownames(forecasts.tvp)=paste(rep(2017:2019,each=4),
paste0("Q",1:4))

    for (i in 12:1) {
      endi = N - i
      X0 = tail(head(X, endi),68)
      Y0 = tail(head(Y, endi),68)

      # Generating initial values
      ols = lm(Y0 ~ X0)
      start.vals  =  c(log(var(Y0)),  log(summary(ols)$coeffi-
cients[1:6, 2]^2))

      # Trying different initial values
      TVP.mle = tryCatch({
        # MLE
        TVP.mle = dlmMLE(
          y = Y0,
```

```
        parm = start.vals,
        x.mat = X0,
        build = buildTVP,
        method = "L-BFGS-B"
    )
}, warning = function(warn) {
    #exp(-6.907755)=0.001
    start.vals[1] = -6.907755
    TVP.mle = dlmMLE(
        y = Y0,
        parm = start.vals,
        x.mat = X0,
        build = buildTVP,
        method = "L-BFGS-B"
    )
    return (TVP.mle)
}, error = function(err) {
    start.vals[1] = -6.907755
    TVP.mle = dlmMLE(
        y = Y0,
        parm = start.vals,
        x.mat = X0,
        build = buildTVP,
        method = "L-BFGS-B"
    )
    return (TVP.mle)
})

# Build TVP
fitted = buildTVP(TVP.mle$par, X0)

# Kalman filter
filtered = dlmFilter(Y0, fitted)

# TVP Forecasting
Y1 = window(Y0, end = c(2019, 4), extend = TRUE)
X(fitted) = tail(X,length(Y1))
fc.tvp = tail(dlmFilter(Y1, fitted)$f,i)

# Seasonal Naive forecasting
fc.snaive = snaive(Y0, h = i)

# ETS forecasting
fit.ets = ets(Y0)
```

```
    fc.ets = forecast(Y0, model = fit.ets, use.initial.values
= FALSE, h = i)

    # ARIMA forecasting
    fit.arima = auto.arima(Y0)
    fc.arima = forecast(Y0, model = fit.arima, h = i)

    for (j in 1:8) {
      if ((12 - i + j) > 12) {
        break
      }
      forecasts.tvp[(12 - i + j), j] = fc.tvp[j]
      forecasts.snaive[(12 - i + j), j] = fc.snaive$mean[j]
      forecasts.ets[(12 - i + j), j] = fc.ets$mean[j]
      forecasts.arima[(12 - i + j), j] = fc.arima$mean[j]
      Y0.h[(12 - i + j), j] = Y[endi + j]
    }
  }

  # Computing forecasting accuracy
  res.arima = exp(forecasts.arima) - exp(Y0.h)
  res.ets = exp(forecasts.ets) - exp(Y0.h)
  res.snaive = exp(forecasts.snaive) - exp(Y0.h)
  res.tvp = exp(forecasts.tvp) - exp(Y0.h)

  MAPE.arima = colMeans(abs(res.arima) * 100 / exp(Y0.h),
na.rm = TRUE)
  MAPE.ets = colMeans(abs(res.ets) * 100 / exp(Y0.h), na.rm
= TRUE)
  MAPE.snaive = colMeans(abs(res.snaive) * 100 / exp(Y0.h),
na.rm = TRUE)
  MAPE.tvp = colMeans(abs(res.tvp) * 100 / exp(Y0.h), na.rm
= TRUE)

  RMSE.arima = sqrt(colMeans((res.arima) ^ 2, na.rm = TRUE))
  RMSE.ets = sqrt(colMeans((res.ets) ^ 2, na.rm = TRUE))
  RMSE.snaive = sqrt(colMeans((res.snaive) ^ 2, na.rm =
TRUE))
  RMSE.tvp = sqrt(colMeans((res.tvp) ^ 2, na.rm = TRUE))

  MASE.arima = colMeans(abs(res.arima) / mean(abs(diff(ex-
p(Y), 4))), na.rm = TRUE)
  MASE.ets = colMeans(abs(res.ets) / mean(abs(diff(exp(Y),
4))), na.rm = TRUE)
```

```
    MASE.snaive = colMeans(abs(res.snaive) / mean(abs(diff(ex-
p(Y), 4))), na.rm = TRUE)
    MASE.tvp = colMeans(abs(res.tvp) / mean(abs(diff(exp(Y),
4))), na.rm = TRUE)

    table.MAPE  =  rbind(MAPE.snaive,  MAPE.ets,  MAPE.arima,
MAPE.tvp)
    table.MAPE = formatC(table.MAPE, format = "f", digits = 3)
    table.MAPE = rbind("",table.MAPE)
    colnames(table.MAPE) = paste0("h=", 1:8)
    rownames(table.MAPE) = c(country, "SNAIVE", "ETS", "SA-
RIMA", "TVP")
    table.MAPE = table.MAPE[,c(1:4,8)]

    table.RMSE = rbind(RMSE.snaive, RMSE.ets, RMSE.arima,
RMSE.tvp)
    table.RMSE = formatC(table.RMSE, format = "f", digits = 0)
    table.RMSE = rbind("",table.RMSE)
    colnames(table.RMSE)=paste0("h=",1:8)
    rownames(table.RMSE) = c(country, "SNAIVE", "ETS", "SA-
RIMA", "TVP")
    table.RMSE = table.RMSE[,c(1:4,8)]

    table.MASE = rbind(MASE.snaive, MASE.ets, MASE.arima,
MASE.tvp)
    table.MASE = formatC(table.MASE, format = "f", digits = 3)
    table.MASE = rbind("",table.MASE)
    colnames(table.MASE)=paste0("h=",1:8)
    rownames(table.MASE) = c(country, "SNAIVE", "ETS", "SA-
RIMA", "TVP")
    table.MASE = table.MASE[,c(1:4,8)]

    table.MAPE.all.countries =rbind(table.MAPE.all.countries,
table.MAPE)
    table.RMSE.all.countries =rbind(table.RMSE.all.countries,
table.RMSE)
    table.MASE.all.countries =rbind(table.MASE.all.countries,
table.MASE)

    # Output: Forecasts
    write.csv(exp(forecasts.snaive),
        paste0("output/forecasts _ SNAIVE _ ", country,
".csv"))
    write.csv(exp(forecasts.ets),
        paste0("output/forecasts _ ETS _ ", country, ".csv"))
    write.csv(exp(forecasts.arima),
```

```
        paste0("output/forecasts _ SARIMA _ ", country,
".csv"))
    write.csv(exp(forecasts.tvp),
        paste0("output/forecasts _ TVP _ ", country, ".csv"))
  }
    # Output: Accuracy tables
    write.csv(table.MAPE.all.countries, "output/table _ MAPE.
csv")
    write.csv(table.RMSE.all.countries, "output/table _ RMSE.
csv")
    write.csv(table.MASE.all.countries, "output/table _ MASE.
csv")

  # Output: estimates and graphs
  for (country in countries) {
    datafile = paste0("data/THA _ ", country, ".csv")
    dat = read.csv(datafile)
    N = nrow(dat)
    ln _ arrivals = log(dat$Arr)
    ln _ income = log(dat$GDP)
    ln _ price = log((dat$CPI _ D / dat$EX _ D) / (dat$CPI _ O /
dat$EX _ O))
    dummies = dat[, 11:ncol(dat)]
    X = cbind(ln _ income, ln _ price, dat$Q1, dat$Q2, dat$Q3,
dummies)
    colnames(X)[1:5] = c("Ln _ Income", "Ln _ Price", "Q1", "Q2",
"Q3")
    X = ts(X, freq = 4, start = c(2000, 1))
    Y = ts(ln _ arrivals, freq = 4, start = c(2000, 1))

    # Sample period for estimation: 2000Q1-2016Q4
    X0 = head(X, 68)
    Y0 = head(Y, 68)

    # Taking OLS estimates as initial values
    ols = lm(Y0 ~ X0)
    start.vals = c(log(var(Y0)), log(summary(ols)$coeffi-
cients[1:6, 2] ^ 2))

    # Trying different initial values
    TVP.mle = tryCatch({
      TVP.mle = dlmMLE(
        y = Y0,
        parm = start.vals,
        x.mat = X0,
```

```
      build = buildTVP,
      method = "L-BFGS-B"
    )
  }, warning = function(warn) {
    start.vals[1] = -6.907755
    TVP.mle = dlmMLE(
      y = Y0,
      parm = start.vals,
      x.mat = X0,
      build = buildTVP,
      method = "L-BFGS-B"
    )
    return (TVP.mle)
  }, error = function(err) {
    start.vals[1] = -6.907755
    TVP.mle = dlmMLE(
      y = Y0,
      parm = start.vals,
      x.mat = X0,
      build = buildTVP,
      method = "L-BFGS-B"
    )
    return (TVP.mle)
})

loglik = -TVP.mle$value
n.coef = length(start.vals)
AIC = 2 * n.coef - 2 * loglik
BIC = log(length(X0)) * n.coef - 2 * loglik

fitted = buildTVP(TVP.mle$par, X0)
filtered = dlmFilter(Y0, fitted)
smoothed = dlmSmooth(filtered)

beta.mat = filtered$m[-1, ]
colnames(beta.mat) = c("Intercept", colnames(X0))

mse.list = dlmSvd2var(smoothed$U.S, smoothed$D.S)
se.mat = t(sapply(
  mse.list,
  FUN = function(x)
    sqrt(diag(x))
))
se.mat = se.mat[-1, ]
```

```
t.mat = beta.mat / se.mat
p.mat = 2 * pt(q = abs(t.mat),
          df = 67,
          lower.tail = F)
p.mat = ts(p.mat, freq = 4, start = c(2000, 1))

table.estimates = t(rbind(tail(beta.mat, 1), tail(se.mat,
1), tail(p.mat, 1)))
  colnames(table.estimates) = c("Final State", "Standard
Error", "P value")

p.stars = rep("", ncol(p.mat))
for (k in 1:ncol(p.mat)) {
  if (table.estimates[k, 3] < 0.01)
    p.stars[k] = "***"
  else if (table.estimates[k, 3] < 0.05)
    p.stars[k] = "**"
  else if (table.estimates[k, 3] < 0.1)
    p.stars[k] = "*"
}
beta.stars = paste0(formatC(table.estimates[, 1], format =
"f", digits = 3), p.stars)
  se.brack = formatC(table.estimates[, 2], format = "f",
digits = 3)
se.brack = paste0("[", se.brack, "]")
AIC = formatC(AIC, format = "f", digits = 3)
BIC = formatC(BIC, format = "f", digits = 3)
table.estimates.formatted = matrix(t(cbind(beta.stars,
se.brack)), ncol = 1, byrow = TRUE)
rownames(table.estimates.formatted) = rep(rownames(table.
estimates), each = 2)
colnames(table.estimates.formatted) = country
table.estimates.formatted = rbind(table.estimates.format-
ted, AIC, BIC)
write.csv(
  table.estimates.formatted,
  paste0("output/table_estimates_", country, ".csv")
)

# Generating graphs
par(mfrow = c(2, 3), mar = c(2, 2, 2, 2))
plot(
  ts(filtered$m[-1, 1], freq = 4, start = c(2000, 1)),
  main = "Intercept",
  font.main = 3,
```

```
        xlab = "",
        ylab = ""
    )
    plot(
        ts(filtered$m[-1, 2], freq = 4, start = c(2000, 1)),
        main = expression('ln'*italic(income)),
        xlab = "",
        ylab = ""
    )
    plot(
        ts(filtered$m[-1, 3], freq = 4, start = c(2000, 1)),
        main = expression('ln'*italic(price)),
        xlab = "",
        ylab = ""
    )
    plot(
        ts(filtered$m[-1, 4], freq = 4, start = c(2000, 1)),
        main = "Q1",
        font.main = 3,
        xlab = "",
        ylab = ""
    )
    plot(
        ts(filtered$m[-1, 5], freq = 4, start = c(2000, 1)),
        main = "Q2",
        font.main = 3,
        xlab = "",
        ylab = ""
    )
    plot(
        ts(filtered$m[-1, 6], freq = 4, start = c(2000, 1)),
        main = "Q3",
        font.main = 3,
        xlab = "",
        ylab = ""
    )
}
```

5

VECTOR AUTOREGRESSIVE MODELS

Zheng Chris Cao

5.1 Introduction

Macroeconomists are often tasked with describing and summarising macroeconomic data, making macroeconomic forecasts, quantifying what we do or do not know about the true structure of the economy and advising macroeconomic policymakers (Stock & Watson, 2001). In macroeconomics, a threshold concept that describes the complex interrelations among economic variables is *cumulative causation*, which refers to a self-reinforcing process whereby an initial shock triggers subsequent changes in other variables in the economic system through feedback loops. Vector autoregressive (VAR) models hold the promise of capturing the rich dynamics and interconnected nature of multiple economic variables by providing a coherent and credible approach to data description, forecasting, structural inference and policy analysis (Stock & Watson, 2001).

VAR models have been applied in tourism demand research since the early 2000s; for example, see Song, Romilly and Liu (2000). These studies are not limited to unrestricted VAR models but also incorporate cointegration analysis in the form of vector error correction models (VECM) (e.g., Lim & McAleer, 2001) and structural analysis in the form of structural VAR (e.g., De Mello & Nell, 2005).

Empirically, each tourism destination country can be perceived as a single system within which interactions take place between tourism demand and other economic variables that characterise the local economy. In a global setting, which is characterised by the interconnectedness of destination countries and tourist-originating countries, cumulative causation can be readily transmitted across borders. The transmission can take place through various channels. As summarised by Chudik and Pesaran (2016),

DOI: 10.4324/9781003269366-5

these include sharing scarce resources (such as oil and other commodities), political and technological developments, the movements of labour and capital across countries, and cross-border trade in financial assets as well as trade in goods and services. In addition, there might be residual interdependencies due to unobserved interactions and spillover effects not properly captured by the common interaction channels listed above.

To model the interdependencies among multiple countries, researchers need to handle the *curse of dimensionality* in the estimation of a vast number of coefficients. Initially proposed by Pesaran et al. (2004), the global VAR (GVAR) approach offers a relatively simple yet effective method for modelling complex high-dimensional systems such as the global economy. In the context of tourism, this approach enables research into the global tourism demand system (e.g., Cao, Li, & Song, 2017; Gunter & Zekan, 2021), which encompasses a host of tourism demand variables and macroeconomic determinants for multiple destination countries and treats all variables as *endogenous*.

Furthermore, a recent development in VAR models is the use of Bayesian statistics. Many of the macroeconomic databases used in modelling practice, including tourism statistics, provide relatively short sample periods, rendering VAR estimations less precise. To enhance forecast accuracy, many researchers impose additional restrictions on their estimations, which may help reduce the variance of unrestricted least squares estimators. As Kilian and Lütkepohl (2017) noted, the Bayesian approach provides a formal framework for incorporating such extraneous information (i.e., priors) into estimations and inferences. It also reduces the need for estimating a large number of coefficients. The Bayesian approach to VAR modelling has long attracted the attention of tourism researchers; for example, see Wong, Song, and Chon (2006) and Assaf et al. (2019).

This chapter explores how VAR models are applied in tourism demand modelling and forecasting. Section 5.2 reviews a range of VAR models, from the classic VAR model to the recently developed GVAR model and their Bayesian counterparts (i.e., Bayesian VAR and Bayesian GVAR). Section 5.3 demonstrates an application of VAR models using global tourism demand data and evaluates the models' forecasting performance. Section 5.4 reflects on VAR modelling and proposes future research directions.

5.2 Methods

VAR models relax the assumption of exogeneity imposed on independent variables in many econometric models. Developed by Sims (1980), a VAR model is a k-equation, k-variable linear model in which each variable is explained by its own lagged values plus the current and past values of the remaining $k - 1$ variables, whilst allowing for deterministic terms such as intercepts, trends and dummy variables (Song & Witt, 2006; Stock & Watson, 2001).

5.2.1 The VAR model

A classic VAR(p) model, where p is the lag order, can be written as

$$Y_t = \sum_{l=1}^{p} A_l Y_{t-l} + C_0 + C_1 t + U_t \tag{5.1}$$

$$U_t \sim IID(\mathbf{0},\ \Sigma) \tag{5.2}$$

where Y_t is a $k \times 1$ vector of k endogenous variables, A_l is a $k \times k$ matrix of coefficients to be estimated, C_0 is a $k \times 1$ vector of intercepts, C_1 is a $k \times 1$ vector of coefficients on the trend terms and U_t is a $k \times 1$ vector of innovations or shocks. Moreover, dummy variables can be added to Equation (5.1) in the same manner as the trend term. The variables in Y_t are endogenous variables (justified either by theory or simply due to lack of evidence of exogeneity) in a system, such that changes in one variable can cumulatively cause changes to the other variables. The lag order p can be selected based on, among other criteria, the Akaike information criterion, the Schwarz Bayesian information criterion or the Hannan–Quinn criterion (Song, Witt, & Li, 2009: 42). In total, there are k equations to be estimated. Assuming U_t to be contemporaneously correlated but not autocorrelated, each equation in the system can be individually estimated with the ordinary least squares estimator or the seemingly unrelated regression estimator (Song & Witt, 2006).

More generally, VAR models can be extended to include exogenous variables, as follows:

$$Y_t = \sum_{l=1}^{p} A_l Y_{t-l} + BZ_t + C_0 + C_1 t + U_t \tag{5.3}$$

where Z_t is a $d \times 1$ vector of d exogenous variables and B is a $k \times d$ matrix of coefficients to be estimated. Equation (5.3) is called a VAR with exogenous variables (VARX) model. Unlike Equation (5.1), where the k equations explain the causal relationships among k endogenous variables, Equation (5.3) uses $k + d$ variables to explain the k relationships.

Cointegration analysis can be incorporated into the above VAR models, which are then specified as VECMs:

$$\Delta Y_t = \sum_{l=1}^{p-1} A_l \Delta Y_{t-l} + \Pi Y_{t-1} + C_0 + C_1 t + U_t \tag{5.4}$$

where ΠY_{t-1} is the error correction vector. If the elements of Y_t are $I(0)$, Π will be a full rank $k \times k$ matrix. If the elements of Y_t are $I(1)$ and not cointegrated, then $\Pi = 0$ and a VAR model in first differences will be a more appropriate specification than a VECM. If the elements of Y_t are $I(1)$ and cointegrated with rank $(\Pi) = r$ ($0 < r < k$), then Π can be expressed as $\Pi = \alpha\beta'$. Both α and β are $k \times r$ full column rank matrices, and there are r cointegrating relations, i.e., $\xi_t = \beta'Y_t$, which are $I(0)$. ξ_t captures the deviations from equilibrium, and α is the matrix of adjustment or feedback coefficients, which measure how strongly the deviations from equilibrium feed back into the system (Garratt, Lee, Pesaran, & Shin, 2012: 117–118). As in the classic VAR model, Equation (5.4) can also be extended to include exogenous variables, as described in Pesaran, Shin, and Smith (2000).

Whilst Π can be estimated unrestrictedly, α and β are not necessarily unique. It is possible to choose any non-singular $r \times r$ matrix, Q, and write $\Pi = \alpha\beta' = \left(\alpha Q'^{-1}\right)\left(Q'\beta'\right) = \alpha_*\beta_*'$, such that $\alpha_* = \alpha Q'^{-1}$ and $\beta_* = \beta Q$ constitute observationally equivalent alternative structures. To identify β, at least r^2 restrictions are needed, formed from r restrictions on each of the r cointegrating relations (Garratt, Lee, Pesaran, & Shin, 2012, p. 36). One often-used restriction is a normalisation scheme of imposing an $r \times r$ identity matrix on β'. Other subjective identification schemes are also plausible. In fact, the restrictions can be drawn from economic theories and other a priori information, which add economic interpretability to the cointegrating relations (Garratt, Lee, Pesaran, & Shin, 2012: 36–37; Juselius, 2006: 120).

To determine the number of cointegrating relations, r, the Johansen Maximum Likelihood (JML) procedure can be adopted. This procedure is based on estimating the significance of the characteristic roots of matrix Π (Song, Witt, & Li, 2009, p. 129). The rank of a matrix is the same as the number of characteristic roots that are different from zero. In the JML procedure, two statistics can be calculated:

$$\lambda_{trace} = -T \sum_{i=r+1}^{m} in\left(1 - \hat{\lambda}_i\right) \tag{5.5}$$

$$\lambda_{max} = -T\ln\left(1 - \hat{\lambda}_{r+1}\right) \tag{5.6}$$

where $\hat{\lambda}_i$ are the estimated values of the characteristic roots or eigenvalues from matrix Π in Equation (5.4), and T is the total number of observations. The first test statistic λ_{trace} is the trace test. The null hypothesis is that there are at most r cointegrating relations, i.e., $\text{rank}(\Pi) \leq r$, whereas the alternative hypothesis is there are more than r cointegrating relations, i.e., $\text{rank}(\Pi) > r$. The second test statistic λ_{max} is known as the maximal eigenvalue test. Its null hypothesis is that the rank of Π is r, and the alternative hypothesis is that the rank is $r + 1$. In practice, λ_{trace} and λ_{max} very often suggest different numbers of cointegrating relations. It is then at the discretion of the researcher to decide what value r should take, after considering both the test statistics and economic interpretability.

In the cointegrating relations, $\beta' Y_t$, which is $I(0)$ if the variables of Y_t are cointegrated, it is possible to add deterministic terms such as intercept C_0 and trend $C_1 t$. Let

$$C_0 = \alpha \beta_0 + \gamma_0 \qquad (5.7)$$
$$C_1 = \alpha \beta_1 + \gamma_1 \qquad (5.8)$$

where α has the same meaning as in $\Pi = \alpha \beta'$. The derivations of β_0, β_1, γ_0 and γ_1 are explained in Juselius (2006, pp. 95–99).

There are five cases under which Equations (5.7) and (5.8) can be incorporated into Equation (5.4) (Juselius, 2006, p. 100; Song, Witt, & Li, 2009, pp. 129–130).

Case I: Y_t does not have deterministic trends and the cointegration equations do not have intercepts, i.e., $C_0 = 0$ and $C_1 = 0$. Hence, $\Pi Y_{t-1} + C_0 + C_1 t = \alpha \beta' Y_{t-1}$.

Case II: Y_t does not have deterministic trends but the cointegration equations have intercepts, i.e., $\beta_0 \neq 0$, $\gamma_0 = 0$ and $C_1 = 0$. Hence, $\Pi Y_{t-1} + C_0 + C_1 t = \alpha \left(\beta' Y_{t-1} + \beta_0 \right)$.

Case III: Y_t has deterministic trends but the cointegration equations only have intercepts, i.e., $\beta_0 \neq 0$, $\gamma_0 \neq 0$ and $C_1 = 0$. Hence, $\Pi Y_{t-1} + C_0 + C_1 t = \alpha \left(\beta' Y_{t-1} + \beta_0 \right) + \gamma_0$.

Case IV: Y_t has deterministic trends and the cointegration equations have intercepts and deterministic trends, i.e., $\beta_0 \neq 0$, $\gamma_0 \neq 0$, $\beta_1 \neq 0$ and $\gamma_1 = 0$. Hence, $\Pi Y_{t-1} + C_0 + C_1 t = \alpha \left(\beta' Y_{t-1} + \beta_0 + \beta_1 t \right) + \gamma_0$.

Case V: Y_t has quadratic trends and the cointegration equations have intercepts and deterministic trends, i.e., $\beta_0 \neq 0$, $\gamma_0 \neq 0$, $\beta_1 \neq 0$ and $\gamma_1 \neq 0$. Hence, $\Pi Y_{t-1} + C_0 + C_1 t = \alpha \left(\beta' Y_{t-1} + \beta_0 + \beta_1 t \right) + \gamma_0 + \gamma_1 t$.

Of the above five cases, *Case III* and *Case IV* are commonly used in economics.

One major usage of VAR models is to simulate the impulse responses of endogenous variables in the face of a shock to the ith variable. For simplicity, consider a VAR(1) model:

$$Y_t = A_1 Y_{t-1} + U_t \qquad (5.9)$$

By iterative substitution for n times, Equation (5.9) can be rearranged as follows:

$$Y_t = \sum_{i=0}^{n} A_1^i U_{t-i} + A_1^{n+1} Y_{t-n+1} \qquad (5.10)$$

If the time series data are stationary, i.e., $0 < |A_1| < 1$, then $\lim_{n \to \infty} A_1^n = 0$, and Equation (5.10) can be written as follows:

$$Y_t = \sum_{i=0}^{\infty} A_1^i U_{t-i} \qquad (5.11)$$

Equation (5.11) is called a vector moving average form, where the vector of dependent variables is represented by an infinite sum of lagged random errors weighted by an exponentially diminishing coefficient. Hence, the endogenous variables of Y_t can be expressed by sequences of shocks to the VAR system. Equation (5.11) can capture the impacts of unitary changes in the error terms (i.e., shocks) on the endogenous variables.

5.2.2 The GVAR model

An issue with the classic VAR model is that whilst the number of coefficients to be estimated grows exponentially when more endogenous variables are included, as each variable is represented in k equations, the number of observations tends to be limited relative to the number of coefficients. The reduction in the degrees of freedom makes it difficult to estimate a high-dimensional VAR model. In response to this issue, Pesaran, Schuermann, and Weiner (2004) proposed the GVAR model, the global high-dimensional version of the VAR model, which is suitable for a large multiple cross-sectional setting. Dees, Mauro, Pesaran, and Smith (2007) further developed the approach within a global common factor framework.

The GVAR approach entails a two-stage procedure: (1) treating each cross section in a global system as an individual VAR model and estimating the coefficients for each model; and (2) stacking the individual VAR models to form the GVAR system.

Suppose that in a global system, there are N countries (i.e., cross sections). In the first stage, each country-specific model is specified as a VARX*(p_i, q_i) model:

$$\phi_i\left(L, \; p_i\right)x_{it} = a_{i0} + a_{i1}t + \Lambda_i\left(L, \; q_i\right)x_{it}^* + \Upsilon_i\left(L, \; q_i\right)d_t + u_{it} \qquad (5.12)$$

Let x_{it} denote a $k_i \times 1$ vector of endogenous variables belonging to country $i \in \{1,..., N\}$. x_{it} is also called *domestic variables* in relation to country i. x_{it}^* is a $k_i^* \times 1$ vector of *foreign variables* specific to country i, which is supposed to capture the influence of country i's trade partners. x_{it}^* is calculated as cross-sectional averages of the foreign counterparts of country i's domestic variables:

$$x_{it}^* = \sum_{j=1}^{N} w_{ij}x_{jt} \qquad (5.13)$$

where x_{jt} represents the domestic variables of country $j \in \{1,..., N\}$, and w_{ij} is the weight for country j (e.g., the share of country j's trade with country i among country i's total trade with the global system). In tourism demand research, the weight can be the share of tourist arrivals or the share of tourism expenditures. Preferably the weights are non-random (i.e., predetermined) and granular (i.e., compared with the global system, each country's weight is small, and no country dominates the system) (Bussiere, Chudik, & Sestieri, 2009). w_{ij} satisfies $w_{ii} = 0, \forall i = 1,..., N$, and

$$\sum_{j=1}^{N} w_{ij} = 1, \forall i,\ j = 1,..., N.$$ Equation (5.13) is a data shrinkage method that

addresses the dimensionality problem. d_t is a $k_d \times 1$ vector of *observable global common factors*, which apply to all of the country-specific VARX* models. As an aside, Equation (5.12) can incorporate cointegration analysis and be specified in its error correction representation VECMX* (see Dees, Mauro, Pesaran, & Smith, 2007 for technical details).

Domestic variables (x_{it}), *foreign variables* (x_{it}^*) and *observable global common variables* (d_t) capture the different channels through which the cross-border transmission of business cycles takes place. Broadly, the transmission can be caused by observable global common shocks (e.g., changes in oil prices); it can arise as a result of unobserved global common factors (e.g., diffusion of technological progress and political developments); or it can be due to specific national or sectoral shocks. In a factor model framework, Dees, Mauro, Pesaran, and Smith (2007) showed that *foreign variables* are proxies for unobserved global common factors.

In Equation (5.12), $\Phi_i(L, p_i) = I_{k_i} - \sum_{l=1}^{p_i} \Phi_l L^l$ is a $k_i \times k_i$ matrix of unknown

coefficients on *domestic variables*; $\Lambda_i(L, q_i) = \sum_{l=0}^{q_i} \Lambda_l L^l$ is a $k_i \times k_i^*$ matrix of

unknown coefficients on *foreign variables*; and $Y_i(L, q_i) = \sum_{l=0}^{q_i} Y_l L^l$ is a $k_i \times k_d$

matrix of unknown coefficients on *global common variables*. L is the lag operator, and p_i and q_i respectively denote the lag order of *domestic variables* and the lag order of *foreign* and *global common variables*. p_i and q_i can be different. $\Phi_i(L, p_i)$, $\Lambda_i(L, q_i)$ and $Y_i(L, q_i)$, together with a_{i0} and a_{i1}, are the coefficients to be estimated in the first stage. Last, u_{it} is a $k_i \times 1$ vector of idiosyncratic country-specific shocks, and is assumed to be serially uncorrelated with a zero mean and a non-singular covariance matrix

$$\sum_{ii} = (\sigma_{ii,\,ls}),$$ where $\sigma_{ii,\,ls} = cov(u_{ilt},\,u_{ist})$ with l and s denoting the lth and

sth variables, respectively. More compactly, $u_{it} \sim i.i.d.\left(0, \sum_{ii}\right)$.

As noted by Dees, Mauro, Pesaran, and Smith (2007), in the first stage's country-specific VARX* models, x_{it} (*domestic variables*) is treated as *endogenous*, whereas x_{it}^* (*foreign variables*) is assumed to be *weakly exogenous*, which means that x_{it}^* is long-run forcing for x_{it} but there is no long-run feedback from x_{it} to x_{it}^*. Lagged short-run feedback between the two sets of variables is, however, allowed. This weak exogeneity is in line with the assumption that most countries in the global system are perceived as small open economies, in the sense that they are operating under the influence of a global economic environment, which in turn is not subject to a particular country's influence. d_t (*Observable global common variables*) is also assumed to be *weakly exogenous* and treated in a similar manner to x_{it}^* (*foreign variables*).

Once $\Phi_i(L,\ p_i)$, $\Lambda_i(L,\ q_i)$, $Y_i(L,\ q_i)$, a_{i0} and a_{i1} are estimated for all country-specific VARX* models, the second stage can proceed. Let $x_t = (x'_{1t},\ x'_{2t},\ ...,\ x'_{Nt})'$, which is a $k\times 1$ vector that collects all of the domestic variables across N countries, with $k = \sum_{i=1}^{N} k_i$ denoting the total number of variables. Given that $x_{it}^* = \sum_{j=1}^{N} w_{ij} x_{jt}$, apparently x_t contains all of the variables that are used to construct each country-specific VARX* model.

In the second stage, all of the elements in x_t are treated as *endogenously* determined from the standpoint of the global VAR system.

The second stage involves re-arranging Equation (5.12) as follows:

$$B_i(L,\ p_i,\ q_i) x_t = a_{i0} + a_{i1}t + Y_i(L,\ q_i) d_t + u_{it} \tag{5.14}$$

where $B_i(L,\ p_i,\ q_i) = \left[\Phi_i(L,\ p_i) E'_i,\ -\Lambda_i(L,\ q_i) W'_i\right]$. E_i is a $k\times k_i$ selection matrix that selects vector x_{it}, namely, $x_{it} = E'_i x_t$. W_i is merely a $k\times k_i^*$ matrix that collects the weights w_{ij} used in calculating the *foreign variables*, such that $x_{it}^* = W'_i x_t$.

Let $p = max\{max\ p_i,\ max\ q_i\}$, $\forall i = 1,...,\ N$, and construct $B_i(L,\ p)$ from $B_i(L,\ p_i,\ q_i)$ by augmenting $p - p_i$ or $p - q_i$ additional terms in powers of L by zeros; similarly, construct $Y_i(L,\ p)$. Then Equation (5.14) becomes

$$B_i(L,\ p) x_t = a_{i0} + a_{i1}t + Y_i(L,\ p) d_t + u_{it} \tag{5.15}$$

The next step is to stack Equation (5.15) for all $i = 1,...,\ N$, such that

$$G(L,\ p) x_t = a_0 + a_1 t + Y(L,\ p) d_t + u_t \tag{5.16}$$

where $u_t = (u'_{1t},\ ...,\ u'_{Nt})'$, $a_0 = (a'_{10},\ ...,\ a'_{N0})'$, $a_1 = (a'_{11},\ ...,\ a'_{N1})'$,

$$Y(L,\ p) = \begin{pmatrix} Y_1(L,\ p) \\ \vdots \\ Y_N(L,\ p) \end{pmatrix} \text{and } G(L,\ p) = \begin{pmatrix} B_1(L,\ p) \\ \vdots \\ B_N(L,\ p) \end{pmatrix}.$$

Eqution (5.16) is the GVAR model that explains the causal relationships among all $k = \sum_{i=1}^{N} k_i$ variables in the global system.

To obtain the reduced form of the GVAR model, Equation (5.16) can be further transformed into

$$G(L, p)x_t = G_0 x_t - \sum_{j=1}^{p} G_j x_{t-j} = a_0 + a_1 t + \sum_{j=0}^{p} Y_j d_{t-j} + u_t \qquad (5.17)$$

Moving $\sum_{j=1}^{p} G_j x_{t-j}$ to the right-hand side and then pre-multiplying both sides of the above equation by G_0^{-1}, which is a non-singular matrix, gives

$$x_t = G_0^{-1} a_0 + G_0^{-1} a_1 t + \sum_{j=1}^{p} G_0^{-1} G_j x_{t-j} + \sum_{j=0}^{p} G_0^{-1} Y_j d_{t-j} + G_0^{-1} u_t$$

$$= b_0 + b_1 t + \sum_{j=1}^{p} F_j x_{t-j} + \sum_{j=0}^{p} \Gamma_j d_{t-j} + \varepsilon_t \qquad (5.18)$$

where $b_0 = G_0^{-1} a_0$, $b_1 = G_0^{-1} a_1$, $F_j = G_0^{-1} G_j$, $\Gamma_j = G_0^{-1} Y_j$ for $j = 1, 2, \ldots, p$ and $\varepsilon_t = G_0^{-1} u_t$.

For impulse response analysis, Pesaran, Schuermann, and Weiner (2004) proposed using the generalised impulse response (GIR) functions, instead of the more common orthogonalised impulse response (OIR) functions. Consider the reduced form GVAR model in Equation (5.18), and for simplicity, let the lag orders be 1:

$$x_t = b_0 + b_1 t + Fx_{t-1} + \Gamma_0 d_t + \Gamma_1 d_{t-1} + \varepsilon_t \qquad (5.19)$$

For predetermined values of d_t ($t = T + 1, T + 2 \ldots$), it can be solved as follows:

$$x_{T+n} = F^n x_T + \sum_{\tau=0}^{n-1} F^{\tau} \left[b_0 + b_1 (T + n - \tau) \right]$$

$$+ \sum_{\tau=0}^{n-1} F^{\tau} \left[\Gamma_0 d_{T+n-\tau} + \Gamma_1 d_{T+n-\tau-1} \right] \qquad (5.20)$$

$$+ \sum_{\tau=0}^{n-1} F^{\tau} \varepsilon_{T+n-\tau}$$

The point forecasts of x_{T+n}, conditional on the initial state of the system and the exogenous global variables, are given by

$$
\begin{aligned}
x_{T+n}^{f} &= E\left(x_{T+n} | x_T, \bigcup_{\tau=1}^{n} d_{T+\tau} \right) \\
&= F^n x_T + \sum_{\tau=0}^{n-1} F^\tau \left[b_0 + b_1 (T+n-\tau) \right] \\
&\quad + \sum_{\tau=0}^{n-1} F^\tau \left[\Gamma_0 d_{T+n-\tau} + \Gamma_1 d_{T+n-\tau-1} \right]
\end{aligned}
\tag{5.21}
$$

Under the assumption that u_t is normally distributed,

$$
x_{T+n} | x_T, \bigcup_{\tau=1}^{n} d_{T+\tau} \sim N\left(x_{T+n}^{f}, \Omega_n \right)
\tag{5.22}
$$

where $\Omega_n = \sum_{\tau=0}^{n-1} F^\tau G_0^{-1} \Sigma G_0^{-1} F'^{\tau}$ and Σ is the $k \times k$ variance-covariance matrix of shocks u_t. Σ_{ij}, which measures the dependence of shocks in country i on shocks in country j, is defined as $\Sigma_{ij} = cov(u_{it}, u_{jt})$. A typical element of Σ_{ij} is denoted by $\sigma_{ij, ls} = cov(u_{ilt}, u_{jst})$, which is the covariance of the lth variable in country i with the sth variable in country j.

According to Pesaran, Schuermann, and Weiner (2004), the GIR function that denotes the jth shock in u_t (corresponding to the lth variable in the ith country) is given by

$$
GI_{x:u_{il}}\left(n, \sqrt{\sigma_{ii, ll}}, I_{t-1} \right) = E\left(x_{t+n} | u_{ilt} = \sqrt{\sigma_{ii, ll}}, I_{t-1} \right) - E\left(x_{t+n} | I_{t-1} \right)
\tag{5.23}
$$

where $I_t = (x_t, x_{t-1}, \ldots)$ is the information set at time $t-1$, and d_t is assumed to be given exogenously. On the assumption that u_t has a multivariate normal distribution, and using Equation (5.20), it can be derived that

$$
\psi_j^g (n) = \frac{1}{\sqrt{\sigma_{ii, ll}}} F^n G_0^{-1} \Sigma \, \zeta_j
\tag{5.24}
$$

where ζ_j is a $k \times 1$ selection vector with unity as its jth element (corresponding to a particular shock in a particular country), and zeros otherwise. Equation (5.24) measures the effect of one standard error shock to the jth equation (corresponding to the lth variable in the ith country) at time t on the expected values of $\mathbf{x}$ at time $t + n$.

5.2.3 Bayesian approaches

As discussed above, when the number of coefficients in a VAR model is large relative to the number of observations, asymptotic theory will typically be an unreliable guide for the finite sample estimation properties (George, Sun, & Ni, 2008). Bayesian approaches address this issue by imposing priors on the VAR model to reduce the number of coefficients to be estimated whilst improving the significant uncertainty about the future paths projected by the model.

In a primer of Bayesian statistics, van de Schoot et al. (2021) described the typical Bayesian workflow, which consists of three main steps: (1) capturing available knowledge about a given parameter in a statistical model via the *prior distribution*, expressed as a probability density function (PDF); (2) determining the likelihood function using parameter information available in the observed data, expressed as the conditional probability of the data given the model parameters; and (3) combining both the prior distribution and the likelihood function using Bayes' theorem in the form of the *posterior distribution*, which is the probability of the model parameters conditional on the observed data. The posterior distribution reflects one's updated knowledge, balancing prior knowledge with observed data, and is used to conduct inferences.

For the general VAR model in Equation (5.1), Bayesian VAR (BVAR) estimation centres around forming prior distributions for the matrices of lag coefficients A_l ($l = 1, 2, ..., p$) and the covariance matrix Σ. A popular prior is the Minnesota prior introduced by Litterman (1979). In the tourism demand literature, this prior is used by Wong, Song, and Chon (2006), Gunter and Önder (2015), Ampountolas (2019) and others.

The Minnesota prior assumes that each variable follows an independent random walk process, possibly with drift:

$$Y_t = C_0 + Y_{t-1} + U_t \tag{5.25}$$

which represents the macroeconomic behaviour of an economic variable. As described by Giannone, Lenza, and Primiceri (2015) and Kuschnig and Vashold (2021a), the prior is imposed by setting the following moments for the prior distribution of the coefficients:

$$\mathrm{E}\left[(A_s)_{ij} \mid \Sigma\right] = \begin{cases} 1, i = j \text{ and } s = 1 \\ 0, \text{ otherwise} \end{cases} \tag{5.26}$$

$$cov\left[(A_s)_{ij}, (A_r)_{gh} \mid \Sigma\right] = \begin{cases} \lambda^2 \dfrac{1}{s^\alpha} \dfrac{\Sigma_{ig}}{\psi_j / (d-k-1)}, h = j \text{ and } r = s \\ 0, \qquad\qquad\qquad\quad \text{otherwise} \end{cases} \tag{5.27}$$

where A_s and A_r are the coefficient matrices of the sth and rth lags, k is the number of endogenous variables given in Equation (5.1), d is the prior degrees of freedom and Ψ is a diagonal matrix of hyperparameters. The hyperparameter λ controls the tightness of the prior, i.e., it weighs the relative importance of the prior and data. For $\lambda \to 0$, the prior outweighs any information in the data, and the posterior approaches the prior. As $\lambda \to \infty$, the posterior distribution mirrors the sample. Governing the variance decay with increasing lag order, α controls the degree of shrinkage for more distant observations. Finally, ψ_j, the jth variable of Ψ, controls the prior's standard deviation on the lags of all of the variables other than the dependent variable.

Another popular prior is stochastic search variable selection (SSVS). As described by George, Sun, and Ni (2008), SSVS treats each possible set of restrictions as a distinct sub-model and then uses priors to describe the uncertainty across all of the sub-models. This can be done by assigning commonly used prior variances to the parameters that should be included in a model and prior variances close to zero to irrelevant parameters. As a result of this process, relevant parameters are estimated in the usual way, and posterior draws of irrelevant variables are close to zero and thus have no significant effect on forecasts or impulse responses. In modelling practice, a hierarchical prior can be added, where the relevance of a variable is assessed in each step of the sampling algorithm. Under such a setup, the posterior distribution will increase the prior weights on the restrictions that are best supported by the observed data. Although it is typically not feasible to exhaustively calculate all of the sub-model posterior probabilities, many of the higher posterior probability sub-models can be found through a stochastic search using Markov chain Monte Carlo algorithms.

In the context of GVAR modelling, Bayesian GVAR (BGVAR) is adopted by researchers in economics and tourism. Cuaresma, Feldkircher, and Huber (2016) implemented the Minnesota prior. It is assumed that the endogenous variables a priori follow random walk processes at the country-specific (i.e., cross-sectional) level, and the prior mean is set to one for the first own lag of the endogenous variables in the level, and zero for contemporaneous and lagged foreign variables and higher lag orders of the endogenous variables. The prior variance of the coefficients is set according to whether the variable is endogenous, weakly exogenous (i.e., foreign variable at the country-specific level) or deterministic. Cuaresma, Feldkircher, and Huber (2016) also implemented SSVS. Unlike the Minnesota prior, which applies a symmetric and equal degree of shrinkage across equations, SSVS allows for more flexibility in the specification of the prior variance-covariance matrix on the coefficients. As an alternative to the Minnesota prior and SSVS, Assaf et al. (2019) followed another strand of literature and adopted the Bayesian variant of the least absolute shrinkage and selection operator (LASSO) as priors for the BGVAR model. They found that the BGVAR model unequivocally outperforms other VAR models.

5.3 Application

To illustrate how VAR models can be applied to tourism research, we construct classic VAR, BVAR, GVAR and BGVAR models to forecast the tourism exports of Thailand, a major tourist destination. Methodologically, we treat Thailand as a single VAR system and use VAR and BVAR models in the forecasting exercise. In a global setting, we use GVAR and BGVAR models to account for the influence of the external economic environment on Thailand's tourism exports. We then evaluate the forecast accuracy of these models against three benchmark models: seasonal naïve (SNAIVE), seasonal autoregressive integrated moving average (SARIMA) and exponential smoothing (ETS) models, consistent with other chapters.

5.3.1 A global tourism demand system

Our data set corresponds to a global system consisting of 24 major economies around the world, as listed in Table 5.1. From the perspective of GVAR modelling, each country is an individual VAR system, and the 24 countries altogether constitute a GVAR system. The selection of countries is based on data availability and their use in Dees, Mauro, Pesaran, and Smith (2007).

Following Cao, Li, and Song (2017), we use real tourism exports ($rtex$), real GDP index (y) and exchange rate-adjusted consumer price index (CPI) (p) as endogenous variables. As indicated in Table 5.2, the raw data are collected from the following international macroeconomic databases: Balance of Payments Statistics and International Financial Statistics of the International Monetary Fund (IMF). In addition, for GVAR and BGVAR modelling, a weight matrix is constructed using bilateral trade flows between the 24 countries. The data source for these bilateral trade flows is the IMF's Direction of Trade Statistics database. The sample period is 2000Q1–2019Q4. All of the variables are log-transformed before the models are estimated, and the forecasts are then rid of the logarithms before being evaluated.

In the GVAR and BGVAR settings, for each country the variables are arranged as *domestic variables* (i.e., x_{it}) and *foreign variables* (i.e., x^*_{it}) in the following manner: $x_{it} = (rtex_{it},\ y_{it},\ p_{it})$ and $x^*_{it} = (rtex^*_{it},\ y^*_{it},\ p^*_{it})$, where

$$rtex^*_{it} = \sum_{j=1}^{N} w_{ij} rtex, \quad y^*_{it} = \sum_{j=1}^{N} w_{ij} y_{jt} \text{ and } p^*_{it} = \sum_{j=1}^{N} w_{ij} p_{jt}; \quad N \text{ is the number of}$$

TABLE 5.1 Sampled countries in the global tourism demand system

Australia	Austria	Brazil	Canada	China	France
Germany	India	Indonesia	Italy	Japan	Korea
Malaysia	Mexico	Netherlands	New Zealand	Philippines	Singapore
Spain	Sweden	Thailand	Turkey	UK	USA

TABLE 5.2 Description of endogenous variables

Variable	Definition	Source	Mean	Median	Maximum	Minimum	Std dev.	Observations
rtex	Tourism exports in constant price and constant US dollars (base year 2010), in millions of US dollars, seasonally adjusted	Balance of Payments Statistics, IMF	7,061.14	4,661.44	44,596.96	509.27	7,100.00	1,920
y	Real GDP index, base year 2010 = 100	International Financial Statistics, IMF	100.92	100.21	206.69	35.72	21.87	1,920
p	CPI (adjusted by exchange rate against US dollar), base year 2010 = 100	International Financial Statistics, IMF	90.06	92.64	129.39	30.67	19.21	1,920

Note: *rtex* is measured using nominal travel credits (in millions of US dollars) deflated by exchange rate-adjusted CPI. Missing values are imputed in R using the *imputeTS* package. Seasonal adjustment is carried out using the *seasonal* package.

countries in the global system; w_{ij} is the bilateral trade weight that country j accounts for among all of country i's trade partners; and $w_{ij} = 0$ where $i = j$. For the classic VAR and BVAR, only x_{it} for Thailand is used and treated as endogenous variables.

Descriptively, Figure 5.1 shows the developments of real tourism exports in each of the sampled countries. The tourism market of many countries saw a marked growth after 2010, a sign of healthy recovery from the global financial crisis of 2008. For Thailand, its real tourism exports (our variable of interest) grew steadily throughout the sample period. It is worth noting that the evolution of real tourism exports is susceptible to not only volatility in tourism demand per se but also volatility in prices and exchange rates. As a result, the fluctuations in real tourism exports, as depicted in Figure 5.1, are occasionally dramatic.

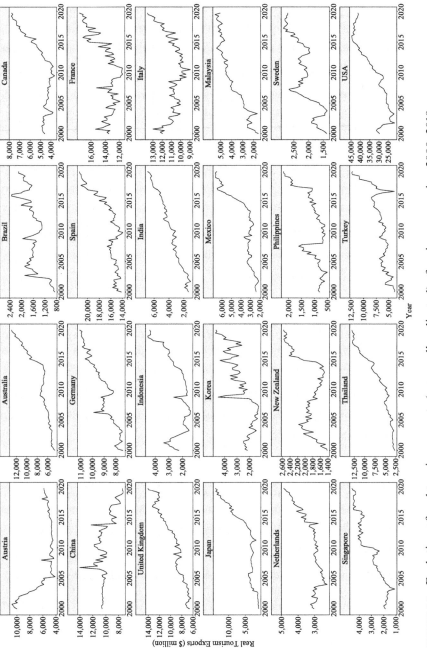

FIGURE 5.1 Evolution of real tourism exports (seasonally adjusted) of major economies, 2000–2019

5.3.2 Forecast evaluation

In executing the forecasts, we divide the sample data into a training set (2000Q1–2016Q4) and a test set (2017Q1–2019Q4). A rolling window scheme (also known as the "evaluation on a rolling forecasting origin", see Hyndman & Athanasopoulos, 2018) is adopted. We evaluate seven competing models (SNAIVE, SARIMA, ETS, VAR, GVAR, BVAR and BGVAR models) in terms of ex post out-of-sample predictive means of Thailand's real tourism exports over forecasting horizons of 1, 2, 3, 4 and 8 quarters. The evaluation is based on the forecasts from 2017Q1 to 2019Q4.

The modelling and forecasting exercises are implemented in R, using prewritten packages. Specifically, classic VAR models are constructed using the *vars* package (https://cran.r-project.org/package=vars), developed by Pfaff (2008). GVAR modelling is implemented using the *GVARX* package (https://cran.r-project.org/package=GVARX), developed by Ho (2020). It should be noted that to carry out GVAR forecasting, one may also use the open-source toolbox (https://sites.google.com/site/gvarmodelling/) written by Smith and Galesi (2014). The toolbox is accessible and easy to use, with a comprehensive range of built-in analytics. For Bayesian analysis, BVAR modelling is implemented using the *BVAR* package (https://cran.r-project.org/package=BVAR), developed by Kuschnig and Vashold (2021b). BGVAR modelling is implemented using the *BGVAR* package (https://cran.r-project.org/package=BGVAR), developed by Böck, Feldkircher, and Huber (2020). Both the *BVAR* and *BGVAR* packages allow the Minnesota prior to be imposed, but the *BGVAR* package also provides the option of an SSVS prior. For illustration purposes, we use the Minnesota prior. The benchmark models are implemented using the *forecast* package (https://cran.r-project.org/web/packages/forecast/index.html), developed by Hyndman et al. (2022) and Hyndman and Khandakar (2008).

The results of the forecast evaluation are reported in Table 5.3. Overall, the univariate time series benchmark models perform fairly well, especially over short-term horizons. According to mean absolute percentage error (MAPE) and mean absolute scaled error (MASE), the SNAIVE model performs the best in two-step-ahead and three-step-ahead forecasts. Root mean square error (RMSE) suggests that the SNAIVE model is better than the other models in one-step-ahead and two-step-ahead forecasts. The performance of SARIMA and ETS models is similar to that of the SNAIVE model, although they both have slightly higher forecast errors.

Among the VAR models, the BVAR and BGVAR models consistently outperform their frequentist counterparts. Their forecast accuracy is close to that of the time series benchmark models. According to MAPE and MASE, the BVAR model is better than all of its rival models in one-step-ahead and eight-step-ahead forecasts, and BGVAR is the best in four-step-ahead forecasts. This finding is corroborated by RMSE, although this measure suggests that BVAR performs the best in eight-step-ahead

TABLE 5.3 Forecasting performance evaluation

	Forecasting horizon				
	1	2	3	4	5
MAPE (%)					
SNAIVE	2.189	3.360	4.272	5.087	10.923
SARIMA	2.388	3.634	4.730	6.472	14.287
ETS	2.166	3.892	5.335	6.775	10.110
VAR	3.003	5.352	6.875	8.637	15.313
GVAR	2.946	5.700	7.587	9.813	22.407
BVAR	2.015	3.761	5.092	6.562	9.573
BGVAR	2.492	3.655	4.334	4.146	11.285
MASE					
SNAIVE	0.504	0.781	0.994	1.186	2.523
SARIMA	0.550	0.844	1.098	1.504	3.305
ETS	0.501	0.903	1.244	1.577	2.367
VAR	0.700	1.248	1.604	2.007	3.581
GVAR	0.686	1.331	1.775	2.282	5.183
BVAR	0.465	0.872	1.186	1.524	2.240
BGVAR	0.578	0.851	1.011	0.972	2.546
RMSE					
SNAIVE	329	530	697	837	1,617
SARIMA	345	587	824	1,045	2,039
ETS	357	591	790	1,003	1,543
VAR	425	737	988	1,265	2,148
GVAR	432	789	1,057	1,357	3,114
BVAR	335	563	766	991	1,497
BGVAR	391	532	650	608	2,310

Note: RMSE is scale dependent, whereas MAPE and MASE are not. The forecasts are for Thailand's real tourism exports, which are in the region of 10,000 million US dollars. Hence, the values of RMSE are quite large compared with the other two accuracy measures.

forecasts only and that BGVAR outperforms the other models in both three-step-ahead and four-step-ahead forecasts. In comparison, the forecasting performance of the classic VAR and GVAR is less accurate, as they generate much higher forecast errors.

The pattern shown in Table 5.3 corroborates the findings of previous studies such as Wong, Song, and Chon (2006), Song, Smeral, Li, and Chen (2008) and Gunter and Zekan (2021). These studies also observe that frequentist VAR models are less accurate than univariate time series models, although VAR models can considerably improve their performance by imposing Bayesian priors. Among our seven competing models, the GVAR model is typically the least accurate. This is in line with Gunter and Zekan

(2021). They also observe that the GVAR model ranks behind VAR, SNA-IVE and autoregressive integrated moving average (ARIMA) models, especially when the forecasting horizon stretches beyond three quarters.

It is important to note that the evaluation in Table 5.3 is based on forecasts for Thailand only, so the results could be different for forecasts made for other countries. As Wong, Song, and Chon (2006) noted, there is no indication that univariate time series models always outperform econometric models such as the VAR model in all forecasting situations. Econometric models tend to be more accurate in forecasting directional changes in tourism demand than simple time series models. From the perspective of economic intuition, Gunter and Zekan (2021) commented that time series models such as the ARIMA model are hardly economically interpretable and cannot answer questions about what drives tourism demand in a certain direction. In contrast, VAR models are well suited to adding economic interpretability to the modelling process.

5.4 Conclusion and future directions

This chapter reviews a popular class of macroeconometric models called VAR models, which are designed to capture the interrelations between economic variables. In a VAR model, each variable is treated as endogenous and is explained by its own lagged values as well as the remaining variables in the model. In recent years, VAR models have undergone rapid development and their capability has expanded. Notably, the GVAR approach is well suited to modelling a large high-dimensional system with multiple cross sections. Moreover, the incorporation of Bayesian techniques substantially improves the forecasting performance of VAR models.

This chapter covers not only frequentist classic VAR and GVAR models but also their Bayesian counterparts (i.e., BVAR and BGVAR). As an illustration, this chapter uses both frequentist and Bayesian VAR models to forecast tourism demand for Thailand, and then evaluates their forecasting performance against three commonly used univariate time series models.

Unsurprisingly, we find that the classic VAR and GVAR models are not as accurate as the benchmarks, which is consistent with the tourism demand literature. However, by imposing Bayesian priors, BVAR and BGVAR models greatly improve the forecast accuracy of VAR and GVAR models. The performance of BVAR and BGVAR models is closely comparable to the benchmark models in almost all forecasting horizons. In particular, the BVAR model outperforms all of the competing models in one-step-ahead and eight-step-ahead forecasts, whilst the BGVAR model outperforms its rivals in four-step-ahead forecasts. Although VAR models may not always outperform time series models, in tourism demand research they still deserve attention because they offer an analytical framework that can embed economics theories in the modelling process. With respect to the choice between frequentist and Bayesian methods, there is no one-size-fits-all answer. As Kilian and Lütkepohl (2017) commented, researchers should rely on their own preferences and the convenience of implementation.

Future research in tourism demand could take advantage of the vast range of advanced VAR models available. Closely related to the GVAR model, spatial VAR methods (e.g., Ramajo, Márquez, & Hewings, 2017) are also able to model multi-regional/multi-country interrelations, with a weight matrix based on geographical criteria. Another development in VAR models is the panel VAR (PVAR) model, which has garnered attention in recent years. It allows for individual heterogeneity by introducing fixed effects in VAR models (Xu & Reed, 2019). Focusing on temporal patterns, regime-switching VAR (RS-VAR) models (e.g., Huarng, Yu, & Solé Parellada, 2011; Yamaka, Pastpipatkul, & Sriboonchitta, 2015) are well suited to capturing the cyclical asymmetry of the different phases of business cycles. They have already been further extended to the GVAR setting as RS-GVAR models (e.g., Binder & Gross, 2013). Other advanced developments include mixed-frequency VAR models (e.g., Ghysels, 2016) and threshold VAR models (e.g., Afonso, Baxa, & Slavík, 2018). All of these methods enrich the capability of VAR models and render VAR modelling a valuable tool in tourism demand research.

Self-study questions

1   For a classic VAR model, what are the issues if an increasing number of lagged terms are included in the model?
2   In a GVAR model, foreign variables are treated as weakly exogenous to country-specific VARX* systems. How do we test for the weak exogeneity of foreign variables?
3   What are the advantages of Bayesian approaches to VAR modelling?

References

Afonso, A., Baxa, J., & Slavík, M. (2018). Fiscal developments and financial stress: A threshold VAR analysis. *Empirical Economics, 54*(2), 395–423. doi:10.1007/s00181-016-1210-5

Ampountolas, A. (2019). Forecasting hotel demand uncertainty using time series Bayesian VAR models. *Tourism Economics, 25*(5), 734–756. doi:10.1177/1354816618801741

Assaf, A. G., Li, G., Song, H., & Tsionas, M. G. (2019). Modeling and forecasting regional tourism demand using the Bayesian global vector autoregressive (BGVAR) model. *Journal of Travel Research, 58*(3), 383–397. doi:10.1177/0047287518759226

Binder, M., & Gross, M. (2013). *Regime-switching global vector autoregressive models.* European Central Bank Working Paper Series No. 1569. Retrieved 3

February 2022 from https://www.ecb.europa.eu/pub/pdf/scpwps/ecbwp1569. pdf.

Böck, M., Feldkircher, M., & Huber, F. (2020). *BGVAR: Bayesian Global Vector Autoregressions*. R package version 2.4.3. https://CRAN.R-project.org/package=BGVAR.

Bussiere, M., Chudik, A., & Sestieri, G. (2009). Modelling global trade flows: Results from a GVAR model. *SSRN Electronic Journal*. doi:10.2139/ssrn.1456883

Cao, Z., Li, G., & Song, H. (2017). Modelling the interdependence of tourism demand: The global vector autoregressive approach. *Annals of Tourism Research, 67*, 1–13. doi:10.1016/j.annals.2017.07.019

Chudik, A., & Pesaran, M. H. (2016). Theory and practice of GVAR modelling. *Journal of Economic Surveys, 30*(1), 165–197. doi:10.1111/joes.12095

Cuaresma, J. C., Feldkircher, M., & Huber, F. (2016). Forecasting with global vector autoregressive models: A Bayesian approach. *Journal of Applied Econometrics, 31*(7), 1371–1391. doi:10.1002/jae.2504

De Mello, M. M., & Nell, K. S. (2005). The forecasting ability of a cointegrated VAR system of the UK tourism demand for France, Spain and Portugal. *Empirical Economics, 30*(2), 277–308. doi:10.1007/s00181-005-0241-0

Dees, S., Mauro, F. D., Pesaran, M. H., & Smith, L. V. (2007). Exploring the international linkages of the euro area: a global VAR analysis. *Journal of Applied Econometrics, 22*(1), 1–38. doi:10.1002/jae.932

Garratt, A., Lee, K., Pesaran, M. H., & Shin, Y. (2012). *Global and national macroeconometric modelling: A long-run structural approach*. Oxford University Press.

George, E. I., Sun, D., & Ni, S. (2008). Bayesian stochastic search for VAR model restrictions. *Journal of Econometrics, 142*(1), 553–580. doi:10.1016/j.jeconom.2007.08.017

Ghysels, E. (2016). Macroeconomics and the reality of mixed frequency data. *Journal of Econometrics, 193*(2), 294–314. doi:10.1016/j.jeconom.2016.04.008

Giannone, D., Lenza, M., & Primiceri, G. E. (2015). Prior selection for vector autoregressions. *Review of Economics and Statistics, 97*(2), 436–451. doi:10.1162/rest_a_00483

Gunter, U., & Önder, I. (2015). Forecasting international city tourism demand for Paris: Accuracy of uni- and multivariate models employing monthly data. *Tourism Management, 46*, 123–135. doi:10.1016/j.tourman.2014.06.017

Gunter, U., & Zekan, B. (2021). Forecasting air passenger numbers with a GVAR model. *Annals of Tourism Research, 89*, 103252. doi:10.1016/j.annals.2021.103252

Ho, T. (2020). *GVARX: Perform global vector autoregression estimation and inference*. R package version 1.3. https://CRAN.R-project.org/package=GVARX

Huarng, K. H., Yu, T. H. K., & Solé Parellada, F. (2011). An innovative regime switching model to forecast Taiwan tourism demand. *The Service Industries Journal, 31*(10), 1603–1612. doi:10.1080/02642069.2010.485637

Hyndman, R., Athanasopoulos, G., Bergmeir, C., Caceres, G., Chhay, L., O'Hara-Wild, M., Petropoulos, F., Razbash, S., Wang, E., & Yasmeen, F. (2022). *Forecast: Forecasting Functions for Time Series and Linear Models*. R package version 8.16. https://pkg.robjhyndman.com/forecast/.

Hyndman, R. J., & Athanasopoulos, G. (2018). *Forecasting: Principles and practice*. OTexts.

Hyndman, R. J., & Khandakar, Y. (2008). Automatic time series forecasting: The forecast package for R. *Journal of Statistical Software, 27*, 1–22. doi:10.18637/jss.v027.i03

Juselius, K. (2006). *The cointegrated VAR model: methodology and applications.* Oxford University Press.

Kilian, L., & Lütkepohl, H. (2017). *Structural vector autoregressive analysis.* Cambridge University Press. doi:10.1017/9781108164818

Kuschnig, N., & Vashold, L. (2021a). BVAR: Bayesian vector autoregressions with hierarchical prior selection in R. *Journal of Statistical Software, 100*, 1–27. doi:10.18637/jss.v100.i14

Kuschnig, N., & Vashold, L. (2021b). *BVAR: Hierarchical Prior Selection in R.* R package version 1.0.2. https://CRAN.R-project.org/package=BVAR.

Lim, C., & McAleer, M. (2001). Cointegration analysis of quarterly tourism demand by Hong Kong and Singapore for Australia. *Applied Economics, 33*(12), 1599–1619. doi:10.1080/00036840010014012

Litterman, R. B. (1979). *Techniques of forecasting using vector autoregressions (Working Papers 115).* Federal Reserve Bank of Minneapolis. doi:10.21034/wp.115

Pesaran, M. H., Schuermann, T., & Weiner, S. M. (2004). Modeling regional interdependencies using a global error-correcting macroeconometric model. *Journal of Business & Economic Statistics, 22*(2), 129–162. doi:10.1198/073500104000000019

Pesaran, M. H., Shin, Y., & Smith, R. J. (2000). Structural analysis of vector error correction models with exogenous I (1) variables. *Journal of Econometrics, 97*(2), 293–343. doi:10.1016/s0304-4076(99)00073-1

Pfaff, B. (2008). VAR, SVAR and SVEC models: Implementation within R package vars. *Journal of Statistical Software, 27*, 1–32. doi:10.1016/s0304-4076(99)00073-1

Ramajo, J., Márquez, M. A., & Hewings, G. J. (2017). Spatiotemporal analysis of regional systems: A multiregional spatial vector autoregressive model for Spain. *International Regional Science Review, 40*(1), 75–96. doi:10.1177/0160017615571586

Sims, C. A. (1980). Macroeconomics and reality. *Econometrica: Journal of the Econometric Society, 48*(*1*), 1–48. doi:10.2307/1912017

Smith, L. V., & Galesi, A. (2014). *GVAR Toolbox 2.0.* https://sites.google.com/site/gvarmodelling/gvar-toolbox.

Song, H., Romilly, P., & Liu, X. (2000). An empirical study of outbound tourism demand in the UK. *Applied Economics, 32*(5), 611–624. doi:10.1080/000368400322516

Song, H., Smeral, E., Li, G., & Chen, J. L. (2008). *Tourism forecasting: Accuracy of alternative econometric models revisited* (No. 326). WIFO Working Papers.

Song, H., & Witt, S. F. (2006). Forecasting international tourist flows to Macau. *Tourism Management, 27*(2), 214–224. doi:10.1016/j.tourman.2004.09.004

Song, H., Witt, S. F., & Li, G. (2009). *The advanced econometrics of tourism demand.* Routledge. doi:10.4324/9780203891469

Stock, J. H., & Watson, M. W. (2001). Vector autoregressions. *Journal of Economic Perspectives, 15*(4), 101–115. doi:10.1257/jep.15.4.101

van de Schoot, R., Depaoli, S., King, R., Kramer, B., Märtens, K., Tadesse, M. G., Vannucci, M., Gelman, A., Veen, D., Willemsen, J., & Yau, C. (2021). Bayesian statistics and modelling. *Nature Reviews Methods Primers, 1*(1), 1–26. doi:10.1038/s43586-020-00001-2

Wong, K. K., Song, H., & Chon, K. S. (2006). Bayesian models for tourism demand forecasting. *Tourism Management, 27*(5), 773–780. doi:10.1016/j.tourman.2005.05.017

Xu, X., & Reed, M. (2019). Perceived pollution and inbound tourism for Shanghai: A panel VAR approach. *Current Issues in Tourism, 22*(5), 601–614. doi:10.4324/9781003133568-8

Yamaka, W., Pastpipatkul, P., & Sriboonchitta, S. (2015, October). Business cycle of international tourism demand in Thailand: A Markov-switching Bayesian vector error correction model. In *International Symposium on Integrated Uncertainty in Knowledge Modelling and Decision Making* (pp. 415–427). Springer, Cham. doi:10.1007/978-3-319-25135-6_38

APPENDIX

R CODE

```
rm(list=ls())
graphics.off()

library(lubridate)    # for use in dealing with date-time
data
```

Chunk 1. Read data and create data frames

```
#  "GVAR": country-specific endogenous variables
#          rtex: real tourism exports ($ million)
#          y: real GDP index (2010 = 100)
#          pi: CPI (adjusted by exchange rate against USD)
(2010 = 100)
#  "Weight": weight matrix
#           elements in each row are trade shares of part-
ner countries
#           each row sums to unity (i.e., 1)

load("Chapter5_Data.RData")
lnGVAR <- GVAR
lnGVAR[,c(3:5)] <- log(lnGVAR[,c(3:5)])   # take logarithm
```

Chunk 2. Preparation

```
#  Create a template data frame to record each model's
forecasts
df_sheets <- data.frame(matrix(nrow = 20, ncol = 6))
colnames(df_sheets ) <- c("Time", "1-step ahead",
                          "2-step ahead", "3-step ahead",
                          "4-step ahead", "8-step ahead")
df_sheets[,1] <- as.yearqtr("2015-01-01") + 0:19/4
```

```
#  Extract Thailand data for benchmarks, VAR and BVAR
models
 df _ thai <- lnGVAR[lnGVAR$country == "TH",]
 df _ thai <- ts(df _ thai[,c(3:5)], start = c(2000,1), end =
c(2019, 4), freq = 4)

 #  Forecast horizons
 horizon <- c(1, 2, 3, 4, 8)
```

Chunk 3. Benchmark models: (1) No-change naive; (2) SARIMA;
(3) ETS

```
 library(forecast)
```

Chunk 3.1 No-change naive

```
 tmp _ f _ naive <- df _ sheets   # temporary sheet

 for (i in 1:20) {
   # i loop over rolling windows
   train <- window(df _ thai[,"rtex"],
                   start = 2000.00 + (i-1)/4, end = 2014.75
+ (i-1)/4)

     for (j in 1:length(horizon)) {
       # j loop over five horizons
       h <- horizon[j]   # h-step ahead
       if (i+h-1 <= 20) {
         fcst _ naive <- naive(train, h = h)
         tmp _ f _ naive[i+h-1,j+1] <- fcst _ naive[["mean"]][[h]]
       } else {
         next
       }
     }
 }

 tmp _ f _ naive[,2:6] <- exp(tmp _ f _ naive[,2:6])   # un-log
forecasts
 fcst _ naive <- tmp _ f _ naive  # forecasts
 rm(tmp _ f _ naive, train)

 print(fcst _ naive)  # print forecasts
```

Chunk 3.2 SARIMA

```
 tmp _ f _ sarima <- df _ sheets  # temporary sheet

 fit _ sarima <- auto.arima(window(df _ thai[,"rtex"], end =
c(2014,4), freq = 4),
                           ic = "aic",
```

```
                       seasonal = TRUE,
                       stepwise = FALSE,
                       approximation = FALSE)
  order <- arimaorder(fit_sarima)

  for (i in 1:20) {
    # i loop over rolling windows
    train <- window(df_thai[,"rtex"],
                   start = 2000.00 + (i-1)/4, end = 2014.75
+ (i-1)/4)
    model_sarima <- arima(train, order = order[1:3], seasonal
= order[4:6])

    for (j in 1:length(horizon)) {
      # j loop over five horizons
      h <- horizon[j]   # h-step ahead
      if (i+h-1 <= 20) {
        fcst_sarima <- forecast(model_sarima, h = h)
        tmp_f_sarima[i+h-1,j+1] <- fcst_sarima[["mean"]][[h]]
      } else {
        next
      }
    }
  }

  tmp_f_sarima[,2:6] <- exp(tmp_f_sarima[,2:6])   # un-log
forecasts
  fcst_sarima <- tmp_f_sarima   # forecasts
  rm(tmp_f_sarima, train)

  print(fcst_sarima)   # print forecasts
```

Chunk 3.3 ETS

```
  tmp_f_ets <- df_sheets   # temporary sheet

  for (i in 1:20) {
    # i loop over rolling windows
    train <- window(df_thai[,"rtex"],
                   start = 2000.00 + (i-1)/4, end = 2014.75
+ (i-1)/4)
    model_ets <- ets(train,
                     model = "ZZZ",
                     ic = "aic",
                     use.initial.values = TRUE)
```

```
  for (j in 1:length(horizon)) {
    # j loop over five horizons
    h <- horizon[j]   # h-step ahead
    if (i+h-1 <= 20) {
      fcst _ ets <- forecast(model _ ets, h = h, PI = FALSE)
      tmp _ f _ ets[i+h-1,j+1] <- fcst _ ets[["mean"]][[h]]
    } else {
      next
    }
  }
}
```

```
  tmp _ f _ ets[,2:6]   <-   exp(tmp _ f _ ets[,2:6])      # un-log
forecasts
  fcst _ ets <- tmp _ f _ ets  # forecasts
  rm(tmp _ f _ ets, train)
```

```
  print(fcst _ ets)  # print forecasts
```

Chunk 4. VAR modelling: (1) classic VAR; (2) BVAR; (3) GVAR; (4) BGVAR

Chunk 4.1 Classic vector autoregression (VAR)

```
library(vars)
```

```
  tmp _ f _ var <- df _ sheets  # temporary sheet
```

```
  p <- VARselect(window(df _ thai[,c(1:3)], end = c(2014,4), freq
= 4),
                    lag.max = 4,
                    type = "both",
                    season = 4)[["selection"]][["SC(n)"]]  # select
order of lags
```

```
  for (i in 1:20) {
    # i loop over rolling windows
    train <- window(df _ thai[,c(1:3)],
                    start = 2000.00 + (i-1)/4, end = 2014.75
+ (i-1)/4)
    model _ var <- VAR(train,
                    p = p,
                    type = c("both"),
                    season = 4)
```

```
    for (j in 1:length(horizon)) {
      # j loop over five horizons
```

```
      h <- horizon[j]    # h-step ahead
      if (i+h-1 <= 20) {
         fcst _ var <- predict(model _ var, n.ahead = h, ci =
0.95)
         tmp _ f _ var[i+h-1,j+1] <- fcst _ var[["fcst"]][["rtex"]]
[h,1]
      } else {
        next
      }
    }
  }

  tmp _ f _ var[,2:6]   <-  exp(tmp _ f _ var[,2:6])      # un-log
forecasts
  fcst _ var <- tmp _ f _ var  # forecasts
  rm(tmp _ f _ var, train)

  print(fcst _ var)  # print forecasts
```

Chunk 4.2 Bayesian vector autoregression (BVAR)

```
library(BVAR)

tmp _ f _ bvar <- df _ sheets  # temporary sheet
set.seed(1234)

#  Setting priors
minnesota <- bv _ mn(lambda = bv _ lambda(mode = 0.5),
                 alpha = bv _ alpha(mode = 1))
priors <- bv _ priors(hyper = "auto", mn = minnesota)

#  Estimation and forecast
for (i in 1:20) {
  # i loop over rolling windows
  train <- window(df _ thai,
              start = 2000.00 + (i-1)/4, end = 2014.75
+ (i-1)/4)
    model _ bvar <- bvar(train,
                    lags = 4,
                    n _ draw = 10000L,
                    n _ burn = 5000L,
                    n _ thin = 2L,
                    priors = priors,
                    verbose = FALSE)

    for (j in 1:length(horizon)) {
```

```
        # j loop over five horizons
        h <- horizon[j]    # h-step ahead
        if (i+h-1 <= 20) {
          fcst _ bvar <- predict(model _ bvar, horizon = h)
          fcst _ result <- as.matrix(fcst _ bvar[["quants"]][,,1])
          tmp _ f _ bvar[i+h-1,j+1] <- fcst _ result[2,h]
        } else {
          next
        }
      }
    }


  tmp _ f _ bvar[,2:6]  <-  exp(tmp _ f _ bvar[,2:6])    # un-log
forecasts
  fcst _ bvar <- tmp _ f _ bvar # forecasts
  rm(tmp _ f _ bvar, train)


  print(fcst _ bvar)  # print forecasts
```

Chunk 4.3 Global vector autoregression (GVAR)

The forecast in this section is based on the first stage of GVAR model-ling. An alternative, tractable way of implementing GVAR forecast is to use the GVAR Toolbox developed by Smith and Galesi (2014).

```
  library(GVARX)


  tmp _ f _ gvar <- df _ sheets  # temporary sheet


  tmp <- lnGVAR
  names(tmp)[1:2] <- c("ID", "Time")  # set names as required
by the package
  tmp$ID <- as.character(tmp$ID)
  tmp$Time  <-  as.character(as.Date(tmp$Time,  format  =  "%y
Q%q"))


  #  Time-variant weight matrix 2000-2019
  WeightALL <- split(Weight[,3:26], f = Weight$Time)


  #  Foreign variables for Thailand, used as exogenous vari-
ables in forecast
  exo  <-  GVAR _ Ft(data  =  tmp,weight.matrix  =  WeightALL)
[[21]]
  exo <- ts(exo, start = c(2000,1), end = c(2019, 4), freq = 4)
  exo <- cbind(exo, stats::lag(exo, k = -1))
  exo <- window(exo, start = 2015.00, end = 2019.75)
```

```
  colnames(exo) <- c("F.rtex.Lag0", "F.y.Lag0", "F.pi.Lag0",
                     "F.rtex.Lag1","F.y.Lag1", "F.pi.Lag1")
  exo <- as.data.frame(exo)

  #  Estimation and forecast
  for (i in 1:20) {
    # i loop over rolling windows
    train _ idx <- as.yearqtr(tmp$Time, format = "%Y-%m-%d")
>= 2000.00 + (i-1)/4 & as.yearqtr(tmp$Time, format = "%Y-%m-%d")
<= 2014.75 + (i-1)/4
    train <- tmp[which(train _ idx),]

    p <- 2
    FLag <- 2
    lag.max <- 4
    type <- "const"
    ic <- "SC"

    w _ yrs <- as.character(unique(year(train$Time)))
    weight.matrix <- WeightALL[w _ yrs]

    model _ gvar  <-  GVARest(data  =  train,p,FLag,lag.max,-
type,ic,weight.matrix)

    # Extract VARX* model for Thailand, on which the fore-
cast is based
    thai _ gvar <- model _ gvar[["gvar"]][[21]]

    for (j in 1:length(horizon)) {
      # j loop over five horizons
      h <- horizon[j]   # h-step ahead
      if (i+h-1 <= 20) {
        fcst _ gvar <- predict(thai _ gvar,
                               dumvar = exo[i:(i+h-1),],
                               n.ahead = h,
                               ci = 0.95)
        tmp _ f _ gvar[i+h-1,j+1] <- fcst _ gvar[["fcst"]][["TH.
rtex"]][h,1]
      } else {
        next
      }
    }
  }
```

```
  tmp _ f _ gvar[,2:6]  <-  exp(tmp _ f _ gvar[,2:6])     # un-log
forecasts
  fcst _ gvar <- tmp _ f _ gvar  # forecasts
  rm(tmp _ f _ gvar, train)

  print(fcst _ gvar)  # print forecasts
```
Chunk 4.4 Bayesian global vector autoregression (BGVAR)
```
  library(BGVAR)

  tmp _ f _ bgvar <- df _ sheets  # temporary sheet
  set.seed(1234)

  # Weight matrix 2014
  matrname <- colnames(Weight)[3:26]
  Weight2014 <- as.matrix(Weight[Weight$Time == "2014",c(3:26)])
  rownames(Weight2014) <- matrname

  # Data input should be a list object
  # Convert the data set (data frame) into a list
  df2list <- split(lnGVAR[,c(2:5)], f = lnGVAR$country)
  df2list <- sapply(names(df2list),
                    function(x) xts(df2list[[x]][,c(2:4)],
                                order.by = as.yearqtr(d-
f2list[[x]][[1]]),
                                    "%Y/Q%q"),
                    simplify=FALSE)
  df2list <- df2list[c(matrname)]

  # Estimation and forecast
  for (i in 1:20) {
    # i loop over rolling windows
    train <- sapply(names(df2list),
                    function(x) window(df2list[[x]],
                                index = index
(df2list[[x]]),
                                    start = as.yearqtr
(2000.00 + (i-1)/4),
                                    end = as.yearqtr(2014.
75 + (i-1)/4)),
                    simplify = FALSE)
    model _ bgvar <- bgvar(Data = train,
                        W = Weight2014,
                        plag = 2,
                        draws = 5000,
```

```
                    burnin = 2500,
                    prior = "MN",
                    SV = TRUE,
                    trend = FALSE,
                    thin = 2)

  for (j in 1:length(horizon)) {
    # j loop over five horizons
    h <- horizon[j]    # h-step ahead
    if (i+h-1 <= 20) {
      fcst _ bgvar <- predict(model _ bgvar, n.ahead = h)
      fcst _ result <- as.matrix(fcst _ bgvar[["fcast"]][,,4])
      tmp _ f _ bgvar[i+h-1,j+1] <- fcst _ result["TH.rtex",h]
    } else {
      next
    }
  }
}

tmp _ f _ bgvar[,2:6] <- exp(tmp _ f _ bgvar[,2:6])   # un-log
forecasts
fcst _ bgvar <- tmp _ f _ bgvar  # forecasts
rm(tmp _ f _ bgvar, train)

print(fcst _ bgvar)  # print forecasts
```

6

SPATIOTEMPORAL ECONOMETRIC MODELS

Xiaoying Jiao and Jason Li Chen

6.1 Introduction

Globalisation, in the forms of global markets, production, competition, and communication, facilitates the growing interdependence between national economies and broader interconnections across the world (Dwyer, 2015). As with any economic activity, the tourism industry is connected and interdependent across destinations through different channels. These connections or dependencies can be understood as spillover, defined as an effect that unintentionally spreads from an origin to a target through an explicit transmission channel (Elhorst, Gross, & Tereanu, 2018). Yang and Wong (2012) identified several reasons why tourism flows to one destination influence flows to other destinations. From the supply side, these include demonstration and competition effects from productivity spillover, market access spillover, joint promotion, and one-off events. Multi-destination travel patterns also contribute to a demand-side factor that generates spillover effects in tourist flows. For example, due to Schengen visa arrangements and convenient transportation between countries, tourists from long-haul source markets tend to visit multiple destinations in a single trip to Europe (Jiao, Li & Chen, 2020). Studies have also identified spillover effects in terms of regional tourism growth (Capone & Boix, 2008). These supply-side and demand-side factors contribute to the existence of spillovers in tourism demand. Intuitively, destinations tend to unintentionally generate spillovers, which can positively or negatively affect neighbouring destinations (Yang & Wong, 2012).

However, most studies have treated destinations in isolation, whereas in reality they are interconnected in various ways. The change in economic conditions can only capture the direct effects on tourism demand in a

DOI: 10.4324/9781003269366-6

particular destination. Without considering spillover from other destinations, effects are often overestimated or underestimated, which can lead to prediction failure (LeSage & Fischer, 2008). By effectively capturing the spatial and temporal dependencies in tourism demand between destinations in a systematic framework, spatiotemporal models can overcome this limitation and explicitly account for the magnitude and significance of spillover effects.

The development of spatial models in the field of general regional science typically begins with cross-sectional data that consider interactions across units but neglect temporal information. Spatial panel data models incorporate the time dimension of cross-sectional units and enable cross-learning of information obtained from both space and time dimensions within a system. Spatiotemporal econometric models (i.e., dynamic spatial models) with both space and time dimensions can take many different forms and can often be differentiated by the type of spatial spillover effects that are incorporated. In the space dimension, interaction effects can be distinguished as endogenous effects among the dependent variables (i.e., spatial lag on dependent variable), exogeneous effects among the independent variables (i.e., spatial lag on independent variable), and interaction effects among error terms (i.e., spatial lag on error term). Details of these effects and the different types of spatial models are explained in the following sections.

In the context of tourism demand, many studies (e.g., Yang & Fik, 2014; Majewska, 2015) have applied spatial econometric models and confirmed the existence of spillover effects in tourism flows and growth. The existence of spillover effects provides evidence of regional co-development (both positive and negative) of nearby destinations' tourism industries (Ma, Hong, & Zhang, 2015; Majewska, 2015). Apart from tourist arrivals, spatial econometric models have also been applied to supply and demand in the hotel and Airbnb industry. Adam and Mensah (2014) assessed the perceived spatial agglomeration effects in hotel location choices. Gunter, Önder, and Zekan (2020) applied a spatial Durbin model (SDM) to estimate the spillover effects of Airbnb demand on New York City. The above two studies confirm the existence of spatial spillover effects in hotels and Airbnb listings in nearby locations. From the supply side, Mao and Yang (2016) evaluated the foreign direct investment spillovers in the Chinese hotel industry. Chica-Olmo et al. (2020) and Gyódi and Nawaro (2021) both focused on the spatial spillover effects of Airbnb pricing.

However, applications in tourism demand forecasting are still uncommon. Long et al. (2019) made the first attempt to use a dynamic spatiotemporal autoregressive model for this purpose. They forecasted tourist arrivals in 341 cities in China and demonstrated superior forecasting performance against non-spatial and static alternatives. Yang and Zhang (2019) conducted spatiotemporal forecasting to predict tourism demand in 29 Chinese provincial regions and found results consistent with Long et al. (2019). Jiao et al. (2020) and Jiao et al. (2021) attempted to introduce local estimation into the spatiotemporal model, which allows for varying numbers of neighbours and parameter estimation to fully reflect spatial heterogeneity. These two studies also made methodological advancements by developing the general nested spatiotemporal (GNST) model, which incorporates all possible lags in both space and time dimensions. Empirical results of forecasting quarterly arrivals in Europe have confirmed the superiority of the locally estimated GNST model against other global and non-spatial benchmarks (Jiao et al., 2021).

This chapter aims to introduce the family of spatiotemporal econometric models and its applications in tourism demand forecasting by illustrating the complete process of applying the models to an empirical case study, including model specification, calibration, estimation, and forecasting. In addition, due to spatial feedback and spillover effects across destinations, regression coefficients alone are not adequate to explain the marginal effects of explanatory variables. Therefore, the direct, indirect, and total effects are also discussed to evaluate the impact of explanatory variables on dependent variables across destinations (LeSage & Pace, 2009; Li et al., 2016).

6.2 Methods

The rationale behind the formulation of spatial autoregressive (SAR) and spatial econometric models can be understood as the incorporation of spatial spillover effects into the traditional and simple linear ordinary least square (OLS) regression model. The manner of this incorporation (i.e., on the dependent variable, independent variable, or error term) determines the type of spatial model (Jiao et al., 2020). Thus, illustrating this family of spatial models begins with an OLS regression model as follows:

$$Y_t = \beta X_t + \alpha + \varepsilon_t \tag{6.1}$$

where Y_t and X_t represent the value of the dependent variable and the independent variable, respectively, ε_t represents the disturbance term, and β and α represent the estimated parameters. Equation (6.1) considers only the direct effects of the explanatory variables without considering any spatial interactions from neighbouring units, which tends to underestimate the direct effects and comprise forecasting performance when involving panel data. Spatiotemporal econometric models overcome this limitation through the incorporation of endogenous interaction effects on the dependent variable (Y), exogenous interaction effects on the independent variables (X), and interaction effects on the error terms (ε) (Elhorst, 2014). The SAR model, the spatial lag of X (SLX) model, and the spatial error model

(SEM) are three types of spatial models with one of the above three inter-action effects incorporated, respectively. The SAR model can be expressed as follows:

$$Y_t = \lambda W Y_t + \beta X_t + \mu + \alpha + \varepsilon_t \tag{6.2}$$

As a panel data model, Y_t denotes an $N \times 1$ vector of the dependent variable where N represents the number of units or locations included in the panel; X_t is an $m \times N$ matrix of explanatory variables in which m represents the number of explanatory variables; ε_t represents the disturbance term; and λ, β, μ, and α are estimated parameters. Equations (6.1) and (6.2) substan-tially differ in the terms $\lambda W Y_t$ and μ. $\lambda W Y_t$ is the spatially lagged depen-dent variable which denotes the endogenous interaction effects such that W represents the spatial weight matrix that indicates the geographical re-lationships across different locations within the panel. The spatial effects among dependent variables indicate that the dependent variable for one specific agent is jointly determined with those of the neighbouring loca-tions (Vega & Elhorst, 2013). μ is an $N \times 1$ vector of spatial fixed effects that reflect the spatial heterogeneity of each unit.

The spatial weight matrix can take many forms, though the k-nearest neighbours method has been used most frequently (Li et al., 2016). $W_{ij} = 1$ if location i and location j are neighbours, and $W_{ij} = 0$ otherwise. The num-ber of neighbours k is determined by experimentation, wherein various spatial weight matrices (i.e., different k) are applied to the spatial econo-metric model with estimation and forecasting done using the matrix that yields the best model fitness measured by residual variance (Elhorst et al., 2013) or in-sample mean absolute percentage error (MAPE) (Jiao et al., 2021). After specifying the number of neighbours, the spatial weight ma-trix is row-normalised for easier interpretation (Long et al., 2019).

Apart from the spatial effects, temporal effects can also be incorpo-rated into the modelling procedure to reflect time lapses in both depen-dent and independent variables. Following the theoretical foundation of evaluating tourism demand, a dynamic SAR model with fixed effects can be specified by incorporating a time-lagged dependent variable as follows:

$$Y_t = \lambda W Y_t + \rho Y_{t-1} + \beta X_t + \mu + \alpha + \varepsilon_t \tag{6.3}$$

where ρY_{t-1} represents the time-lagged dependent variable, which indi-cates that the value of the dependent variable at time t depends on that at time $t-1$. The other variables and parameters are the same as those in Equation (6.2). This dynamic SAR model with fixed effects is used in the following empirical study.

The SAR, SLX, and SEM models allow for only one type of spatial spillover effect such that only one spatially lagged variable is incorporated into the spatial models. However, multiple spatial interactions can be implemented into the spatial model structure. For example, the SDM further extends the SAR by the addition of a spatially lagged independent variable (WX_t). Alternatively, the SAR combined model additionally incorporates the interaction effects among the error terms to estimate an SAR coefficient. The GNST model developed in Jiao et al. (2021) represents the most general spatiotemporal econometric model yet, and incorporates all possible spatial and temporal lags. The spatiotemporal econometric models are estimated by the maximum likelihood method.

Although cross-sectional spatial models have been widely applied, empirical applications of spatial panel data remain rare due to the computational difficulties of the underlying algorithms and the lack of user-friendly software prior to the availability of comprehensive and publicly available codes written in MATLAB by Elhorst (2003) and built upon the work of LeSage (1999). However, as MATLAB is not free and has complicated syntax, further spatial panel applications have been facilitated by the R package 'splm' (Millo & Piras, 2012) within the opensource R platform (Bivand et al., 2021). The empirical applications in the following sections thus use R with the package 'splm'. The packages 'spdep' and 'plm' are also needed to generate spatial weight matrices and summarise results.

6.3 Application

6.3.1 Data

The empirical application of spatial econometric models in tourism demand forecasting uses quarterly inbound tourist arrivals data from 16 Asian destinations from 2004Q1 to 2017Q4 due to data completeness. Thus, the impact of the Covid-19 pandemic is not considered in this empirical study. The descriptive statistics of the quarterly arrivals are presented in Table 6.1. Asian destinations are used due to their close linkage and connectivity. Economic expansion, globalisation, universal connectivity, and social adaptation have rapidly occurred in Southeast Asia in the past decade (Todd, Leask & Fyall, 2015). Furthermore, the formation of the Great Bay Area by the Chinese government has facilitated intra-regional movement of goods and people and the cooperative development of the tourism industry in cities in Guangdong Province, Hong Kong, and Macao (Kirillova et al., 2020). Moreover, tourists from long-haul source markets tend to visit multiple destinations in Asia (e.g., Hong Kong and Macao; Singapore, Malaysia, and Thailand), which also indicates the existence of spatial interactions across Asian destinations.

The dependent variable used in this application is the log-transformed arrivals $(\ln y_t)$. The explanatory variables (X_t) include log-transformed tourism price $(\ln price_t)$ and log-transformed tourist income $(\ln income_t)$,

TABLE 6.1 Descriptive statistics of quarterly tourist arrivals

Destination	Observations	Mean	SD
Mainland China	56	17.299	0.086
Hong Kong	56	16.075	0.378
Japan	56	14.742	0.507
South Korea	56	14.625	0.378
Macao	56	15.671	0.207
Sri Lanka	56	12.277	0.595
Nepal	56	11.778	0.462
Maldives	56	12.254	0.380
Cambodia	56	13.438	0.522
Indonesia	56	14.438	0.327
Laos	56	13.290	0.550
Malaysia	56	15.549	0.186
Myanmar	56	11.646	0.776
Philippines	56	13.719	0.328
Singapore	56	14.932	0.249
Thailand	56	15.374	0.392

Note: The arrivals figures are in natural logarithm form.

which have been identified as major influencing factors affecting demand (Li et al., 2005). As shown in Equation (6.3), a spatially lagged dependent variable ($W\ln y_t$) and a time-lagged dependent variable ($\ln y_{t-1}$) are also incorporated into the dynamic SAR model. Tourism price is calculated as CPI_t / EX_t, in which CPI_t represents the consumer price index (CPI) and EX_t signifies the value of national currency per US dollar of the focal destination (base year = 2010). Normally, origin country income or private consumption are used as key indicators in tourism demand functions, but as source markets are not specified in the arrivals data, the rest of the world real GDP (base year = 2010) is used as a proxy of tourist income, where all countries other than the focal destination are identified as the source markets of international arrivals. Quarterly tourist arrivals data are obtained from the national statistical offices of the destinations, and the economic indicators are obtained from the International Monetary Fund. To capture seasonality, seasonal differences are conducted for all variables prior to the model estimation and forecasting process.

6.3.2 Model estimation

The dynamic SAR model with fixed effects is estimated using data from 2004Q1 to 2014Q4 from a panel of 16 Asian destinations. The model estimation results are presented in Table 6.2. Both the spatial lag ($W\ln y_t$) and the temporal lag ($\ln y_{t-1}$) of tourist arrivals are significant and positive, which indicates the positive effect of arrivals in the previous period and arrivals in neighbouring destinations. The price variable ($\ln price_t$) is also significant at the 0.01 level. The negative sign of its coefficient indicates that tourist arrivals are negatively influenced by the tourism price at the destination, which is consistent with previous tourism demand studies (Song et al., 2003). The rest of the world real GDP ($\ln income_t$) is positive but insignificant. This variable can be understood as a proxy of income in the tourism demand modelling structure. This lack of significance probably results from the inability to capture the exact income level of tourists in the major source markets of a specific destination in the panel.

6.3.3 Spillover effects

Contrary to traditional OLS regression models, regression coefficients alone cannot fully explain the influence of explanatory variables on dependent variables because of spatial feedback and spatial spillover effects (Li et al., 2016). Therefore, direct, indirect, and total effects are calculated to estimate these spillover effects. Direct effects measure the direct impact of changing one explanatory variable on the focal destination, whereas indirect effects can be understood as the spillover effects that represent either the impact of changing one explanatory variable in a region on the dependent variable in other regions or the feedback effects on a particular region from the changes in other regions. The total effects are the sum of the direct and indirect effects. The calculations of the impacts in a dynamic SAR model can be illustrated using Equations (6.4) and (6.5). Equation (6.4) can be obtained by rearranging Equation (6.3) to move Y_t to the left side and all other terms to the right side, where I is an $N \times N$ identity matrix with 1s on the diagonal and 0s elsewhere. The matrix of partial

TABLE 6.2 Model estimation results

	Coefficient	Estimate	Significance
$W\ln y_t$	λ	0.074	0.009 ***
$\ln y_{t-1}$	ρ	0.565	0.000 ***
$\ln income_t$	β_1	0.099	0.190
$\ln price_t$	β_2	−0.042	0.000 ***
Residual variance		0.012	
No. of fixed effects		16	

Note: *, **, and *** denote significance at the 0.1, 0.05, and 0.01 levels, respectively.

derivatives of Y_t with respect to $m^{th}X_t$ from region 1 to region N represents the effect of changes as presented in Equation (6.5).

$$Y_t = (I - \lambda W)^{-1}(\rho Y_{t-1} + \beta X_t + \mu + \varepsilon_t) \tag{6.4}$$

$$\left[\frac{\partial E(Y)}{\partial X_{1m}} \cdots \frac{\partial E(Y)}{\partial X_{Nm}}\right] = (I - \lambda W)^{-1}\beta_m \tag{6.5}$$

Direct effects are measured by the average of the diagonal elements of Equation (6.5), whereas indirect effects are measured by the average of the off-diagonal elements. This calculation of spillover effects also demonstrates a global definition of spillovers as proposed by LeSage and Pace (2009) because the indirect effects are very sensitive to the specification of the spatial weight matrix if they are reported for each single unit. The measurements of the level and significance of the spillover effects are applicable to most spatial econometric models other than the SEM model, which provides no explicit information about spillovers apart from the disturbance process.

Table 6.3 presents the spatial effects of the explanatory variables and the time-lagged dependent variable. The spatial effects are inherently global, which means that a change in x at any location transmits to all other locations due to the existence of the SAR coefficient λ (i.e., the inverse matrix multiplied by β_m in Equation (6.5)). As illustrated in LeSage and Pace (2011), these global spillover effects include feedbacks caused by the impact passing through neighbouring units back to the original unit. According to Table 6.3, the tourist arrivals in the previous period have a significant positive direct effect on the current arrivals and a significant positive spillover effect on neighbouring regions before returning to the original destination. Consistent with the regression coefficient, the price variable generates significant negative direct and indirect effects on the tourist arrivals, considering the spillover effects across destinations. The income variable does not have significant direct or indirect effects, which also results in a non-significant total effect. Thus, the change in rest of the world GDP does not greatly influence tourist arrivals in Asian destinations.

TABLE 6.3 Global spatial effects of explanatory variables

Variable	Direct effect	Indirect effect	Total effect
$\ln y_{t-1}$	0.566***	0.044**	0.611***
$\ln income_t$	0.099	0.008	0.107
$\ln price_t$	−0.042***	−0.003**	−0.045***

Note: *, **, and *** denote significance at the 0.1, 0.05, and 0.01 levels, respectively.

6.3.4 Forecasting

Following the model estimation, out-of-sample forecasts are generated for the 16 destinations in one, two, three, four, and eight horizons based on the rolling window method. The dynamic SAR model with fixed effects is estimated globally. Therefore, one set of parameter estimates is used for all destinations, where the uniqueness of each destination is reflected by only destination-specific spatial fixed effects. The forecasts are generated using Equation (6.4). To evaluate the forecasting performance, consistent with other chapters, three individually estimated benchmark models, the seasonal autoregressive integrated moving average (SARIMA), exponential smoothing (ETS) and seasonal naïve (SNAIVE) models, are applied to quarterly arrivals in the 16 Asian destinations. Forecasting performance is evaluated using MAPE, root mean square error (RMSE), and mean absolute scaled error (MASE).

TABLE 6.4 Forecasting performance evaluation measured by MAPE (%)

	Forecasting horizon				
	1	2	3	4	8
SNAIVE	12.634	12.794	12.621	12.219	17.935
ETS	9.270	10.741	12.045	12.820	20.573
SARIMA	9.444	11.454	12.671	14.663	23.738
SAR	12.674	12.450	11.926	17.062	18.073

TABLE 6.5 Forecasting performance evaluation measured by RMSE

	Forecasting horizon				
	1	2	3	4	8
SNAIVE	544,590	550,376	548,564	546,116	815,959
ETS	350,791	449,554	538,550	597,411	979,206
SARIMA	350,422	470,384	571,460	642,769	1,005,741
SAR	558,046	555,093	562,988	769,592	916,915

TABLE 6.6 Forecasting performance evaluation measured by MASE

	Forecasting horizon				
	1	2	3	4	8
SNAIVE	1.386	1.403	1.423	1.411	2.287
ETS	0.979	1.143	1.304	1.435	2.496
SARIMA	0.976	1.161	1.320	1.565	2.663
SAR	1.326	1.299	1.287	1.984	2.140

Tables 6.4−6.6 present the average forecasting performance of the dynamic SAR model and three benchmark models in forecasting quarterly tourist arrivals in 16 Asian destinations. For short-term forecasts, the dynamic SAR model outperforms the SNAIVE model in most cases in terms of MAPE and MASE, but the performance is inferior to the SARIMA and ETS models. However, in the longer term (i.e., eight-step-ahead), the spatial model outperforms the SARIMA and ETS models according to all three measures, which indicates that the dynamic SAR model with fixed effects generates more accurate long-term forecasting results of tourist arrivals in Asian destinations than the two benchmarks. The forecasting performance of the SAR model is not as good as the other benchmarks according to RMSE, which might indicate the existence of large variance for specific individual destinations.

This empirical application of the dynamic SAR model is only an initial attempt at forecasting tourist arrivals in Asian destinations using panel data for the purpose of simple and straightforward illustration. One reason why the spatiotemporal econometric model did not consistently outperform the time series benchmarks might be the global estimation of the model, where spatial heterogeneity is reflected only through destination-specific spatial fixed effects. This is contrary to the local estimation and forecasting applied in Jiao et al. (2020) and Jiao et al. (2021), which used substantially more complicated procedures. In local estimation, each destination is individually estimated with a destination-specific bandwidth that determines the size of the sub-sample and number of neighbours, and, subsequently, the spatial weight matrix. As opposed to global models that assume the same panel, number of neighbours, and coefficients for all destinations, local models allow for differences in all specifications for each destination. Particularly for larger panels, this generally improves the forecasting accuracy of local estimation and provides more consistent superiority compared with the individually estimated time series benchmarks.

Other future research directions include the specification of source markets for tourist arrivals data. When tourist arrivals series in Origin-Destination (O-D) pairs can be obtained to generate model estimations and forecasts, the income and price variables can be more accurately specified with identified source markets. Finally, spatial econometric model selection is worth further discussion. As concluded by most tourism forecasting studies, no single type of model outperforms the others in all situations. No study has empirically tested forecasting capability among the family of spatial models, though this would be a fruitful future research direction to seek further improvement of forecasting accuracy using spatial econometric models.

6.4 Conclusion and future directions

This chapter presents an overview of the family of spatial econometric models and uses the most frequently used spatiotemporal form of spatial model. The dynamic SAR model with fixed effects is empirically applied as a representative model for forecasting tourist arrivals in 16 Asian destinations using a global panel. A full procedure of model calibration, model estimation, spillover effects calculation, and forecasting is presented with empirical results. The forecasting results are benchmarked with three time series models using MAPE, RMSE, and MASE as the evaluation criteria. Although the forecasting performance evaluation varies with different measures, the SAR model shows relatively stable accuracy in three-step-ahead and eight-step-ahead forecasts compared to other benchmark models in terms of MAPE and MASE. In addition, the current empirical study has shed some light on future research directions. Particularly for larger panels, local estimation reflects spatial heterogeneity more explicitly, and its application should further improve forecasting accuracy (Jiao et al., 2020, 2021). O-D pair tourist arrivals within a panel may also further improve forecasting results. Finally, future research could focus on spatial model selection in different cases to accurately capture the types of spillover effects based on real-world situations and thus provide more practical implications.

Self-study questions

1   What are the three different types of interaction effects in spatiotemporal econometric models?
2   What type of spatiotemporal econometric models cannot estimate spillover effects?
3   What is the most general form of spatiotemporal econometric models thus far?

References

Adam, I., & Mensah, E. A. (2014). Perceived spatial agglomeration effects and hotel location choice. *Anatolia, 25*(1), 49–60. https://doi.org/10.1080/13032917.2013.822818

Bivand, R., Millo, G., & Piras, G. (2021). A review of software for spatial econometrics in R. *Mathematics, 9*(11), 1276. https://doi.org/10.3390/math9111276

Capone, F., & Boix, R. (2008). Sources of growth and competitiveness of local tourist production systems: An application to Italy (1991–2001). *The Annals of Regional Science, 42*(1), 209–224. https://doi.org/10.1007/s00168-007-0133-7

Chica-Olmo, J., González-Morales, J. G., & Zafra-Gómez, J. L. (2020). Effects of location on Airbnb apartment pricing in Málaga. *Tourism Management, 77*, 103981. https://doi.org/10.1016/j.tourman.2019.103981

Dwyer, L. (2015). Globalization of tourism: Drivers and outcomes. *Tourism Recreation Research, 40*(3), 326–339. https://doi.org/10.1080/02508281.2015.1075723

Elhorst, J. P. (2003). Specification and estimation of spatial panel data models. *International Regional Science Review, 26*(3), 244–268. https://doi.org/10.1177/0160017603253791

Elhorst, J. P. (2014). Dynamic Spatial Panels: Models, Methods and Inferences. In J. P. Elhorst (Ed.), *Spatial Econometrics: From Cross-Sectional Data to Spatial Panels* (pp. 95–119). Springer. https://doi.org/10.1007/978-3-642-40340-8_4

Elhorst, J. P., Gross, M., & Tereanu, E. (2018). *Spillovers in Space and Time: Where Spatial Econometrics and Global VAR Models Meet* (SSRN Scholarly Paper ID 3134525). Social Science Research Network. https://papers.ssrn.com/abstract=3134525

Elhorst, P., Zandberg, E., & De Haan, J. (2013). The impact of interaction effects among neighbouring countries on financial liberalization and reform: A dynamic spatial panel data approach. *Spatial Economic Analysis, 8*(3), 293–313. https://doi.org/10.1080/17421772.2012.760136

Gunter, U., Önder, I., & Zekan, B. (2020). Modeling Airbnb demand to New York City while employing spatial panel data at the listing level. *Tourism Management, 77*, 104000. https://doi.org/10.1016/j.tourman.2019.104000

Gyódi, K., & Nawaro, Ł. (2021). Determinants of Airbnb prices in European cities: A spatial econometrics approach. *Tourism Management, 86*, 104319. https://doi.org/10.1016/j.tourman.2021.104319

Jiao, X., Chen, J. L., & Li, G. (2021). Forecasting tourism demand: Developing a general nesting spatiotemporal model. *Annals of Tourism Research, 90*, 103277. https://doi.org/10.1016/j.annals.2021.103277

Jiao, X., Li, G., & Chen, J. L. (2020). Forecasting international tourism demand: A local spatiotemporal model. *Annals of Tourism Research, 83*, 102937. https://doi.org/10.1016/j.annals.2020.102937

Kirillova, K., Park, J., Zhu, M., Dioko, L., & Zeng, G. (2020). Developing the coopetitive destination brand for the Greater Bay Area. *Journal of Destination Marketing & Management, 17*, 100439. https://doi.org/10.1016/j.jdmm.2020.100439

LeSage, J. P. (1999). *The theory and practice of spatial econometrics*. Toledo, OH: University of Toledo.

LeSage, J. P., & Fischer, M. M. (2008). Spatial growth regressions: Model specification, estimation and interpretation. *Spatial Economic Analysis, 3*(3), 275–304. https://doi.org/10.1080/17421770802353758

LeSage, J., & Pace, R. K. (2009). *Introduction to Spatial Econometrics*. Chapman and Hall/CRC. https://doi.org/10.1201/9781420064254

LeSage, J. P., & Pace, R. K. (2011). Pitfalls in higher order model extensions of basic spatial regression methodology. *Review of Regional Studies, 41*(1), 13–26.

Li, G., Song, H., & Witt, S. F. (2005). Recent developments in econometric modeling and forecasting. *Journal of Travel Research, 44*(1), 82–99. https://doi.org/10.1177/0047287505276594

Li, H., Chen, J. L., Li, G., & Goh, C. (2016). Tourism and regional income inequality: Evidence from China. *Annals of Tourism Research, 58*, 81–99. https://doi.org/10.1016/j.annals.2016.02.001

Long, W., Liu, C., & Song, H. (2019). Pooling in tourism demand forecasting. *Journal of Travel Research, 58*(7), 1161–1174. https://doi.org/10.1177/0047287518800390

Ma, T., Hong, T., & Zhang, H. (2015). Tourism spatial spillover effects and urban economic growth. *Journal of Business Research, 68*(1), 74–80. https://doi.org/10.1016/j.jbusres.2014.05.005

Majewska, J. (2015). Inter-regional agglomeration effects in tourism in Poland. *Tourism Geographies, 17*(3), 408–436. https://doi.org/10.1080/14616688.2014.997279

Mao, Z. & Yang, Y. (2016). FDI spillovers in the Chinese hotel industry: The role of geographic regions, star-rating classifications, ownership types, and foreign capital origins. *Tourism Management, 54*, 1–12. https://doi.org/10.1016/j.tourman.2015.10.011

Millo, G., & Piras, G. (2012). splm: Spatial panel data models in R. *Journal of Statistical Software, 47*, 1–38. https://doi.org/10.18637/jss.v047.i01

Song, H., Wong, K. K. F., & Chon, K. K. S. (2003). Modelling and forecasting the demand for Hong Kong tourism. *International Journal of Hospitality Management, 22*(4), 435–451. https://doi.org/10.1016/S0278-4319(03)00047-1

Todd, L., Leask, A., & Fyall, A. (2015). *Destination Competitiveness: A Comparative Study of Hong Kong, Macau, and Singapore.* Cognizant Communication Corporation. https://doi.org/10.3727/108354215X14464845877832

Vega, S. H., & Elhorst, J. P. (2013, August). On spatial econometric models, spillover effects, and W. *In 53rd ERSA Congress, Palermo, Italy.*

Yang, Y., & Fik, T. (2014). Spatial effects in regional tourism growth. *Annals of Tourism Research, 46*, 144–162.

Yang, Y., & Wong, K. K. F. (2012). A spatial econometric approach to model spillover effects in tourism flows. *Journal of Travel Research, 51*(6), 768–778. https://doi.org/10.1177/0047287512437855

Yang, Y., & Zhang, H. (2019). Spatial-temporal forecasting of tourism demand. *Annals of Tourism Research, 75*, 106–119. https://doi.org/10.1016/j.annals.2018.12.024

APPENDIX

R CODE

```
##Chapter 6 code

  ##read data
  #setwd("~/R/tourism forecasting book chapter")
  data _ full       =       read.csv("data _ sd.csv",header       =
TRUE,fileEncoding="UTF-8-BOM")
  data _ or         =         read.csv("data.csv",header         =
TRUE,fileEncoding="UTF-8-BOM")
  coord=read.csv("longlat.csv",header = FALSE)
  library(splm)
  library(plm)
  library(spdep)
  library(geosphere)
  library(matlib)

  ##Generate spatial weight matrices

  N = 16
  #number of neighbours
  for (k in 1:(N-1)){
    w _ mat = matrix(0,N,N)
    for (n in 1:N){
      dist _ all = matrix(0,1,N)
      for (n.hat in 1:N){
        point1 = as.numeric(coord[n,])
        point2 = as.numeric(coord[n.hat,])
        my _ points <- matrix(c(point1, point2), nrow = 2,by-
row = TRUE)
```

```
        colnames(my _ points) <- c("longitude", "latitude")
        rownames(my _ points) <- c("point _ 1", "point _ 2")
        dist = distHaversine(my _ points)
        dist _ all[1,n.hat] = dist


    }
      nn  =  sapply(1:(k+1),  function(x)  which(dist _ all  ==
sort(dist _ all)[x]))
      w _ mat[n,nn] = 1
      w _ mat[n,n] = 0
      w _ mat _ norm = w _ mat/k

  }
    write.table(w _ mat _ norm,paste("WR",k,".csv",sep = ""),row.
names = FALSE,col.names = FALSE,sep = ",")
  }

  ##Choose spatial weight matrix

  selection = matrix(0,(N-1),2)
  len = nrow(data _ full)
  data _ estimate = data _ full[1:(len - 12*N),]
  y = data _ estimate$ln _ arriv
  for (k in 1:(N-1)){
    w = read.csv(paste("WR",k,".csv",sep = ""),header = FALSE)
    matw = matrix(unlist(w),ncol = N, nrow = N)
    fm2 <- ln _ arriv ~ ln _ arriv _ tl + ln _ income + ln _ price
    mod2 <- spml(fm2, data = data _ estimate, index = c("id",
"year"),listw = spdep::mat2listw(matw),
            model="within", spatial.error="none", lag=TRUE)
    selection[k,1] = mod2$sigma2  #residual variance
    mape2 = mean(abs(y-mod2$fitted.values)/y)
    selection[k,2] = mape2
  }
  kmod2 _ rv = which.min(selection[,1])
  kmod2 _ mape = which.min(selection[,2])

  ##Coefficients and spatial effects
  k = kmod2 _ mape
  w = read.csv(paste("WR",k,".csv",sep = ""),header = FALSE)
  matw = matrix(unlist(w),ncol = N, nrow = N)
  fm2 <- ln _ arriv ~ ln _ arriv _ tl + ln _ income + ln _ price
  mod2 <- spml(fm2, data = data _ estimate, index = c("id",
"year"),listw = spdep::mat2listw(matw),
            model="within", spatial.error="none", lag=TRUE)
  print(summary(mod2))
```

```
  impac1 <- spatialreg::impacts(mod2, listw = spdep::mat2list-
w(matw, style = "W"), time = 17)
  print(summary(impac1, zstats=TRUE, short=TRUE))

  ##Forecasting
  k = kmod2 _ mape
  w = read.csv(paste("WR",k,".csv",sep = ""),header = FALSE)
  matw = matrix(unlist(w),ncol = N, nrow = N)
  fn = 12
  len = nrow(data _ full)
  endQ = (len - 12*N)
  ynot = data _ or$ln _ arriv
  qnot = length(ynot)
  explan = c("ln _ arriv _ tl","ln _ income","ln _ price")
  horizons = c(1:8)
  all = sum(13-horizons)
  forecast _ s1 = matrix(0,16,all)
  for (i in 0:11){
    for (h in horizons){
      if ((i+h)<13){
        tend = endQ+i*N
        train = data _ full[(1+i*N):tend,]
          fm1 <- ln _ arriv ~ ln _ arriv _ tl + ln _ income +
ln _ price
          mod1 <- spml(fm1, data = train, index = c("id",
"year"),listw = spdep::mat2listw(matw),
                        model="within", spatial.error="none",
lag=TRUE)
        if (h == 1){
          data _ f = data _ full[(tend+1+(h-1)*N):(tend+h*N),]
        }else{
          data _ f = data _ full[(tend+1+(h-1)*N):(tend+h*N),]
          data _ f$ln _ arriv _ tl = predicts
        }
        effect = effects.splm(mod1)
        lamda = mod1$coefficients[1]
        B = inv(diag(N)-lamda*matw)
        con = effect$INTTable[1]
        sfe = effect$SETable[,1]
        coeff = mod1$coefficients[-1]
        dat = data _ f[,explan]
        ft = matrix(0,N,1)
        for (j in 1:N){
          ft[j] = sum(coeff*dat[j,])+con+sfe[j]
        }
        forecast = B%*%ft
```

```
ind = rep(0,8)
h_not = 13-horizons
for (a in 2:8){
  ind[a] = sum(h_not[1:(a-1)])
}
h_hat = h
indexM = ind[h_hat]+i+1
if (h==8){
  ty1 = qnot-16*N+i*N+1+3*N
  ty2 = ty1+N
  yo = ynot[ty1:ty2]
  for (p in 1:N){  ·
    forecast_s1[p,indexM] = exp(forecast[p]+
forecast_4[p])*exp(yo[p])
  }
}else{
  ty1 = qnot-16*N+i*N+1+(h-1)*N
  ty2 = ty1+N
  yo = ynot[ty1:ty2]
  for (p in 1:N){
    forecast_s1[p,indexM] = exp(forecast[p])*exp(yo[p])
  }
}
predicts = forecast
if (h == 4){
  forecast_4 = forecast
}
      }
    }
  }
}
forecast_1 = forecast_s1[,1:12]
forecast_2 = forecast_s1[,13:23]
forecast_3 = forecast_s1[,24:33]
forecast_4 = forecast_s1[,33:41]
col.n = ncol(forecast_s1)
forecast_8 = forecast_s1[,(col.n-4):col.n]
write.csv(forecast_1,"forecastSARh1.csv",row.names = FALSE)
write.csv(forecast_2,"forecastSARh2.csv",row.names = FALSE)
write.csv(forecast_3,"forecastSARh3.csv",row.names = FALSE)
write.csv(forecast_4,"forecastSARh4.csv",row.names = FALSE)
write.csv(forecast_8,"forecastSARh8.csv",row.names = FALSE)

#Performance (mape, rmse, mase)
yt = as.numeric(data_or$ln_arriv_t1[1:N])
ytt = as.numeric(data_or$ln_arriv)
```

```
  yAll = c(yt,ytt)
  yAll = matrix(exp(yAll),nrow = N,ncol = 56)
  n = N
  steps = c(1,2,3,4,8)
  performance = matrix(0, n, 15)
  for (j in steps){
    test = yAll[,(44+j):56]
    forecast = read.csv(paste("forecastSARh",j,".csv",sep =
""),header = TRUE)
    mape1 = matrix(0, n, 1)
    rmse1 = matrix(0, n, 1)
    mase1 = matrix(0,n,1)
    for (i in 1:16){
      ypred = as.numeric(as.character(forecast[i,]))
      ytrue =as.numeric(as.character(test[i,]))
      mape1[i,1] = mean(abs(ypred-ytrue)*100/ytrue)
      rmse1[i,1] = sqrt(mean((ypred-ytrue)^2))
      lnY = as.numeric(yAll[i,])
      MASE.denominator = mean(abs(diff(lnY, 4)))
      mase1[i,1] = mean(abs(ypred-ytrue)/MASE.denominator)
    }

    if (j == 8){
      index = 5
    } else{
      index = j
    }
    performance[,1+3*(index-1)] = mape1
    performance[,2+3*(index-1)] = rmse1
    performance[,3+3*(index-1)] = mase1

  }

  # destination-level performance (take average to calculate
overall performance)
  write.csv(performance, "performance _ SAR.csv",row.names=F)

  #average performance
  average = colMeans(performance)
  print(average)
```

7

MIXED-FREQUENCY MODELS

Han Liu, Ying Liu, and Peihuang Wu

7.1 Introduction

In the previous chapters, the explanatory variables used in forecasting tourism arrivals to Thailand are quarterly explanatory variables, such as tourist income and relative tourism price. In fact, most of the explanatory variables are processed at the same frequency as tourism demand due to the limitation of traditional econometric models allowing variables with only the same frequency (Song & Li, 2008; Wu, Song, & Shen, 2017).

With the rapid development of the internet, big data have become increasingly important in both academia and business (Chen, Chiang, & Storey, 2012; Xiang, Schwartz, Gerdes, & Uysal, 2015) and multiple internet data sources have been introduced in previous tourism demand forecasting research, including search query data, blogs, social networks, and photo/video sharing (Berthon, Pitt, Plangger, & Shapiro, 2012; Fesenmaier, Xiang, Pan, and Law, 2010; Li et al., 2018a; Li et al., 2021). The most popular internet data source used in tourism demand forecasting is search query data (Pan & Yang, 2016; Rivera, 2016). For example, Google Trends data were applied by Pan, Wu, and Song (2012) to forecast weekly hotel room demand. Choi and Varian (2012) used Google Trends data to demonstrate improved tourism demand forecast accuracy for Hong Kong from nine source markets. Data are also often acquired from the Baidu Index and other search engines, and many studies have used search engine data to forecast tourism demand. For example, Yang, Pan, Evans, and Lv (2015) used web search query volume to predict visitor numbers for Hainan province, a popular tourist destination in China. Xu and Reed (2017) examined the interaction between perceived pollution and inbound tourism in mainland China with monthly Google Trends data on pollution concerns.

DOI: 10.4324/9781003269366-7

Sun, Wei, Tsui, and Wang (2019) proposed a forecasting framework that included both Google Trends and Baidu Index data to forecast tourist arrivals in Beijing. Liu et al. (2021) used Baidu Index data to forecast tourist arrivals from mainland China to Hong Kong.

Google Trends and Baidu Index data are respectively provided weekly and daily at their highest frequencies, which exceed the number of tourist arrivals typically captured by lower frequencies. As most econometric models in tourism demand can only use variables that are measured at the same frequency, high-frequency variables must be converted to the same low frequencies by aggregating them to fit the traditional econometric models. However, high-frequency data usually contain rich information and can be collected and released more rapidly. Directly aggregating these data not only loses potentially valuable information but also causes delays in tourism demand forecasting (Bangwayo-Skeete & Skeete, 2015; Havranek & Zeynalov, 2021). In addition, data frequency mismatch seems inevitable as the explanatory variables for tourism demand forecasting grow more diversified.

Fortunately, two types of mixed-frequency models have been developed to deal with these problems. The mixed-frequency vector autoregressive (MF-VAR) approach proposed by Zadrozny (1988), Mittnik and Zadrozny (2005) and Mariano and Murasawa (2010) is a well-established method that treats all of the time series as being generated at the highest frequency. The MF-VAR model is designed for accurate posterior Bayesian inference and can systematically analyse the two-way dynamics between the low-frequency target variable and the high-frequency explanatory variables (Schorfheide & Song, 2015). It has been used extensively to improve the forecast accuracy of time series. For example, Brave, Butters, and Justiniano (2019) tested the performance of the medium-large mixed-frequency Bayesian vector autoregressive (MF-BVAR) model in forecasting US GDP and found that the predictive ability of the model compared favourably with surveys by professional predictors in a data-rich environment. Schorfheide and Song (2020) used the MF-VAR model to generate US macroeconomic forecasts during the COVID-19 pandemic and predicted that the shock of the pandemic would cause a long-term economic depression. In the context of tourism research, Liu and Song (2018) evaluated Granger causality between tourism demand and economic growth in Hong Kong using the MF-VAR model, showing short-term bidirectional causality and that the relationship changes over time. Liu et al. (2021) used the MF-VAR model to test whether the relationship between Hong Kong tourism demand and economic growth will change in the presence of economic policy uncertainty, and found that tourism demand is highly sensitive to economic policy uncertainty.

However, the MF-VAR model has complicated estimation methods and an excess of parameters to estimate, such that expanding the dataset causes the computational burden to increase exponentially (Song & Witt, 2006). Alternatively, the mixed data sampling (MIDAS) model proposed by Ghysels, Santa-Clara, and Valkanov (2004) provides a new method to resolve the frequency mismatch problem by explaining low-frequency variables with exogenous variables of higher frequency in the absence of any aggregation procedure and within a parsimonious framework. This allows direct estimation of equations with variables sampled at different frequencies. The earliest proposed MIDAS model importantly introduced a polynomial weight function to restrict the number of parameters, the choice of which greatly influences the final performance of the model. The most commonly used polynomial weight functions include the Almon, polynomial, the exponential Almon polynomial, and the Beta polynomial. MIDAS regressions have been widely used to forecast macroeconomic and financial variables (Andreou, Ghysels, & Kourtellos, 2013; Baumeister, Guérin, & Kilian, 2015; Clements & Galvão, 2008; Engle, Ghysels, & Sohn, 2013) but have only recently been adopted to forecast tourism demand (Bangwayo-Skeete & Skeete, 2015; Wen, Liu, Song, & Liu, 2021).

As research problems become more complex, they increasingly require mixed-frequency data analysis methods. As a result, some expansions of the MIDAS model have been proposed. For example, given that explanatory and dependent variables typically have minimal frequency mismatch in macroeconomic studies, frequency alignment does not bring too many parameters to the estimation process. In this case, a polynomial weight function is not necessary to reduce the number of parameters. Foroni, Marcellino, and Schumacher (2015) proposed the unrestricted MIDAS (U-MIDAS) model and found that it outperformed the MIDAS model in applications involving small differences in sampling frequencies. Furthermore, Clements and Galvão (2008) added an autoregressive (AR) term to MIDAS regression (MIDAS-AR) as an independent variable with a low-frequency lag.

With increasingly diverse factors influencing tourism, incorporating as many predictors as possible into tourism demand forecasting models improves accuracy. However, the greater number of variables in models increases, the difficulty of parameter estimation and can cause the curse of dimensionality. That is, the number of parameters to be estimated can be larger than the length of the data sample resulting in exponentially growing computational cost (Winschel & Krätzig, 2010; Nakajima & Sueishi, 2020). Combining MIDAS regressions with factor estimators, Marcellino and Schumacher (2010) proposed nine Factor MIDAS approaches, including the Factor MIDAS and Factor U-MIDAS models. The Factor MIDAS model can be built by the two-step method of extracting common factors and constructing a mixed-frequency data model, the former of which can reduce the dimensionality of the data and solve the curse of dimensionality. The MIDAS model also has other extensions. Ghysels and Ozkan

(2015) constructed the augmented distributed lag MIDAS (ADL-MIDAS) model with consideration of the impact of the lags of each variable to explore the influence of high-frequency financial and macroeconomic indicators and their lags on low-frequency fiscal expenditure and revenue. Miller (2014) proposed the Cointegrating MIDAS (CoMIDAS) model to analyse mixed-frequency data with cointegration relationships. In consideration of the time-varying nature of economic variables, Pan, Wang, Wang, and Yang (2018) constructed the time-varying parameter MIDAS (TVP-MIDAS) model to forecast the US GDP.

A growing number of interdisciplinary researchers have utilised the MIDAS model or its extended forms, although it was first applied in macroeconomics. Clements and Galvão (2008) improved the accuracy of quarterly GDP growth forecasts using the MIDAS model with monthly business cycle indicators. Marcellino and Schumacher (2010) considered three alternative MIDAS approaches (basic, smoothed and unrestricted) for nowcasting and forecasting low-frequency GDP with a large set of high-frequency indicators. Kuzin, Marcellino, and Schumacher (2011) conducted a recursive forecast of quarterly GDP in the Euro area using the MIDAS approach. Barsoum and Stankiewicz (2015) developed the Markov-switching MIDAS model with an unrestricted lag polynomial (MS-U-MIDAS) by combining the unrestricted MIDAS with the Markov-switching approach and used it to forecast GDP growth. Other than for GDP, it has been used to forecast inflation. Monteforte and Moretti (2013) presented a MIDAS regression to forecast monthly Euro area inflation with daily data from the financial market and found that the mixed-frequency method had a superior predictive performance. Li et al. (2015) used five groups of Google search data to forecast the Chinese consumer price index (CPI) using the MIDAS model. The MIDAS regressions have also been used in the financial literature. For example, Ghysels, Ghysels, Valkanov, and Serrano (2009) found that the MIDAS model outperformed several other models in long-term forecasts of stock return volatility. Fang, Yu, and Li (2017) used the modified dynamic conditional correlation-MIDAS (DCC-MIDAS) model to investigate the long-term correlation between US stock and bond markets as influenced by the economic policy uncertainty (EPU) index. Xu, Bo, Jiang, and Liu (2019) developed the novel multiple factors generalised autoregressive conditional heteroscedasticity MIDAS (GARCH-MIDAS) model to investigate the usefulness of Google Trends data for forecasting stock market volatility.

The application of the MIDAS model to tourism research has also become more widespread. Bangwayo-Skeete and Skeete (2015) applied the MIDAS-AR model to forecast monthly tourism demand in several major Caribbean tourist destinations with weekly Google search data. Havranek and Zeynalov (2021) combined the MIDAS model with Google Trends data to forecast tourist arrivals in Prague and found that the mixed-frequency model significantly outperformed alternatives. Liu et al. (2021) compared the usefulness of official statistical data and online search engine data in tourism demand forecasting using the least absolute shrinkage and selection operator MIDAS (LASSO-MIDAS) model. Wen et al. (2021) combined the seasonal autoregressive integrated moving average (ARIMA) model with the MIDAS model to construct the MIDAS-ARIMA model and investigated its performance in forecasting monthly tourism demand in Hong Kong from mainland China with daily Baidu Index data. The extensive application of MIDAS-type models in tourism demand forecasting has proven that this method effectively resolves the problem of frequency mismatch. While various innovative extensions are also under constant development, they often require more complex forms and are proposed for specific problems. In this chapter, we therefore introduce and demonstrate the application of several basic MIDAS-type models in tourism demand forecasting, including the basic MIDAS, U-MIDAS, MIDAS-AR, Factor MIDAS and Factor U-MIDAS models.

For consistency with the previous chapters, we use the quarterly GDP of origin markets and tourism prices in Thailand relative to source markets to forecast quarterly tourist arrivals in Thailand from mainland China, Malaysia, Russia and the USA. The monthly search query data are also added to tourism demand forecasting. Data for mainland China are from the Baidu Index, while data for the other three source markets come from Google Trends. The Factor MIDAS and Factor U-MIDAS models address the multicollinearity problem as there are many search keywords. Through the application of multiple mixed-frequency models, we test the role of MIDAS-type models in tourism demand forecasting.

The remainder of this chapter is organised as follows. The MIDAS, U-MIDAS, MIDAS-AR, Factor MIDAS and Factor U-MIDAS models are presented in Section 7.2. Section 7.3 provides empirical examples to test the performance of these models as well as the results of tourism demand forecasting in Thailand from four source markets: mainland China, Malaysia, Russia and the USA. In Section 7.4, we conclude this chapter and propose future directions. Finally, self-study questions are provided at the end of the chapter. The data and R code are also provided, should readers wish to run these codes in RStudio.

7.2 Methods

MIDAS-type models have two main advantages in forecasting. First, they can enhance forecast accuracy through the direct use of high-frequency information, thus avoiding the information loss of full sample data and artificial data caused by data frequency compression (Clements & Galvão, 2008). Second, they can use the most recent high-frequency data to perform short-term nowcasts on low-frequency data, which avoids the time lag in the release of low-frequency data (Foroni & Marcellino, 2014). In this way, they allow timely forecasting and nowcasting of tourism demand and improve the timeliness and accuracy of nowcasts (Kuzin et al., 2011). The following section focuses on the basic MIDAS model with its extended variants and explicates the estimation methods of these mixed-frequency models.

7.2.1 The basic MIDAS model

The MIDAS model is a single-equation approach wherein the left side of the equation is the low-frequency dependent variable y_t, $t = 1,2,\cdots,T$, and the right side is the high-frequency explanatory variable x_τ, $\tau = 1/m, 2/m,\cdots,T$. The frequency difference between the high- and low-frequency variables, typically expressed as m, is defined as a frequency mismatch. In each low-frequency period from t to $(t+1)$, there are m high-frequency variables x_τ that can be observed at $\tau = t, t+1/m,\ldots,t+(m-1)/m$. For example, if y_t is quarterly and x_τ is monthly, then $m = 3$. The MIDAS method uses a distributed lag of polynomials to ensure parsimonious specifications. The frequency alignment of high-frequency x_τ can be written in matrix notation as follows:

$$\mathbf{X}_\tau = \begin{bmatrix} x_1 & x_{1-1/m} & \cdots & x_{1-l/m} \\ x_2 & x_{2-1/m} & \cdots & x_{2-l/m} \\ \vdots & \vdots & \ddots & \vdots \\ x_t & x_{t-1/m} & \cdots & x_{t-l/m} \\ \vdots & \vdots & \ddots & \vdots \\ x_T & x_{T-1/m} & \cdots & x_{T-l/m} \end{bmatrix} \tag{7.1}$$

where l represents the maximum lag order corresponding to the explanatory variable x_τ, which depends on the frequency mismatch m. Through the frequency alignment process, both sides of the MIDAS equation have the same frequency. To explore the dynamic influence of x_τ on y_t, a regression model between the two variables must be established:

$$y_t = \alpha_0 + \alpha_1 B\left(L^m; \theta\right) x_\tau + \xi_t \tag{7.2}$$

Equation (7.2) is the most basic form of the MIDAS model, and the corresponding h -step forward prediction model is

$$y_t = \alpha_{0,h} + \alpha_{1,h} B\left(L^m; \theta_h\right) x_{\tau-h} + \xi_t \tag{7.3}$$

where $B(L^m; \theta_h) = \sum_{j=0}^{l} B(j; \theta_h) L^{j/m}$, $L^{j/m}$ is the lag operator and $L^{1/m} x_{t-h}$

$= x_{t-h-1/m}$. Then $B\left(L^m; \theta_h\right) x_{\tau-h} = \sum_{j=0}^{l} B(j; \theta_h) L^{j/m} x_{\tau-h} = \sum_{j=0}^{l} w(j; \theta_h) x_{t-h-j/m}$, where $w(j;\theta_h)$ is the polynomial weight function, ξ_h is the corresponding parameter vector and ξ_t is a disturbance term. The most commonly used weight polynomial functions including Almon, exponential Almon and Beta are proposed by Ghysels, Sinko, and Valkanov (2007). The specific analysis of three commonly used weight polynomials is expressed as follows:

(1) The Almon lag polynomial (Almon, 1965) can be expressed as:

$$w(j;\theta) = \frac{\theta_1 j + \theta_2 j^2 + \cdots + \theta_q j^q + \cdots + \theta_Q j^Q}{\sum\limits_{j=1}^{l} \left(\theta_1 j + \theta_2 j^2 + \cdots + \theta_q j^q + \cdots + \theta_Q j^Q\right)} \tag{7.4}$$

(2) The exponential Almon lag polynomial can be expressed as:

$$w(j;\theta) = \frac{e^{\theta_1 j + \theta_2 j^2 + \cdots + \theta_q j^q + \cdots + \theta_Q j^Q}}{\sum\limits_{j=1}^{l} e^{\theta_1 j + \theta_2 j^2 + \cdots + \theta_q j^q + \cdots + \theta_Q j^Q}} \tag{7.5}$$

where Q represents the number of parameters in the exponential Almon polynomial weight function, such that $\theta = (\theta_1, \theta_2)$ and typically $Q = 2$. Although only two parameters are considered, the exponential Almon lag polynomial is the most commonly used polynomial function and can generate a wide variety of weights.

In the case of a given polynomial weight function $w(j;\theta)$, the weight sequence obtained from the estimation result $\theta = (\theta_1, \theta_2)$ reflects the number of explanatory variables that affect the dependent variable y_t and automatically identifies the maximum lag order l. Introducing the polynomial weight function $w(j;\theta)$ in the MIDAS model can not only reduce the number of parameters to be estimated but also automatically select the appropriate maximum lag order l.

(3) The weight function of Beta is a polynomial function with only two parameters, but it can also construct a wide variety of weight functions. The Beta polynomial is more often used in financial market forecasting and analysis and can be expressed as follows:

$$w(j;\theta) = \frac{f\left(\frac{j}{l};\theta_1,\theta_2\right)}{\sum\limits_{j=1}^{l} f\left(\frac{j}{l};\theta_1,\theta_2\right)} \tag{7.6}$$

where $f\left(\dfrac{j}{l};\theta_1,\theta_2\right)=\dfrac{\Gamma(\theta_1+\theta_2)}{\Gamma(\theta_1)\Gamma(\theta_2)}\left(\dfrac{j}{l}\right)^{\delta_1-1}\left(1-\dfrac{j}{l}\right)^{\delta_2-1}$, and $\Gamma(\theta_1)=\displaystyle\int_0^\infty e^{-j/l}\left(\dfrac{j}{l}\right)^{\theta_1-1}$

$d\left(\dfrac{j}{l}\right);\Gamma(\theta_2)=\displaystyle\int_0^\infty e^{-j/l}\left(\dfrac{j}{l}\right)^{\theta_2-1}d\left(\dfrac{j}{l}\right)$

The introduction of the polynomial weight function leads to nonlinear characteristics in the MIDAS model, thus precluding the ordinary least squares (OLS) estimation method. Alternatively, nonlinear least squares (NLS), maximum likelihood estimation (MLE) and generalised method of moments (GMM) estimation methods can be used to estimate the MIDAS model. Among these methods, NLS is most frequently used for parameter estimation due to its stable statistical properties.

7.2.2 The unrestricted MIDAS model

Foroni et al. (2015) derived the U-MIDAS regression model from the general dynamic linear model. It assumes that the left side of the equation is the low-frequency dependent variable y_t. The lag process can be expressed as $B^L y_t = y_{t-1}$, where B^L is the low-frequency lag operator. The right side of the equation is the high-frequency explanatory variable x_τ and its lag process can be expressed as $B^H x_\tau = x_{\tau-1/m}$, where B^H is the high-frequency lag operator. The frequency difference between the high- and low-frequency variables is also expressed as m. Through the process of frequency alignment, the general form of the U-MIDAS regression model can be obtained as follows:

$$y_t = \alpha_0 + \sum_{j=0}^{l}\alpha_j x_{t-j/m-h} + \xi_t \tag{7.7}$$

where ξ_t is a white noise. When $h=0$, Equation defines the contemporaneous relationship between y_t and $x_{t-j/m}$, while when $h>0$, it can be used for h-step ahead forward forecasts where h represents the number of steps.

The model only uses the frequency alignment technique and omits the polynomial weight function, which avoids weight function selection and nonlinear parameter estimation. Parameter estimation can be accomplished with the basic OLS method. However, the forecasting performance of the U-MIDAS model is limited by the frequency difference between the dependent and explanatory variables and thus the model is only effective when the frequency mismatch is small (Foroni et al., 2015). As the number of parameters to be estimated increases with frequency difference, the rising estimation difficulty of the U-MIDAS model results in estimation deviation and overfitting, reducing its generalisability and forecast accuracy.

7.2.3 The MIDAS-AR model

The right side of the basic MIDAS model contains only high-frequency data, ignoring the impact of the lagged dependent variables and other same frequency variables on the forecasts. In fact, forecasting models often include AR terms in the response variable. The introduction of the AR term in the MIDAS model was first proposed by Ghysels et al. (2007) and further elaborated by Clements and Galvão (2008). By adding a low-frequency lag of the dependent variable y_{t-1} to Equation of the basic MIDAS model, we obtain the MIDAS-AR regression model:

$$y_t = \alpha_0 + \lambda y_{t-1} + \alpha_1 B\left(L^m; \theta\right) x_\tau + \xi_t \tag{7.8}$$

The model can be rewritten as:

$$y_t = \alpha_0 (1-\lambda)^{-1} + \alpha_1 (1-\lambda L)^{-1} B\left(L^m; \theta\right) x_\tau + (1-\lambda L)^{-1} \xi_t \tag{7.9}$$

The polynomial acting on the high-frequency explanatory variable x_τ consists of the high-frequency lag operator L^m, the polynomial weight function $B\left(L^m; \theta\right)$, the low-frequency lag operator L. To effectively eliminate seasonal effects, the dynamic autoregressive structure of $(1-\lambda L)$ was introduced in Equation as a common factor by Clements and Galvão (2008):

$$y_t = \alpha_0 + \lambda y_{t-1} + \alpha_1 B\left(L^m; \theta\right)(1-\lambda L) x_\tau + \xi_t \tag{7.10}$$

7.2.4 The Factor (U)-MIDAS models

This chapter aims to generate tourism demand forecasts in Thailand from four source markets by incorporating high-frequency data. There are many other extended forms of the MIDAS model, such as the Factor MIDAS (Marcellino & Schumacher, 2010), the Markov-switching MIDAS (Guérin & Marcellino, 2013), the DCC-MIDAS (Fang et al., 2017) and the GARCH-MIDAS (Xu, Bo, Jiang, & Liu, 2019). When using search engine data in tourism demand forecasting, it is necessary to consider many factors simultaneously, which increases the number of selected keywords. Furthermore, while high-dimensional and high-frequency data provide more available information for accurate forecasting, they also bring the curse of dimensionality.

The factor mixed-frequency model is currently the mainstream method for solving the two modelling problems of frequency mismatch and the curse of dimensionality because it can reduce dimensionality and use the original data without loss of information. The restricted and unrestricted Factor MIDAS models proposed by Marcellino and Schumacher (2010) are the most commonly used methods, and are introduced in this section. The factor mixed-frequency model used in this section can be implemented by a two-step method that first extracts common factors and then builds the mixed-frequency model.

In the first step, a factor augmented model proposed by Stock and Watson (2002) is used to extract common factors from the high-frequency time-series dataset $\mathbf{X}_t$:

$$\mathbf{X}_t = \Lambda\mathbf{F}_t + \mathbf{u}_t \tag{7.11}$$

where $\mathbf{X}_t$ is the N - dimensional vector of endogenous variables, $\mathbf{F}_t$ is the r-dimensional factor vector, the $(N \times r)$ factor loading matrix Λ represents the common components of each variable, and $\mathbf{u}_t$ is a heterogeneous error vector.

In the second step, the extracted factors are embedded in the mixed-frequency model to obtain the Factor MIDAS and Factor U-MIDAS models.

(1) The Factor MIDAS model

The Factor MIDAS model imposes weight constraints on explanatory variables such that each variable has only one coefficient to be estimated. It can be expressed as follows:

$$y_t = \alpha_0 + \sum_{k=1}^{K} \alpha_k B_k\left(L_m; \theta\right) \hat{f}_{k,t-h/m}^{(m)} + \varepsilon_t \tag{7.12}$$

where $B(L_m; \theta) = \sum_{j=0}^{l} w(j; \theta) L^{j/m}$ is the weight lag polynomial and $L^{j/m}$ is the lag operator. The weight lag polynomial of the MIDAS model is often expressed as the following two-parameter exponential Almon polynomial weight function:

$$w(j; \theta) = \frac{e^{\left(\theta_1 j + \theta_2 j^2\right)}}{\sum_{j=1}^{l} e^{\left(\theta_1 j + \theta_2 j^2\right)}} \tag{7.13}$$

(2) The Factor U-MIDAS model

Similar to the difference between the MIDAS and U-MIDAS models, the Factor U-MIDAS model can be expressed as follows:

$$y_t = \alpha_0 + \sum_{k=1}^{K} \sum_{j=0}^{l} \alpha_{k,j} \hat{f}_{k,t-j/m-h}^{(m)} + \xi_t \tag{7.14}$$

where $\left\{ \hat{f}_{k,t-j/m-h}^{(m)} \right\}_{j=0}^{l}$ denotes the low-frequency matrix formed through frequency alignment of the i th high-frequency factor, K is the number of factors, l is the lag order of each factor and h is the forecasting horizon of the explanatory variable.

Through the extraction of common factors from high-frequency variables and datasets, the Factor (U)-MIDAS model can resolve the curse of dimensionality by reducing the number of data dimensions.

7.3 Application

7.3.1 Data

The log transformation of the dependent variable, quarterly tourist arrivals (*Arr*), the log transformation of explanatory variables including real GDP and the relative tourism price of Thai tourism (*price*$_t$) and three seasonal dummy variables (Q1, Q2 and Q3) used in this chapter are consistent with the variables used in this book. Given the availability and generalisability of high-frequency data, monthly search query data are used to test the forecasting performance of MIDAS-type models. Specifically, Baidu Index data, the primary search engine in China, are used to forecast tourism demand in Thailand from mainland China. The daily Baidu Index data are sampled from the beginning of their availability in January 2011 to December 2019. The analyses in this chapter use monthly aggregate Baidu Index data. For the other source markets, Google search query data are used for forecasting from the beginning of their availability in January 2004 to December 2019.

As mentioned, researchers' prior knowledge and intuition are the most common methods of selecting search queries (Brynjolfsson, Geva, & Reichman, 2014; Yang et al., 2015). In this chapter, search queries relate to six aspects of tourism planning: lodging, dining, attractions, transportation, tours and shopping (Li et al., 2018b; Li, Pan et al., 2017; Wen et al., 2021). The same initial search queries are selected for Malaysia, Russia and the USA. Then, the pool of search queries is expanded by adding those that are strongly correlated with the initial keywords using the related queries section of Google Trends. Language requires particular consideration when retrieving data from each source market using the local language. For example, the search term applied to retrieve Google Trend data from Russia should be translated to the local vernacular since the search volume obtained by English keywords is relatively small (Önder & Gunter, 2016). Therefore, the initial search queries are subsequently translated into Russian via Google Translate before being searched. Similarly, the initial keywords are translated into Chinese for Baidu and then expanded by using a demand map interface provided by Baidu. The final search queries used for forecasting tourism demand in Thailand from four source markets are shown in Table 7.1.

7.3.2 Forecasting strategy

A rolling forecasting scheme is used to generate forecasts to align with the forecasting strategy of previous chapters and increase the reliability of the forecasting results. We provide multi-step-ahead rolling forecasts for different forecasting horizons $h = \{1,2,3,4,8\}$. However, setting the window size of the sample somewhat differs from previous chapters due to differences in the availability of the Baidu Index and Google search query data. Google search query data from January 2004 (2004Q1) to December 2014 (2014Q4) are used for modelling while those from January 2015 (2015Q1) to December 2019 (2019Q4) are used for generating forecasts, as in previous

TABLE 7.1 Search queries related to the six aspects of tourism planning

(A) Google search queries used for Malaysia, Russia and the USA			
Tourism	**Thailand tourism**	Shopping	**Thailand shopping***
	Thailand vacation		**Bangkok shopping***
	Thailand weather		**Phuket shopping***
	Bangkok weather	Attractions	**Thailand attractions***
	Phuket weather		Thailand beaches
Transportation	**Thailand airline**	Lodging	**Thailand hotels**
	Thailand airways		**Bangkok hotels**
	Thailand map		**Phuket hotels**
Dinning	**Thailand food**		
	Thailand restaurant		
(B) Baidu search queries used for mainland China			
Tourism	**Thailand tourism**	Dinning	**Thailand speciality**
	Thailand travel tips		**Bangkok Food**
	Thailand weather	Shopping	**Bangkok shopping**
	Bangkok weather	Attractions	**Thailand attractions**
	Thailand self-guided tour tips		Thailand tourists attractions
	Phuket weather		Taj Mahal
Transportation	**Thailand airline**		Phuket
	Thailand airways	Lodging	**Thailand hotels**
	Thailand map		**Bangkok hotels**
	Thailand airport		**Phuket hotels**

Note: Keywords in bold indicate the seed keywords specified; "*" indicates that the keyword cannot be found in Google Trends when the search occurs in Russia.

chapters. Baidu Index data from January 2011 (2011Q1) to December 2016 (2016Q4) are used for modelling and data from January 2017 (2017Q1) to December 2019 (2019Q4) are used for forecasting because of data limit.

The basic MIDAS and U-MIDAS models should have been added as benchmarks, but the curse of dimensionality caused by the large number of keywords and the limited dataset made these models ineffective. Therefore, the seasonal naïve (SNAIVE) model, the seasonal autoregressive integrated moving average (SARIMA) model, the exponential smoothing (ETS) model and the low-frequency Factor OLS model are used as benchmarks to test the forecasting performance of the other MIDAS-type models. In addition, the mean absolute percentage error (MAPE), root mean square error (RMSE) and mean absolute scaled error (MASE) are used to evaluate forecast accuracy. The maximum lag of the explanatory variables is set to 3, and the two-parameter exponential Almon polynomial weight function is used, as suggested by Ghysels et al. (2007).

7.3.3 Empirical results

The multi-step-ahead rolling forecasting results of tourism demand in Thailand from the USA are shown in Table 7.2. The SARIMA model performs well at very short-term forecasting horizons. As the forecasting horizon extends, the MIDAS-type models perform better than the benchmark models, which confirms the findings of previous studies that search queries provide useful information for forecasting tourism demand (Bangwayo-Skeete & Skeete, 2015). Furthermore, the performance of the Factor U-MIDAS model is superior to that of the Factor MIDAS model for three- and eight-step-ahead forecasts in terms of MAPE and MASE. These results confirm the finding of Foroni et al. (2015) that the forecasting performance of the U-MIDAS model may exceed that of the MIDAS model when the maximum number of lags of high-frequency data and the differences in sampling frequencies are sufficiently small.

The one- to eight-step-ahead forecasting results of tourism demand in Thailand from Russia are shown in Table 7.3. Although the MAPE results show that the SNAIVE model performs well in almost all cases, the MIDAS-type models outperform the benchmark models in short-term and long-term forecasting in terms of RMSE and MASE. These results indicate that large error terms may be produced by the SNAIVE model in some forecast periods, as outliers can significantly affect the RMSE (Fildes, 1992; Fildes, Wei, & Ismail, 2011). The forecasting results in the case of Russia indicate that the MIDAS-type models can improve the long-term forecast accuracy by directly estimating variables sampled at different frequencies.

Tables 7.4 and 7.5 show the forecasting results of tourism demand in Thailand from Malaysia and mainland China using Google Trends and

TABLE 7.2 Forecasting performance for tourist arrivals from the USA to Thailand

	Forecasting horizon				
	1	2	3	4	8
MAPE (%)					
SNAIVE	5.703	5.563	5.098	4.839	9.991
ETS	4.238	3.371	4.049	5.210	10.266
SARIMA	2.139	2.752	3.860	3.889	7.694
Factor OLS	6.304	4.859	4.282	3.558	7.204
Factor U-MIDAS	3.766	3.612	2.969	3.119	5.565
Factor MIDAS	4.416	3.915	3.516	3.099	6.068
RMSE					
SNAIVE	17,100	16,757	15,602	15,539	32,289
ETS	13,164	11,093	15,184	16,889	33,369
SARIMA	8,791	10,342	12,543	14,091	27,491
Factor OLS	19,333	16,039	20,369	11,726	22,618
Factor U-MIDAS	11,971	14,376	11,531	10,443	19,437
Factor MIDAS	13,884	13,924	13,934	10,529	20,948
MASE					
SNAIVE	0.898	0.874	0.817	0.806	1.738
ETS	0.658	0.532	0.662	0.878	1.791
SARIMA	0.338	0.424	0.617	0.642	1.338
Factor OLS	0.984	0.755	0.729	0.574	1.230
Factor U-MIDAS	0.574	0.599	0.485	0.504	0.979
Factor MIDAS	0.680	0.614	0.576	0.493	1.074

TABLE 7.3 Forecasting performance for tourist arrivals from Russia to Thailand

	Forecasting horizon				
	1	2	3	4	8
MAPE (%)					
SNAIVE	9.800	8.259	7.474	7.783	13.722
ETS	12.641	12.990	7.634	8.662	18.965
SARIMA	13.769	17.054	10.568	11.410	18.613
Factor OLS	10.971	15.632	14.190	15.289	28.230
Factor U-MIDAS	10.173	15.603	12.497	11.879	22.730
Factor MIDAS	9.844	12.545	11.230	10.040	17.456
RMSE					
SNAIVE	60,723	49,666	50,755	53,441	72,672
ETS	55,331	57,840	34,753	47,745	70,403
SARIMA	57,133	64,421	50,679	56,255	58,813
Factor OLS	47,819	70,468	69,174	69,992	124,770

(*Continued*)

Forecasting horizon

	1	2	3	4	8
Factor U-MIDAS	42,126	66,724	66,566	40,641	57,880
Factor MIDAS	44,001	59,930	63,114	43,055	56,216
MASE					
SNAIVE	0.627	0.496	0.487	0.527	0.936
ETS	0.731	0.667	0.432	0.527	0.998
SARIMA	0.768	0.798	0.572	0.705	0.849
Factor OLS	0.594	0.884	0.748	0.905	1.581
Factor U-MIDAS	0.531	0.839	0.658	0.545	0.820
Factor MIDAS	0.533	0.705	0.618	0.545	0.785

TABLE 7.4 Forecasting performance for tourist arrivals from Malaysia to Thailand

	Forecasting horizon				
	1	2	3	4	8
MAPE (%)					
SNAIVE	7.859	7.559	7.349	8.114	18.818
ETS	7.612	9.149	11.961	11.091	17.184
SARIMA	9.565	8.403	10.906	9.065	15.940
Factor OLS	7.519	6.807	7.495	8.979	8.721
Factor U-MIDAS	7.200	5.688	7.831	9.952	7.537
Factor MIDAS	7.147	5.982	7.637	9.341	6.483
RMSE					
SNAIVE	114,911	117,014	119,366	125,817	227,894
ETS	88,747	111,056	150,652	136,170	216,052
SARIMA	115,473	124,150	146,510	123,694	206,094
Factor OLS	76,178	80,329	86,711	103,271	118,707
Factor U-MIDAS	73,526	67,057	85,096	110,387	88,178
Factor MIDAS	72,515	69,176	81,597	100,954	80,119
MASE					
SNAIVE	0.925	0.917	0.905	1.000	2.436
ETS	0.869	1.064	1.403	1.313	2.242
SARIMA	1.088	1.041	1.332	1.118	2.099
Factor OLS	0.825	0.781	0.876	1.048	1.158
Factor U-MIDAS	0.777	0.642	0.879	1.164	0.964
Factor MIDAS	0.760	0.673	0.855	1.082	0.839

Baidu Index data, respectively. The performance of the MIDAS-type models exceeds that of other benchmarks across almost all forecasting horizons, illustrating the sustained stability of these models as the forecasting horizon extends. The forecast results also demonstrate that the

TABLE 7.5 Forecasting performance for tourist arrivals from mainland China to Thailand

	Forecasting horizons				
	1	2	3	4	8
MAPE (%)					
SNAIVE	13.194	13.683	15.039	15.606	14.882
ETS	10.403	17.555	15.973	20.327	14.971
SARIMA	13.336	21.466	28.469	30.183	42.790
Factor OLS	17.582	19.618	10.145	12.621	15.895
Factor U-MIDAS	10.510	12.679	6.940	15.340	18.527
Factor MIDAS	11.176	9.179	13.176	16.745	15.081
RMSE					
SNAIVE	435,305	451,019	473,032	490,637	465,626
ETS	332,511	549,552	467,524	652,590	466,131
SARIMA	441,046	622,911	856,296	879,481	1,200,052
Factor OLS	590,427	701,317	397,136	431,332	472,194
Factor U-MIDAS	328,692	393,352	270,101	480,094	575,418
Factor MIDAS	349,788	322,825	635,814	599,474	401,767
MASE					
SNAIVE	0.840	0.875	0.961	0.996	0.926
ETS	0.632	1.051	1.025	1.287	0.932
SARIMA	0.862	1.349	1.783	1.866	2.678
Factor OLS	1.089	1.319	0.664	0.786	0.983
Factor U-MIDAS	0.651	0.767	0.442	0.962	1.215
Factor MIDAS	0.686	0.556	0.843	1.020	0.962

information contained in search query data from both Google Trends and the Baidu Index improves tourism demand forecasting. Overall, the empirical results demonstrate the robustness and validity of the forecasting performance of MIDAS-type models for all source markets.

7.4 Conclusion and future directions

This chapter presents tourism demand forecasting with data sampled at different frequencies. The MIDAS models can directly accommodate variables sampled at different frequencies. They are a simple, parsimonious and flexible class of time-series models that allow the left- and right-hand side variables of the regression to be sampled at different frequencies.

This chapter provides an overview of various MIDAS techniques in tourism demand forecasting, followed by an empirical study to test the performance of these models. As in previous chapters, mainland China, Malaysia, Russia and the USA are selected as source markets to forecast tourism demand in Thailand. Monthly Baidu Index data are used to forecast tourism demand in Thailand from mainland China and monthly Google search query data are used to forecast tourism demand in Thailand from the other source markets. The empirical results show that the MIDAS-type models outperform the benchmark models in almost all cases, which confirms that MIDAS-type models are effective tools to increase forecast accuracy and decrease forecast failure risk when using data sampled at different frequencies. The results have important implications for future research, as high-frequency data related to people's behaviours in searching for tourism information is becoming freely available with the widespread use of the internet. To forecast tourism demand using these high-frequency data, it is important to account for mixed-frequency models. This chapter thus provides a framework for readers who would like to use mixed-frequency data for tourism demand forecasting.

Various possibilities should be considered in future research. First, only two types of high-frequency search query data are used in this chapter to test the performance of MIDAS-type models. Future researchers could consider other forms of big data, such as online review data, which may be useful for tourism demand forecasting. Second, only monthly search query data are used to forecast tourism demand to ensure the consistency of data frequency across different source markets. Weekly, daily and hourly data could also be considered for use in future research. Third, the short sampling period and long-term forecasts limit the maximum lag order setting for the explanatory variables in the model, as Baidu Index data are only available since 2011. Various possibilities for parameter settings could be considered in future studies.

Self-study questions

1   List and discuss the differences between the mixed-frequency models provided in this chapter.
2   Combine R code provided in this chapter to discuss why the maximum lag order setting for explanatory variables is limited in this chapter.
3   Modify the code to substitute polynomial weight functions other than the exponential Almon polynomial function that can be applied in the MIDAS model, and discuss the influence of different polynomial weight functions on the forecasting results.
4   In practice, do any particular mixed-frequency models outperform others?

References

Almon, S. (1965). The distributed lag between capital appropriations and expenditures. *Econometrica: Journal of the Econometric Society, 33*(1), 178–196. https://doi.org/https://doi.org/10.2307/1911894

Andreou, E., Ghysels, E., & Kourtellos, A. (2013). Should macroeconomic forecasters use daily financial data and how? *Journal of Business & Economic Statistics, 31*(2), 240–251. https://doi.org/10.1080/07350015.2013.767199

Bangwayo-Skeete, P. F., & Skeete, R. W. (2015). Can Google data improve the forecasting performance of tourist arrivals? Mixed-data sampling approach. *Tourism Management, 46*, 454–464. https://doi.org/10.1016/j.tourman.2014.07.014

Barsoum, F., & Stankiewicz, S. (2015). Forecasting GDP growth using mixed-frequency models with switching regimes. *International Journal of Forecasting, 31*(1), 33–50. https://doi.org/10.1016/j.ijforecast.2014.04.002

Baumeister, C., Guérin, P., & Kilian, L. (2015). Do high-frequency financial data help forecast oil prices? The MIDAS touch at work. *International Journal of Forecasting, 31*(2), 238–252. https://doi.org/https://doi.org/10.1016/j.ijforecast.2014.06.005

Berthon, P. R., Pitt, L. F., Plangger, K., & Shapiro, D. (2012). Marketing meets Web 2.0, social media, and creative consumers: Implications for international marketing strategy. *Business Horizons, 55*(3), 261–271. https://doi.org/https://doi.org/10.1016/j.bushor.2012.01.007

Brave, S. A., Butters, R. A., & Justiniano, A. (2019). Forecasting economic activity with mixed frequency BVARs. *International Journal of Forecasting, 35*(4), 1692–1707. https://doi.org/https://doi.org/10.1016/j.ijforecast.2019.02.010

Brynjolfsson, E., Geva, T., & Reichman, S. (2014). Using crowd-based data selection to improve the predictive power of search trend data. Paper presented at the International Conference on Information Systems (ICIS 2014), Auckland, New Zealand.

Chen, H., Chiang, R. H., & Storey, V. C. (2012). Business intelligence and analytics: From big data to big impact. *MIS Quarterly, 36*(4), 1165–1188. https://doi.org/https://doi.org/10.2307/41703503

Choi, H., & Varian, H. A. L. (2012). Predicting the present with Google Trends. *Economic Record, 88*, 2–9. https://doi.org/https://doi.org/10.1111/j.1475-4932.2012.00809.x

Clements, M. P., & Galvão, A. B. (2008). Macroeconomic forecasting with mixed-frequency data. *Journal of Business & Economic Statistics, 26*(4), 546–554. https://doi.org/https://doi.org/10.1198/073500108000000015

Engle, R. F., Ghysels, E., & Sohn, B. (2013). Stock market volatility and macroeconomic fundamentals. *Review of Economics and Statistics, 95*(3), 776–797. https://doi.org/https://doi.org/10.1162/REST_a_00300

Fang, L., Yu, H., & Li, L. (2017). The effect of economic policy uncertainty on the long-term correlation between US stock and bond markets. *Economic Modelling, 66*, 139–145. https://doi.org/10.1016/j.econmod.2017.06.007

Fesenmaier, D. R., Xiang, Z., Pan, B., & Law, R. (2010). A framework of search engine use for travel planning. *Journal of Travel Research, 50*(6), 587–601. https://doi.org/https://doi.org/10.1177/0047287510385466

Fildes, R. (1992). The evaluation of extrapolative forecasting methods. *International Journal of Forecasting, 8*(1), 81–98. https://doi.org/https://doi.org/10.1016/0169-2070(92)90009-X

Fildes, R., Wei, Y., & Ismail, S. (2011). Evaluating the forecasting performance of econometric models of air passenger traffic flows using multiple error measures. *International Journal of Forecasting, 27*(3), 902–922. https://doi.org/https://doi.org/10.1016/j.ijforecast.2009.06.002

Foroni, C., & Marcellino, M. (2014). A comparison of mixed frequency approaches for nowcasting Euro area macroeconomic aggregates. *International Journal of Forecasting, 30*(3), 554–568. https://doi.org/10.1016/j.ijforecast.2013.01.010

Foroni, C., Marcellino, M., & Schumacher, C. (2015). Unrestricted mixed data sampling (MIDAS): MIDAS regressions with unrestricted lag polynomials. *Journal of the Royal Statistical Society: Series A (Statistics in Society), 178*(1), 57–82.

Ghysels, E., & Ozkan, N. (2015). Real-time forecasting of the US federal government budget: A simple mixed frequency data regression approach. *International Journal of Forecasting, 31*(4), 1009–1020. https://doi.org/10.1016/j.ijforecast.2014.12.008

Ghysels, E., Santa-Clara, P., & Valkanov, R. (2004). The MIDAS touch: Mixed data sampling regression models. *CIRANO Working Paper.*

Ghysels, E., Sinko, A., & Valkanov, R. (2007). MIDAS regressions: Further results and new directions. *Econometric Reviews, 26*(1), 53–90. https://doi.org/10.1080/07474930600972467

Ghysels, E., Valkanov, R. I., & Serrano, A. R. (2009). Multi-period forecasts of volatility: Direct, iterated, and mixed-data approaches. *Working paper, Department of Economics, UNC at Chapel Hill.*

Guérin, P., & Marcellino, M. (2013). Markov-Switching MIDAS Models. *Journal of Business & Economic Statistics, 31*(1), 45–56. https://doi.org/10.1080/07350015.2012.727721

Havranek, T., & Zeynalov, A. (2021). Forecasting tourist arrivals: Google Trends meets mixed-frequency data. *Tourism Economics, 27*(1), 129–148. https://doi.org/10.1177/1354816619879584

Kuzin, V., Marcellino, M., & Schumacher, C. (2011). MIDAS vs. mixed-frequency VAR: Nowcasting GDP in the euro area. *International Journal of Forecasting, 27*(2), 529–542. https://doi.org/10.1016/j.ijforecast.2010.02.006

Li, J., Xu, L., Tang, L., Wang, S., & Li, L. (2018a). Big data in tourism research: A literature review. *Tourism Management, 68*, 301–323. https://doi.org/https://doi.org/10.1016/j.tourman.2018.03.009

Li, S., Chen, T., Wang, L., & Ming, C. (2018b). Effective tourist volume forecasting supported by PCA and improved BPNN using Baidu index. *Tourism Management, 68*, 116–126. https://doi.org/https://doi.org/10.1016/j.tourman.2018.03.006

Li, X., Law, R., Xie, G., & Wang, S. (2021). Review of tourism forecasting research with internet data. *Tourism Management, 83*, 104245. https://doi.org/https://doi.org/10.1016/j.tourman.2020.104245

Li, X., Pan, B., Law, R., & Huang, X. K. (2017). Forecasting tourism demand with composite search index. *Tourism Management, 59*, 57–66. https://doi.org/https://doi.org/10.1016/j.tourman.2016.07.005

Li, X., Shang, W., Wang, S., & Ma, J. (2015). A MIDAS modelling framework for Chinese inflation index forecast incorporating Google search data. *Electronic Commerce Research and Applications, 14*(2), 112–125. https://doi.org/10.1016/j.elerap.2015.01.001

Liu, H., Liu, Y., Li, G., & Wen, L. (2021). Tourism demand nowcasting using a LASSO-MIDAS model. *International Journal of Contemporary Hospitality Management, 33*(6), 1922–1949. https://doi.org/https://doi.org/10.1108/IJCHM-06-2020-0589

Liu, H., Liu, Y., & Wang, Y. (2021). Exploring the influence of economic policy uncertainty on the relationship between tourism and economic growth with an

MF-VAR model. *Tourism Economics, 27*(5), 1081–1100. https://doi.org/https://doi.org/10.1177/1354816620921298

Liu, H., & Song, H. (2018). New evidence of dynamic links between tourism and economic growth based on mixed-frequency Granger causality tests.*Journal of Travel Research, 57*(7), 899–907. https://doi.org/https://doi.org/10.1177/0047287517723531

Marcellino, M., & Schumacher, C. (2010). Factor MIDAS for nowcasting and forecasting with ragged-edge data: A model comparison for German GDP. *Oxford Bulletin of Economics and Statistics, 72*(4), 518–550. https://doi.org/10.1111/j.1468-0084.2010.00591.x

Mariano, R. S., & Murasawa, Y. (2010). A coincident index, common factors, and monthly real GDP. *Oxford Bulletin of Economics and Statistics, 72*(1), 27–46. https://doi.org/10.1111/j.1468-0084.2009.00567.x

Miller, J. I. (2014). Mixed-frequency cointegrating regressions with parsimonious distributed lag structures. *Journal of Financial Econometrics, 12*(3), 584–614. https://doi.org/10.1093/jjfinec/nbt010

Mittnik, S., & Zadrozny, P. (2005). Forecasting quarterly German GDP at monthly intervals using monthly IFO business conditions data. In J.-E. Sturm & T. Wollmershäuser (Eds.), *Ifo survey data in business cycle and monetary policy analysis* (pp. 19–48): Springer-Verlag. https://doi.org/10.1007/3-7908-1605-1_2

Monteforte, L., & Moretti, G. (2013). Real-time forecasts of inflation: The role of financial variables. *Journal of Forecasting, 32*(1), 51–61. https://doi.org/10.1002/for.1250

Nakajima, Y., & Sueishi, N. (2020). Forecasting the Japanese macroeconomy using high-dimensional data. *The Japanese Economic Review*, forthcoming. https://doi.org/10.1007/s42973-020-00041-z

Önder, I., & Gunter, U. (2016). Forecasting tourism demand with Google Trends for a major European city destination. *Tourism Analysis, 21*(2–3), 203–220. https://doi.org/https://doi.org/10.3727/108354216X14559233984773

Pan, B., Wu, D. C., & Song, H. (2012). Forecasting hotel room demand using search engine data. *Journal of Hospitality and Tourism Technology, 3*(3), 196–210. https://doi.org/https://doi.org/10.1108/17579881211264486

Pan, B., & Yang, Y. (2016). Forecasting destination weekly hotel occupancy with big data. *Journal of Travel Research, 56*(7), 957–970. https://doi.org/https://doi.org/10.1177/0047287516669050

Pan, Z., Wang, Q., Wang, Y., & Yang, L. (2018). Forecasting US real GDP using oil prices: A time-varying parameter MIDAS model. *Energy Economics, 72*, 177–187. https://doi.org/10.1016/j.eneco.2018.04.008

Rivera, R. (2016). A dynamic linear model to forecast hotel registrations in Puerto Rico using Google Trends data. *Tourism Management, 57*, 12–20. https://doi.org/https://doi.org/10.1016/j.tourman.2016.04.008

Schorfheide, F., & Song, D. (2015). Real-time forecasting with a mixed-frequency VAR. *Journal of Business & Economic Statistics, 33*(3), 366–380. https://doi.org/https://doi.org/10.1080/07350015.2014.954707

Schorfheide, F., & Song, D. (2020). Real-time forecasting with a (standard) mixed-frequency VAR during a pandemic. *FRB of Philadelphia Working Paper No. 20–26*. https://doi.org/http://dx.doi.org/10.21799/frbp.wp.2020.26

Song, H., & Li, G. (2008). Tourism demand modelling and forecasting - A review of recent research. *Tourism Management, 29*(2), 203–220. https://doi.org/https://doi.org/10.1016/j.tourman.2007.07.016

Song, H., & Witt, S. F. (2006). Forecasting international tourist flows to Macau. *Tourism Management, 27*(2), 214–224. https://doi.org/https://doi.org/10.1016/j. tourman.2004.09.004

Stock, J. H., & Watson, M. W. (2002). Forecasting using principal components from a large number of predictors. *Journal of the American Statistical Association, 97*(460), 1167–1179. https://doi.org/10.1198/016214502388618960

Sun, S., Wei, Y., Tsui, K.-L., & Wang, S. (2019). Forecasting tourist arrivals with machine learning and internet search index. *Tourism Management, 70*, 1–10. https://doi.org/10.1016/j.tourman.2018.07.010

Wen, L., Liu, C., & Song, H. (2019). Forecasting tourism demand using search query data: A hybrid modelling approach. *Tourism Economics, 25*(3), 309–329. https://doi.org/10.1177/1354816618768317

Wen, L., Liu, C., Song, H., & Liu, H. (2021). Forecasting tourism demand with an improved mixed data sampling model. *Journal of Travel Research, 60*(2), 336–353. https://doi.org/10.1177/0047287520906220

Winschel, V., & Krätzig, M. (2010). Solving, estimating, and selecting nonlinear dynamic models without the curse of dimensionality. *Econometrica, 78*(2), 803–821. https://doi.org/10.3982/ECTA6297

Wu, D. C., Song, H., & Shen, S. (2017). New developments in tourism and hotel demand modeling and forecasting. *International Journal of Contemporary Hospitality Management, 29*(1), 507–529. https://doi.org/10.1108/IJCHM-05-2015-0249

Xiang, Z., Schwartz, Z., Gerdes, J. H., & Uysal, M. (2015). What can big data and text analytics tell us about hotel guest experience and satisfaction? *International Journal of Hospitality Management, 44*, 120–130. https://doi.org/10.1016/j. ijhm.2014.10.013

Xu, Q., Bo, Z., Jiang, C., & Liu, Y. (2019). Does Google search index really help predicting stock market volatility? Evidence from a modified mixed data sampling model on volatility. *Knowledge-Based Systems, 166*, 170–185. https://doi. org/10.1016/j.knosys.2018.12.025

Xu, X., & Reed, M. (2017). Perceived pollution and inbound tourism in China. *Tourism Management Perspectives, 21*, 109–112. https://doi.org/10.1016/j. tmp.2016.12.006

Yang, X., Pan, B., Evans, J. A., & Lv, B. (2015). Forecasting Chinese tourist volume with search engine data. *Tourism Management, 46*, 386–397. https://doi. org/10.1016/j.tourman.2014.07.019

Zadrozny, P. (1988). Gaussian likelihood of continuous-time ARMAX models when data are stocks and flows at different frequencies. *Econometric Theory, 4*(1), 108–124. https://doi.org/https://doi.org/10.1017/S0266466600011890

APPENDIX

R CODE

```
############################################################
  # Contents:
  # 1.  Initialize
  # 2.  Sub function
  # 3.  Read data
  # 4.  Set parameters
  # 5.  Rolling forecast
  # 6.  Results
############################################################

############################################################
  # 1.  Initialize
############################################################
  setwd() # Users need to add their own paths
  getwd()
  rm(list=ls())
  start.time <- proc.time()[3]

  library(midasr)
  library(forecast)
  library(RSpectra)
  library(zoo)

  set.seed(20220120)

############################################################
  # 2.  Sub-function
############################################################
  # (1) Data standardization
```

```
fNorm <- function(mX){
  N <- ncol(mX)
  T <- nrow(mX)
  mXnorm <- mX
  vm <- numeric(N)
  vs <- vm

  for (j in 1:N){
    vX <- mXnorm[,j]
    m <- mean(vX, na.rm = TRUE)
    s <- sd(vX, na.rm = TRUE)
    vX <- (vX - m) / s
    mXnorm[,j] <- vX
    vm[j] <- m
    vs[j] <- s
  }
  return (list(mXnorm,vm,vs))
}

# (2) Function of factor estimation
factorest <- function(mK,r) {
  T <- nrow(mK)
  N <- ncol(mK)
  eig <- eigs _ sym(mK%*%t(mK), r, which = "LM", sigma =
NULL, lower = TRUE)
  # veigval <- eig$values
  meigvec <- eig$vectors
  Ftil <- sqrt(T) * meigvec # estimated factors
  Ftil <- as.matrix(Ftil)
  Lamtil <- 1/T * t(mK) %*% Ftil
  Rsdm <- mK - Ftil %*% t(Lamtil)
  Rsd <- 1/N * 1/T * sum(diag(t(Rsdm)%*%Rsdm))
  return(list(Ftil,Lamtil,Rsd))
}

# (3) BNIC function for selecting the best factor number
BNic2 <- function(data,maxrrr){
  TT <- nrow(data)
  NN <- ncol(data)

  Cnt <- min(sqrt(TT),sqrt(NN))
  ICp2v <- numeric(maxrrr)

  rrr <- 1
  while (rrr <= maxrrr) {
    facrsd <- factorest(data,rrr)
    Rsd <- facrsd[[3]]
    ICp2 <- log(Rsd) + rrr * (NN+TT)/(NN*TT) * log(Cnt^2)
```

```
      ICp2v[rrr] <- ICp2
      rrr <- rrr + 1
    }
    rrhat2 <- which.min(ICp2v)
    return(rrhat2)
  }

###############################################################
  # 3. Read data
###############################################################
  Monthly <- read.csv(file = "THA _ USA _ Monthly.csv", string-
sAsFactors = FALSE)

  Quarterly <- read.csv(file = "THA _ USA.csv", stringsAsFac-
tors = FALSE)

  VA <- Quarterly[ ,c("Date", "Arr")]; VA$Arr <- log(VA$Arr);
  X.Q <- Quarterly[ ,c("Date", "GDP", "P _ D")]; X.Q$GDP <- log(X.
Q$GDP); X.Q$P _ D <- log(X.Q$P _ D);
  XQ.dummy <- Quarterly[,c("Q1","Q2","Q3")]

###############################################################
  # 4. Set parameters
###############################################################
  m <- 3 # frequency ratio:m
  lags <- 3 # maximum lag orders:l

  # dependent variable
  insam.x <- c(which(Monthly$Date=="2004M4"): which(Monthly$-
Date=="2016M9")) # including lags
  insam.qx    <-    c(which(X.Q$Date=="2004Q4"):    which(X.
Q$Date=="2016Q3"))

  # explanatory variable
  insam.y    <-    c(which(VA$Date=="2005Q1"):    which(VA$-
Date=="2016Q4")) # 1-step-ahead
  outsam.y    <-    c(which(VA$Date=="2017Q1"):
which(VA$Date=="2019Q4"))

  roltim <- length(outsam.y)
  lnY = ts(VA[which(VA$Date=="2005Q1"):nrow(VA),]$Arr, freq =
4, start = c(2005, 1)) # used to calculate the MAPE value

###############################################################
  # 5. Rolling forecast
###############################################################
  # (1) setup the storage space
```

```
  forecasts.snaive  <-  forecasts.sarima  <-  forecasts.ets  <-
forecasts.fols  <-  forecasts.fumidas  <-  forecasts.fmidas  <-
Y0.h <- matrix(NA,12,8)
  colnames(forecasts.snaive)      <-      colnames(forecasts.sa-
rima)<- colnames(forecasts.ets)  <-  colnames(forecasts.fols)
<- colnames(forecasts.fumidas)  <-  colnames(forecasts.fmidas)
<- paste0("h=",1:8)

  rownames(forecasts.snaive)      <-      rownames(forecasts.sa-
rima)<- rownames(forecasts.ets)  <-  rownames(forecasts.fols)
<- rownames(forecasts.fumidas)  <-  rownames(forecasts.fmidas)
<- paste(rep(2017:2019,each=4), paste0("Q",1:4))

  # (2) rolling window
  # (1) SNaive, SARIMA, and ETS model
  N <- nrow(VA[which(VA$Date=="2005Q1"):nrow(VA),])
  Y <- ts(VA[which(VA$Date=="2005Q1"):nrow(VA),]$Arr, freq = 4,
start = c(2005, 1))

  for (i in 12:1) {
    endi = N - i
    Y0 = tail(head(Y, endi),48)
    # SARIMA forecasting
    fit.sarima = auto.arima(Y0)
    fc.sarima = forecast(Y0, model = fit.sarima, h = i)

    # ETS forecasting
    fit.ets = ets(Y0)
    fc.ets = forecast(Y0,
                model = fit.ets,
                use.initial.values = TRUE,
                h = i)

    # Seasonal Naive forecasting
    fc.snaive = snaive(Y0, h = i)

    for (j in 1:8) {
      if ((12 - i + j) > 12)
        break
      forecasts.sarima[(12 - i + j), j] = fc.sarima$mean[j]
      forecasts.ets[(12 - i + j), j] = fc.ets$mean[j]
      forecasts.snaive[(12 - i + j), j] = fc.snaive$mean[j]
      Y0.h[(12 - i + j), j] = Y[endi + j]
    }
  }
```

```
# (2.2) Factor OLS, Factor UMIDAS and Factor MIDAS model
for (h in 1:8){ # h-step-ahead forecast

  for (a in 1:(roltim-h+1)){
    # split the sample into insample and out-of-sample
    # dependent variable
    in.y <- (insam.y + h - 1) + a - 1
    out.y <- in.y[1]:(max(in.y) + 1)

    # inpendent variable
    in.mx <-  insam.x + (a-1)*m
    out.mx <- in.mx[1]:(max(in.mx) + m)

    in.qx <- insam.qx + a-1
    out.qx <- in.qx[1]:(max(in.qx) + 1)

    # insample and out-of-sample data
    xm.in <- Monthly[in.mx, ]
    xm.out <- Monthly[out.mx, ]

    xq.in <- cbind(X.Q[in.qx, -ncol(X.Q)], X.Q$GDP[in.qx-1],
X.Q$P _ D[in.qx], X.Q$P _ D[in.qx-1])
    xq.out <- cbind(X.Q[out.qx, -ncol(X.Q)], X.Q$GDP[out.qx-1],
X.Q$P _ D[out.qx], X.Q$P _ D[out.qx-1])
    colnames(xq.in)  <- colnames(xq.out) <- c("Date", "GDP",
"GDP.l1", "P _ D", "P _ D.l1")

    ylags.in <- cbind(VA[in.qx, ], VA$Arr[in.qx-1], VA$Arr[in.
qx-2])
    ylags.out <- cbind(VA[out.qx, ], VA$Arr[out.qx-1], VA$Ar-
r[out.qx-2])
    colnames(ylags.in)  <- colnames(ylags.out) <- c("Date",
"ylags.1", "ylags.2", "ylags.3")

    y.in  <- VA[in.y, ]
    y.out <- VA[out.y, ]

  ####################### FA-OLS model #######################
    xmin.ols <- rollapply(xm.in[ ,-1], width = 3, mean, by = 3)
    xmout.ols <- rollapply(xm.out[ ,-1], width = 3, mean,
by = 3)

    # decide the number of factors
    rhat <- 1

    # extract factor from variables
```

```
      inF.ols <- as.matrix(factorest(fNorm(xmin.ols)[[1]], rhat)
[[1]])
        outF.ols <- as.matrix(factorest(fNorm(xmout.ols)[[1]],
rhat)[[1]])

      inF.ols <- mls(inF.ols, 0:(lags-1), 1); outF.ols <- mls(outF.
ols, 0:(lags-1), 1);
        xin.ols <- as.matrix(cbind(tail(inF.ols, length(in.y)),
xq.in[ ,-1], ylags.in[ ,-1], XQ.dummy[in.qx,]))
      xout.ols <- as.matrix(cbind(tail(outF.ols, length(out.y)),
xq.out[ ,-1], ylags.out[ ,-1], XQ.dummy[out.qx,]))

      FOLS.reg <- lm(y.in$Arr ~., data=data.frame(xin.ols))

      pre.ols <- FOLS.reg$coefficients[1] + tail(xout.ols, 1)
%*% FOLS.reg$coefficients[-1] # predict(FOLS.reg, newdata =
data.frame(tail(xout.ols,1)))
      forecasts.fols[a+h-1, h] <- pre.ols

  ###################### FA-UMIDAS model #################
#####
      # Extracted factors
      inF <- as.matrix(fNorm(xm.in[ ,-1])[[1]])
      outF <- as.matrix(fNorm(xm.out[ ,-1])[[1]])

      # decide the number of factors
      rhat <- 1 # BNic2(inF,1)

      # construct the factors
      inF <- as.matrix(factorest(inF, rhat)[[1]])
      outF <- as.matrix(factorest(outF, rhat)[[1]])

      inF.l <- matrix(NA, nrow(inF)/m, ncol(inF)*(lags))
      outF.l <- matrix(NA, nrow(outF)/m, ncol(outF)*(lags))

      inF.l[ ,1:lags] <- mls(inF, 0:(lags-1), m)
      outF.l[ ,1:lags] <- mls(outF, 0:(lags-1), m)

      xin.all <- as.matrix(cbind(tail(inF.l, length(in.y)),
xq.in[, -1], ylags.in[, -1], XQ.dummy[in.qx, ]))
        xout.all <- as.matrix(cbind(tail(outF.l, length(out.y)),
xq.out[, -1], ylags.out[, -1], XQ.dummy[out.qx, ]))

      FUMIDAS.reg <- lm(y.in$Arr ~., data=data.frame(xin.all))

      pre.faumidas <- FUMIDAS.reg$coefficients[1] + tail(xout.
all, 1) %*% FUMIDAS.reg$coefficients[-1]
```

```
        forecasts.fumidas[a+h-1, h] <- pre.faumidas

####################### FA-MIDAS model ################
########
        iniv <- numeric(rhat*2)

        ini1 <- 1
         odd <- seq(1, length(iniv), 2); even <- seq(2, length
(iniv), 2)
        iniv[odd] <- 1
        iniv[even] <- -3

        # the data used for MIDAS model
        new.l <- (in.qx[1] - (nrow(inF)/m - length(in.y))):max(in.qx)
      yy <- VA$Arr[(in.y[1] - (nrow(inF)/m - length(in.y))):max(in.y)]
        xq.in.midas <- X.Q[new.l, ]; ylags.in.midas <- VA[new.l, ];
    xq.in.dummy <- XQ.dummy[new.l, ];

        # the estimation of the Factor MIDAS model
        FMIDAS <- midas_r(yy ~ mls(inF, 0:(lags-1), 3, nealmon)
+ mls(xq.in.midas[ ,"GDP"], 0:1, 1, "*") + mls(xq.in.midas[
,"P_D"], 0:1, 1, "*") + mls(ylags.in.midas[ ,"Arr"], 0:2, 1, "*")
+ mls(xq.in.dummy[ ,"Q1"], 0, 1,"*") + mls(xq.in.dummy[ ,"Q2"],
0, 1,"*") + mls(xq.in.dummy[ ,"Q3"], 0, 1,"*"),
                        start = list(inF = c(ini1, iniv[1:2])))

        estconst <- FMIDAS$opt$par[1]
        estalmonp <- FMIDAS$opt$par[2:(3*rhat+1)]
        esty <- FMIDAS$opt$par[(3*rhat+2):length(FMIDAS$opt$par)]

        # Weight function
        fun <- nealmon(p=estalmonp, d=lags)
         pre.famidas <- t(as.matrix(c(estconst, fun, esty))) %*%
as.matrix(c(1, tail(xout.all, 1)))

        forecasts.fmidas[a+h-1, h] <- pre.famidas

    }

  }
  #########################################################
  # 6. Results ###########################################
  res.sarima = exp(forecasts.sarima) - exp(Y0.h)
  res.ets = exp(forecasts.ets) - exp(Y0.h)
  res.snaive = exp(forecasts.snaive) - exp(Y0.h)
  res.fols = exp(forecasts.fols) - exp(Y0.h)
```

```
  res.fumidas = exp(forecasts.fumidas) - exp(Y0.h)
  res.fmidas = exp(forecasts.fmidas) - exp(Y0.h)

  MAPE.sarima = colMeans(abs(res.sarima) * 100 / exp(Y0.h),
na.rm = T)
  MAPE.ets = colMeans(abs(res.ets) * 100 / exp(Y0.h), na.rm = T)
  MAPE.snaive = colMeans(abs(res.snaive) * 100 / exp(Y0.h),
na.rm = T)
  MAPE.fols = colMeans(abs(res.fols) * 100 / exp(Y0.h), na.rm = T)
  MAPE.fumidas = colMeans(abs(res.fumidas) * 100 / exp(Y0.h),
na.rm = T)
  MAPE.fmidas = colMeans(abs(res.fmidas) * 100 / exp(Y0.h),
na.rm = T)

  MASE.denominator = mean(abs(diff(exp(lnY), 4)))
  MASE.sarima = colMeans(abs(res.sarima) / MASE.denominator,
na.rm = TRUE)
  MASE.ets = colMeans(abs(res.ets) / MASE.denominator, na.rm
= TRUE)
  MASE.snaive = colMeans(abs(res.snaive) / MASE.denominator,
na.rm = TRUE)
  MASE.fols = colMeans(abs(res.fols) / MASE.denominator, na.rm
= TRUE)
  MASE.fumidas = colMeans(abs(res.fumidas) / MASE.denomina-
tor, na.rm = TRUE)
  MASE.fmidas = colMeans(abs(res.fmidas) / MASE.denominator,
na.rm = TRUE)

  RMSE.sarima = sqrt(colMeans((res.sarima) ^ 2, na.rm = TRUE))
  RMSE.ets = sqrt(colMeans((res.ets) ^ 2, na.rm = TRUE))
  RMSE.snaive = sqrt(colMeans((res.snaive) ^ 2, na.rm = TRUE))
  RMSE.fols = sqrt(colMeans((res.fols) ^ 2, na.rm = TRUE))
  RMSE.fumidas = sqrt(colMeans((res.fumidas) ^ 2, na.rm =
TRUE))
  RMSE.fmidas = sqrt(colMeans((res.fmidas) ^ 2, na.rm = TRUE))

  # output the results
  MAPE.all <- cbind(MAPE.snaive, MAPE.sarima, MAPE.ets, MAPE.
fols, MAPE.fumidas, MAPE.fmidas)
  RMSE.all <- cbind(RMSE.snaive, RMSE.sarima, RMSE.ets, RMSE.
fols, RMSE.fumidas, RMSE.fmidas)
  MASE.all <- cbind(MASE.snaive, MASE.sarima, MASE.ets, MASE.
fols, MASE.fumidas, MASE.fmidas)

  forevalue <- t(rbind(MAPE.all, RMSE.all, MASE.all))
  forecasts.all <- exp(cbind(Y0.h, forecasts.snaive, fore-
casts.sarima, forecasts.ets, forecasts.fols, forecasts.fumi-
das, forecasts.fmidas))
```

8

HYBRID FORECASTING MODELS

Mingming Hu, Mei Li, and Xin Zhao

8.1 Introduction

Accurate tourism demand forecasts serve as important references for tourism policymakers in both the government and private sectors (Shen, Li, & Song, 2011). Many models have been used for forecasting tourism demand, each with unique characteristics, advantages, and disadvantages, and no single model can accurately predict tourism demand under all conditions (Li, Song, & Witt, 2005). Hybrid models have thus piqued researchers' interest: these models possess enhanced prediction accuracy by capitalising on different models' strengths.

A hybrid model is one that combines two or more statistical and/or artificial intelligence (AI) techniques to obtain a result (Fajardo-Toro, Mula, & Poler, 2019). This model type is intended to compensate for the pitfalls of individual methods and generate synergy in the prediction. Related studies generally fall into two categories. Some focus on hybridising different models. For example, Fritz, Brandon, and Xander (1984) combined a traditional econometric model – the spectral residual model – with the autoregressive integrated moving average (ARIMA) model and forecast the US state of Florida airline visitors to demonstrate that combining forecasts could improve accuracy. Chu (1998) later developed a combined seasonal ARIMA (SARIMA) and sine wave nonlinear regression forecasting model to predict inbound tourism demand to Singapore, and the prediction effect of the model of Fritz et al. (1984) was further confirmed. Coshall (2009) integrated the ARIMA model with generalised autoregressive conditional heteroskedastic (GARCH) models and compared their forecasting accuracy with exponential smoothing (ETS) and the NAIVE model. The results showed that hybrid models between the

DOI: 10.4324/9781003269366-8

ARIMA-GARCH and Holt–Winters models yielded the best forecasts across nearly all sample countries and horizons. Athanasopoulos and Hyndman (2008) applied a regression framework to estimate important economic relationships in domestic tourism demand and then used an innovative state–space with exogenous variables to forecast this demand. Their findings indicated that the proposed models performed well. Hassani, Silva, Antonakakis, Filis, and Gupta (2017) used a method like that of Athanasopoulos and Hyndman (2008) and, after comparison with other models, found that the recurrent singular spectrum analysis model was the most efficient, as measured by the lowest overall forecasting error. The above studies considered time series with identical timings to combine forecasts, but forecasting performance will likely improve even further if different time aggregations are used. Andrawis, Atiya and El-Shishiny (2011) verified this supposition by integrating long-run ETS and short-run ETS to forecast tourism numbers for inbound tourism to Egypt. The empirical evidence suggested that this blended strategy did increase forecasting accuracy.

Various interrelated factors influence tourism demand. It is therefore difficult to make accurate predictions by using individual methods, and it is challenging to discern the precise features of time series data. AI-based methods were introduced to solve this problem. Many scholars have confirmed that hybrid AI-based and other models have greater forecasting accuracy than benchmark models. These hybrid models include a hybridisation of the SARIMA model with the support vector regression (SVR) model (Abellana, Rivero, Aparente, & Rivero, 2021; Cang, 2014); the SARIMA model with long short-term memory (LSTM; Wu, Ji, He & Tso, 2021); the ARIMA model with the multilayer perceptron model (Nor, Nurul, & Rusiman, 2018); the ARIMA model with grey models (Nguyen, Shu, Huang, & Hsu, 2013); the Grey–Markov model with neural networks (Hu et al., 2019); the ARIMA model with a back propagation neural network (BPNN; Liao, Jin, Luo, Ren, & Gao, 2013); the SARIMA model with a convolutional neural network (CNN; He, Ji, Wu, & Tso, 2021); and the nonlinear autoregressive with exogenous variable model with an ARIMA model with exogenous variables (ARIMAX; Wen et al., 2019). Few studies, however, compare hybrid models. The few that do include Aslanargun, Mammadov, Yazici, and Yolacan (2007), Chen (2011), and Oh and Morzuch (2005), who compared different hybrid models to determine which produced the lowest prediction error.

Other scholars have proposed hybrid models to examine different forecasting methods and identify the most suitable approach for model hybridisation. A typical example is Wong, Song, Witt, and Wu (2007), who combined four models: the autoregressive distributed lag model (ADLM), the ARIMA model, the error correction model (ECM), and the vector autoregressive (VAR) model. They then examined three linear combination methods: (a) simple average (SA), (b) variance–covariance, and (c) discounted mean square forecasting error. The results revealed that combining forecasts can considerably reduce the risk of forecasting failure. Shen et al. (2011) examined the same three combined methods with multiple-step-ahead forecasting horizons and seven single forecasting techniques: the ADLM, two ECMs, the VAR model, the time-varying parameter model, the seasonal NAIVE (SNAIVE) model, and the SARIMA model. The empirical results provided further evidence for the efficiency of combination forecasts and the superiority of these forecasts across different time horizons in the tourism demand context when compared to individual forecasts. Cang and Yu (2014) conducted further research on combination versus individual tourism demand forecasts: they utilised the same three methods as in Wong et al. (2007) and Shen et al. (2008) in combination with the SVR neural network, the ARIMA model, Winters' multiplicative ETS model, and the NAIVE model. They also used the Mutual Information algorithm to select the optimal subset of individual models from available options without needing to test all possible model combinations. The combination of individual models from the optimal subset significantly outperformed the combination of all available models. Wan and Song (2018) combined the NAIVE, historical average, ADLM, and VAR models separately and considered four linear approaches: (a) SA, (b) the Akaike information criterion (AIC), (c) the Bayesian information criterion (BIC), and (d) constrained linear opinion pooling. They also examined one nonlinear approach, the simple geometric mean, and found that combined approaches – especially nonlinear ones – were sensitive to the quality of forecasts in the pool. To identify the most suitable model combination method, Gunter and Önder (2016) integrated four models – the VAR, moving average (MA), ETS, and NAIVE models– and compared several forecast combination methods: (a) uniform weights, (b) Bates–Granger weights, (c) forecast-encompassing tests with uniform weights, and (d) forecast-encompassing tests with Bates–Granger weights. According to the empirical results, a univariate benchmark performed best for shorter forecasting horizons (h = 1, 2 months ahead), whereas forecast combination methods including prediction information from Google Analytics were preferable for longer forecasting horizons (h = 3, 6, 12).

Another group of scholars incorporated optimisation technology into models. Tourist flows have intricate nonlinear variations, which complicates the detection of relationships between later tourist flows and current influencing variables based on single models. Neural network–based models have unique drawbacks in setting parameters. Certain optimisation algorithms have proven effective in enhancing prediction accuracy by identifying optimal values of model parameters. Studies suggest that combining specific optimisation algorithms and models can further improve prediction accuracy. Hybrid models mainly involve integrating seasonal SVR with an adaptive genetic algorithm (Chen, Liang, Hong, & Gu, 2015); SVR with the Bat algorithm and inclusion of search engine data (Zhang,

Huang, Li, & Law, 2017); SVR with the chaotic genetic algorithm (Hong, Dong, Chen, & Wei, 2011); BPNN with a fruit fly optimisation algorithm based on web search data (Li, Lu, Liang, & Wang, 2019); least-squares support vector machine (SVM) with particle swarm optimisation (Li et al., 2019; Shabri, 2016); and CNN-LSTM with a genetic algorithm (Lu et al., 2020). Additionally, certain optimisation algorithms have also been utilised to choose the parameters for combined models and have been found to be effective in forecasting tourism demand. Coshall and Charlesworth (2011) combined the ARIMA, GARCH, ETS, and NAIVE 2 models using a goal programming approach for model integration. Shen, Liu, Lien, Lee, and Yang (2019) combined feature selection and SVR to forecast tourist arrivals to Singapore, with particle swarm optimisation used to adjust the SVR parameters to more effectively predict travel demand. Pai, Hung, and Lin (2014) combined fuzzy c-means with logarithm least-squares SVR technologies, and used genetic algorithms simultaneously to optimally select model parameters.

Tourist behaviour is inherently complex, and tourism demand is characterised by volatility and elasticity, obstacles to forecasting performance with quantitative models. It is therefore necessary to construct models with a high degree of flexibility, and researchers have proposed introducing the judgemental method into tourism demand forecasting. Lin (2013) proposed a web-based tourism demand forecasting system (TDFS) integrating statistical forecasts and expert judgement. In an initial stage of the Delphi survey, panellists were invited to adjust quarterly visitor arrival forecasts, and statistical forecasts produced via VAR models were presented on a web page in tabular and graphic forms. Integrating expert judgement into statistical forecasts led to apparent gains, particularly in the short term. Song, Gao, and Lin (2013) adopted the same TDFS and performed an experiment with postgraduate students and staff from the School of Hotel and Tourism Management at the Hong Kong Polytechnic University to test the reliability of the TDFS Statistical Adjustment module. They used ETS via the state–space model to forecast price-related variables. This combination of quantitative and judgemental forecasts improved overall forecasting accuracy.

Table 8.1 summarises studies on hybrid models in tourism demand forecasting. ARIMA/SARIMA and AI models are the models most frequently used in hybrid modelling. This study introduces a hybrid model combining the SARIMA, ETS, SNAIVE, and BPNN models. The SARIMA, ETS, and SNAIVE models have been used in previous studies to analyse linear relationships and seasonal characteristics, and BPNN models have been used successfully in nonlinear estimations. Combining these four model types enables the observation and prediction of linear and nonlinear relationships.

TABLE 8.1 Summary of studies on hybrid models

Author (year)	Research area	Data type	Hybrid models
Fritz, Brandon & Xander (1984)	Air arrivals into the US state of Florida	Quarterly	SR + ARIMA
Chu (1998)	Tourist arrivals in Singapore	Monthly	SARIMA + Sine wave regression
Oh & Morzuch (2005)	Travellers' arrivals to Singapore	Monthly	ARIMA with different parameters + Winters' model
Aslanargun et al. (2007)	Tourist arrivals to Turkey	Monthly	MLP + MLP; MLP + RBFN
Wong, Song, Witt & Wu (2007)	Tourism demand for Hong Kong by residents from ten major origin countries/regions	Quarterly	SARIMA + VAR + ECM + ADLM
Athanasopoulos & Hyndman (2008)	Australian domestic tourism	Quarterly	State–space models + ETS
Lee, Song & Mjelde (2008)	Foreign tourist arrivals to South Korea and interventions	Quarterly	Delphi method + SARIMA, ETS
Coshall (2009)	Outbound UK tourism numbers by air to the twelve most frequently visited destinations	Quarterly	ARIMA + GARCH
Andrawis et al. (2011)	Tourism numbers for inbound tourism to Egypt	Monthly	Long-run ETS + Short-run ETS
Chen (2011)	Outbound travelling population from 6 areas in Taiwan	Monthly	ARIMA + SVR; NAIVE + SVR; ETS + SVR
Hong, Dong, Chen & Wei (2011)	Total number of tourist arrivals in Barbados	Yearly	SVR model + SVR
Coshall & Charlesworth (2011)	Outbound tourism numbers by air from the UK to the eighteen most popular destinations in Europe	Quarterly	ARIMA + GARCH + ETS + NAIVE 2
Shen, Li & Song (2011)	UK outbound tourism demand for seven major destinations	Quarterly	ADLM + ECM + VAR + TVP + SNAIVE+ SARIMA
Liao, Jin, Luo, Ren & Gao (2013)	Quantity of tourists in Jiuzhaigou Valley	Monthly	ARIMA + BPNN

(Continued)

Author (year)	Research area	Data type	Hybrid models
Nguyen, Shu, Huang & Hsu (2013)	Inbound tourism demand in Vietnam	Monthly	ARIMA + BPNN
Lin (2013)	Visitor arrivals to Hong Kong	Quarterly	Delphi method + VAR
Song, Gao & Lin (2013)	Tourist arrivals, tourist expenditure, and the demand for hotel rooms in Hong Kong	Quarterly; annually	Delphi method + ADLM
Cang & Yu (2014)	UK inbound visitor numbers	Quarterly	SVR + ARIMA + WMES + The NAIVE
Cang (2014)	UK inbound visitor arrivals	Quarterly	SARIMA + SVR
Pai, Hung & Lin (2014)	Tourist arrivals	Yearly	FCM + LLS-SVR
Chen, Liang, Hong & Gu (2015)	Tourist flow volume during seven different holidays in Mountain Huangshan	Daily	SSVR + AGA
Gunter & Önder (2016)	Tourism demand to Vienna	Monthly	VAR + MA + ETS + NAIVE 1
Shabri (2016)	Number of tourists arriving in Malaysia from Singapore	Monthly	EEMD + LSSVM
Hassani, Silva, Antonakakis, Filis & Gupta (2017)	International tourist arrivals in European countries	Monthly	SSA + ETS
Zhang, Huang, Li & Law (2017)	Hainan's tourist volumes	Monthly	BA + SVR
Wan & Song (2018)	Number of visitor arrivals to Hong Kong	Quarterly	The NAIVE + HA + ADLM + VAR
Nor, Nurul & Rusiman (2018)	Tourist arrivals in Malaysia	Monthly	ARIMA + ANN
Hu, Jiang & Lee (2019)	Foreign tourists from six economies to Taiwan; Foreign tourists to China from eight economies	Yearly	The Grey–Markov model + ANN
Wen, Liu & Song (2019)	Tourist arrivals in Hong Kong from Chinese mainland	Monthly	ARIMAX + ANN
Athanasopoulos, Song & Sun (2018)	Tourist arrivals to Australia from six origin countries	Quarterly	ADLM + Bagging

Li, Lu, Liang & Wang (2019)	Mount Huangshan daily visitors and Baidu index data	Daily	FOA + BPNN
Li, Liang, Lu, Li, Zhao & Wang (2020)	Mountain Huangshan daily tourist flow data	Yearly	LSSVM + PSO
Shen, Liu, Lien, Lee & Yang (2019)	Visitors to Singapore from five countries	Yearly	FS+SVR + PSO
Abellana, Rivero, Aparente & Rivero (2021)	Inbound tourist arrivals to the Philippines	Yearly	SARIMA+SVR
Lu, Rui, Liang, Jiang, Zhao & Li (2020)	Huangshan daily tourist flow data	Daily	GA + CNN + LSTM
Shabri, Samsudin & Yusoff (2020)	Tourist arrivals to Langkawi Island in Malaysia	Monthly	Fourier series + DNN
Wu, Ji, He & Tso (2021)	Macau tourist arrivals	Daily	SARIMA + LSTM
He, Ji, Wu & Tso (2021)	Tourist arrivals in Macau from 6 major countries and regions	Daily	SARIMA+ CNN+LSTM

Note: AGA: Adaptive Genetic Algorithm; ANN: Artificial Neural Network; BA: Bat Algorithm; DNN: Deep Neural Networks; EEMD: Ensemble Empirical Mode Decomposition; FCM: Fuzzy *c*-means method; FOA: Fruit Fly Optimisation Algorithm; FS: Feature Selection; GA: Genetic Algorithm; HA: Historical Average; LLS-SVR: Logarithm Least-Squares Support Vector Regression; LSSVM: Least-Squares Support Vector Machine; LSTM: Long-Short-Term Memory Network; MLP: Multilayer Perceptron; PSO: Particle Swarm Optimisation; RBFN: Radial Basis Function Networks; SR: Spectral Residual; SSA: Singular Spectrum Analysis; SSVR: Support Vector Regression with seasonal index adjustment; WMES: Winters' Multiplicative Exponential Smoothing.

8.2 Methods

The SARIMA, ETS, SNAIVE, BPNN, and hybrid models are used to analyse the time series data used in this study.

8.2.1 The SARIMA model

ARMA family models are frequently used in tourism demand forecasting (Song, Qiu, & Park, 2019). The general form of a seasonal ARIMA (i.e., SARIMA) model is written as follows (Aslanargun et al., 2007):

ARIMA (p, d, q) $(P, D, Q)s$,

where p is the number of parameters in the autoregressive (AR) model, d denotes the differencing degree, q is the number of parameters in the MA model, P is the number of parameters in the AR seasonal model, D is the seasonal differencing degree, Q is the number of parameters in the MA seasonal model, and S is the period of seasonality. The SARIMA model of Box and Jenkins (1970) is formulated as follows:

$$\varphi(B)\phi(B^s)(1-B)(1-B^s)^D Y_t = \Theta_0 + \theta(B)\Theta(B^s)\varepsilon_t \tag{8.1}$$

where

B is the backshift operator;

S denotes the seasonal order;

ε_t is the error term with a mean of zero and a variance of σ^2;

$(1-B)^d$ denotes the non-seasonal differencing of order d;

$\left(1-B^S\right)^D$ denotes the seasonal differencing of order D;

$\varnothing(B)$ is the p-order non-seasonal AR model;

$\theta(B)$ is the q-order non-seasonal MA model;

$\Phi\left(B^S\right)$ is the P-order seasonal AR model; and

$\Theta\left(B^S\right)$ is the Q-order seasonal MA model.

8.2.2 The ETS model

The ETS model contains different versions. They develop an exponential smoothing method by including level, trend, seasonality, and smoothing (Hyndman, Akram, & Archibald, 2008; Hyndman, Koehler, Snyder, & Grose, 2002). This method has two formats: additive and multiplicative. A general ETS model can be written as *ETS (e, t, s)*, where e denotes the error type ('A', 'M', or 'Z'), with 'A' denoting an additive error, 'M' indicating a multiplicative error, and 'Z' automatically selecting the type of error. t denotes the trend type ('N', 'A', 'M', or 'Z'), with 'N' indicating no trend, 'A' representing an additive trend, 'M' denoting a multiplicative trend, and 'Z' automatically selecting the type of trend. s denotes the seasonality type ('N', 'A', 'M', or 'Z'), with 'N' for no seasonality, 'A' for additive seasonality, 'M' for multiplicative seasonality, and 'Z' automatically selecting the type of seasonality. For example, 'ETS(A, N, N)' is simple exponential smoothing with additive errors and 'ETS(M, A, M)' is the multiplicative Holt–Winters' method with multiplicative errors. The ets() function of the 'forecast' package (Hyndman et al., 2019) in the R software package is utilised to automatically determine the parameters.

8.2.3 The SNAIVE model

The SNAIVE model is used for data with dramatic seasonal variability. The model sets each prediction equal to the previous observation for the same season (e.g., the same month during the previous year). The predicted value at time $T+h$ is then written as follows:

$$\hat{y}_{T+h|T} = y^{T+h-km} \tag{8.2}$$

where m denotes period length and k is the integer element of $(h-1)/m$ (e.g., the number of years in the forecast period up to time $T+h$). Take monthly data as an example. All future February predictions are equal to the February observations of the previous year. For quarterly data, all future second quarter predictions are equal to the second quarter observations of the previous year. Similar rules apply to other months, quarters, and cycle lengths.

8.2.3 The BPNN model

The BPNN method was first introduced to tourism demand forecasting in the late 1990s. Empirical evidence shows that BPNN generally outperforms the traditional time series and econometric models used in tourism forecasting (Chen, Lai, & Yeh, 2012; Law, 2000; Law & Au, 1999; Li, Chen, Wang, & Ming, 2018; Pattie & Snyder, 1996).

In the BPNN model, back propagation is a learning mode requiring supervised learning, which is mainly reflected in the training process of BPNN – a feedforward network is a kind of structure, which is reflected in the network architecture of BPNN. A typical feedforward neural network is shown in Figure 8.1. It contains three parts: an input layer, a hidden unit layer, and an output layer. The input layer is mainly used to obtain input information, and the size depends on the number of input variables. The hidden layer performs 'feature extraction', adjusting the connecting weight so that the neural units of the hidden layer respond to certain patterns. The output layer is used to connect with the hidden layer and output the results, adjusting the connecting weights to form the correct response to different hidden layer neuron stimuli.

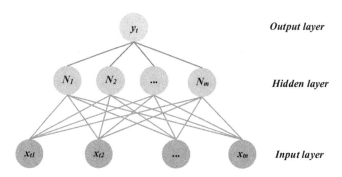

FIGURE 8.1 Topology of a three-layer BPNN model

The specific modelling and forecasting steps are as follows:

1 *Divide the sample.* Divide the sample into a training set, validation set, and test set.
2 *Pre-process the data.* A BPNN model has unique requirements for the training sample data: if the range of input or output data changes too much, it will affect the convergence of connecting weights and the model's stability. Therefore, data should be normalised according to the characteristics of the data to be predicted. A common adjustment is to use the maximum values X_{max} and minimum values X_{min}, often formulated as follows:

$$X_k = \frac{X_k - X_{min}}{X_{max} - X_{min}} \tag{8.3}$$

3 *Design the network architecture.* This process primarily involves parameter selection, such as choosing the number of hidden-layer nodes, the number of input nodes, the number of output nodes, the activation function, and the threshold.
4 *Initialise the network.* Randomly assign weights and thresholds.
5 *Start training.* Input the divided data and start training the network. When the training error is lower than the specified error, the training is terminated.
6 *Validate the network.* Validate the parameters and adjust them as needed.
7 *Forecasting and evaluation.* Produce the forecasts and evaluate the forecasting performance of the model.

8.2.4 The hybrid model

Model setting. The procedure of the hybrid model in this study is shown in Figure 8.2. In this hybrid model, the SARIMA, ETS, and SNAIVE models are used to capture linear and seasonal components of tourism demand data. The BPNN model is used to capture data features that the SA-RIMA, ETS, and SNAIVE models cannot interpret. In the modelling process for the SARIMA, ETS, and SNAIVE models, 'tourism demand' is regarded as a unique variable. The procedure for setting the BPNN model is as follows:

First, following Wen, Liu, and Song (2019), a typical three-layer BPNN is utilised in this study, including an input layer, a hidden layer, and an output layer. The hidden unit layer is set to 1. In the output layer, current tourism demand y_t is taken as output. In the input layer, *tourist arrivals, price, income* (measured by GDP), one-step-ahead forecasts from the SA-RIMA, ETS, and SNAIVE models, and seasonal dummy variables are used as inputs in the BPNN model. The inputs at time t are summarised as follows:

- y with lag 1 y_{t-1};
- *price* with lag 1 $price_{t-1}$;
- *income* with lag 1 $income_{t-1}$;
- One-step-ahead prediction from the SARIMA model, $\widehat{AOP}_t$;
- One-step-ahead prediction from the ETS model, $\widehat{EOP}_t$;
- One-step-ahead prediction from the SNAIVE model, $\widehat{NOP}_t$; and
- Seasonal dummy variables Qs, including seasonal factors Q_{1t}, Q_{2t}, Q_{3t}, and Q_{4t}.

where y_{t-1}, $price_{t-1}$, and $income_{t-1}$ represent tourism demand, tourist income, and the tourism price at time $t-1$, respectively; $\widehat{AOP}_t$, $\widehat{EOP}_t$, and $\widehat{NOP}_t$ are one-step-ahead forecasts from the SARIMA, ETS, and SNAIVE models at time t, respectively; Q_{1t}, Q_{2t}, Q_{3t}, and Q_{4t} are seasonal dummy variables at time t. The data sources of tourism demand, tourist income, the tourism price, and seasonal dummy variables Q_{1t}, Q_{2t}, and Q_{3t} for each source market of Thailand (mainland China, Malaysia, Russia, and the USA) are included in the data source of this book. Q_{4t} is generated by the self-coding by R attached at the end of this chapter.

Second, the sigmoid function is selected as the activation function in the BPNN model to extract nonlinear information:

$$f(x) = \frac{1}{1+e^{-x}} \tag{8.4}$$

Third, the number of neurons in the hidden layer is set from 1 to 10 and the threshold is set with six values, namely, 0.005, 0.01, 0.02, 0.03, 0.04, and 0.05. A validation set is used to select the optimal values for the number of nodes in the hidden layer and the threshold by comparing the forecasting performance on this validation set.

Dataset setting. Each group of collected time series data is divided into three datasets: a training set, a validation set, and a testing set for the hybrid model. The initial dataset setting is shown in Figure 8.3. The initial

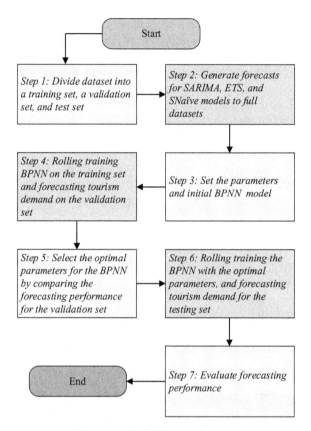

FIGURE 8.2 Proposed hybrid model

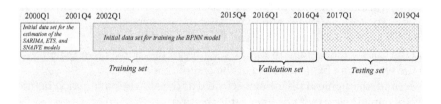

FIGURE 8.3 Sample division of datasets

training dataset is used to estimate or train the SARIMA, ETS, SNAIVE, and BPNN models, the validation set is used to select the optimal parameter for the BPNN model, and the testing set is used to evaluate the forecasting performance of the hybrid model. When training the BPNN model, it is necessary to input the results generated from the SARIMA, ETS, and SNAIVE models. The training set is therefore divided into two parts. The first comprises the observations that form the initial estimation set for the

SARIMA, ETS, and SNAIVE models. The second comprises the observations that construct the training set for the BPNN model.

Following the previous chapter, the SNAIVE, SARIMA, and ETS models are used as benchmark models to assess the proposed hybrid model's performance. Consistent with other chapters, MAPE, root mean square error (RMSE), and mean absolute scaled error (MASE) are used as prediction accuracy evaluation criteria.

8.3 Application

8.3.1 The modelling process

As described in Chapter 2, the datasets for each original country/region include data from 2000Q1 to 2019Q4 and contain 80 quarterly observations, and this study sets tourism demand y as the dependent variable, with explanatory variables *price, income*, and seasonal dummy variables Q. The 'auto.arima', 'ets', and 'snaïve' functionalities in R's forecast library enable automatic estimation of the SARIMA, ETS, and SNAIVE parameters, respectively. The first extending window is set to 8, and the SARIMA, ETS, and SNAIVE models are used to perform a one-step-ahead forecast. The first window contains tourist arrivals from 2000Q1 to 2001Q4. These data are used to estimate the SARIMA, ETS, and SNAIVE models to predict the value of 2002Q1. By extending the window, the following 71 forecast values from 2002Q2 to 2019Q4 are predicted by the SARIMA, ETS, and SNAIVE models.

Data from 2002Q1 to 2019Q4 are divided into a training set, a validation set, and a testing set for the BPNN model. During the validation process, the data from 2002Q1 to 2015Q4 are used as the initial training sets to forecast tourist arrivals in 2016Q1; the window is then rolled by one quarter each time until the validation set (2016Q1 to 2016Q4) is exhausted. The forecasting accuracy of the validation set is measured by RMSE. Figures 8.4–8.7 show the values of RMSE for different parameter combinations (the number of neurons in the hidden layer and the threshold) in four different markets. The optimal parameters of the BPNN model are then selected. During the forecasting process, the data from 2002Q1 to 2016Q4 are initially used as the training set. The BPNN model with optimal parameters is trained using samples from this training set. The value of 2017Q1 is then forecast by the trained BPNN model, and the training and forecasting window rolls until the testing set is exhausted.

8.3.2 Empirical results

In this study, SARIMA, ETS, and SNAIVE models are implemented via the 'auto.arima', 'ets', and 'snaïve' functionalities of R's 'forecast' library,

CHN_RMSE

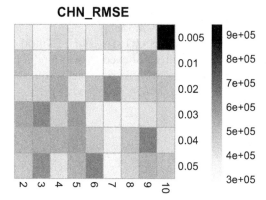

FIGURE 8.4 The values of RMSE for different parameters combinations (mainland China)

MAL_RMSE

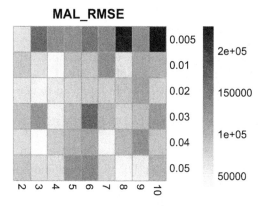

FIGURE 8.5 The values of RMSE for different parameters combinations (Malaysia)

and the BPNN model is built using the 'neuralnet' functionality in R's 'neuralnet' library and the 'predict' functionality. Through the above modelling process, one-, two-, three-, four-, and eight-step-ahead forecasts are generated by the hybrid forecasting model.

Tables 8.2–8.4 summarise the forecasting results of the hybrid, SNA-IVE, SARIMA, and ETS models for tourism demand from four source markets to Thailand. The results show that the hybrid model outperforms most benchmark models among different source markets and different accuracy measures. For details, the hybrid model consistently outperforms the benchmark models when forecasting one-step-ahead tourist arrivals

RUS_RMSE

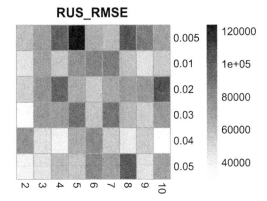

FIGURE 8.6   The values of RMSE for different parameters combinations (Russia)

USA_RMSE

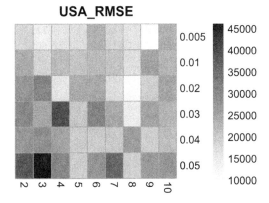

FIGURE 8.7   The values of RMSE for different parameters combinations (USA)

from mainland China, Malaysia, and the USA. It also consistently outperforms the benchmark models when forecasting eight-step-ahead tourist arrivals from mainland China, Russia, and the USA. Besides, for all individual source markets, the hybrid model can also outperform most of the benchmark models among all accuracy measures except in the case of Russia. The results are consistent with previous studies indicating that hybrid models generate strong forecasting performances (Hu et al., 2019; Li et al., 2019; Liao et al., 2013; Nguyen et al., 2013; Nor et al., 2018; Wen et al., 2019). The results from the four analysed source markets consistently

TABLE 8.2 Forecasting performance evaluation measured by MAPE (%)

	Forecasting horizon				
	1	2	3	4	8
Mainland China					
SNAIVE	13.194	13.683	15.039	15.606	14.882
ETS	12.201	16.127	15.163	13.312	15.984
SARIMA	14.753	13.945	16.658	17.642	21.033
Hybrid model	11.795	21.380	11.168	12.740	10.930
Malaysia					
SNAIVE	7.859	7.559	7.349	8.114	18.818
ETS	7.973	8.113	8.193	8.448	5.081
SARIMA	8.339	8.032	8.422	7.148	8.964
Hybrid model	7.432	6.980	9.018	10.683	8.342
Russia					
SNAIVE	9.800	8.259	7.474	7.783	13.722
ETS	9.956	12.781	16.648	13.287	26.609
SARIMA	12.221	16.511	15.800	19.900	46.633
Hybrid model	12.185	14.919	11.010	9.986	6.039
USA					
SNAIVE	5.703	5.563	5.098	4.839	9.991
ETS	3.956	3.919	4.345	6.008	11.263
SARIMA	4.553	7.014	8.247	9.483	14.186
Hybrid model	3.301	3.795	3.201	2.975	3.726

TABLE 8.3 Forecasting performance evaluation measured by RMSE

	Forecasting horizon				
	1	2	3	4	8
Mainland China					
SNAIVE	435,305	451,019	473,032	490,637	465,626
ETS	361,836	454,310	454,610	469,960	496,274
SARIMA	431,710	440,885	532,880	515,603	596,629
Hybrid model	346,034	576,812	349,313	394,749	308,159
Malaysia					
SNAIVE	114,911	117,014	119,366	125,817	227,894
ETS	86,084	96,150	108,836	92,312	64,159

SARIMA	98,563	100,908	116,794	107,835	131,294
Hybrid model	89,330	97,239	109,977	125,786	131,120
Russia					
SNAIVE	60,723	49,666	50,755	53,441	72,672
ETS	40,284	35,219	69,387	61,388	92,175
SARIMA	44,255	51,003	58,842	75,123	150,857
Hybrid model	66,440	79,264	67,192	64,101	34,102
USA					
SNAIVE	17,100	16,758	15,602	15,539	32,290
ETS	12,734	13,027	16,326	19,637	36,930
SARIMA	17,164	22,540	26,103	30,561	45,171
Hybrid model	10,188	12,757	12,420	10,744	11,572

TABLE 8.4 Forecasting performance evaluation measured by MASE

	Forecasting horizon				
	1	*2*	*3*	*4*	*8*
Mainland China					
SNAIVE	1.624	1.691	1.858	1.926	1.790
ETS	1.472	1.916	1.885	1.678	2.002
SARIMA	1.777	1.631	1.963	2.117	2.503
Hybrid model	1.405	2.508	1.368	1.544	1.234
Malaysia					
SNAIVE	1.033	1.024	1.010	1.117	2.720
ETS	0.974	1.016	1.069	1.076	0.727
SARIMA	1.052	1.049	1.121	0.983	1.326
Hybrid model	0.961	0.933	1.181	1.412	1.251
Russia					
SNAIVE	0.830	0.656	0.644	0.698	1.239
ETS	0.657	0.633	1.191	0.912	1.725
SARIMA	0.802	0.959	0.968	1.237	3.059
Hybrid model	1.046	1.088	0.959	0.808	0.519
USA					
SNAIVE	0.962	0.936	0.875	0.863	1.862
ETS	0.646	0.652	0.768	1.078	2.110
SARIMA	0.773	1.144	1.409	1.684	2.624
Hybrid model	0.552	0.641	0.562	0.514	0.654

demonstrate that hybridising the neural network with other time series models does indeed improve forecasting performance.

8.4 Conclusion and future directions

A large body of literature suggests that hybrid forecasting models are useful in capturing different characteristics of time series data. This study introduces a hybrid SARIMA, ETS, SNAIVE, and BPNN model to forecast tourism demand and assumes the model's capacity to capture linear, seasonal, and nonlinear features of tourism demand data. The SARIMA, ETS, and SNAIVE models are used to identify linear and seasonal characteristics, whereas the BPNN model serves to identify nonlinear attributes and make corresponding predictions. When comparing the forecasting accuracy of the SNAIVE, SARIMA, and ETS models with the forecasts generated from the hybrid model, the hybrid model outperforms most of the benchmark models for both short-term and long-term forecasting. These results are consistent with those found in the literature (Hu et al., 2019; Li et al., 2019; Liao et al., 2013; Nguyen et al., 2013; Nor et al., 2018; Wen et al., 2019), which suggests that hybrid modelling can more effectively generate accurate forecasts than individual models.

For future research, more factors that affect tourism demand should be mined and introduced into hybrid forecasting models to enhance the models' explanatory power. At the same time, higher-frequency data should also be concluded to forecast tourism demand. Moreover, various AI models should be applied when generating hybrid models to achieve higher forecasting accuracy.

Self-study questions

1 Attempt to use monthly/weekly data to conduct one-step-ahead forecasting using this hybrid model.
2 Attempt to utilise another AI model and combine it with seasonal autoregressive integrated moving average model incorporating explanatory variables (SARIMAX) to generate a new hybrid forecasting model.

References

Abellana, D. P. M., Rivero, D. M. C., Aparente, M. E., & Rivero, A. (2021). Hybrid SVR-SARIMA model for tourism forecasting using PROMETHEE II as a selection methodology: A Philippine scenario. *Journal of Tourism Futures, 7*(1), 78–97. https://doi.org/10.1108/JTF-07-2019-0070

Andrawis, R. R., Atiya, A. F., & El-Shishiny, H. (2011). Combination of long term and short term forecasts, with application to tourism demand forecasting.

International Journal of Forecasting, 27(3), 870–886. https://doi.org/10.1016/j. ijforecast.2010.05.019

Aslanargun, A., Mammadov, M., Yazici, B., & Yolacan, S. (2007). Comparison of ARIMA, neural networks and hybrid models in time series: Tourist arrival forecasting. *Journal of Statistical Computation and Simulation, 77*(1), 29–53. https://doi.org/10.1080/10629360600564874

Athanasopoulos, G., & Hyndman, R. J. (2008). Modelling and forecasting Australian domestic tourism. *Tourism Management, 29*(1), 19–31. https://doi. org/10.1016/j.tourman.2007.04.009

Athanasopoulos, G., Song, H., & Sun, J. A. (2018). Bagging in tourism demand modeling and forecasting. *Journal of Travel Research.* https://doi. org/10.1177/0047287516682871

Box, G. E. P., & Jenkins, G. M. (1970). Time series analysis forecasting and control. *Chapman-Hall /crc Boca Raton, 2*(3), 131–133.

Cang, S. (2014). A comparative analysis of three types of tourism demand forecasting models: Individual, linear combination and non-linear combination. *International Journal of Tourism Research, 16(6),* 596–607. https://doi. org/10.1002/jtr.1953

Cang, S., & Yu, H. (2014). A combination selection algorithm on forecasting. *European Journal of Operational Research, 234*(1), 127–139. https://doi.org/10.1016/j. ejor.2013.08.045

Chen, C. F., Lai, M. C., & Yeh, C. C. (2012). Forecasting tourism demand based on empirical mode decomposition and neural network. *Knowledge-Based Systems, 26,* 281–287. https://doi.org/10.1016/j.knosys.2011.09.002

Chen, K. Y. (2011). Combining linear and nonlinear model in forecasting tourism demand. *Expert Systems with Applications, 38*(8), 10368–10376. https://doi. org/10.1016/j.eswa.2011.02.049

Chen, R., Liang, C. Y., Hong, W. C., & Gu, D. X. (2015). Forecasting holiday daily tourist flow based on seasonal support vector regression with adaptive genetic algorithm. *Applied Soft Computing, 26,* 435–443. https://doi.org/10.1016/j. asoc.2014.10.022

Chu, F. L. (1998). Forecasting tourism: A combined approach. *Tourism Management, 19*(6), 515–520. https://doi.org/10.1016/S0261-5177(98)00053-3

Coshall, J. T. (2009). Combining volatility and smoothing forecasts of UK demand for international tourism. *Tourism Management, 30*(4), 495–511. https://doi. org/10.1016/j.tourman.2008.10.010

Coshall, J. T., & Charlesworth, R. (2011). A management orientated approach to combination forecasting of tourism demand. *Tourism Management, 32*(4), 759–769. https://doi.org/10.1016/j.tourman.2010.06.011

Fajardo-Toro, C. H., Mula, J., & Poler, R. (2019). Adaptive and hybrid forecasting models—A review. *Engineering Digital Transformation,* 315–322. https://doi. org/10.1007/978-3-319-96005-0_38

Fritz, R. G., Brandon, C., & Xander, J. (1984). Combining time series and econometric forecast of tourism activity. *Annals of Tourism Research, 11*(2), 219–229. https://doi.org/10.1016/0160-7383(84)90071-9

Gunter, U., & Önder, I. (2016). Forecasting city arrivals with Google Analytics. *Annals of Tourism Research, 61,* 199–212. https://doi.org/10.1016/j.annals. 2016.10.007

Hassani, H., Silva, E. S., Antonakakis, N., Filis, G., & Gupta, R. (2017). Forecasting accuracy evaluation of tourist arrivals. *Annals of Tourism Research, 63*, 112–127. https://doi.org/10.1016/j.annals.2017.01.008

He, K., Ji, L., Wu, C. W. D., & Tso, K. F. G. (2021). Using SARIMA–CNN–LSTM approach to forecast daily tourism demand. *Journal of Hospitality and Tourism Management, 49*, 25–33. https://doi.org/10.1016/j.jhtm.2021.08.022

Hong, W. C., Dong, Y., Chen, L. Y., & Wei, S. Y. (2011). SVR with hybrid chaotic genetic algorithms for tourism demand forecasting. *Applied Soft Computing, 11*(2), 1881–1890. https://doi.org/10.1016/j.asoc.2010.06.003

Hu, Y. C., Jiang, P., & Lee, P. C. (2019). Forecasting tourism demand by incorporating neural networks into Grey–Markov models. *Journal of the Operational Research Society, 70*(1), 12–20. https://doi.org/10.1080/01605682.2017.1418150

Hyndman, R. J., Akram, M., & Archibald, B. C. (2008). The admissible parameter space for exponential smoothing models. *Annals of the Institute of Statistical Mathematics, 60*(2), 407–426. https://doi.org/https://doi.org/10.1007/s10463-006-0109-x

Hyndman, R., Athanasopoulos, G., Bergmeir, C., Caceres, G., Chhay, L., O'Hara-Wild, M., & Razbash, S. (2019). Package "forecast." Retrieved from https://cran.r-project.org/web/packages/forecast/forecast.pdf.

Hyndman, R. J., Koehler, A. B., Snyder, R. D., & Grose, S. (2002). A state space framework for automatic forecasting using exponential smoothing methods. *International Journal of Forecasting, 18*(3), 439–454. https://doi.org/10.1016/S0169-2070(01)00110-8

Law, R. (2000). Back-propagation learning in improving the accuracy of neural network-based tourism demand forecasting. *Tourism Management, 21*(4), 331–340. https://doi.org/10.1016/S0261-5177(99)00067-9

Law, R., & Au, N. (1999). A neural network model to forecast Japanese demand for travel to Hong Kong. *Tourism Management, 20*(1), 89–97. https://doi.org/10.1016/S0261-5177(98)00094-6

Lee, C. K., Song, H. J., & Mjelde, J. W. (2008). The forecasting of International Expo tourism using quantitative and qualitative techniques. *Tourism Management, 29*(6), 1084–1098. https://doi.org/10.1016/j.tourman.2008.02.007

Li, G., Song, H., & Witt, S. F. (2005). Recent developments in econometric modelling and forecasting. *Journal of Travel Research, 44*, 82–99. https://doi.org/10.1177/0047287505276594

Li, K., Liang, C., Lu, W., Li, C., Zhao, S., & Wang, B. (2020). Forecasting of short-term daily tourist flow based on seasonal clustering method and PSO-LSSVM. *ISPRS* International Journal of Geo-Information, 9(11), 676. https://doi.org/10.3390/ijgi9110676

Li, K., Lu, W., Liang, C., & Wang, B. (2019). Intelligence in tourism management: A hybrid FOA-BP method on daily tourism demand forecasting with web search data. *Mathematics, 7*(6), 531. https://doi.org/10.3390/math7060531

Li, S., Chen, T., Wang, L., & Ming, C. (2018). Effective tourist volume forecasting supported by PCA and improved BPNN using Baidu index. *Tourism Management, 68*, 116–126. https://doi.org/10.1016/j.tourman.2018.03.006

Liao, Z., Jin, M., Luo, Y., Ren, P., & Gao, H. (2013). Research on prediction of tourists' quantity in Jiuzhaigou Valley scenic based on ABR@ G integration model. *International Journal of Environment and Pollution, 51*(34), 176–191. https://doi.org/10.1504/IJEP.2013.054028

Lin, V. S. (2013). Improving forecasting accuracy by combining statistical and judgmental forecasts in tourism. *Journal of China Tourism Research, 9*(3), 325–352. https://doi.org/10.1080/19388160.2013.812901

Lu, W., Rui, H., Liang, C., Jiang, L., Zhao, S., & Li, K. (2020). A method based on ga-cnn-lstm for daily tourist flow prediction at scenic spots. *Entropy, 22*(3), 261. https://doi.org/10.3390/e22030261

Nguyen, T. L., Shu, M. H., Huang, Y. F., & Hsu, B. M. (2013). Accurate forecasting models in predicting the inbound tourism demand in Vietnam. *Journal of Statistics and Management Systems, 16*(1), 25–43. https://doi.org/10.1080/09720 510.2013.777570

Nor, M. E., Nurul, A. I., & Rusiman, M. S. (2018). A hybrid approach on tourism demand forecasting. In *Journal of Physics: Conference Series* (Vol. 995, No. 1, p. 012034). IOP Publishing. https://doi.org/10.1088/1742-6596/995/1/012034

Oh, C. O., & Morzuch, B. J. (2005). Evaluating time series models to forecast the demand for tourism in Singapore: Comparing within sample and postsample results. *Journal of Travel Research, 43*(4), 404–413. https://doi.org/10.1177/0047287505274653

Pai, P. F., Hung, K. C., & Lin, K. P. (2014). Tourism demand forecasting using novel hybrid system. *Expert Systems with Applications, 41*(8), 3691–3702. https://doi.org/10.1016/j.eswa.2013.12.007

Pattie, D. C., & Snyder, J. (1996). Using a neural network to forecast visitor behavior. *Annals of Tourism Research, 23*(1), 151–164. https://doi.org/10.1016/0160-7383(95)00052-6

Shabri, A. (2016). A hybrid of EEMD and LSSVM-PSO model for tourist demand forecasting. *Indian Journal of Science and Technology, 36*(9), 1–6. https://doi.org/10.17485/ijst/2016/v9i36/97773

Shabri, A., Samsudin, R., & Yusoff, Y. (2020, May). Combining Deep Neural Network and Fourier Series for Tourist Arrivals Forecasting. In IOP Conference Series: Materials Science and Engineering (Vol. 864, No. 1, p. 012094). IOP Publishing.https://doi.org/10.1088/1757-899X/864/1/012094

Shen, M. L., Liu, H. H., Lien, Y. H., Lee, C. F., & Yang, C. H. (2019). Hybrid approach for forecasting tourist arrivals. In *Proceedings of the 2019 8th International Conference on Software and Computer Applications* (pp. 392–396). https://doi.org/10.1145/3316615.3316628

Shen, S., Li, G., & Song, H. (2008). An assessment of combining tourism demand forecasts over different time horizons. *Journal of Travel Research, 47(2)*, 197–207. https://doi.org/10.1177/0047287508321199

Shen, S., Li, G., & Song, H. (2011). Combination forecasts of international tourism demand. *Annals of Tourism Research, 38*(1), 72–89. https://doi.org/10.1016/j.annals.2010.05.003

Song, H., Gao, B. Z., & Lin, V. S. (2013). Combining statistical and judgmental forecasts via a web based tourism demand forecasting system. *International Journal of Forecasting, 29*(2), 295–310. https://doi.org/10.1016/j.ijforecast.2011.12.003

Song, H., Qiu, R. T., & Park, J. (2019). A review of research on tourism demand forecasting: Launching the Annals of Tourism Research Curated Collection on tourism demand forecasting. *Annals of Tourism Research, 75*, 338–362. https://doi.org/10.1016/j.annals.2018.12.001

Wan, S., & Song, H. (2018). Forecasting turning points in tourism growth. *Annals of Tourism Research, 72*, 156–167. https://doi.org/10.1016/j.annals.2018.07.010

Wen, L., Liu, C., & Song, H. (2019). Forecasting tourism demand using search query data: A hybrid modelling approach. *Tourism Economics, 25*(3), 309–329. https://doi.org/10.1177/1354816618768317

Wong, K. K., Song, H., Witt, S. F., & Wu, D. C. (2007). Tourism forecasting: To combine or not to combine? *Tourism Management, 28*(4), 1068–1078. https://doi.org/10.1016/j.tourman.2006.08.003

Wu, D. C. W., Ji, L., He, K., & Tso, K. F. G. (2021). Forecasting tourist daily arrivals with a hybrid Sarima–Lstm approach. *Journal of Hospitality & Tourism Research, 45*(1), 52–67. https://doi.org/10.1177/1096348020934046

Zhang, B., Huang, X., Li, N., & Law, R. (2017). A novel hybrid model for tourist volume forecasting incorporating search engine data. *Asia Pacific Journal of Tourism Research, 22*(3), 245–254. https://doi.org/10.1080/10941665.2016.1232742

APPENDIX

R CODE

```
#Hybrid model for Chapter 8
  install.packages("forecast")
  install.packages("neuralnet")
  library("forecast")
  library("neuralnet")
  ##Loading data from local file
  setwd("data/MAL25")
  THA _ CHN<-read.csv('THA _ CHN.csv')
  THA _ MAL<-read.csv('THA _ MAL.csv')
  THA _ RUS<-read.csv('THA _ RUS.csv')
  THA _ USA<-read.csv('THA _ USA.csv')
  ##Adding the dummy of Q4 into data
  Q4<-rep(c(0,0,0,1),times=20)
  THA _ CHN<-cbind(THA _ CHN[1:80,1:10],Q4,THA _ CHN[1:80,11:16])
  THA _ MAL<-cbind(THA _ MAL[1:80,1:10],Q4,THA _ MAL[1:80,11:13])
  THA _ RUS<-cbind(THA _ RUS[1:80,1:10],Q4,THA _ RUS[1:80,11:12])
  THA _ USA<-cbind(THA _ USA[1:80,1:10],Q4,THA _ USA[1:80,11:14])
  prepared _ data<-list(4)
  original _ data<-list(China=THA _ CHN[,2:11],Malaysia=THA _
MAL[,2:11],
                 Russia=THA _ RUS[,2:11],USA=THA _ USA[1:80,2:11])
  rm(THA _ CHN,THA _ MAL,THA _ RUS,THA _ USA)
  ##calculating price of China, Malaysia, Russia and USA
  for (market in 1:4){
    datamatrix<-original _ data[[market]]
    for (i in 1:80){
            datamatrix[i,11]<-(datamatrix[i,4]/datamatrix[i,6])/
(datamatrix[i,3]/datamatrix[i,5])
```

```
    }
    prepared _ data[[market]]<-datamatrix[,c(1,2,7:11)]
  }
  forecast _ values<-array(NA,dim = c(4,4,12,8))
  hidddot<-array(NA,dim = c(4,2))
  RMSE<-array(data = NA,dim = c(4,8,50,10))
  set.seed(1234)
  for (market in 1:4){
    vt=Sys.time()
    print(vt)
    datamatrix<-prepared _ data[[market]]
    #benchmark
    for (k in 1:12){
      arrival _ ts<-ts(log(prepared _ data[[market]][k:(67+k),1]),
frequency = 4)
      h<-min(13-k,8)
      ##to get multi-step forecast of Seasonal Naive
      model1<-snaive(arrival _ ts)
      forecast _ valuesue<-forecast(model1,h)$mean
                          forecast _ values[market,1,k,1:h]<-as.
numeric(forecast _ valuesue[1:h])
      ##to get multi-step forecast of ETS
      model2<-ets(arrival _ ts)
      forecast _ valuesue<-forecast(model2,h)$mean
                          forecast _ values[market,2,k,1:h]<-as.
numeric(forecast _ valuesue)
      ##to get multi-step forecast of Seasonal ARIMA
      model3<-auto.arima(arrival _ ts)
      forecast _ valuesue<-forecast(model3,h)$mean
                          forecast _ values[market,3,k,1:h]<-as.
numeric(forecast _ valuesue)
    }
    foreca<-matrix(NA, nrow = 80,ncol = 24)
    for (k in 1:72){
      arrival _ ts<-ts(prepared _ data[[market]][1:(7+k),1],fre-
quency = 4)
      h<-8
      ##to get multi-step forecast of SARIMA
      model1<-auto.arima(arrival _ ts)
      forecast _ valuesue<-forecast(model1,h)$mean
      foreca[(8+k),1:8]<-forecast _ valuesue
      ##to get multi-step forecast of ETS
      model2<-ets(arrival _ ts)
      forecast _ valuesue<-forecast(model2,h)$mean
      foreca[(8+k),9:16]<-forecast _ valuesue
```

```
      ##to get multi-step forecast of SNAIVE
      model3<-snaive(arrival _ ts)
      forecast _ valuesue<-forecast(model3,h)$mean
      foreca[(8+k),17:24]<-forecast _ valuesue
   }
  datamatrix<-cbind(datamatrix,foreca)
  for (step in c(1,2,3,4,8)){
    ##output of hybrid model
    train _ output<-datamatrix[(8+step):80,1]
    ##input of hybrid model
    train _ input<-data.frame(datamatrix[8:(80-step),c(2,7)],
                       datamatrix[9:(81-step),(7+step)],
                       datamatrix[9:(81-step),(15+step)],
                       datamatrix[(8+step):80,3:6],
                       datamatrix[8:(80-step),1],
                       datamatrix[9:(81-step),(23+step)])
  BP _ input _ and _ output<-cbind(train _ output,train _ input)
  colnames(BP _ input _ and _ output)<-c("arrive","Price _
        lag _ step","Income _ lag _ step","arima _ forecast",
        "ets _ forecast","D1","D2","D3","D4","arrive _ lag _
        step","snaive _ forecast")
  maxs<-apply(BP _ input _ and _ output,2,max)
  mins<-apply(BP _ input _ and _ output,2,min)
  BP _ input _ and _ output _ s<-as.data.frame(scale
(BP _ input _ and _ output,
                                        center =
mins,scale = maxs-mins))
  flag<-100000000000
  ##searching the best parameter of hybrid model by using
RMSE
    for (thre in c(0.005,0.01,0.02,0.03,0.04,0.05)){
      for (hidd in seq(2,10,1)){
        validation<-c()
        for (k in 1:4){
           hybrid _ module<-neuralnet(arrive~.,data = BP _
input _ and _ output _ s[k:(73-step-12-5+k),], threshold = thre,
hidden = hidd, act.fct="logistic", stepmax=100000, linear.
output=TRUE)
           validation[k]<-predict(hybrid _ module,BP _ input _
and _ output _ s[(73-step-12-4+k),2:11])*(maxs[1]-mins[1])+mins[1]
```

```
            }
            real<-train _ output[(73-step-15):(73-step-12)]
            RMSE[market,step,thre*1000,hidd]<-accuracy(ts(valida-
tion),real)[2]
          validation _ rmse<-accuracy(ts(validation),real)[2]
          if (validation _ rmse<flag){
               flag<-validation _ rmse
               thre _ flag<-thre
               hidd _ flag<-hidd
          }
        }
      }
      hidddot[market,]<-c(thre _ flag,hidd _ flag)
      thre<-thre _ flag
      hidd<-hidd _ flag
      hybird _ predict<-c()
      ##forecasting by using best parameter
      for (k in 1:12){
      hybrid _ module<-neuralnet(arrive~.,data = BP _ input _ and _
output _ s[k:(73-step-12-1+k),], threshold = thre, hidden =
hidd, act.fct="logistic", stepmax=100000, linear.output=TRUE)
            hybird _ predict[k]<-predict(hybrid _ module,BP _ input _
and _ output _ s[(73-step-12+k),2:11])*(maxs[1]-mins[1])+mins[1]
         }
         forecast _ values[market,4,1:(13-step),step]<-hybird _ pre-
dict[step:12]
         }
       }
       ###Computing forecasting accuracy of SARIMA,ETS,SNAIVE and
Hybrid model in China, Malaysia, Russia and USA
       result<-array(NA,dim = c(4,4,8,3))
       for (market in 1:4){
         for (model in 1:4){
           for (step in c(1,2,3,4,8)){
             print(c(market,model,step))
             denominator<-mean(abs(diff(prepared _ data
[[market]]$Arr, 4)))
             if (model==1|2|3) {
             residuals<-exp(forecast _ values[market,mod-
el,1:(13-step),step])-prepared _ data[[market]][(68+step):80,1]
```

```
            result[market,model,step,1:2]<-accuracy(exp(-
forecast _ values[market,model,1:(13-step),step]),prepared _
data[[market]][(68+step):80,1])[c(5,2)]
          }
        if (model==4){
          residuals<-forecast _ values[market,mod-
el,1:(13-step),step]-prepared _ data[[market]][(68+step):80,1]
          result[market,model,step,1:2]<-accuracy(forecast _
values[market,model,1:(13-step),step],prepared _ data[[market]]
[(68+step):80,1])[c(5,2)]
          }
        result[market,model,step,3]<-mean(abs(residuals)/
denominator)


      }
    }
  }


  ###Output: Forecasts and accuracy tables
  ###save MAPE
  MAPE<-rbind(c("*"),result[1,,c(1,2,3,4,8),1],c("*"),re-
sult[2,,c(1,2,3,4,8),1],c("*"),result[3,,c(1,2,3,4,8),1],c("*"),re-
sult[4,,c(1,2,3,4,8),1])
  colnames(MAPE)<-c("one _ step","two _ step","three _ step","-
four _ step","eight _ step")
  rownames(MAPE)<-c("mainland      China","SNAIVE","ETS","SARI-
MA","Hybrid     model","Malaysia","SNAIVE","ETS","SARIMA","Hybrid
model","Russia","SNAIVE","ETS","SARIMA","Hybrid              mod-
el","USA","SNAIVE","ETS","SARIMA","Hybrid model")
  write.csv(MAPE,file = "MAPE.csv")
  ##save RMSE
  RMSE<-rbind(c("*"),result[1,,c(1,2,3,4,8),2],c("*"),re-
sult[2,,c(1,2,3,4,8),2],c("*"),result[3,,c(1,2,3,4,8),2],c("*"),re-
sult[4,,c(1,2,3,4,8),2])
  colnames(RMSE)<-c("one _ step","two _ step","three _ step","-
four _ step","eight _ step")
  rownames(RMSE)<-c("mainland China","SNAIVE","ETS","SARIMA",
"Hybrid    model","Malaysia","SNAIVE","ETS","SARIMA","Hybrid    mod-
el","Russia","SNAIVE","ETS","SARIMA","Hybridmodel","USA","SNAIVE",
"ETS","SARIMA","Hybrid model")
  write.csv(RMSE,file = "RMSE.csv")
  ##save MASE
  MASE<-rbind(c("*"),result[1,,c(1,2,3,4,8),3],c("*"),result[2,
,c(1,2,3,4,8),3],c("*"),result[3,,c(1,2,3,4,8),3],c("*"),result[4
,,c(1,2,3,4,8),3])
```

```
colnames(MASE)<-c("one _ step","two _ step","three _ step","-
four _ step","eight _ step")
rownames(MASE)<-c("mainland China","SNAIVE","ETS","SARIMA",
"Hybrid model","Malaysia","SNAIVE","ETS","SARIMA","Hybrid mod-
el","Russia","SNAIVE","ETS","SARIMA","Hybrid model","USA","SNA-
IVE","ETS","SARIMA","Hybrid model")
write.csv(MASE,file = "MASE.csv")
```

9

DENSITY FORECASTING

Long Wen

9.1 Introduction

Tourism demand forecasting studies often focus on point forecasting. However, point forecasts cannot provide any information about the degree of uncertainty associated with the forecasts (Kim et al., 2011), which is essential for optimal decision making. Interval forecasts incorporate the uncertainties of forecasts into the generation of forecast intervals, corresponding to a prescribed confidence level. Although interval forecasts are more informative than point forecasts, they provide no information about what the tails of the forecasts look like. For a complete description of the uncertainty associated with a forecast, density forecasts can be used to forecast the probability distribution of the possible future values of the random variable of interest. Density forecasts contain all of the information provided by point and interval forecasts. In fact, point forecasts are often just the means of the density forecasts.

The differences between point, interval and density forecasts can be illustrated using the example of a forecast that has been generated for the growth rate of tourism demand, with a normal distribution with a mean of 0.1 and a standard deviation of 0.1. The corresponding point, 90% interval and density forecasts for this example are shown in Figure 9.1. The point forecast in this case is often equal to 0.1 (the mean), the 90% interval forecast can be constructed by $0.1 \pm 1.645 \times 0.1$ and the density forecast is the normal distribution itself with a mean of 0.1 and a standard deviation of 0.1. All of the information contained by point and interval forecasts can be generated using density forecasts.

Density forecasts allow users to derive the forecasts of the probabilities of any event of interest. This is relevant in the context of tourism demand

DOI: 10.4324/9781003269366-9

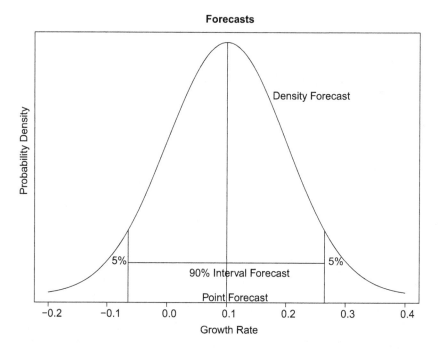

FIGURE 9.1   Point, interval and density forecasts

forecasting because the users often need to make decisions, such as decisions about staffing, pricing and investment in infrastructure projects, based on forecasts about the probability of a specific event occurring (e.g., the probability of demand exceeding current capacity). Therefore, if density forecasts are used properly, they can help achieve optimal decision making subject to specific loss functions.

Density forecasts have gained popularity in various fields, such as weather (Leutbecher & Palmer, 2008; Palmer, 2012), population (Raftery et al., 2014), epidemiology (Alkema et al., 2007) and economics and finance (Garratt et al., 2011; Groen et al., 2013; Tay & Wallis, 2000). In finance, risk measures, such as value-at-risk (VaR), can be generated using density forecasts. VaR is a good example of a specific event of interest in the financial industry. The Survey of Professional Forecasters was first established in 1968 (Croushore, 1993) to produce macroeconomic density forecasts in the USA. Many other countries, such as the UK, Australia, Brazil, Canada, Norway, the Philippines, South Africa, Thailand and Turkey, have since started producing macroeconomic density forecasts (Hammond, 2012).

Few studies attempt to investigate density forecasting in a tourism context. Wan, Song and Ko (2016) first investigated the use of the probability integral transform (PIT) to evaluate the distributional assumption in density forecasts of tourism demand in Hong Kong. A histogram-based evaluation technique proposed by Diebold, Gunther, and Tay (1998) can be used to check the null hypothesis of the joint uniformity of PITs. This is an absolute evaluation method concerning the statistical compatibility between density forecasts and observations. Song et al. (2019) further used proper scoring rules to compare the performance of several alternative models in generating density forecasts for tourism demand in Hong Kong.

9.2 Methods

In this section, different ways to generate density forecasts and how to evaluate them are discussed.

9.2.1 Generation of density forecasts

Different models may impose different assumptions on error terms, leading to density forecasts with different distributions. Of focus here are two commonly used models in tourism demand forecasting, namely, seasonal autoregressive integrated moving average (SARIMA) and dynamic regression (DR) models, both of which assume that errors are normally distributed.

The SARIMA model can accommodate autoregressive, moving average terms and differencing for both seasonal and non-seasonal frequencies. The general form of the SARIMA(p, d, q)(P, D, Q)$_m$ model can be expressed as

$$\Phi\left(B^m\right)\phi(B)\left(1-B^m\right)^D(1-B)^d\, y_t = \delta + \Theta\left(B^m\right)\theta(B)u_t, \tag{9.1}$$

where u_t is a white noise process with a mean of zero and a fixed variance of σ^2; m is the order of periodicity; B is the backshift operator; $\left(1-B^m\right)^D$ and $(1-B)^d$ are seasonal and annual differencing order terms; $\Phi(x)$ and $\Theta(x)$ are the seasonal components of polynomials of orders P and Q, respectively; and $\phi(x)$ and $\theta(x)$ are the non-seasonal components of polynomials of orders p and q, respectively. An automatic procedure can be used to select the orders (Hyndman & Khandakar, 2008). Seasonal differencing order D is first chosen based on a measure of seasonal strength. If the seasonal strength is larger than 0.64, seasonal differencing is selected (Wang et al., 2006). Then the order of non-seasonal differencing d is chosen based on the Kwiatkowski–Phillips–Schmidt–Shin unit-root test (Kwiatkowski et al., 1992). Finally, the order of autoregressive and moving average terms p, q, P and Q are chosen based on the corrected Akaike information criterion using a stepwise procedure to traverse the model space. The parameters are estimated using maximum likelihood estimation.

A typical linear regression model can be expressed as

$$y_t = \beta_0 + \beta_1 x_{1,t} + \ldots + \beta_K x_{K,t} + \mu_t \tag{9.2}$$

where $x_{1,t}, \ldots, x_{K,t}$ are regressors, such as the income level in the origin country and the relative price of the destination to that of the source markets. The error term, μ_t, is often assumed to be white noise. However, the model can be extended to allow the errors to have autocorrelation and follow a SARIMA model. As a result, it becomes a DR model and can be written as

$$y_t = \beta_0 + \beta_1 x_{1,t} + \ldots + \beta_K x_{K,t} + \eta_t \tag{9.3}$$

$$\Phi\left(B^m\right)\phi(B)\left(1 - B^m\right)^D (1 - B)^d \, \eta_t = \delta + \Theta\left(B^m\right)\theta(B)\varepsilon_t \tag{9.4}$$

where ϵ_t is white noise. It can also be estimated in a similar way as the SARIMA model, except that it involves a linear regression in the first step. The spurious regression problem is addressed by unit-root tests and differencing if needed. For error terms with $d > 0$, the DR model is the same as using differenced variables in the regression model. For example, a DR model with an error following a SARIMA(1,1,1) model

$$(1 - \phi_1 B)(1 - B)\eta_t = (1 + \theta_1 B)\varepsilon_t \tag{9.5}$$

can be rewritten as

$$y_t' = \beta_0 + \beta_1 x_{1,t}' + \ldots + \beta_K x_{K,t}' + \eta_t' \tag{9.6}$$

$$(1 - \phi_1 B)\eta_t' = (1 + \theta_1 B)\varepsilon_t \tag{9.7}$$

To illustrate the generation of forecasts, consider a simple example of the AR(1) model

$$y_t = \phi y_{t-1} + u_t \tag{9.8}$$

Given data up to time T, y_{T+1} can be written as

$$y_{T+1} = \phi y_T + u_{T+1} \tag{9.9}$$

Its point forecast, which is its conditional mean (minimising the expected squared forecast error) given data up to time T, can be expressed as

$$\hat{y}_{T+1|T} = E\left(y_{T+1} \mid Y_T\right) = \phi E\left(y_T \mid Y_T\right) + E\left(u_{T+1} \mid Y_T\right) = \phi y_T \tag{9.10}$$

where $Y_T = [y_1, y_2, \ldots, y_T]$. Similarly, the point forecast of time $T+2$ can be calculated as

$$\hat{y}_{T+2|T} = \phi^2 y_T \tag{9.11}$$

In general,

$$\hat{y}_{T+h|T} = \phi^h y_T \tag{9.12}$$

Given the assumption that u_t s are normally distributed, the forecasts are also normally distributed, and the conditional variance can be calculated to generate the predictive density or density forecast.

$$Var(y_{T+1} | Y_T) = Var(u_{T+1}) = \sigma^2 \tag{9.13}$$
$$Var(y_{T+2} | Y_T) = Var(u_{T+2} + \phi u_{T+1}) = \sigma^2(1+\phi^2) \tag{9.14}$$

In general,

$$Var(y_{T+h} | Y_T) = \sigma^2(1+\phi^2+\ldots+\phi^{2(h-1)}) = \sigma^2 \frac{1-\phi^{2h}}{1-\phi^2} \tag{9.15}$$

for stationary cases. Therefore, given data up to time T, the density forecast of time $T+h$ is then $N\left(\phi^h y_T, \sigma^2 \frac{1-\phi^{2h}}{1-\phi^2}\right)$ for an AR(1) model.

For SARIMA models, the calculations become more complicated, but density forecasts can always be generated in a similar way for a particular forecasting horizon. For DR models, the forecasts of $x_{1,T+h},\ldots,x_{K,T+h}$ can be used to generate the density forecasts of y_{T+h}, often referred to as ex ante forecasts. Alternatively, the true values of $x_{1,T+h},\ldots,x_{K,T+h}$ can be used, and the resulting forecasts of y_{T+h} are ex post forecasts. In this chapter, ex post density forecasts are generated for DR models.

In the context of tourism demand forecasting, it is common to use log transformation on the variables before the modelling process. The point forecasts of the transformed data are then generated and need to be transformed back to the original scale before forecast accuracy is evaluated. In the case of density forecasts, the implication of data transformation is beyond the change of scale and imposes a change of distribution on the forecasts of the original variable. Again, using AR(1) as an example, assuming that the model is applied to log-transformed data instead of the original scale, the model specification essentially becomes

$$\ln(y_t) = \phi \ln(y_{t-1}) + u_t \tag{9.16}$$

As a result, the forecast of time $T+1$ given data up to time T is then

$$\ln(y_{T+1})|Y_T = [\phi \ln(y_T) + u_{T+1}]|Y_T \sim N(\phi \ln(y_T), \sigma^2) \tag{9.17}$$

This suggests that the forecast of a log-transformed variable follows a normal distribution. Therefore, the density forecast of y_{T+1} follows a lognormal distribution. This applies similarly to other models that have normally distributed errors fitted to log-transformed data.

9.2.2 Evaluation of density forecasts

The goal of density forecasting is to maximise the sharpness of the predictive distributions, subject to calibration (Gneiting et al., 2007). The notion of calibration refers to the statistical compatibility of the density forecasts and the realisations. If the model is correctly specified, the observed realisations should resemble random draws from the density forecasts. Sharpness refers to the concentration of density forecasts and can be assessed by the widths of the associated prediction intervals.

Various methods have been proposed in the literature to evaluate density forecasts. PITs have been used to check the generated density forecasts, and the realisations are compatible. To simplify the notations, assume that a density forecast is generated for observation y_t, given data up to a certain time point before t. The PIT of y_t can be defined as

$$z_t = \int_{-\infty}^{y_t} p_t(u)\,du = P_t(y_t) \tag{9.18}$$

where $p_t(y_t)$ is the probability density function (PDF) of the forecast of y_t. If the true PDF of y_t is $f_t(y_t)$ and $p_t(y_t) = f_t(y_t)$, the PIT z_t is uniformly distributed on the interval [0,1] ($z_t \sim U(0,1)$). Furthermore, if a sequence of one-step-ahead density forecasts coincides with true densities, the sequence of PITs is independently, identically and uniformly distributed $U(0,1)$ (Diebold et al., 1998). A histogram-based evaluation technique can be used to check the uniformity of PITs. The bins should have similar heights if the density forecasts are correctly generated. Various formal tests have been proposed to test for independence and uniformity (Berkowitz, 2001; Hong & White, 2005). Although such tests provide information regarding the statistical compatibility between density forecasts and realisations, it is difficult to select and compare models when multiple models or none of the models pass the test. In contrast, scoring rules are useful for comparisons to evaluate and rank density forecasts. In addition, proper scoring rules can be used to assess calibration and sharpness simultaneously and to encourage forecasters to provide honest and careful quotes (Gneiting & Katzfuss, 2014; Gneiting & Raftery, 2007).

A scoring rule assigns a numerical value to each density forecast and realised value pair. Generally, the scores are taken to be negatively oriented penalties, which means that a lower score indicates a better forecast. Models can be ranked based on their average scores over the evaluation of density forecasts. One of the most used proper scoring rules is a logarithmic score (LS; Good, 1952). It is defined as

$$LS(f,y) = -\log f(y) \tag{9.19}$$

where f is the PDF of the forecast and y is the realised value. If the density forecasts generated by a model are close to the true densities, the LSs tend to have low values on average.

Another popular proper scoring rule is the continuous rank probability score (CRPS; Matheson & Winkler, 1976). It is defined as

$$\mathrm{CRPS}(F,y) = \int \left(F(z) - 1\left\{y \le z\right\}\right)^2 dz \tag{9.20}$$

where F is the cumulative distribution function (CDF) of the forecast and $1\left\{y \le z\right\}$) is an indicator function that is equal to 1 if $y \le z$ and 0 otherwise. The CRPS measures the average absolute distance between F and the empirical CDF of the realisation, which is a step function at y.

A density forecast can take the form of a specific distribution with certain parameters or a sample of simulated point forecasts. For example, in weather forecasting applications, density forecasts consist of simulated sample values that are generated by numerical weather prediction models with different model physics and initial conditions. The calculation of the LS requires a predictive PDF, which can be obtained via nonparametric kernel density estimation using a simulated sample of point forecasts. However, this estimator is only valid under stringent theoretical assumptions and can be highly sensitive to the choice of the bandwidth tuning parameter if the realisation falls into the tails of the simulated forecast distribution (Krüger et al., 2021). CRPS values can be calculated by first calculating empirical CDF from the simulated sample. If F is a point forecast, the empirical CDF becomes a step function at the value of the point forecast and the CRPS is reduced to the absolute error. Therefore, the CRPS offers a direct method of comparing point and density forecasts. To facilitate the comparison between different density forecasts, as well as between density and point forecasts, the CRPS is used as the scoring rule in the following applications.

9.3 Application

9.3.1 Evaluation of point and density forecasts

Four different model settings are adopted to generate the point and density forecasts, namely, each of the two models (SARIMA and DR) with and without log transformation. Point and density forecasts are generated for each model setting, resulting in eight different sets of forecasts for each country. These forecasts are denoted as follows:

- SARIMA.P: The point forecasts generated by the SARIMA model.
- SARIMA.D: The density forecasts generated by the SARIMA model.

- SARIMA.LOG.P: The point forecasts generated by the SARIMA model fitted on the log-transformed series, which are then transformed back to the original scale.
- SARIMA.LOG.D: The density forecasts generated by the SARIMA model fitted on the log-transformed series, which are then transformed back to the original scale.
- DR.P: The point forecasts generated by the DR model.
- DR.D: The density forecasts generated by the DR model.
- DR.LOG.P: The point forecasts generated by the DR model fitted on the log-transformed series, which are then transformed back to the original scale.
- DR.LOG.D: The density forecasts generated by the DR model fitted on the log-transformed series, which are then transformed back to the original scale.

A rolling window approach is used to generate and evaluate the forecasts recursively. First, the data for the period 2000Q1–2014Q4 are used for model estimation, and one- to eight-step-ahead forecasts are generated and evaluated using the actual data. Then the second round of forecasts is generated and evaluated after re-estimating the model using data for the period 2000Q2–2015Q1. This is repeated until the last round, during which the data for the period 2004Q4–2019Q3 are used for model estimation and one-step-ahead forecasts are generated and evaluated for 2019Q4.

The performance of the density forecasts for arrivals from mainland China are presented in Table 9.1. All of the density forecasts outperform their point counterparts, and, generally, the improvement of the density forecasts over point forecasts becomes larger as the forecasting horizon

TABLE 9.1 Average CRPS across different forecasting horizons for arrivals from mainland China

Method	Forecasting horizon							
	1	2	3	4	5	6	7	8
SARIMA.P	331,387	468,760	544,887	522,491	677,575	610,651	686,849	670,518
SARIMA.D	256,485	363,968	423,634	367,361	501,905	452,959	511,864	480,752
SARIMA.LOG.P	458,933	425,759	605,361	636,588	877,903	893,160	1,013,371	906,435
SARIMA.LOG.D	321,525	323,325	395,429	391,020	517,376	503,573	546,567	490,077
DR.P	395,713	499,540	540,322	447,607	434,697	405,916	382,991	389,223
DR.D	330,760	411,330	419,008	330,725	332,342	288,117	273,269	286,680
DR.LOG.P	398,674	454,568	535,309	613,863	795,734	806,197	767,035	638,917
DR.LOG.D	278,688	326,775	367,925	414,414	521,154	525,407	512,376	477,893

increases. When comparing the density forecasts generated by the alternative model settings, DR.D outperforms the other models for forecasting horizons longer than three. For shorter forecasting horizons, the performance of the different model settings is similar. However, DR.D shows much better forecasting performance than the density forecasts generated by the other models over forecasting horizons longer than four. Log transformation improves the forecasting performance for shorter forecasting horizons (shorter than four). In contrast, for longer forecasting horizons, log transformation worsens the forecasting performance. This is true for both the point and density forecasts. The DR models perform better than the SARIMA models for the data from the original scale, but they show similar performance for the data from the log-transformed scale.

The results for arrivals from Malaysia are shown in Table 9.2. The same pattern as for mainland China can be observed when comparing the point forecasts with the density forecasts, with the density forecasts outperforming their point counterparts and the differences increasing when the forecasting horizon increases. In terms of the density forecasts, the best model is SARIMA.D, which outperforms the other models for six out of eight forecasting horizons. Whereas DR.D and DR.LOG.D demonstrate similar forecasting performance, the SARIMA models perform worse on the data from the log-transformed scale. As a result, the SARIMA.LOG.D model performs worse overall than the density forecasts generated by the DR models. This is different from the case of mainland China, where the effect is different for different forecasting horizons.

The results for Russia are presented in Table 9.3. As with mainland China and Malaysia, it is clear that the density forecasts outperform the point forecasts, and the differences widen as the forecasting horizon increases. The DR.D models perform the best overall, especially over longer

TABLE 9.2 Average CRPS across different forecasting horizons for arrivals from Malaysia

Method	Forecasting horizon							
	1	2	3	4	5	6	7	8
SARIMA.P	83,764	86,448	84,995	72,621	103,826	84,350	96,507	81,413
SARIMA.D	58,499	58,429	62,941	52,870	72,978	61,994	71,156	62,399
SARIMA.LOG.P	77,611	86,853	93,583	93,678	101,124	105,879	106,149	102,542
SARIMA.LOG.D	55,199	64,428	69,978	71,996	75,995	77,116	81,121	78,980
DR.P	82,313	100,921	89,910	88,602	101,312	101,158	98,753	93,528
DR.D	59,163	71,949	67,258	65,293	71,607	73,670	73,107	70,433
DR.LOG.P	88,593	102,931	10,3070	101,267	99,606	108,254	101,296	86,371
DR.LOG.D	59,807	71,763	70,688	68,290	71,018	75,641	71,975	64,137

TABLE 9.3 Average CRPS across different forecasting horizons for arrivals from Russia

Method	Forecasting horizon							
	1	2	3	4	5	6	7	8
SARIMA.P	77,910	69,591	53,242	52,697	110,679	134,169	111,334	123,786
SARIMA.D	59,155	50,932	40,649	39,322	78,839	97,154	84,483	91,099
SARIMA.LOG.P	59,926	61,818	60,068	90,031	136,515	126,955	164,387	211,210
SARIMA.LOG.D	42,473	44,007	46,049	63,408	92,388	78,636	88,991	119,360
DR.P	57,983	51,971	41,633	57,637	85,445	83,610	74,765	87,073
DR.D	44,577	37,628	30,112	42,435	65,951	56,835	49,868	61,473
DR.LOG.P	54,249	50,962	44,186	68,348	109,257	91,247	104,712	130,538
DR.LOG.D	38,567	36,375	33,991	49,443	72,542	59,424	63,039	84,980

forecasting horizons. Except for DR.D, the performance of the point forecasts deteriorates quickly as the forecasting horizon increases. The log transformation effects are similar to the effects for the case of mainland China, with the log transformation generally improving the forecasting performance over short forecasting horizons and worsening the performance over longer forecasting horizons. The DR models perform better than the SARIMA models over all of the forecasting horizons.

Lastly, the results for the USA are shown in Table 9.4. The same pattern can be observed when comparing the density and point forecasts as for the previous cases. In terms of the density forecasts, except for the one-step-ahead forecasts, DR.LOG.D performs best and the DR models consistently outperform their SARIMA counterparts, with the improvements increasing as the forecasting horizon increases. Log transformation improves the forecasting performance of the DR models over all of the forecasting horizons, but it only improves the forecasting performance of the SARIMA models over longer forecasting horizons.

9.3.2 Discussion

Proper scoring rules, such as the CRPS, provide a means of comparing the density forecasts generated by alternative model settings and conducting a direct comparison between density and point forecasts. The point and density forecasts for arrivals from four source markets in Thailand are generated and evaluated. Although the results vary across the different origins, there are some highlights. First, the density forecasts always outperform their point counterparts, and the difference widens as the forecasting horizon increases. This indicates that in terms of the CRPS, point forecasts

TABLE 9.4 Average CRPS across different forecasting horizons for arrivals from the USA

Method	Forecasting horizon							
	1	2	3	4	5	6	7	8
SARIMA.P	11,152	15,833	18,234	20,007	26,862	30,287	32,011	35,383
SARIMA.D	7,606	10,706	12,790	14,944	19,558	22,209	24,341	27,249
SARIMA. LOG.P	9,040	14,274	17,463	21,421	25,772	30,001	32,252	37,075
SARIMA. LOG.D	7,957	10,716	12,902	15,364	18,578	20,810	23,054	25,927
DR.P	11,449	15,152	16,757	18,774	23,698	25,059	25,622	27,020
DR.D	8,089	10,422	11,843	13,434	17,884	19,318	20,221	21,493
DR.LOG.P	11,703	14,672	16,506	18,504	21,994	23,480	24,868	24,578
DR.LOG.D	7,889	9,607	10,924	1,2342	15,243	16,258	16,925	17,251

(whose CDFs can be viewed as step functions at the point forecasts) are inferior to density forecasts. Density forecasts provide a complete description of predictive density, and they can provide useful information to decision makers with various forms of loss functions.

Except for Malaysia, the DR models (either original or log-transformed scale) show the best forecasting performance. The information used to generate the forecasts by the SARIMA and DR models is different, as the true values of regressors, such as the income and relative price variables, are used to generate the ex post density forecasts for the DR models. In this respect, it is not surprising that the DR models outperform the SARIMA models in most cases.

The effect of log transformation on the density forecasts varies across different origins and different forecasting horizons. Studies find that using log transformation can improve the point forecasts generated by time series models if the transformation can stabilise the variance of the underlying series (Lütkepohl & Xu, 2012). However, if it cannot, log transformation can negatively affect the accuracy of point forecasts. The results here show that except for the case of the USA, log transformation worsens the forecasting performance over longer forecasting horizons for both time series and econometric models. However, log transformation improves the forecasting performance of the DR models in the case of the USA.

9.4 Conclusion and future directions

Point forecasts are often generated and evaluated in tourism demand forecasting studies. However, they do not provide any information about the uncertainty associated with the forecasts. The point forecast often uses the mean of a predictive density and is only optimal for a group of restricted loss functions, such as the quadratic loss function, and may be inadequate for decision makers that have different forms of loss functions. Density forecasts can provide a complete description of the predictive distribution of the forecasts, and they can be used for various purposes, such as generating the predicted probability of any event of interest to the decision makers.

This chapter demonstrates the generation and evaluation of density forecasts. Some proper scoring rules are introduced that can be used to assess calibration and sharpness simultaneously and encourage honest forecasting. The CRPS is used here to evaluate the density forecasts and the comparison between the point and density forecasts. It is found that density forecasts always perform better than their point counterparts, suggesting that density forecasts are superior to point forecasts when they are evaluated by the CRPS.

The performance of time series (SARIMA) and econometric (DR) models are evaluated and compared. The econometric models are found to perform better in most cases. The ex post density forecasts generated by the DR models utilise the true values of regressors in the future, and these models therefore have more information when generating the forecasts compared with the SARIMA models.

The role of log transformation in density forecasting is investigated. The effect of log transformation varies across different origins and depends on the characteristics of the series in consideration.

In this chapter, some empirical data sets are used to investigate the forecasting performance of different models and the role of log transformation in density forecasts. However, the varied results indicate that series with different characteristics can give rise to different results and conclusions. A simulation study can be conducted to investigate the performance of different model settings when the true data generating process is known.

SARIMA and DR models are used with different model settings to investigate the effects of log transformation on density forecasts. However, the results may differ for other types of models and can depend on the characteristics of the series. This warrants further investigation. A simulation study can also be conducted to investigate the effects of log transformation and bootstrapping with different data generating processes.

When calculating the variance of density forecasts, most of the uncertainties come from the error terms. However, there are also uncertainties from the parameter estimation (some of these uncertainties are addressed in the DR model) and model specification. These sources of uncertainties are not accounted for and can lead to under-dispersed density forecasts. Methods such as bootstrapping can be used to account for these uncertainties and further improve the performance of density forecasts.

Self-study questions

1 Discuss the differences between point, interval and density forecasts.
2 Discuss the effect of the assumed distribution of the error term on density forecasts.
3 Why does it make sense to use LS and CRPS to assess density forecasts?
4 How can bootstrapping be used to address uncertainty in the parameters and model specification?

References

Alkema, L., Raftery, A. E., & Clark, S. J. (2007). Probabilistic projections of HIV prevalence using Bayesian melding. *The Annals of Applied Statistics*, 229–248. https://doi.org/10.1214/07-AOAS111

Berkowitz, J. (2001). Testing density forecasts, with applications to risk management. *Journal of Business & Economic Statistics, 19*(4), 465–474. https://doi.org/10.1198/07350010152596718

Croushore, D. D. (1993). Introducing: The survey of professional forecasters. *Business Review-Federal Reserve Bank of Philadelphia, 6*, 3.

Diebold, F. X., Gunther, T. A., & Tay, A. S. (1998). Evaluating density forecasts with applications to financial risk management. *International Economic Review, 39*(4), 863–883. https://doi.org/10.2307/2527342

Garratt, A., Mitchell, J., Vahey, S. P., & Wakerly, E. C. (2011). Real-time inflation forecast densities from ensemble Phillips curves. *The North American Journal of Economics and Finance, 22*(1), 77–87. https://doi.org/10.1016/j.najef.2010.09.003

Gneiting, T., Balabdaoui, F., & Raftery, A. E. (2007). Probabilistic forecasts, calibration and sharpness. *Journal of the Royal Statistical Society: Series B (Statistical Methodology), 69*(2), 243–268. https://doi.org/10.1111/j.1467-9868.2007.00587.x

Gneiting, T., & Katzfuss, M. (2014). Probabilistic forecasting. *Annual Review of Statistics and Its Application, 1*, 125–151. https://doi.org/10.1146/annurev-statistics-062713-085831

Gneiting, T., & Raftery, A. E. (2007). Strictly proper scoring rules, prediction, and estimation. *Journal of the American Statistical Association, 102*(477), 359–378. https://doi.org/10.1198/016214506000001437

Good, I. J. (1952). Rational decisions. *Journal of the Royal Statistical Society. Series B (Methodological)*, 107–114. https://doi.org/10.1111/j.2517-6161.1952.tb00104.x

Groen, J. J. J., Paap, R., & Ravazzolo, F. (2013). Real-time inflation forecasting in a changing world. *Journal of Business & Economic Statistics, 31*(1), 29–44. https://doi.org/10.1080/07350015.2012.727718

Hammond, G. (2012). *State of the art of inflation targeting.* Centre for Central Banking Studies, Bank of England. https://ideas.repec.org/b/ccb/hbooks/29.html

Hong, Y., & White, H. (2005). Asymptotic distribution theory for nonparametric entropy measures of serial dependence. *Econometrica, 73*(3), 837–901. https://doi.org/10.1111/j.1468-0262.2005.00597.x

Hyndman, R. J., & Khandakar, Y. (2008). Automatic time series forecasting: The forecast package for R. *Journal of Statistical Software, Articles, 27*(3), 1–22. https://doi.org/10.18637/jss.v027.i03

Kim, J. H., Wong, K., Athanasopoulos, G., & Liu, S. (2011). Beyond point forecasting: Evaluation of alternative prediction intervals for tourist arrivals. *International Journal of Forecasting, 27*(3), 887–901. https://doi.org/10.1016/j.ijforecast.2010.02.014

Krüger, F., Lerch, S., Thorarinsdottir, T., & Gneiting, T. (2021). Predictive inference based on Markov chain Monte Carlo output. *International Statistical Review, 89*(2), 274–301. https://doi.org/10.1111/insr.12405

Kwiatkowski, D., Phillips, P. C. B., Schmidt, P., & Shin, Y. (1992). Testing the null hypothesis of stationarity against the alternative of a unit root. *Journal of Econometrics, 54*(1), 159–178. https://doi.org/10.1016/0304-4076(92)90104-Y

Leutbecher, M., & Palmer, T. N. (2008). Ensemble forecasting. *Journal of Computational Physics, 227*(7), 3515–3539. https://doi.org/10.1016/j.jcp.2007.02.014

Lütkepohl, H., & Xu, F. (2012). The role of the log transformation in forecasting economic variables. *Empirical Economics, 42*(3), 619–638. https://doi.org/10.1007/s00181-010-0440-1

Matheson, J. E., & Winkler, R. L. (1976). Scoring rules for continuous probability distributions. *Management Science, 22*(10), 1087–1096. https://doi.org/10.1287/mnsc.22.10.1087

Palmer, T. N. (2012). Towards the probabilistic Earth-system simulator: A vision for the future of climate and weather prediction. *Quarterly Journal of the Royal Meteorological Society, 138*(665), 841–861. https://doi.org/10.1002/qj.1923

Raftery, A. E., Alkema, L., & Gerland, P. (2014). Bayesian population projections for the United Nations. *Statistical Science: A Review Journal of the Institute of Mathematical Statistics, 29*(1), 58–68. https://doi.org/10.1214/13-STS419

Song, H., Wen, L., & Liu, C. (2019). Density tourism demand forecasting revisited. *Annals of Tourism Research, 75*, 379–392. https://doi.org/10.1016/j.annals.2018.12.019

Tay, A. S., & Wallis, K. F. (2000). Density forecasting: A survey. *Journal of Forecasting, 19*(4), 235–254. https://doi.org/10.1002/1099-131X(200007)19:4<235::AID-FOR772>3.0.CO;2-L

Wan, S. K., Song, H., & Ko, D. (2016). Density forecasting for tourism demand. *Annals of Tourism Research, 60*(Supplement C), 27–30. https://doi.org/10.1016/j.annals.2016.05.012

Wang, X., Smith, K., & Hyndman, R. (2006). Characteristic-based clustering for time series data. *Data Mining and Knowledge Discovery, 13*(3), 335–364. https://doi.org/10.1007/s10618-005-0039-x

APPENDIX

R CODE

```r
library(forecast)
  library(scoringRules)
  #Read data
  data _ CHN <- read.csv("THA _ CHN.csv")
  data _ MAL <- read.csv("THA _ MAL.csv")
  data _ RUS <- read.csv("THA _ RUS.csv")
  data _ USA <- read.csv("THA _ USA.csv")
  country _ names <- c("China","Malaysia","Russia","USA")
  #Data preperation
  data _ all <- list(data _ CHN,data _ MAL,data _ RUS,data _ USA)
  names(data _ all) <- country _ names
  for (i in 1:length(data _ all)){
    data _ country <- data _ all[[i]]
    Rep <- data _ country["CPI _ D"]/data _ country["EX _ D"]/
      (data _ country["CPI _ O"]/data _ country["EX _ O"])
    data _ country["Rep"] <- Rep
    data _ country _ ts <- ts(data _ country[,-1],start=c(2000,1)
,end=c(2019,4),frequency = 4)
    data _ country _ ts _ sub <- data _ country _ ts[,c(1:2,
                                        ncol(data _ coun-
try _ ts),10:(ncol(data _ country _ ts)-1))]
    data _ all[[i]] <- data _ country _ ts _ sub
  }
  model _ names  =  c('sari _ p','sari _ d','l _ sari _ p','l _ sa-
ri _ d',
            'sarix _ p','sarix _ d','l _ sarix _ p','l _ sarix _ d')
  fore _ scores = list()
```

```
fore _ detailed _ scores = list()
set.seed(123456789)
for (i in 1:length(data _ all)){
  data _ ts <- data _ all[[i]]
  arr _ ts = data _ ts[,"Arr"]
  sarima _ point = matrix(,20,8)
  sarima _ den = matrix(,20,8)
  log _ sarima _ point = matrix(,20,8)
  log _ sarima _ den = matrix(,20,8)
  sarimax _ point = matrix(,20,8)
  sarimax _ den = matrix(,20,8)
  log _ sarimax _ point = matrix(,20,8)
  log _ sarimax _ den = matrix(,20,8)
  for (qt in 1:20){
    #Set estimation and forecasting data set
    ts _ est = window(data _ ts, start = c(2000, qt), end =
c(2015, qt - 1))
    ts _ fore = window(data _ ts, start = c(2015, qt), end =
c(2019, 4))
    len _ eval = min(8,21-qt)
    y _ fore = ts _ fore[1:len _ eval,'Arr']
    #SARIMA model
    sarima _ fit = auto.arima(ts _ est[,'Arr'])
     sarima _ fore = forecast(sarima _ fit, h = len _ eval,
level = 95)
    sarima _ mean = sarima _ fore$mean
  sarima _ se = (sarima _ fore$upper-sarima _ fore$lower)/1.96/2
                  sarima _ point[qt,    1:len _ eval]    =
crps _ sample(y _ fore,matrix(sarima _ mean,len _ eval,1))
    sarima _ den[qt, 1:len _ eval] = crps(
      y _ fore,
      family = "norm",
      mean = c(sarima _ mean),
      sd = c(sarima _ se)
    )
    #Log SARIMA model
    log _ sarima _ fit = auto.arima(log(ts _ est[,'Arr']))
    log _ sarima _ fore = forecast(log _ sarima _ fit, h =
len _ eval, level = 95)
    log _ sarima _ mean = log _ sarima _ fore$mean
    log _ sarima _ se = (log _ sarima _ fore$upper
- log _ sarima _ fore$lower)/1.96/2
      log _ sarima _ exp _ mean = exp(log _ sarima _ mean +
                  0.5 * log _ sarima _ se ^ 2)
```

```
      log _ sarima _ point[qt, 1:len _ eval] = crps _ sample(y _
fore,matrix(log _ sarima _ exp _ mean,len _ eval, 1))
      log _ sarima _ den[qt, 1:len _ eval] = crps(
        y _ fore,
        family = "lnorm",
        meanlog = c(log _ sarima _ mean),
        sdlog = c(log _ sarima _ se)
      )
      #SARIMAX model
    all _ zero _ col <- apply(ts _ est, 2, function(x) all(x==0))
    ts _ est _ reg <- ts _ est[,!all _ zero _ col]
    # ts _ fore _ reg <- ts _ fore[,!all _ zero _ col]
    ts _ fore _ reg = window(data _ ts[,!all _ zero _ col], start
= c(2015, qt), end = c(2019, 4))
      sarimax _ fit = auto.arima(ts _ est _ reg[,1],
                    xreg=ts _ est _ reg[,2:ncol(ts _ est _ reg)])
      sarimax _ fore = forecast(sarimax _ fit,
                            xreg=as.matrix(as.data.frame(ts _
fore _ reg)[1:len _ eval,2:ncol(ts _ fore _ reg)]),
                             h = len _ eval, level = 95)
      sarimax _ mean = sarimax _ fore$mean
            sarimax _ se  =  (sarimax _ fore$upper-sarimax _
fore$lower)/1.96/2
                  sarimax _ point[qt,   1:len _ eval]   =
crps _ sample(y _ fore,matrix(sarimax _ mean,len _ eval,1))
      sarimax _ den[qt, 1:len _ eval] = crps(
        y _ fore,
        family = "norm",
        mean = c(sarimax _ mean),
        sd = c(sarimax _ se)
      )
      #log SARIMAX model
      log _ sarimax _ fit = auto.arima(log(ts _ est _ reg[,1]),
                        xreg=cbind(log(ts _ est _ reg[,2:3]),
                            ts _ est _ reg[,4:ncol
                            (ts _ est _ reg)]))
      log _ sarimax _ fore = forecast(log _ sarimax _ fit,
xreg = as.matrix(cbind(as.data.frame(log(ts _ fore _ reg))[,2:3],
                        as.data.frame(ts _ fore _ reg
                        )[,4:ncol(ts _ fore _ reg)])[1:len _ eval,]),
                      h = len _ eval, level = 95)
      log _ sarimax _ mean = log _ sarimax _ fore$mean
```

```
            log _ sarimax _ se   =   (log _ sarimax _ fore$upper
- log _ sarimax _ fore$lower)/1.96/2
      log _ sarimax _ exp _ mean = exp(log _ sarimax _ mean +
                            0.5 * log _ sarimax _ se ^ 2)
      log _ sarimax _ point[qt, 1:len _ eval] = crps _ sample(y _
fore,matrix(log _ sarimax _ exp _ mean,len _ eval, 1))
      log _ sarimax _ den[qt, 1:len _ eval] = crps(
        y _ fore,
        family = "lnorm",
        meanlog = c(log _ sarimax _ mean),
        sdlog = c(log _ sarimax _ se)
      )
    }
    #Calculate Mean CRPS
    crps _ ls = list(sarima _ point,sarima _ den,log _ sarima _
point,log _ sarima _ den,
                      sarimax _ point,sarimax _ den,log _ sari-
max _ point,log _ sarimax _ den)
    fore _ detailed _ scores[[country _ names[i]]]=crps _ ls
    crps _ mean _ mat = matrix(,8,8)
    for (k in 1:length(crps _ ls)){
      crps _ mean _ mat[k,] = colMeans(crps _ ls[[k]],na.rm=TRUE)
    }
    rownames(crps _ mean _ mat)=model _ names
    colnames(crps _ mean _ mat)=paste0('h', seq(8))
    fore _ scores[[country _ names[i]]]=crps _.mean _ mat
  }
```

10

FORECAST COMBINATIONS

Doris Chenguang Wu, Chenyu Cao, and Shujie Shen

10.1 Introduction

Tourism-related businesses and policymakers rely on accurate tourism demand forecasting to manage capacity, to allocate resources and prices in the short term (Jiao & Chen, 2019), and to guide infrastructure construction and policy planning in the long term. Due to the volatility of determining factors and external disturbances, however, the tourism market often undergoes fluctuations that drive researchers to try and predict future tourism demand (Song et al., 2019), despite the difficulty. Thus, scholars have proposed various forecasting methods.

As Bates and Granger (1969) posited, forecasting models can contain different information, make different assumptions about the relationship between variables, and be combined to utilise information from various sources. As there is no single model that performs best in all situations by all criteria or over all horizons (Li et al., 2005; Wong et al., 2007), combining single models reduces the risk in model selection (Zhang, 2003).

In the tourism literature, various studies empirically verified the impact of forecast combinations on improved performance. Examples include Shen et al. (2008), Song et al. (2009), and Wong et al. (2007). These scholars found that forecast combinations performed better than, at minimum, the worst single model, while having the potential to outperform the best single models. Scholars have proposed a wide range of methods and practices concerning the construction of forecast combinations. Combinations can be obtained using different individual models, explanatory variables, estimation windows, forecasting horizons, and methods for determining the weights.

DOI: 10.4324/9781003269366-10

10.1.1 Rationale and superiority of forecast combinations

In the tourism demand forecasting literature, multiple studies have indicated that the performance of different forecasting models varies with the origin/destination pairs and forecasting horizons (Wong et al., 2007). There is also no single criterion for determining the most suitable forecasting model for specific forecasting tasks. To address this issue and obtain better forecasting performance, researchers have turned to forecast combinations. Scholars began combining forecasts in 1969 when Bates and Granger (1969) published their seminal work, which led to a large number of studies on forecast combinations across various fields. In their work, they combined two sets of forecasts and found that the composite forecasts had lower errors than component ones. By making use of all possible information contained in various individual forecasting models, forecast combinations help improve forecasting performance (Bates & Granger, 1969; Bunn, 1989; Winkler, 1989). Flores and White (1989) suggested that when individual models contain different information or are based on different assumptions and none of them provide consistently ideal forecast accuracy, combinations can generate better forecasts. Armstrong (2001) noted diversity as a strength of forecast combinations, which can help researchers avoid a narrow focus. By combining different models and their forecasts, researchers can incorporate the advantages of each model (Wong et al., 2007). Hendry and Clements (2004) offered several explanations regarding the superiority of forecast combinations relative to individual models, including that individual models provide new pieces of non-overlapping information, that combinations can deal better with structural breaks, and that individual models are possibly mis-specified. As Zhang (2003) stated, the validity of a single forecasting model for future uses might be challenged by factors of sampling variation, model uncertainty, and structural change, while combining models can easily alleviate the difficulty and risk of model selection.

Scholars have repeatedly examined the effect of combination techniques on forecasting performance in the field of tourism demand forecasting. As the first scholars to include modern econometric forecasting models as individual models, Wong et al. (2007) showed that combined models do not always outperform the best individual models, but always outperform the worst individual ones. Wong et al. (2007) only took one-step-ahead forecasts into consideration while subsequent studies have examined the performance of combination techniques for different forecasting horizons (Shen et al., 2008; Song et al., 2009). In the empirical analysis of Shen et al. (2008), all forecasts yielded by combination models were superior to individual models, across all forecasting horizons. Meanwhile, Song et al. (2009) found that combined forecasts are significantly better than the average individual models across all horizons. Song et al. (2009) also found that combinations may be more beneficial for forecasting at longer horizons. In general, forecast combinations are clearly preferred over single models, as they can reduce forecast failure risk and provide better forecast accuracy.

10.1.2 Practices for implementing forecast combinations

Just like single-model forecasting, differences in origin/destination pairs can affect forecast results of combination techniques while different combination methods also generate various levels of accuracy (Wong et al., 2007). Therefore, scholars have examined numerous combination methods in tourism demand forecasting. As stated by Armstrong (2001), diversity in underlying forecasting models is usually achieved by utilising different individual models, different explanatory variables, or non-overlapping estimation periods. Wong et al. (2007), Song et al. (2009), and Shen et al. (2011) included both time-series models and econometric models as individual models when examining the efficiency of combination methods in tourism demand forecasting. Volatility models, borrowed from the field of finance, were also examined as component models and applied to generate tourism demand forecast combinations (Coshall, 2009). In addition, Jungmittag (2016) combined forecasts across different estimation windows, which mitigated the problem of structural break, and showed that the combined method mostly outperformed single-window forecasts in the case of air travel demand.

There are various ways to achieve 'diversity'. For example, Andrawis et al. (2011) combined forecasts at different horizons, which captured the dynamics at different time scales and added information diversity to the model. Based on the idea that both linear and nonlinear models have distinct strengths in tracking the linear and nonlinear aspects of time series, Chen (2011) decomposed a time series into a linear autocorrelation part and a nonlinear part, used linear models to fit the linear part of the time series, which resulted in residuals containing only nonlinear components, and then used nonlinear models to fit the residuals. Altogether, Chen (2011) used three linear models and two nonlinear models to make six combinations, which were better able to forecast turning points in the time series. Several scholars have sought to extend the capability of forecast combinations by using nonparametric individual models (Cheng & Liu, 2014; Hu, 2021; Hu et al., 2021). Some studies have also made combinations of interval forecasts (Hu, 2021; Li et al., 2019). Interval forecasting provides more information about the variation of forecasts compared with point forecasting. Li et al. (2019) combined the density forecasts of multiple forecasting models to generate combined intervals, whereas Hu (2021) used neural networks to generate intervals based on point forecasts of individual grey models.

Regarding which individual forecasting models should be included in a combination, Coshall (2009) adopted the encompassing test

(Holden & Thompson, 1997) to determine whether combining models is worthwhile and whether all component models in the combination contribute unique information. Shen et al. (2008), however, showed that the encompassing test made no significant contribution to forecast accuracy. Cang and Yu (2014) proposed an algorithm that selects the optimal subset from all available individual models, based on information theory. Their algorithm provides a theoretical basis for model selection and is able to decrease computation load and save time compared to the practice of experimenting with all possible combinations. Andrawis et al. (2011) also proposed two more flexible methods for forecast combinations. The first involves determining whether to use combinations based on individual model performance. When there is one dominant (in terms of ex ante forecasting performance) individual model, simply using the dominant model instead of combining them can help achieve better performance; when all individual models perform similarly, combinations will be more beneficial. The second practice involves combining combined forecasts. Given that a linear combination of linearly combined forecasts is essentially another linear combination, it becomes meaningful when nonlinear forecast combination methods are included.

Combining forecasts requires forecasters to determine the weight for each forecast generated by each individual model. The most frequently used statistical combination methods are simple average, variance-covariance, and discounted mean square forecast error (MSFE) methods. Most studies with linear forecast combinations have used these methods (Cang & Yu, 2014; Shen et al., 2008; Song et al., 2009; Wong et al., 2007). In the context of international tourism, Shen et al. (2011) examined three additional combination methods: Granger and Ramanathan regression (Granger & Ramanathan, 1984), the shrinkage method (Clemen & Winkler, 1986), and the time-varying parameter combination method with Kalman filtering (Sessions & Chatterjee, 1989). However, Cang (2011) argued that in tourism forecasting, the relationships between variables are nonlinear, especially for data with seasonal patterns; linear models are only capable of approximating the real-world nonlinear relationship. Therefore, Cang (2011, 2014) proposed an array of nonlinear combination methods to obtain combination weights that provide better accuracy, including multilayer perceptron neural networks and radial basis function. Other nonlinear combination methods include support vector regression neural networks (Cang, 2014), back-propagation neural network (Chen, 2011), support vector regression (Chen, 2011), fuzzy integral (Hu et al., 2021), and the composite method of artificial neural networks and the K-means clustering algorithm (Jun et al., 2018). In addition to statistical methods for determining weights, scholars have applied multi-criteria decision-making methods to tourism forecast combinations. Coshall and Charlesworth (2011) adopted a pre-emptive goal programming approach in which criteria are met in order of importance, i.e., the most important criterion is met first, the next most important criterion is met second, and so on. Wu et al. (2020) adopted a stochastic frontier analysis technique to obtain the weights, with which the authors were able to simultaneously consider multiple accuracy measures when evaluating combination model performance. In addition, Chan et al. (2010) applied one of the quality control tools, the cumulative sum technique, to combine tourism forecasts. The method was able to detect small shifts in data and Chan et al. (2010) used it to identify changes in time-series trends and determine the timing of updating weights.

In this chapter, we combine forecasts of six individual forecasting models introduced in previous chapters. We adopt four combination methods, namely, simple average, variance-covariance, discounted MSFE, and shrinkage methods, and evaluate and compare the performance of both individual models and combination models. Our empirical results show that forecast combination is an effective tool to improve forecasting accuracy.

10.2 Methods

Using the dataset of tourism demand for Thailand from its two short-haul source markets (mainland China and Malaysia) and two long-haul source markets (Russia and the USA), we illustrate how to develop forecast combinations and evaluate the performance of different combination methods. The data sample available for this chapter covers the 2015Q1–2019Q4 period. Individual forecasts for 2015Q1–2016Q4 are used for combination weight calculations, and combined forecasts for 2017Q1–2019Q4 and the corresponding actual values are used for performance evaluation (Figure 10.1). For one-step-ahead forecasting, we adopt a fixed estimation window of 2015Q1–2016Q4 to calculate the weights of combined forecasts for 2017Q1–2019Q4. To maintain consistency with previous chapters, we also adopt the five forecasting horizons, namely, one, two, three, four, and eight steps ahead, to generate forecast combinations.

In this chapter, we chose four methods, namely, simple average, variance-covariance, discounted MSFE, and shrinkage methods, to demonstrate how to carry out forecast combinations and performance evaluations. Simple averages serve as a benchmark and assist with model accuracy comparisons between individual and combination methods, as well as comparisons across combination methods.

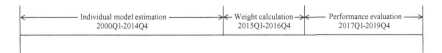

| Individual model estimation | Weight calculation | Performance evaluation |
| 2000Q1-2014Q4 | 2015Q1-2016Q4 | 2017Q1-2019Q4 |

FIGURE 10.1 Data sample allocation

10.2.1 Simple average method

Despite being the simplest of all combination methods, simple average has performed best or almost best in many studies (Clemen, 1989) and has often been used as a benchmark or baseline model. As the arithmetic mean of all component forecasts, it can be delineated as

$$\widehat{y_t^c} = \frac{\sum_{i=1}^{K} \widehat{y_t^i}}{K} \tag{10.1}$$

where $\widehat{y_t^c}$ is the combination forecast at time t and $\widehat{y_t^i}$ is the forecast generated by individual model i among all K individual models.

10.2.2 Variance-covariance method

First proposed by Bates and Granger (1969), the variance-covariance method assigns unequal weights to individual forecasts based on their respective historical performance (Song et al., 2009; Wong et al., 2007). The aim of the method is to minimise the variance, or error variance, of the combination forecast (Shen et al., 2008; Wong et al., 2007). The estimator of the weights when combining two forecasts can be expressed as

$$w_2 = \frac{\sum_{t=1}^{n} e_{1t}^2 - \sum_{t=1}^{n} e_{1t}e_{2t}}{\sum_{t=1}^{n} e_{1t}^2 + \sum_{t=1}^{n} e_{2t}^2 - 2\sum_{t=1}^{n} e_{1t}e_{2t}} \tag{10.2}$$

$$w_1 = 1 - w_2 \tag{10.3}$$

where w_1, w_2 are the weights respectively assigned to the two forecasts, e_{1t}, e_{2t} are forecast errors at a certain time t, and n is the number of forecasts used for weights calculation.

However, Coshall (2009) argued that Equation (10.2) is overly complex and Andrawis et al. (2011) suggested that the estimation of covariance might affect the accuracy of the combination forecast. One way to address such a concern is to simply neglect the covariance terms and use the following weighting scheme:

$$w_2 = \frac{\sum_{t=1}^{n} e_{1t}^2}{\sum_{t=1}^{n} e_{1t}^2 + \sum_{t=1}^{n} e_{2t}^2} \tag{10.4}$$

proposed by Bates and Granger (1969), and which sets the weights to be inversely proportional to the mean squared error.

For cases of more than two individual forecasts, Fritz et al. (1984) proposed the following

$$
w_i = \frac{\left[\sum_{t=1}^{n} e_{it}^2\right]^{-1}}{\sum_{j=1}^{K}\left[\sum_{t=1}^{n} e_{jt}^2\right]^{-1}}
\tag{10.5}
$$

for the weight for the ith forecasting model among all K models.

10.2.3 Discounted MSFE method

This method was proposed by Bates and Granger (1969) and is also based on the mean square error. Its main idea is to assign more weight to more recent forecasts. The weight assigned to individual forecasting model i can be expressed as

$$
w_i = \frac{\left[\sum_{t=1}^{n} \beta^{n-t+1} e_{it}^2\right]^{-1}}{\sum_{j=1}^{K}\left[\sum_{t=1}^{n} \beta^{n-t+1} e_{jt}^2\right]^{-1}}
\tag{10.6}
$$

where β is the discounting factor, which ranges from 0 to 1; K is the number of individual models; and n is the number of data points used for weight calculation. In this study, we adopt a β of 0.9.

10.2.4 Shrinkage method

This method is used together with other weight calculation methods to force the combination weights to shrinkage towards equal weighting. There are two approaches, namely, the Bayesian method (Diebold & Pauly, 1990) and the linear method (Stock & Watson, 2004). We follow the linear method in conjunction with the variance-covariance approach. If we let w_i denote the weight for model i obtained via the variance-covariance method, then the weight when applying the shrinkage method for model i will be:

$$
w_i^* = \lambda w_i + (1-\lambda)\left(\frac{1}{K}\right)
\tag{10.7}
$$

where $\lambda = \max\left[0, \, 1 - \kappa \left[K / [n-1-K]\right]\right]$; κ is the amount of shrinkage, which ranges from 0 to 1; K is the number of individual models; and n is the number of data points used for weight calculation.

10.3 Application

To reduce forecast failure risk and improve forecast accuracy, we apply forecast combinations to tourism demand forecasting. To demonstrate the construction and its effect on forecast accuracy of combination forecasts, we draw on the Thailand tourism demand dataset and forecasts generated from various individual models illuminated in previous chapters, using four weight calculation methods, three metrics of accuracy (mean absolute percentage error (MAPE), root mean square error (RMSE), and mean absolute scaled error (MASE)), and five forecasting horizons.

The individual forecasting models evaluated in this chapter include the autoregressive distributed lag model (ADLM) (Chapter 3), the time-varying parameter (TVP) model (Chapter 4), the hybrid model (Chapter 8), and three benchmark models (i.e., the seasonal naïve (SNAIVE), ETS, and the seasonal autoregressive integrated moving average (SARIMA) models). To enhance the validity of subsequent performance comparisons, we first calculate the accuracy for each of the six individual forecasts along with the mean of these six accuracy values, using observations over 2017Q1–2019Q4. The mean represents the expected accuracy one could achieve when choosing a model randomly from these six options. When combining forecasts, we also consider the effects of the number of component models on the accuracy of combined forecasts. As such, we take all K-combinations (K denotes the number of component models included in the forecast combinations) from the six individual forecasts and compute the mean of the three accuracy metrics over all K-combinations for each K. The computed mean represents the expected accuracy one could achieve by choosing K models randomly from the six models. The value of K ranges from 2 to 6.

Table 10.1 reports the forecasting performance of six individual models and the simple average combination method measured by MAPEs. The best individual model varies across four source markets and over five forecasting horizons, and no single model outperforms the others in all cases. For example, when one-step-ahead forecasts are considered, the ADLM performs best for the mainland China case (MAPE = 7.166%), while the hybrid model performs best for the Malaysia case (MAPE = 7.432%). This conclusion is consistent with prior studies.

Regarding the simple average combination, the mean values of the MAPEs for single-model forecasts and combined forecasts are compared in Table 10.1. The MAPE means of the combined forecasts are lower than the MAPE means of single models for all combination cases and for all source markets. Taking mainland China as an example, in the one-step-ahead forecast case, the MAPEs for all combination forecasts range from 8.916% to 9.925%. These values are all lower than the mean of MAPEs of

TABLE 10.1 Forecasting performance evaluation of the simple average combination method measured by MAPE (%)

	Forecasting horizon				
	1	*2*	*3*	*4*	*8*
Mainland China					
SNAIVE	13.194	13.683	15.039	15.606	14.882
ETS	12.201	16.127	15.163	13.312	15.984
SARIMA	14.753	13.945	16.658	17.642	21.033
ADLM	7.166	11.400	11.122	10.900	7.383
TVP	9.418	12.565	15.305	17.507	9.398
HYBRID	11.795	21.380	11.168	12.740	10.930
Mean of individual models	11.421	14.850	14.076	14.618	13.268
Simple average (2)	9.925	13.360	13.391	13.700	9.150
Simple average (3)	9.371	12.726	13.092	13.342	7.375
Simple average (4)	9.166	12.400	12.932	13.194	6.229
Simple average (5)	9.043	12.203	12.848	13.181	5.166
Simple average (6)	8.916	12.150	12.780	13.181	4.463
Malaysia					
SNAIVE	7.859	7.559	7.349	8.114	18.818
ETS	7.973	8.113	8.193	8.448	5.081
SARIMA	8.339	8.032	8.422	7.148	8.964
ADLM	8.401	8.743	8.318	7.099	12.550
TVP	8.306	10.180	7.960	6.685	11.003
HYBRID	7.432	6.980	9.018	10.683	8.342
Mean of individual models	8.052	8.268	8.210	8.029	10.793
Simple average (2)	7.550	7.523	7.489	7.620	9.947
Simple average (3)	7.402	7.246	7.162	7.506	9.737
Simple average (4)	7.367	7.104	6.940	7.477	9.540
Simple average (5)	7.352	6.988	6.730	7.477	9.385
Simple average (6)	7.352	6.949	6.469	7.477	9.237
Russia					
SNAIVE	9.800	8.259	7.474	7.783	13.722
ETS	9.956	12.781	16.648	13.287	26.609
SARIMA	12.221	16.511	15.800	19.900	46.633
ADLM	12.307	12.278	12.900	10.960	11.817
TVP	11.454	12.707	10.371	11.746	15.000
HYBRID	12.185	14.919	11.010	9.986	6.039
Mean of individual models	11.320	12.909	12.367	12.277	19.970
Simple average (2)	9.677	11.198	9.916	10.625	15.311
Simple average (3)	9.088	10.408	8.984	9.871	13.302

(*Continued*)

	Forecasting horizon				
	1	*2*	*3*	*4*	*8*
Simple average (4)	8.823	9.914	8.465	9.445	12.096
Simple average (5)	8.647	9.599	8.159	9.201	11.178
Simple average (6)	8.501	9.361	7.861	9.036	9.600
USA					
SNAIVE	5.703	5.563	5.098	4.839	9.991
ETS	3.956	3.919	4.345	6.008	11.263
SARIMA	4.553	7.014	8.247	9.483	14.186
ADLM	5.268	5.935	5.854	6.102	5.379
TVP	3.535	3.740	4.556	6.078	7.886
HYBRID	3.301	3.795	3.201	2.975	3.726
Mean of individual models	4.386	4.995	5.217	5.914	8.739
Simple average (2)	3.967	4.341	4.417	5.003	6.727
Simple average (3)	3.773	4.082	4.095	4.543	6.112
Simple average (4)	3.659	3.913	3.855	4.309	5.774
Simple average (5)	3.588	3.809	3.714	4.170	5.636
Simple average (6)	3.575	3.702	3.559	4.081	5.541

Note: The values in parentheses indicate the numbers of individual models being combined.

TABLE 10.2 Forecasting performance evaluation of the simple average combination method measured by RMSE

	Forecasting horizon				
	1	*2*	*3*	*4*	*8*
Mainland China					
SNAIVE	435,305	451,019	473,032	490,637	465,626
ETS	361,836	454,310	454,610	469,960	496,274
SARIMA	431,710	440,885	532,880	515,603	596,629
ADLM	239,047	346,058	342,582	332,689	233,116
TVP	306,137	387,623	473,355	487,537	254,365
HYBRID	346,034	576,812	349,313	394,749	308,159
Mean of individual models	353,345	442,785	437,629	448,529	392,362
Simple average (2)	301,950	389,459	401,094	414,258	280,418
Simple average (3)	281,863	369,849	387,264	401,846	232,889
Simple average (4)	271,066	359,534	380,061	395,556	204,871
Simple average (5)	264,304	353,159	375,660	391,775	186,313
Simple average (6)	259,660	348,823	372,696	389,255	174,123

Malaysia

SNAIVE	114,911	117,014	119,366	125,817	227,894
ETS	86,084	96,150	108,836	92,312	64,159
SARIMA	98,563	100,908	116,794	107,835	131,294
ADLM	96,799	111,594	111,151	107,898	156,260
TVP	96,819	113,998	110,378	98,758	140,996
HYBRID	89,330	97,239	109,977	125,786	131,120
Mean of individual models	97,084	106,151	112,750	109,734	141,954
Simple average (2)	88,237	98,123	104,452	102,745	136,600
Simple average (3)	85,010	95,314	101,555	100,414	134,785
Simple average (4)	83,334	93,873	100,077	99,254	133,874
Simple average (5)	82,307	92,995	99,180	98,560	133,327
Simple average (6)	81,613	92,402	98,577	98,099	132,963

Russia

SNAIVE	60,723	49,666	50,755	53,441	72,672
ETS	40,284	35,219	69,387	61,388	92,175
SARIMA	44,255	51,003	58,842	75,123	150,857
ADLM	78,401	53,962	76,022	55,736	65,652
TVP	52,129	50,634	45,894	64,620	52,183
HYBRID	66,440	79,264	67,192	64,101	34,102
Mean of individual models	57,039	53,291	61,349	62,401	77,940
Simple average (2)	48,177	45,727	47,874	52,201	54,263
Simple average (3)	44,496	42,892	42,382	48,511	41,907
Simple average (4)	42,526	41,448	39,317	46,567	34,887
Simple average (5)	41,298	40,578	37,336	45,352	29,810
Simple average (6)	40,461	39,998	35,945	44,522	25,053

USA

SNAIVE	17,100	16,758	15,602	15,539	32,290
ETS	12,734	13,027	16,326	19,637	36,930
SARIMA	17,164	22,540	26,103	30,561	45,171
ADLM	16,907	18,062	18,546	19,978	20,142
TVP	12,345	12,583	15,643	19,383	23,668
HYBRID	10,188	12,757	12,420	10,744	11,572
Mean of individual models	14,407	15,955	17,440	19,307	28,295
Simple average (2)	13,047	14,246	14,942	16,949	23,973
Simple average (3)	12,577	13,689	14,101	16,117	22,461
Simple average (4)	12,339	13,412	13,683	15,698	21,758
Simple average (5)	12,197	13,246	13,432	15,445	21,355
Simple average (6)	12,101	13,135	13,266	15,275	21,110

Note: The values in parentheses indicate the numbers of individual models being combined.

TABLE 10.3 Forecasting performance evaluation of the simple average combination method measured by MASE

	Forecasting horizon				
	1	*2*	*3*	*4*	*8*
Mainland China					
SNAIVE	1.624	1.691	1.858	1.926	1.790
ETS	1.472	1.916	1.885	1.678	2.002
SARIMA	1.777	1.631	1.963	2.117	2.503
ADLM	0.902	1.410	1.418	1.398	0.940
TVP	1.124	1.443	1.896	2.141	1.122
HYBRID	1.405	2.508	1.368	1.544	1.234
Mean of individual models	1.384	1.766	1.732	1.801	1.599
Simple average (2)	1.205	1.581	1.647	1.685	1.124
Simple average (3)	1.140	1.502	1.612	1.640	0.918
Simple average (4)	1.116	1.463	1.593	1.623	0.785
Simple average (5)	1.102	1.440	1.583	1.621	0.660
Simple average (6)	1.087	1.433	1.575	1.621	0.574
Malaysia					
SNAIVE	1.033	1.024	1.010	1.117	2.720
ETS	0.974	1.016	1.069	1.076	0.727
SARIMA	1.052	1.049	1.121	0.983	1.326
ADLM	1.056	1.115	1.103	0.977	1.833
TVP	1.023	1.305	1.074	0.907	1.611
HYBRID	0.961	0.933	1.181	1.412	1.251
Mean of individual models	1.017	1.074	1.093	1.079	1.578
Simple average (2)	0.959	0.986	1.008	1.029	1.476
Simple average (3)	0.942	0.953	0.970	1.016	1.451
Simple average (4)	0.938	0.936	0.944	1.013	1.427
Simple average (5)	0.936	0.922	0.919	1.013	1.409
Simple average (6)	0.936	0.918	0.889	1.013	1.391
Russia					
SNAIVE	0.830	0.656	0.644	0.698	1.239
ETS	0.657	0.633	1.191	0.912	1.725
SARIMA	0.802	0.959	0.968	1.237	3.059
ADLM	1.044	0.836	1.081	0.895	0.943
TVP	0.876	0.832	0.749	0.996	1.025
HYBRID	1.046	1.088	0.959	0.808	0.519
Mean of individual models	0.876	0.834	0.932	0.924	1.418

Simple average (2)	0.764	0.730	0.739	0.807	0.993
Simple average (3)	0.720	0.678	0.666	0.750	0.788
Simple average (4)	0.699	0.640	0.624	0.717	0.656
Simple average (5)	0.684	0.614	0.600	0.697	0.554
Simple average (6)	0.672	0.593	0.583	0.683	0.380
USA					
SNAIVE	0.962	0.936	0.875	0.863	1.862
ETS	0.646	0.652	0.768	1.078	2.110
SARIMA	0.773	1.144	1.409	1.684	2.624
ADLM	0.873	0.977	0.989	1.065	0.955
TVP	0.582	0.609	0.767	1.058	1.377
HYBRID	0.552	0.641	0.562	0.514	0.654
Mean of individual models	0.732	0.827	0.895	1.044	1.597
Simple average (2)	0.665	0.720	0.760	0.890	1.255
Simple average (3)	0.635	0.676	0.707	0.812	1.149
Simple average (4)	0.617	0.647	0.666	0.771	1.094
Simple average (5)	0.606	0.629	0.643	0.746	1.075
Simple average (6)	0.604	0.610	0.613	0.730	1.061

Note: The values in parentheses indicate the numbers of individual models being combined.

the single models (11.421%). Therefore, combined forecasts can enhance forecasting accuracy. The combined forecasts based on six component models yield the best performance, as they enable combinations of all available information. Tables 10.2 and 10.3 list the results with accuracy measured by RMSE and MASE, respectively; similar conclusions can be drawn.

Tables 10.4–10.7 report the MAPEs for all four combination methods for four respective source markets. The numbers in parentheses indicate K, the number of component models. All four combination methods outperform the mean of individual models over all horizons across the four source markets, barring several exceptions in four-step-ahead forecasts for mainland China. For the cases of mainland China and Malaysia, the simple average combination performs best amongst the four combination methods; in the case of Russia, the simple average combination performs best for two- and three-step-ahead forecasts; and for the case of the USA, the simple average combination performs best for one and two-step-ahead forecasts. The RMSE and MASE results are omitted here due to space constraints.

TABLE 10.4 Performance of forecast combinations for mainland China, by MAPE (%)

	Forecasting horizon				
	1	2	3	4	8
Mean of individual models	11.421	14.850	14.076	14.618	13.268
Combination of 2 models					
Simple average (2)	9.925	13.360	13.391	13.700	9.150
Variance-covariance (2)	10.531	14.420	13.701	14.848	10.644
Discounted MSFE (2)	10.639	14.546	13.717	14.825	10.334
Shrink (2)	10.463	14.291	13.657	14.719	10.446
Combination of 3 models					
Simple average (3)	9.371	12.726	13.092	13.342	7.375
Variance-covariance (3)	9.922	13.795	13.309	14.654	8.233
Discounted MSFE (3)	9.993	13.931	13.289	14.610	7.757
Shrink (3)	9.800	13.563	13.251	14.378	7.955
Combination of 4 models					
Simple average (4)	9.166	12.400	12.932	13.194	6.229
Variance-covariance (4)	9.638	13.387	13.117	14.610	7.220
Discounted MSFE (4)	9.697	13.518	13.062	14.578	6.650
Shrink (4)	9.457	13.004	13.038	14.126	6.750
Combination of 5 models					
Simple average (5)	9.043	12.203	12.848	13.181	5.166
Variance-covariance (5)	9.504	13.066	12.982	14.696	6.708
Discounted MSFE (5)	9.570	13.221	12.881	14.674	5.964
Shrink (5)	9.210	12.490	12.889	13.749	5.687
Combination of 6 models					
Simple average (6)	8.916	12.150	12.780	13.181	4.463
Variance-covariance (6)	9.464	12.814	12.844	14.751	6.139
Discounted MSFE (6)	9.522	13.041	12.680	14.732	5.314
Shrink (6)	8.916	12.150	12.780	13.181	4.463

Note: The values in parentheses indicate the numbers of individual models being combined.

TABLE 10.5 Performance of forecast combinations for Malaysia, by MAPE (%)

	Forecasting horizon				
	1	*2*	*3*	*4*	*8*
Mean of individual models	8.052	8.268	8.210	8.029	10.793
Combination of 2 models					
Simple average (2)	7.550	7.523	7.489	7.620	9.947
Variance-covariance (2)	7.682	7.834	7.572	7.763	10.251
Discounted MSFE (2)	7.658	7.763	7.558	7.797	10.194
Shrink (2)	7.660	7.797	7.548	7.746	10.218
Combination of 3 models					
Simple average (3)	7.402	7.246	7.162	7.506	9.737
Variance-covariance (3)	7.610	7.610	7.214	7.641	10.077
Discounted MSFE (3)	7.584	7.499	7.193	7.697	9.970
Shrink (3)	7.563	7.523	7.173	7.606	9.997
Combination of 4 models					
Simple average (4)	7.367	7.104	6.940	7.477	9.540
Variance-covariance (4)	7.603	7.452	7.013	7.597	9.928
Discounted MSFE (4)	7.587	7.358	6.988	7.665	9.809
Shrink (4)	7.522	7.322	6.957	7.548	9.796
Combination of 5 models					
Simple average (5)	7.352	6.988	6.730	7.477	9.385
Variance-covariance (5)	7.608	7.341	6.874	7.580	9.730
Discounted MSFE (5)	7.596	7.282	6.848	7.661	9.630
Shrink (5)	7.448	7.114	6.747	7.516	9.513
Combination of 6 models					
Simple average (6)	7.352	6.949	6.469	7.477	9.237
Variance-covariance (6)	7.616	7.354	6.757	7.576	9.508
Discounted MSFE (6)	7.605	7.297	6.718	7.659	9.409
Shrink (6)	7.352	6.949	6.469	7.477	9.237

Note: The values in parentheses indicate the numbers of individual models being combined.

TABLE 10.6 Performance of forecast combinations for Russia, by MAPE (%)

	Forecasting horizon				
	1	*2*	*3*	*4*	*8*
Mean of individual models	11.320	12.909	12.367	12.277	19.970
Combination of 2 models					
Simple average (2)	9.677	11.198	9.916	10.625	15.311
Variance-covariance (2)	9.987	11.387	10.443	10.246	11.909
Discounted MSFE (2)	9.926	11.450	10.565	10.245	11.918
Shrink (2)	9.928	11.362	10.336	10.239	11.939
Combination of 3 models					
Simple average (3)	9.088	10.408	8.984	9.871	13.302
Variance-covariance (3)	9.160	10.662	9.582	9.511	10.301
Discounted MSFE (3)	9.118	10.783	9.721	9.561	10.317
Shrink (3)	9.104	10.602	9.378	9.453	10.396
Combination of 4 models					
Simple average (4)	8.823	9.914	8.465	9.445	12.096
Variance-covariance (4)	8.764	10.310	9.081	9.330	9.732
Discounted MSFE (4)	8.744	10.477	9.214	9.393	9.610
Shrink (4)	8.739	10.155	8.704	9.175	9.669
Combination of 5 models					
Simple average (5)	8.647	9.599	8.159	9.201	11.178
Variance-covariance (5)	8.623	10.092	8.760	9.406	9.589
Discounted MSFE (5)	8.599	10.263	8.896	9.475	9.455
Shrink (5)	8.626	9.779	8.227	9.122	9.505
Combination of 6 models					
Simple average (6)	8.501	9.361	7.861	9.036	9.600
Variance-covariance (6)	8.593	10.017	8.488	9.541	9.503
Discounted MSFE (6)	8.548	10.211	8.676	9.619	9.317
Shrink (6)	8.501	9.361	7.861	9.036	9.600

Note: The values in parentheses indicate the numbers of individual models being combined.

TABLE 10.7 Performance of forecast combinations for the USA, by MAPE (%)

	Forecasting horizon				
	1	*2*	*3*	*4*	*8*
Mean of individual models	4.386	4.995	5.217	5.914	8.739
Combination of 2 models					
Simple average (2)	3.967	4.341	4.417	5.003	6.727
Variance-covariance (2)	4.053	4.438	4.269	4.889	5.913
Discounted MSFE (2)	4.056	4.442	4.246	4.873	5.948
Shrink (2)	4.037	4.423	4.243	4.897	5.880
Combination of 3 models					
Simple average (3)	3.773	4.082	4.095	4.543	6.112
Variance-covariance (3)	3.998	4.222	3.718	4.369	4.637
Discounted MSFE (3)	3.995	4.215	3.693	4.339	4.634
Shrink (3)	3.939	4.188	3.692	4.392	4.704
Combination of 4 models					
Simple average (4)	3.659	3.913	3.855	4.309	5.774
Variance-covariance (4)	3.983	4.074	3.339	4.088	3.937
Discounted MSFE (4)	3.979	4.059	3.316	4.044	3.936
Shrink (4)	3.863	4.014	3.380	4.140	4.295
Combination of 5 models					
Simple average (5)	3.588	3.809	3.714	4.170	5.636
Variance-covariance (5)	3.983	3.976	3.050	3.921	3.544
Discounted MSFE (5)	3.978	3.940	3.033	3.866	3.545
Shrink (5)	3.728	3.839	3.308	4.055	4.671
Combination of 6 models					
Simple average (6)	3.575	3.702	3.559	4.081	5.541
Variance-covariance (6)	3.992	3.886	2.831	3.794	3.159
Discounted MSFE (6)	3.986	3.835	2.822	3.733	3.167
Shrink (6)	3.575	3.702	3.559	4.081	5.541

Note: The values in parentheses indicate the numbers of individual models being combined.

10.4 Conclusion and future directions

This chapter introduces the rationale and advantages of forecast combination methods for tourism forecasting. We present one application to
demonstrate the practical implications of combination methods for generating more accurate forecasts. As demonstrated, combining component
models outperforms the average of all component models. Forecast combination can therefore boost forecasting accuracy.

Across the four applied combination methods, we find that despite its extreme simplicity, the simple average combination method performs best in some cases (i.e., mainland China and Malaysia). This outcome provides additional evidence that even the simple average method can improve forecast accuracy. More sophisticated combination methods occasionally struggle to outperform this method (Clemen, 1989). The best combination method varies across forecasting horizons, case series, and the number of models being combined.

Several limitations of this work can be addressed in the future. First, this study adopts fixed windows for weight calculation. In subsequent research, scholars should consider using rolling windows for weight calculation. This tactic would allow the most updated information to be introduced into forecast combinations. Second, due to limited data points, only four combination methods are adopted here. Scholars can examine other forecasting methods, such as regression-based combination methods or artificial neural network combination methods, as more data become available. Third, this study focuses on combining point forecasts. Probabilistic forecasts, such as density forecasts or interval forecasts, should be combined in follow-up work to provide more stable probabilistic forecasts with uncertainty information.

Self-study questions

1 Assume that a number of individual forecasts are combined, can we expect this combined forecast to outperform all individual forecasts involved?
2 What are the advantages of forecast combinations over individual models?
3 Compared with weighted average combination methods, what are the advantages of the single average combination method?

References

Andrawis, R. R., Atiya, A. F., & El-Shishiny, H. (2011). Combination of long term and short term forecasts, with application to tourism demand forecasting. *International Journal of Forecasting, 27*(3), 870–886. https://doi.org/10.1016/j.ijforecast.2010.05.019

Armstrong, J. S. (2001). Combining forecasts. In J. S. Armstrong (Ed.), *Principles of forecasting* (pp. 417–439). Boston, MA: Springer.

Bates, J. M., & Granger, C. W. J. (1969). The Combination of Forecasts. *Journal of the Operational Research Society, 20*(4), 451–468. https://doi.org/10.1057/jors.1969.103

Bunn, D. (1989). Forecasting with more than one model. *Journal of Forecasting, 8*(3), 161–166. https://doi.org/https://doi.org/10.1002/for.3980080302

Cang, S. (2014). A comparative analysis of three types of tourism demand forecasting models: individual, linear combination and non-linear combination.

International Journal of Tourism Research, 16(6), 596–607. https://doi.org/10.1002/jtr.1953

Cang, S., & Yu, H. N. (2014). A combination selection algorithm on forecasting. *European Journal of Operational Research, 234*(1), 127–139. https://doi.org/10.1016/j.ejor.2013.08.045

Cang, S. A. (2011). A non-linear tourism demand forecast combination model. *Tourism Economics, 17*(1), 5–20. https://doi.org/10.5367/te.2011.0031

Chan, C. K., Witt, S. F., Lee, Y. C. E., & Song, H. (2010). Tourism forecast combination using the CUSUM technique. *Tourism Management, 31*(6), 891–897. https://doi.org/10.1016/j.tourman.2009.10.004

Chen, K. Y. (2011). Combining linear and nonlinear model in forecasting tourism demand. *Expert Systems with Applications, 38*(8), 10368–10376. https://doi.org/10.1016/j.eswa.2011.02.049

Cheng, D., & Liu, L. B. (2014, Jul 04–06). Forecasting of tourism demand for Guilin based on combined model. *International Joint Conference on Computational Sciences and Optimization* [2014 seventh international joint conference on computational sciences and optimization (cso)]. 7th International Joint Conference on Computational Sciences and Optimization (CSO), Beijing, People's Republic of China.

Clemen, R. T. (1989). Combining forecasts: A review and annotated bibliography. *International Journal of Forecasting, 5*(4), 559–583. https://doi.org/10.1016/0169-2070(89)90012-5

Clemen, R. T., & Winkler, R. L. (1986). Combining economic forecasts. *Journal of Business & Economic Statistics, 4*(1), 39–46. https://doi.org/10.1080/07350015.1986.10509492

Coshall, J. T. (2009). Combining volatility and smoothing forecasts of UK demand for international tourism. *Tourism Management, 30*(4), 495–511. https://doi.org/10.1016/j.tourman.2008.10.010

Coshall, J. T., & Charlesworth, R. (2011). A management orientated approach to combination forecasting of tourism demand. *Tourism Management, 32*(4), 759–769. https://doi.org/10.1016/j.tourman.2010.06.011

Diebold, F. X., & Pauly, P. (1990). The use of prior information in forecast combination. *International Journal of Forecasting, 6*(4), 503–508. https://doi.org/https://doi.org/10.1016/0169-2070(90)90028-A

Flores, B. E., & White, E. (1989). Combining forecasts: Why, when and how. *Journal of Business Forecasting Methods & Systems,* 8(3), 2–5.

Fritz, R. G., Brandon, C., & Xander, J. (1984). Combining time-series and econometric forecast of tourism activity. *Annals of Tourism Research, 11*(2), 219–229. https://doi.org/https://doi.org/10.1016/0160-7383(84)90071-9

Granger, C., & Ramanathan, R. (1984). Improved methods of combining forecasts. *Journal of Forecasting, 3*(2), 197–204. https://doi.org/10.1002/for.3980030207

Hendry, D. F., & Clements, M. P. (2004). Pooling of forecasts. *The Econometrics Journal, 7*(1), 1–31. https://doi.org/10.1111/j.1368-423X.2004.00119.x

Holden, K., & Thompson, J. (1997). Combining forecasts, encompassing and the properties of UK macroeconomic forecasts. *Applied Economics, 29*(11), 1447–1458. https://doi.org/10.1080/000368497326273

Hu, Y.-C., Wu, G., & Jiang, P. (2021). Tourism demand forecasting using nonadditive forecast combinations. *Journal of Hospitality & Tourism Research,* Article 10963480211047857. https://doi.org/10.1177/10963480211047857

Hu, Y. C. (2021). Forecasting the demand for tourism using combinations of forecasts by neural network-based interval grey prediction models. *Asia Pacific Journal of Tourism Research, 26*(12), 1350–1363. https://doi.org/10.1080/109416 65.2021.1983623

Jiao, E. X., & Chen, J. L. (2019). Tourism forecasting: A review of methodological developments over the last decade. *Tourism Economics, 25*(3), 469–492. https://doi.org/10.1177/1354816618812588

Jun, W., Yuyan, L., Lingyu, T., & Peng, G. (2018). Modeling a combined forecast algorithm based on sequence patterns and near characteristics: An application for tourism demand forecasting. *Chaos, Solitons & Fractals, 108*, 136–147. https://doi.org/https://doi.org/10.1016/j.chaos.2018.01.028

Jungmittag, A. (2016). Combination of forecasts across estimation windows: An application to air travel demand. *Journal of Forecasting, 35*(4), 373–380. https://doi.org/10.1002/for.2400

Li, G., Song, H., & Witt, S. F. (2005). Recent developments in econometric modeling and forecasting. *Journal of Travel Research, 44*(1), 82–99. https://doi.org/10.1177/0047287505276594

Li, G., Wu, D. C., Zhou, M. L., & Liu, A. (2019). The combination of interval forecasts in tourism. *Annals of Tourism Research, 75*, 363–378. https://doi.org/10.1016/j.annals.2019.01.010

Sessions, D. N., & Chatterjee, S. (1989). The combining of forecasts using recursive techniques with non-stationary weights. *Journal of Forecasting, 8*(3), 239–251. https://doi.org/https://doi.org/10.1002/for.3980080309

Shen, S. J., Li, G., & Song, H. (2008). An assessment of combining tourism demand forecasts over different time horizons. *Journal of Travel Research, 47*(2), 197–207. https://doi.org/10.1177/0047287508321199

Shen, S. J., Li, G., & Song, H. (2011). Combination forecasts of international tourism demand. *Annals of Tourism Research, 38*(1), 72–89. https://doi.org/10.1016/j.annals.2010.05.003

Song, H., Qiu, R. T. R., & Park, J. (2019). A review of research on tourism demand forecasting. *Annals of Tourism Research, 75*, 338–362. https://doi.org/10.1016/j.annals.2018.12.001

Song, H., Witt, S. F., Wong, K. F., & Wu, D. C. (2009). An empirical study of forecast combination in tourism. *Journal of Hospitality & Tourism Research, 33*(1), 3–29. https://doi.org/10.1177/1096348008321366

Stock, J. H., & Watson, M. W. (2004). Combination forecasts of output growth in a seven-country data set. *Journal of Forecasting, 23*(6), 405–430. https://doi.org/https://doi.org/10.1002/for.928

Winkler, R. L. (1989). Combining forecasts: A philosophical basis and some current issues. *International Journal of Forecasting, 5*(4), 605–609. https://doi.org/https://doi.org/10.1016/0169-2070(89)90018-6

Wong, K. K. F., Song, H., Witt, S. F., & Wu, D. C. (2007). Tourism forecasting: To combine or not to combine? *Tourism Management, 28*(4), 1068–1078. https://doi.org/10.1016/j.tourman.2006.08.003

Wu, J., Cheng, X., & Liao, S. S. (2020). Tourism forecast combination using the stochastic frontier analysis technique. *Tourism Economics, 26*(7), 1086–1107. https://doi.org/10.1177/1354816619868089

Zhang, G. P. (2003). Time series forecasting using a hybrid ARIMA and neural network model. *Neurocomputing, 50*(17), 159–175.

APPENDIX

R CODE

```
# Forecast combination for Chapter 10
  csv_path <- "D:/Documents/Individual Forecasts/"
  fmodels <- c('snaive', 'ets', 'sarima', 'adl', 'tvp', 'hybrid')
  # loading csv files and compute MAPE, MASE, RMSE for in-
dividual forecasts
  # "c" stands for mainland China, "m" for Malaysia, "r" for
Russia, "u" for USA
  for (i in c('c', 'm', 'r', 'u')){
    mape_df <- data.frame(
      method <- c('method'),
      one_step_ahead <- c('one_step_ahead'),
      two_step_ahead <- c('two_step_ahead'),
      three_step_ahead <- c('three_step_ahead'),
      four_step_ahead <- c('four_step_ahead'),
      eight_step_ahead <- c('eight_step_ahead')
    )
    rmse_df <- data.frame(
      method <- c('method'),
      one_step_ahead <- c('one_step_ahead'),
      two_step_ahead <- c('two_step_ahead'),
      three_step_ahead <- c('three_step_ahead'),
      four_step_ahead <- c('four_step_ahead'),
      eight_step_ahead <- c('eight_step_ahead')
    )
    mase_df <- data.frame(
      method <- c('method'),
      one_step_ahead <- c('one_step_ahead'),
      two_step_ahead <- c('two_step_ahead'),
```

```
        three _ step _ ahead <- c('three _ step _ ahead'),
        four _ step _ ahead <- c('four _ step _ ahead'),
        eight _ step _ ahead <- c('eight _ step _ ahead')
    )
    for (j in fmodels){
        dat <- read.csv(paste(csv _ path, i, '.csv', sep = ''),
encoding='utf-8')
        realvalue <- dat[61:80, 1:2]
        forecasts <- read.csv(paste(csv _ path, j, ' _ ', i,
'.csv', sep = ''), encoding='utf-8')
        mape _ vector <- c(j)
        rmse _ vector <- c(j)
        mase _ vector <- c(j)
        Y = ts(dat$Arr, freq = 4, start = c(2000, 1))
        MASE.denominator = mean(abs(diff(Y, 4)), na.rm = T)
        for (k in c(2:6)){
          if (k == 2){
            indeces <- 9:20
          } else if (k == 3){
            indeces <- 10:20
          } else if (k == 4){
            indeces <- 11:20
          } else if (k == 5){
            indeces <- 12:20
          } else if (k == 6){
            indeces <- 16:20
          }
        residual.vector <- forecasts[indeces, k] - real
value[indeces, 2]
        MAPE = mean(abs(residual.vector) * 100 / realval-
ue[indeces, 2])
        mape _ vector <- c(mape _ vector, MAPE)
        RMSE = sqrt(mean((residual.vector) ^ 2))
        rmse _ vector <- c(rmse _ vector, RMSE)
        MASE = mean(abs(residual.vector) / MASE.denominator)
        mase _ vector <- c(mase _ vector, MASE)
      }
    mape _ df <- rbind(mape _ df, mape _ vector)
    rmse _ df <- rbind(rmse _ df, rmse _ vector)
    mase _ df <- rbind(mase _ df, mase _ vector)
  }
```

```
    write.csv(mape_df, paste("D:/Documents/Performance/
mape_", i, ".csv", sep = ''))
    write.csv(rmse_df, paste("D:/Documents/Performance/
rmse_", i, ".csv", sep = ''))
    write.csv(mase_df, paste("D:/Documents/Performance/
mase_", i, ".csv", sep = ''))
  }

  # Simple average
  # Variable BY denotes the # of component models included
in a combination

  for (BY in c(2:6)){
    for (country in c('c', 'm', 'r', 'u')){
      dat <- read.csv(paste(csv_path, country, '.csv', sep = ''),
encoding='utf-8')

      realvalue <- dat[61:80, 1:2]

      Y = ts(dat$Arr, freq = 4, start = c(2000, 1))
      MASE.denominator = mean(abs(diff(Y, 4)), na.rm = T)

      mape_vector <- c(paste0('comb_sa_', BY))
      rmse_vector <- c(paste0('comb_sa_', BY))
      mase_vector <- c(paste0('comb_sa_', BY))

      for (k in c(2:6)){
        data_df <- data.frame(
          adl = rep(0, 20),
          ets = rep(0, 20),
          hybrid = rep(0, 20),
          sarima = rep(0, 20),
          snaive = rep(0, 20),
          tvp = rep(0, 20),
          actual = rep(0, 20)
        )
        data_df['actual'] <- realvalue[, 2]
        for (fmodel in fmodels){
          forecasts <- read.csv(paste(csv_path, fmodel,
'_', country, '.csv', sep = ''), encoding='utf-8')
          data <- forecasts[, k]
          data_df[fmodel] <- data
        }

        mape_for_all_combn <- c(1)
        rmse_for_all_combn <- c(1)
        mase_for_all_combn <- c(1)

        iter <- 1
```

```
for (x in combn(c(1:6), m = BY, simplify = FALSE)){

    simple _ average <- rowMeans(data _ df[, x])

    if (k == 2){
       indeces <- 9:20
    } else if (k == 3){
       indeces <- 10:20
    } else if (k == 4){
       indeces <- 11:20
    } else if (k == 5){
       indeces <- 12:20
    } else if (k == 6){
       indeces <- 16:20
    }

    residual.vector <- simple _ average[indeces] -
realvalue[indeces, 2]

    MAPE = mean(abs(residual.vector) * 100 / realval-
ue[indeces, 2])

    RMSE = sqrt(mean((residual.vector) ^ 2))

    MASE = mean(abs(residual.vector) / MASE.denominator)

    mape _ for _ all _ combn[iter] <- MAPE
    rmse _ for _ all _ combn[iter] <- RMSE
    mase _ for _ all _ combn[iter] <- MASE

    iter <- iter + 1

}

   mape _ vector[k] <- mean(mape _ for _ all _ combn)
   rmse _ vector[k] <- mean(rmse _ for _ all _ combn)
   mase _ vector[k] <- mean(mase _ for _ all _ combn)
}

   write.csv(t(mape _ vector),  paste("D:/Documents/Perfor-
mance/by _ ", BY," _ mape _ SA _ ", country, ".csv", sep = ''))
   write.csv(t(rmse _ vector),  paste("D:/Documents/Perfor-
mance/by _ ", BY," _ rmse _ SA _ ", country, ".csv", sep = ''))
   write.csv(t(mase _ vector),  paste("D:/Documents/Perfor-
mance/by _ ", BY," _ mase _ SA _ ", country, ".csv", sep = ''))
   }
}

# Variance-covariance method (Bates and Granger)

for (country in c('c', 'm', 'r', 'u')){
```

```
for (BY in c(2:6)){

   dat <- read.csv(paste(csv _ path, country, '.csv', sep = ''),
encoding='utf-8')

   realvalue <- dat[61:80, 1:2]

   Y = ts(dat$Arr, freq = 4, start = c(2000, 1))
   MASE.denominator = mean(abs(diff(Y, 4)), na.rm = T)

   mape _ vector <- c(paste0('comb _ bg _ ', BY))
   rmse _ vector <- c(paste0('comb _ bg _ ', BY))
   mase _ vector <- c(paste0('comb _ bg _ ', BY))

   for (k in c(2:6)){
     data _ df <- data.frame(
       adl = rep(0, 20),
       ets = rep(0, 20),
       hybrid = rep(0, 20),
       sarima = rep(0, 20),
       snaive = rep(0, 20),
       tvp = rep(0, 20),
       actual = rep(0, 20)
     )
     data _ df['actual'] <- realvalue[, 2]
     for (fmodel in fmodels){
       forecasts <- read.csv(paste(csv _ path, fmodel,
' _ ', country, '.csv', sep = ''), encoding='utf-8')
       data <- forecasts[, k]
       data _ df[fmodel] <- data
     }
     mape _ for _ all _ combn <- c(1)
     rmse _ for _ all _ combn <- c(1)
     mase _ for _ all _ combn <- c(1)

     iter <- 1

     for (x in combn(c(1:6), m = BY, simplify = FALSE)){

     print(x)

     if (k == 2){
       indeces <- 9:20
       est _ indeces <- 1:8
     } else if (k == 3){
       indeces <- 10:20
       est _ indeces <- 2:9
     } else if (k == 4){
```

```
          indeces <- 11:20
          est _ indeces <- 3:10
        } else if (k == 5){
          indeces <- 12:20
          est _ indeces <- 4:11
        } else if (k == 6){
          indeces <- 16:20
          est _ indeces <- 8:15
        }
        train _ x <- as.matrix(data _ df)[est _ indeces, x]
        train _ y <- data _ df[est _ indeces, 'actual']
        test _ x <- as.matrix(data _ df)[indeces, x]
        test _ y <- data _ df[indeces, 'actual']

        error _ matrix <- train _ y - train _ x
        mse _ matrix <- (t(error _ matrix) %*% error _
matrix)/length(train _ y)

        weights <- diag(mse _ matrix)^(-1)/sum(diag(mse _
matrix)^(-1))
        fitted <- as.vector(test _ x %*% weights)

        residual.vector <- fitted - realvalue[indeces, 2]

        MAPE = mean(abs(residual.vector) * 100 / realval-
ue[indeces, 2])

        RMSE = sqrt(mean((residual.vector) ^ 2))
        MASE = mean(abs(residual.vector) / MASE.denominator)

        mape _ for _ all _ combn[iter] <- MAPE
        rmse _ for _ all _ combn[iter] <- RMSE
        mase _ for _ all _ combn[iter] <- MASE

        iter <- iter + 1
      }
      mape _ vector[k] <- mean(mape _ for _ all _ combn)
      rmse _ vector[k] <- mean(rmse _ for _ all _ combn)
      mase _ vector[k] <- mean(mase _ for _ all _ combn)
    }

    write.csv(t(mape _ vector),  paste("D:/Documents/Perfor-
mance/by _ ", BY," _ mape _ BG _ ", country, ".csv", sep = ''))
    write.csv(t(rmse _ vector),  paste("D:/Documents/Perfor-
mance/by _ ", BY," _ rmse _ BG _ ", country, ".csv", sep = ''))
    write.csv(t(mase _ vector),  paste("D:/Documents/Perfor-
mance/by _ ", BY," _ mase _ BG _ ", country, ".csv", sep = ''))
  }
}
```

```
# The discounted MSFE combination
window _ size <- 8
for (country in c('c', 'm', 'r', 'u')){

    for (BY in c(2:6)){

    dat <- read.csv(paste(csv _ path, country, '.csv', sep = ''),
encoding='utf-8')

    realvalue <- dat[61:80, 1:2]

    Y = ts(dat$Arr, freq = 4, start = c(2000, 1))
    MASE.denominator = mean(abs(diff(Y, 4)), na.rm = T)

    mape _ vector <- c(paste0('comb _ dmsfe _ ', BY))
    rmse _ vector <- c(paste0('comb _ dmsfe _ ', BY))
    mase _ vector <- c(paste0('comb _ dmsfe _ ', BY))

    for (k in c(2:6)){
        data _ df <- data.frame(
          adl = rep(0, 20),
          ets = rep(0, 20),
          hybrid = rep(0, 20),
          sarima = rep(0, 20),
          snaive = rep(0, 20),
          tvp = rep(0, 20),
          actual = rep(0, 20)
        )
        data _ df['actual'] <- realvalue[, 2]
        for (fmodel in fmodels){
          forecasts <- read.csv(paste(csv _ path, fmodel, ' _ ',
country, '.csv', sep = ''), encoding='utf-8')
          data <- forecasts[, k]
          data _ df[fmodel] <- data
        }

        mape _ for _ all _ combn <- c(1)
        rmse _ for _ all _ combn <- c(1)
        mase _ for _ all _ combn <- c(1)

        iter <- 1

        for (x in combn(c(1:6), m = BY, simplify = FALSE)){

          print(x)

          if (k == 2){
            indeces <- 9:20
            est _ indeces <- 1:8
          } else if (k == 3){
```

```
        indeces <- 10:20
        est _ indeces <- 2:9
    } else if (k == 4){
        indeces <- 11:20
        est _ indeces <- 3:10
    } else if (k == 5){
        indeces <- 12:20
        est _ indeces <- 4:11
    } else if (k == 6){
        indeces <- 16:20
        est _ indeces <- 8:15
    }

    train _ x <- as.matrix(data _ df)[est _ indeces, x]
    train _ y <- data _ df[est _ indeces, 'actual']
    test _ x <- as.matrix(data _ df)[indeces, x]
    test _ y <- data _ df[indeces, 'actual']

    error _ matrix <- train _ y - train _ x
    discounting _ factor <- 0.9
    # discounting factor should range from 0 to 1
    # discounting factors used in Shen et al. (2008)
were 0.95, 0.9 and 0.85
    discounting <- discounting _ factor ^ seq(window _
size, 1)
    discounted _ matrix <- diag(discounting) %*% error _
matrix
    discounted _ mse _ matrix <- (t(discounted _ matrix)
%*% error _ matrix)

    weights <- diag(discounted _ mse _ matrix)^(-1)/
sum(diag(discounted _ mse _ matrix)^(-1))
    fitted <- as.vector(test _ x %*% weights)

    residual.vector <- fitted - realvalue[indeces, 2]

    MAPE = mean(abs(residual.vector) * 100 / realval-
ue[indeces, 2])

    RMSE = sqrt(mean((residual.vector) ^ 2))

    MASE = mean(abs(residual.vector) / MASE.denominator)

    mape _ for _ all _ combn[iter] <- MAPE
    rmse _ for _ all _ combn[iter] <- RMSE
    mase _ for _ all _ combn[iter] <- MASE
```

```
      iter <- iter + 1
    }
    mape _ vector[k] <- mean(mape _ for _ all _ combn)
    rmse _ vector[k] <- mean(rmse _ for _ all _ combn)
    mase _ vector[k] <- mean(mase _ for _ all _ combn)
  }
  write.csv(t(mape _ vector), paste("D:/Documents/Perfor-
mance/by _ ", BY," _ mape _ DMSFE _ ", country, ".csv", sep = ''))
  write.csv(t(rmse _ vector), paste("D:/Documents/Perfor-
mance/by _ ", BY," _ rmse _ DMSFE _ ", country, ".csv", sep = ''))
  write.csv(t(mase _ vector), paste("D:/Documents/Perfor-
mance/by _ ", BY," _ mase _ DMSFE _ ", country, ".csv", sep = ''))
  }
}
# Shrinkage method
# This example uses the shrinkage method in conjunction
with the variance-covariance method
for (country in c('c', 'm', 'r', 'u')){
  for (BY in c(2:6)){

    dat <- read.csv(paste(csv _ path, country, '.csv', sep =
''), encoding='utf-8')

    realvalue <- dat[61:80, 1:2]

    Y = ts(dat$Arr, freq = 4, start = c(2000, 1))
    MASE.denominator = mean(abs(diff(Y, 4)), na.rm = T)

    mape _ vector <- c(paste0('comb _ shrink _ ', BY))
    rmse _ vector <- c(paste0('comb _ shrink _ ', BY))
    mase _ vector <- c(paste0('comb _ shrink _ ', BY))

    for (k in c(2:6)){
      data _ df <- data.frame(
        adl = rep(0, 20),
        ets = rep(0, 20),
        hybrid = rep(0, 20),
        sarima = rep(0, 20),
        snaive = rep(0, 20),
        tvp = rep(0, 20),
        actual = rep(0, 20)
      )
      data _ df['actual'] <- realvalue[, 2]
      for (fmodel in fmodels){
```

```
        forecasts <- read.csv(paste(csv_path, fmodel, '_',
country, '.csv', sep = ''), encoding='utf-8')
        data <- forecasts[, k]
        data_df[fmodel] <- data
    }

    mape_for_all_combn <- c(1)
    rmse_for_all_combn <- c(1)
    mase_for_all_combn <- c(1)

    iter <- 1

    for (x in combn(c(1:6), m = BY, simplify = FALSE)){

        print(x)
        if (k == 2){
            indeces <- 9:20
            est_indeces <- 1:8
            horizon <- 1
        } else if (k == 3){
            indeces <- 10:20
            est_indeces <- 2:9
            horizon <- 2
        } else if (k == 4){
            indeces <- 11:20
            est_indeces <- 3:10
            horizon <- 3
        } else if (k == 5){
            indeces <- 12:20
            est_indeces <- 4:11
            horizon <- 4
        } else if (k == 6){
            indeces <- 16:20
            est_indeces <- 8:15
            horizon <- 8
        }

        train_x <- as.matrix(data_df)[est_indeces, x]
        train_y <- data_df[est_indeces, 'actual']
        test_x <- as.matrix(data_df)[indeces, x]
        test_y <- data_df[indeces, 'actual']

        error_matrix <- train_y - train_x
        mse_matrix <- (t(error_matrix) %*% error_
matrix)/length(train_y)

        kappa <- 0.25
```

```
          # kappa is the amount of shrinkage towards equal
weighting
          # larger values correspond to more shrinkage and
smaller lambda (Stock and Watson, 2004)
          # kappa takes a value between 0 and 1 (Shen et al.,
2008)
          # kappa was chosen to be 0.25, 0.5, 0.75 and 1 in
the work of Shen et al. (2008)
          lambda <- max(0, 1 - kappa * (BY / (window_size -
1 - BY)))
          weights <- diag(mse_matrix)^(-1)/
sum(diag(mse_matrix)^(-1))
          weights <- lambda * weights + (1 - lambda) *
(1 / BY)

          fitted <- as.vector(test_x %*% weights)

          residual.vector <- fitted - realvalue[indeces, 2]

          MAPE = mean(abs(residual.vector) * 100 / realval-
ue[indeces, 2])

          RMSE = sqrt(mean((residual.vector) ^ 2))

          MASE = mean(abs(residual.vector) / MASE.denominator)

          mape_for_all_combn[iter] <- MAPE
          rmse_for_all_combn[iter] <- RMSE
          mase_for_all_combn[iter] <- MASE

          iter <- iter + 1

      }
      mape_vector[k] <- mean(mape_for_all_combn)
      rmse_vector[k] <- mean(rmse_for_all_combn)
      mase_vector[k] <- mean(mase_for_all_combn)
    }

    write.csv(t(mape_vector), paste("D:/Documents/Perfor-
mance/by_", BY," _mape_SHRINK_", country, ".csv", sep = ''))
    write.csv(t(rmse_vector), paste("D:/Documents/Perfor-
mance/by_", BY," _rmse_SHRINK_", country, ".csv", sep = ''))
    write.csv(t(mase_vector), paste("D:/Documents/Perfor-
mance/by_", BY," _mase_SHRINK_", country, ".csv", sep = ''))
    }
  }
```

```
# merging csv files generated by previous code

perf _ path <- 'D:/Documents/Performance/'

for (metr in c('mape', 'rmse', 'mase')){
  country <- 'c'
  merged <- read.csv(paste(perf _ path, metr, ' _ ', country,
'.csv', sep = ''), encoding="UTF-8")
  merged <- merged[1:7, 2:7]
  colnames(merged) <- c('method', '1-step-ahead', '2-step-
ahead', '3-step-ahead', '4-step-ahead', '8-step-ahead')
  merged[1, 1:6] <- c(country, '', '', '', '', '')

  merged <- rbind(merged, c('mean _ acc _ for _ ind _ models',
mean(as.numeric(merged[, 2]), na.rm = T),
                                mean(as.numeric(merged[, 3]),
na.rm = T), mean(as.numeric(merged[, 4]), na.rm = T),
                                mean(as.numeric(merged[, 5]),
na.rm = T), mean(as.numeric(merged[, 6]), na.rm = T)))

  for (BY in c(2:6)){
    comb _ perf <- read.csv(paste(perf _ path, 'by _ ', BY,
' _ ', metr, ' _ SA _ ', country, '.csv', sep = ''), encoding=
"UTF-8")
    comb _ perf <- comb _ perf[, 2:7]
    colnames(comb _ perf) <- c('method', '1-step-ahead',
'2-step-ahead', '3-step-ahead', '4-step-ahead', '8-step-ahead')
    merged <- rbind(merged, comb _ perf)
  }

  for (country in c('m', 'r', 'u')){

    ind _ perf <- read.csv(paste(perf _ path, metr, ' _ ',
country, '.csv', sep = ''), encoding="UTF-8")
    ind _ perf <- ind _ perf[1:7, 2:7]
    ind _ perf[1, 1:6] <- c(country, '', '', '', '', '')
    colnames(ind _ perf) <- c('method', '1-step-ahead',
'2-step-ahead', '3-step-ahead', '4-step-ahead', '8-step-ahead')

    merged <- rbind(merged, ind _ perf)

    merged <- rbind(merged, c('mean _ acc _ for _ ind _ mod-
els', mean(as.numeric(ind _ perf[, 2]), na.rm = T),
                                mean(as.numeric(ind _ perf[,
3]), na.rm = T), mean(as.numeric(ind _ perf[, 4]), na.rm = T),
                                mean(as.numeric(ind _ perf[,
5]), na.rm = T), mean(as.numeric(ind _ perf[, 6]), na.rm = T)))

    for (BY in c(2:6)){
```

```
      comb _ perf <- read.csv(paste(perf _ path, 'by _ ', BY,
' _ ', metr, ' _ SA _ ', country, '.csv', sep = ''), encoding=
"UTF-8")
      comb _ perf <- comb _ perf[, 2:7]
      colnames(comb _ perf) <- c('method', '1-step-ahead',
'2-step-ahead', '3-step-ahead', '4-step-ahead', '8-step-ahead')
      merged <- rbind(merged, comb _ perf)
      }

   }
   write.csv(merged, paste("D:/Documents/merged perfor-
mance/", 'all _ ', metr, ".csv", sep = ''))
   }

   perf _ path <- 'D:/Documents/Performance/'

   metr <- 'mape'

   meanofind  <-  read.csv(paste("D:/Documents/merged  perfor-
mance/", 'all _ ', metr, ".csv", sep = ''), encoding="UTF-8")

   meanofind <- meanofind[which (meanofind$method == 'mean _
acc _ for _ ind _ models'), ]

   meanofind <- meanofind[, -1]

   maxofind  <-  read.csv(paste("D:/Documents/merged  perfor-
mance/", 'all _ ', metr, ".csv", sep = ''), encoding="UTF-8")

   maxofind <- maxofind[which (maxofind$method %in% fmodels), ]
   maxofind <- maxofind[, -1]

   colnames(meanofind) <- c('method', '1-step-ahead', '2-step-
ahead', '3-step-ahead', '4-step-ahead', '8-step-ahead')
   colnames(maxofind) <- c('method', '1-step-ahead', '2-step-
ahead', '3-step-ahead', '4-step-ahead', '8-step-ahead')

   iter <- 1
   for (country in c('c', 'm', 'r', 'u')){
     merged <- meanofind[iter,]
     maxofindrow <- c("Max. err. for ind. models")
     for (horizon in 2:6){
       tempcol <- maxofind[(1 + (iter - 1) * 6):(6 + (iter - 1)
* 6), horizon]
       maxofindrow[horizon] <- max(tempcol)
     }
     merged <- rbind(merged, maxofindrow)
     iter <- iter + 1

     for (BY in c(2:6)){
```

```
    merged <- rbind(merged, c(paste0('Combination of ', BY,
' models'), '', '', '', '', ''))
        for (combmethod in c('SA', 'BG', 'DMSFE', 'SHRINK')){
        comb _ perf <- read.csv(paste(perf _ path, 'by _ ', BY,
' _ ', metr, ' _ ', combmethod, ' _ ', country, '.csv', sep = ''),
encoding="UTF-8")
            comb _ perf <- comb _ perf[, 2:7]
            colnames(comb _ perf) <- c('method', '1-step-ahead',
'2-step-ahead', '3-step-ahead', '4-step-ahead', '8-step-ahead')
            merged <- rbind(merged, comb _ perf)
        }
    }
    write.csv(merged, paste("D:/Documents/merged performance/",
'all _ ', metr, ' _ ', country, ' _ combs', ".csv", sep = ''), row.
names = F)
    }
```

11

JUDGEMENTAL FORECASTING

Vera Shanshan Lin and Yuan Qin

11.1 Introduction

Forecasts based on judgement are common. The goal of judgemental fore-casting, also known as qualitative or subjective forecasting, is to incor-porate forecasters' opinions and expertise into the forecasting process. It can be used in a variety of situations, such as when there are no historical data and a forecast is solely based on judgement, as well as when a forecast relies heavily on conventional extrapolative techniques and judgement is used to support model development and/or fine-tune statistical forecasting outcomes (Önkal-Atay et al., 2004; Wright & Goodwin, 1998). Judgemental forecasting has primarily been used in the following three occasions in the general forecasting literature: (a) statistical forecasting methods are not applicable due to data availability issues; (b) statistical forecasts are ob-tained and then adjusted by judgement; and (c) statistical and judgemental forecasts are generated independently and then combined (Hyndman & Athanasopoulos, 2018). Studies have shown that forecasters may use their expertise, subject knowledge, and up-to-date information to improve sta-tistical forecasting performance in the face of unforeseen occurrences such as economic crises, global pandemics, and terrorist attacks (Zhang et al., 2021). Frechtling (2001) cited several reasons for employing judgemental approaches, including (a) a lack of historical data, (b) an unreliable or in-valid time series, (c) a fast-changing macroenvironment, (d) when large disruptions are foreseen, and (e) when long-term projections are sought.

The popularity and acceptance of judgemental forecasting have grown through the years. Judgemental techniques are employed in tourist fore-casting studies to create a definitive and comprehensive picture of future tourism development based on the knowledge, experience, and views of

DOI: 10.4324/9781003269366-11

experts and other stakeholders (Song et al., 2019). Lin and Song (2015b) categorised four approaches to judgemental forecasting in tourism (Figure 11.1), based on the extent to which forecasters are involved: (a) consulting stakeholders, (b) consulting experts, (c) consulting the public, and (d) using judgement-assisted approaches. Tourism planners and decision makers frequently adapt their forecasting methodologies to account for a variety of qualitative impacting factors. As a result, judgemental forecasting methods that incorporate the views and opinions of experts are frequently used in tourism research to produce more meaningful and relevant projections from which to derive effective managerial recommendations (Lin & Song, 2015b). While statistical techniques have steadily gained prominence among the various forecasting methodologies as technology and data quality have improved over the last few decades (Song et al., 2019), integrating judgemental and statistical projections has been shown to improve predictive performance (Song et al., 2013).

The two most prominent judgemental forecasting techniques in tourism, out of several such methodologies, are the Delphi method and scenario writing (Lin & Song, 2015a). The Delphi method is a well-established technique in long-term tourism planning and forecasting (Cunliffe, 2002), and aims to reach consensus estimates by polling a panel of experts (Kauko & Palmroos, 2014). Lin et al. (2014), for example, applied Delphi-based judgemental adjustments to statistical forecasts of inbound tourism demand in Hong Kong and found that these forecasts were more accurate than a

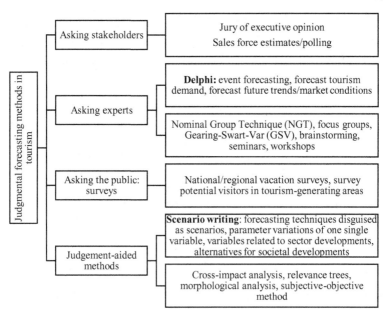

FIGURE 11.1 Judgemental forecasting methods in tourism research
Source: Lin and Song (2015b).

single statistical forecast. von Bergner and Lohmann (2014) utilised an exploratory Delphi poll to identify the most glaring problems facing global tourism until 2020 in terms of the nature, drivers, and effects of those issues. Heiko and Darkow (2010) used a comprehensive Delphi-based scenario method to forecast the future of the logistics services industry until 2025, filling a gap in the knowledge of trends in the field among logistics researchers and practitioners. The Delphi technique has been affirmed to have cognitive value as an effective process for gathering opinions and obtaining knowledge from a group of people with expertise in the field of study (Briedenhann & Butts, 2006; Green & Hunter, 1992; Ziglio, 1996). Mechanistically, it enables different opinions and contradictory attitudes to be incorporated and a useful response to be generated through consensus. Despite these advantages, the Delphi method has limits because it relies on experts' subjective opinion. However, these constraints can be reduced by using well-structured and methodical techniques and approaches to improve predictive performance (Hyndman & Athanasopoulos, 2018).

Based on 46 empirical studies published since 1970, Lin and Song (2015a) have argued that the Delphi approach is mostly employed in three areas: (a) event forecasting, (b) tourism demand forecasting, and (c) trend/market condition forecasting. Although quantitative forecasting methods have gradually become the mainstream method for forecasting tourism demand as technology has advanced, recent studies have shown that following the outbreak of the COVID-19 pandemic, the Delphi technique has regained popularity in the field. Zhang et al. (2021) used a combination of econometric and judgemental methodologies to project inbound tourist arrivals in Hong Kong from 2020Q1 to 2024Q4, forecasting the tourism industry's recovery. Delphi adjustments were applied to baseline forecasts generated by the autoregressive distributed lag-error correction model based on possible recovery scenarios with varying levels of pandemic severity. Liu et al. (2021) forecasted the recovery of tourism demand for 2021 in 20 destinations around the world using a two-step scenario-based judgemental forecasting method. In the first stage, advanced time-series models, artificial intelligence (AI) models, and their combinations generated baseline forecasts. The most accurate forecasts with lowest mean absolute scaled error (MASE) generated in the first stage were then adjusted using the Delphi method to solicit opinions from the study's authors on baseline forecast adjustment coefficients.

Singh et al. (2022) used the Delphi technique to solicit ideas from the tourism and hospitality industry and academic experts about which destination marketing message features (e.g., positive destination attributes, authentic local experience, locals' support, and reminder of the joys of travel) were able to positively affect American visitors' international travel inclinations following the COVID-19 pandemic. Tourism is a dynamic and complex system in which rapid changes and challenging developments occur on a regular basis. Never before has tourism experienced such a

TABLE 11.1 Delphi method process

Stage	Detail
1	Confirm the expert panel.
2	Inform experts about the forecasting work.
3	Obtain initial forecasts and reasoning from experts, and compile and summarise this information to provide feedback.
4	Send feedback to experts on their forecasts, as well as the option to comment further.
5	Iterate the stage until a satisfactory consensus is reached.
6	Construct final forecasts by aggregating the experts' forecasts.

Source: Wright and Goodwin (1998).

downturn, nor has it had to go through such a difficult recovery. According to these studies (Liu et al., 2021; Singh et al., 2022; Zhang et al., 2021), conventional forecasting methods were functionally limited and incapable of producing accurate forecasts in major crisis scenarios, whereas judgemental methods (e.g., the Delphi technique) demonstrated a superior ability to adapt to and cope with a complex context that was full of risks and uncertainties.

A moderator is usually assigned to carry out and manage each procedure in the actual implementation of the Delphi method. In general, the moderator first selects a group of experts in the study's field. Once the experts have been confirmed, they are each sent a questionnaire with instructions to provide comments and responses based on their expertise and experience. After everyone has completed their questionnaires, the facilitator collects and compiles them all and then summarises them to provide feedback. The compiled comments and responses are delivered to each expert for review, with the option of adding further remarks. At the end of each round of expert responses, the facilitator collects all of the questionnaires and determines whether another round of expert opinion is required. This decision depends on whether a broad feeling of consensus is reached. Table 11.1 depicts the Delphi method, as adapted from Wright and Goodwin (1998). Each stage of the Delphi technique has its own set of difficulties. Suggestions and comments about implementation are provided in the following section.

11.2 Methods

11.2.1 Selection of forecasting methods

Although there are numerous alternative methods for forecasting tourism demand, each with its own set of benefits and application contexts, in the context of the COVID-19 pandemic, the primary consideration in selecting a suitable forecasting method should be the certainty of tourism development trends. In circumstances where the future trend of tourist development is fraught with significant uncertainties and hazards, statistical methods are unlikely to maintain the same level of accuracy as in normal times (Liu et al., 2021; Zhang et al., 2021), forcing forecasting to rely solely on judgement. Statistical models, such as non-causal time-series models, econometric models, and AI-based models, as well as their combinations and hybrids, have been widely used in tourism research in recent years, particularly in studies involving big data analytics (Li et al., 2018; Song et al., 2019). Non-causal time-series models produce forecasts based on historical knowledge from a time series. Aside from forecasting, causal or econometric models can be used to investigate the relationship between tourism demand and its determinants. AI-based models can explain non-linear relationships using data-driven and model-free approaches without any prior knowledge of the relationships between input and output variables (Song et al., 2019). Machine learning methods are currently the most commonly used AI approaches in tourism research.

Statistical models are widely used in modern tourism demand forecasting; yet, as previously stated, these methods have limits when dealing with major crises like the COVID-19 pandemic. In this chapter, a Delphi-based pure judgemental forecasting method is used due to the unprecedented impact of the pandemic and the significant uncertainties and hazards associated with the epidemiology and variety of the virus, the vaccine, and regional efforts to prevent and control outbreaks.

11.2.2 Procedure of Delphi-based judgemental forecasting

Delphi studies employ structured survey questionnaires to generate a consensus forecast among a panel of experts. It is crucial to first define the research problem, after which panellists can be identified and the initial survey designed. The initial survey helps to improve and ultimately determine the questionnaire, which is used to obtain expert opinions in the first round of the survey. The responses are then fed back into the reformulated questionnaire, and a second round of surveys is conducted. The process is repeated until the panellists reach an agreement. The two-round Delphi survey procedure is depicted in Figure 11.2.

(1) *Selection of Delphi panellists*
   The first step in using the Delphi method is to choose a group of specialists who can help with the forecasting work. The reliability and authority of forecasting outcomes are determined by the selection of qualified participants. Although there is currently no single definition of 'expert' in the Delphi method literature (Lin & Song, 2015a), von Bergner and Lohmann (2014) provided a fairly concrete definition of a 'tourism expert':

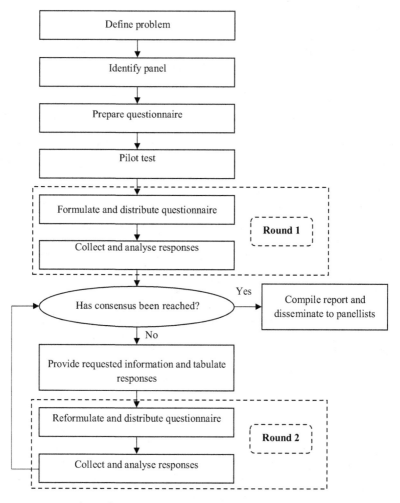

FIGURE 11.2 Design of a two-round Delphi procedure

a respondent with an internationally renowned expertise in tourism research or consulting (i.e., an academic background in different disciplines, membership in relevant research or industry associations, involved in tourism development projects, relevant publications, 10 years or more of professional experience).

(p. 422)

Another issue in confirming an adequate panel of experts is the identification of a group of experts/specialists who represent the desired balance of opinions, knowledge, and experience (Kollwitz, 2011). Rowe and Wright (1999) proposed that, rather than a group of experts concentrating on a specific subject, a heterogeneous group of experts whose unique expertise and experience can be combined to comprehensively reflect the scope of the relevant issue is a better option. Lin and Song (2015a) concluded in their review of Delphi forecasting research:

> in Delphi applications in tourism, the panel often includes stakeholders from different sectors of the tourism industry reflecting a range of experience, knowledge, skills, and perspectives: industry practitioners, tourism and hospitality educators (or academic researchers), professionals from tourism industry associations, government ministries, and non-governmental organizations.
>
> *(p. 1114)*

The majority of studies that use the Delphi method recruit experts using non-probability sampling methods, such as snowball sampling and purposive sampling (Lin & Song, 2015a). Although compared with a probability sample, the sample generated by non-probability sampling methods limits a study's generalisability, it is sometimes the only viable way to proceed in practice.

(2) *Panel size*

The size of the panel is another important factor influencing a study's quality. Lin and Song (2015a) found that the panel size in tourism studies using the Delphi technique ranged from 6 to over 900 since the 1970s, indicating that there is no unified rule specifying the number of experts required to carry out the Delphi method. More importantly, the panel balance, in terms of varied backgrounds and expert capabilities, should be utilised throughout subsequent rounds of the Delphi process rather than the panel size as a determinant of the quality of the study's findings (Wheeller et al., 1990).

Still, several academics have provided guidelines for the proper panel size. According to Hyndman and Athanasopoulos (2018), the average size of a panel is between 5 and 20 experts from a variety of backgrounds. A balanced panel, according to McCleary and Whitney (1994), should include at least ten experts from both professional and academic organisations. The appropriate panel size, according to Sadi and Henderson (2005), is determined by the study's nature, breadth, and topic, as well as the diversification of the experts' domain expertise. For example, Zhang et al. (2021) chose 17 Delphi experts to make adjustments to the baseline statistical forecasts in a study aimed at predicting the recovery of international tourism in Hong Kong amid the COVID-19 pandemic. Seven members of the expert panel specialised in tourism forecasting and destination management and worked at academic institutions in Hong Kong, Macau, and the UK. The remaining ten experts came from the tourism industry and professional associations, with nine of them serving as senior executives in corporations.

(3) *Design of a Delphi survey*

In a study on demand for Hong Kong tourism, Song et al. (2013) used a combination of quantitative and judgemental forecasts. The combined forecasting method's superior forecasting success has been attributed to a variety of reasons, including the provision of feedback to experts following each round of survey, the use of clear Delphi survey instructions, and the inclusion of historical observations. For example, in their study aiming to predict the international tourist recovery in Hong Kong amid the COVID-19 pandemic, Zhang et al. (2021) sent out two rounds of questionnaire surveys by email. A background statement outlined the survey's goals, specific pandemic information such as confirmed cases, travel restrictions, and vaccine development in both the origin regions/countries and Hong Kong, and statistical forecasts for each source market. Some tourism studies have underlined the importance of a pre-test in ensuring the reliability of the Delphi technique. The pre-test serves as a pilot round of the survey, ensuing that the survey instrument performs effectively. According to Lin and Song's (2015a) review, 14 out of 46 studies of tourism using the Delphi technique reported conducting a pre-test before executing their Delphi surveys.

(4) *When to stop*

When a satisfactory level of consensus is reached, the Delphi process comes to an end. The most common ways of evaluating consensus are descriptive statistics and statistical tests (Lin & Song, 2015a). Standard deviation is widely used to measure convergence, while the mean, median, and interquartile range are important statistics for measuring the central tendency. Frechtling (2001), for example, claimed that the interquartile range should not deviate more than 10% from the median to reach group consensus, although some studies (e.g., Austin et al., 2008) have proposed that consensus should be defined as agreement among at least 80% of the experts. The Chi-square test, coefficient of variation (CV), Spearman's rank correlation coefficient, and Wilcoxon rank-sum test are all examples of statistical tests of consensus (Lin & Song, 2015a).

Graphics are recommended for consensus development because they help the Delphi facilitators manage the investigation's iteration and help panellists to locate their points of view within the consensus (Dyck & Emery, 1970). According to Lin and Song (2015a), the number of Delphi rounds ranges between one and four, with two or three rounds being the most common.

(5) *How to aggregate experts' opinions and report results*

To aggregate experts' opinions, quantitative analysis (e.g., the proportion of experts who agree or disagree; the minimum and maximum value, mean, median, mode, and standard deviation of the score) and qualitative analysis (e.g., topic extraction) are used. In addition to the aggregated results of experts' opinions in each round of the survey, the final report should include the research design, panel composition, response rate, and attrition. For example, Singh et al. (2022) used three tables to show their findings after using the Delphi approach to extract message features that positively affected American visitors' international travel intentions following the COVID-19 pandemic. The first table summarises the quality of the survey (e.g., research schedule, panel composition, response rate, and attrition), the second table lists the top 15 message features by frequency of mention and percentage, and the third table displays the agreement proportion, as well as the minimum and maximum values, mean, median, mode and standard deviation of each message feature's score in each round of the survey.

11.3 Application

11.3.1 Design of the Delphi procedure

The forecasting task we are using as an example aimed to forecast quarterly tourist arrivals in Thailand from four source markets (i.e., mainland China, Malaysia, Russia, and the USA) in 2022 and 2023. Two rounds of questionnaire surveys were emailed. The research background, forecast purpose, and official statistics on Thailand's inbound tourist arrivals were provided at the start of each round of the survey. Using mainland China as an example, in Round 1 panellists were asked to provide annual or quarterly judgemental forecasts on the rate of recovery of tourist arrivals in Thailand in comparison to 2019 (see Figure 11.3).

The results of the first round of the survey were collected and analysed. Annual recovery rate projections were converted into quarterly forecasts by assuming a constant recovery rate throughout the year. In Round 2, all panellists were given a statistical summary of the experts' judgemental forecasts, including the mean, minimum, maximum, and standard deviation (see Figure 11.4). Average quarterly recovery rates were utilised to produce the summarised group forecasts from Round 1, which were then relayed back to the panellists in Round 2 along with the accompanying recovery rates. The experts were asked whether they agreed or disagreed with the group's decision, and if they disagreed, they were asked to make additional adjustments. The intention was to repeat the process until a satisfactory consensus was reached. A two-round survey was used in this study.

11.3.2 Profile of Delphi panellists

In total, 12 Delphi experts were asked to forecast the state of Thailand's inbound tourism recovery (see Table 11.2). Two-thirds of the panellists (66.67%) were academics recognised as experts in tourism forecasting and destination

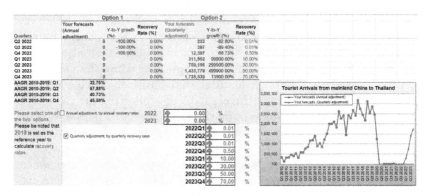

FIGURE 11.3 User interface of the Round 1 questionnaire, mainland China

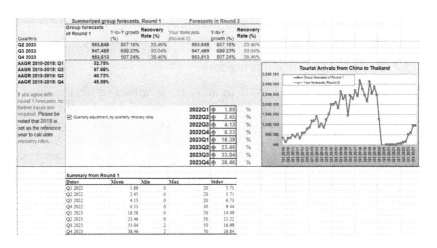

FIGURE 11.4 User interface of the Round 2 questionnaire, mainland China

TABLE 11.2 Composition of the Delphi panel

Sector	Round 1	Round 2
Academic institution	8	7
Industry: exhibitions	1	1
Industry: airlines	1	1
Industry: hotels	1	1
Industry: tourist attractions	1	1
Total	12	11

management. The remaining four panellists represented the exhibition, air-line, hotel, and tourist attraction sectors of the tourism industry. In Round 1, all 12 experts responded, and 11 (91.67%) responded in Round 2.

11.3.3 Delphi consensus and iteration

Table 11.3 shows the mean, minimum and maximum values, standard deviation, and CV of experts' forecasts by source markets and dates. The dispersion of expert judgement was greatly reduced in Round 2: the agreed rate (i.e., the rate of agreement between experts) in the Round 2 survey varied from 66.67% to 75%, and the CV showed a large decrease from Round 1 to Round 2. The Wilcoxon test results displayed a statistically insignificant difference in average recovery rates between the two rounds of the survey, proving that a satisfactory consensus had been reached.

TABLE 11.3 Descriptive statistics: experts' forecasts of recovery rates

Market	Quarter	Mean	Min	Max	Stdev	CV	Consensus rate	Wilcoxon test
Mainland China								
Round 1	Q1 2022	1.89	0.00	20.00	5.71	3.02	66.67%	$z = -1.183$, $p = 0.237$
	Q2 2022	2.45	0.00	20.00	5.71	2.33		
	Q3 2022	4.13	0.00	20.00	6.73	1.63		
	Q4 2022	6.33	0.00	30.00	9.44	1.49		
	Q1 2023	16.38	0.00	50.00	14.49	0.88		
	Q2 2023	23.46	0.00	50.00	15.22	0.65		
	Q3 2023	33.04	1.50	50.00	16.99	0.51		
	Q4 2023	38.46	1.50	70.00	18.84	0.49		
Round 2	Q1 2022	1.73	0.50	1.89	0.42	0.25		
	Q2 2022	2.41	2.00	2.45	0.14	0.06		
	Q3 2022	4.13	4.13	4.13	0.00	0.00		
	Q4 2022	7.12	6.33	15.00	2.61	0.37		
	Q1 2023	16.25	15.00	16.38	0.41	0.03		
	Q2 2023	23.60	23.46	25.00	0.46	0.02		
	Q3 2023	34.13	33.04	45.00	3.61	0.11		
	Q4 2023	39.51	38.46	50.00	3.48	0.09		
Malaysia								
Round 1	Q1 2022	6.58	0.00	40.00	11.90	1.81	75.00%	$z = -0.736$, $p = 0.462$
	Q2 2022	9.13	0.00	40.00	11.57	1.27		
	Q3 2022	12.83	1.00	40.00	12.51	0.97		
	Q4 2022	19.13	1.00	50.00	18.31	0.96		
	Q1 2023	34.58	5.00	60.00	19.00	0.55		
	Q2 2023	41.25	5.00	70.00	20.68	0.50		

(Continued)

Market	Quarter	Mean	Min	Max	Stdev	CV	Consensus rate	Wilcoxon test
	Q3 2023	50.00	5.00	75.00	19.54	0.39		
	Q4 2023	57.50	5.00	80.00	22.71	0.40		
Round 2	Q1 2022	6.17	2.00	6.58	1.38	0.22		
	Q2 2022	8.75	5.00	9.13	1.24	0.14		
	Q3 2022	12.58	10.00	12.83	0.85	0.07		
	Q4 2022	20.11	19.13	30.00	3.28	0.16		
	Q1 2023	34.17	30.00	34.58	1.38	0.04		
	Q2 2023	41.25	41.25	41.25	0.00	0.00		
	Q3 2023	50.00	50.00	50.00	0.00	0.00		
	Q4 2023	57.73	57.50	60.00	0.75	0.01		
Russia								
Round 1	Q1 2022	9.50	1.00	30.00	7.96	0.84	66.67%	$z = -1.260$, $p = 0.208$
	Q2 2022	11.58	5.00	30.00	7.17	0.62		
	Q3 2022	21.46	6.00	80.00	20.07	0.94		
	Q4 2022	21.63	6.00	45.00	12.82	0.59		
	Q1 2023	33.67	9.00	60.00	14.47	0.43		
	Q2 2023	39.92	9.00	60.00	14.96	0.37		
	Q3 2023	58.25	9.00	200.00	47.30	0.81		
	Q4 2023	53.25	9.00	80.00	19.32	0.36		
Round 2	Q1 2022	9.18	7.00	9.50	0.78	0.09		
	Q2 2022	11.30	10.00	11.58	0.64	0.06		
	Q3 2022	20.24	15.00	21.46	2.40	0.12		
	Q4 2022	21.30	18.00	21.63	1.09	0.05		
	Q1 2023	33.79	33.67	35.00	0.40	0.01		
	Q2 2023	40.38	39.92	45.00	1.53	0.04		
	Q3 2023	56.39	45.00	58.25	4.36	0.08		
	Q4 2023	53.32	53.25	54.00	0.23	0.00		
USA								
Round 1	Q1 2022	12.67	2.00	40.00	10.27	0.81	66.67%	$z = -1.122$, $p = 0.262$
	Q2 2022	15.13	2.00	40.00	9.94	0.66		
	Q3 2022	18.13	3.00	40.00	11.25	0.62		
	Q4 2022	23.04	5.00	40.00	13.46	0.58		
	Q1 2023	36.67	10.00	70.00	19.81	0.54		
	Q2 2023	41.67	10.00	70.00	21.25	0.51		

	Q3 2023	50.42	10.00	90.00	26.32	0.52
	Q4 2023	52.83	10.00	80.00	25.68	0.49
Round 2	Q1 2022	11.67	8.00	12.67	1.77	0.15
	Q2 2022	14.92	13.00	15.13	0.64	0.04
	Q3 2022	18.30	18.13	20.00	0.57	0.03
	Q4 2022	23.22	23.04	25.00	0.59	0.03
	Q1 2023	37.42	36.67	45.00	2.51	0.07
	Q2 2023	42.42	41.67	50.00	2.51	0.06
	Q3 2023	51.29	50.42	60.00	2.89	0.06
	Q4 2023	54.39	52.83	70.00	5.18	0.10

Note: Stdev: standard deviation; CV: coefficient of variation.

11.3.4 Analysis of the results

The COVID-19 pandemic outbreak in 2020 and the resulting travel restrictions have had a significant and detrimental influence on Thailand's international inbound tourism market. During the second and third quarters of 2020, no inbound tourists were registered, but once Thailand's inbound restrictions were lifted in the fourth quarter, the country began to attract visitors. Malaysia was the hardest hit of the four source markets, followed by Russia, mainland China, and the USA. Tourist arrivals from mainland China, Malaysia, Russia, and the USA recovered to 0.30%, 0.32%, 5.51%, and 7.85% of the same quarter in 2019, respectively, until the fourth quarter of 2021, with the USA having the highest recovery rate (see Table 11.4).

The experts predicted that the USA will have the highest recovery rate in 2022, while mainland China will have the lowest recovery rate for all four quarters of the same year. Tourist arrivals from mainland China, Malaysia, Russia, and the USA are projected to rebound to 39.51%, 57.73%, 53.32% and 54.39% of their 2019 levels by the fourth quarter of 2024. The panel did not expect any of the four markets to recover to pre-pandemic levels (see Figures 11.5–11.8). Before the pandemic outbreak, strong seasonality could be observed in all four of Thailand's source markets, but no discernible seasonal pattern is predicted for 2022 and 2023.

TABLE 11.4 Delphi forecasting results

Date	Mainland China	Malaysia	Russia	USA
Q1 2019	3,119,622	930,547	615,387	319,790
Q2 2019	2,530,649	1,044,865	210,008	272,650
Q3 2019	2,867,557	1,040,370	145,140	233,638
Q4 2019	2,479,341	1,256,802	512,799	339,778

(Continued)

Date	Mainland China	Malaysia	Russia	USA
Q1 2020	1,247,564	619,400	586,990	210,482
Q2 2020	0	0	0	0
Q3 2020	0	0	0	0
Q4 2020	2,346	51	177	593
Q1 2021	1,520	194	913	2,150
Q2 2021	1,471	635	742	3,178
Q3 2021	2,705	645	845	5,884
Q4 2021	7,347	4,037	28,259	26,668
Q1 2022	53,891	57,384	56,504	37,309
Q2 2022	60,985	91,426	23,721	40,681
Q3 2022	118,550	130,834	29,380	42,745
Q4 2022	176,559	252,789	109,203	78,895
Q1 2023	506,939	317,937	207,926	119,679
Q2 2023	597,195	431,007	84,799	115,670
Q3 2023	978,662	520,185	81,839	119,828
Q4 2023	979,528	725,518	273,415	184,819
Recovery rate				
Q1 2021	0.12%	0.03%	0.16%	1.02%
Q2 2021	0.06%	0.06%	0.35%	1.17%
Q3 2021	0.09%	0.06%	0.58%	2.52%
Q4 2021	0.30%	0.32%	5.51%	7.85%
Q1 2022	1.73%	6.17%	9.18%	11.67%
Q2 2022	2.41%	8.75%	11.30%	14.92%
Q3 2022	4.13%	12.58%	20.24%	18.30%
Q4 2022	7.12%	20.11%	21.30%	23.22%
Q1 2023	16.25%	34.17%	33.79%	37.42%
Q2 2023	23.60%	41.25%	40.38%	42.42%
Q3 2023	34.13%	50.00%	56.39%	51.29%
Q4 2023	39.51%	57.73%	53.32%	54.39%

Note: The 'recovery rate' is calculated by comparison with the 2019 reference year.

11.4 Conclusions and future directions

Delphi is not intended to replace traditional statistical forecasting techniques; rather, it is meant to be used in situations where statistical forecasting methods are ineffective, such as when there are insufficient historical observations, previous trends are disrupted by unexpected shocks, or the market is fraught with risks and uncertainties. When statistical approaches are not reliable, the Delphi method can be used to include expert judgement in the forecasting process, providing managerial insight into the future. In other situations, such as when the market is less volatile or past data is available, the Delphi approach is frequently

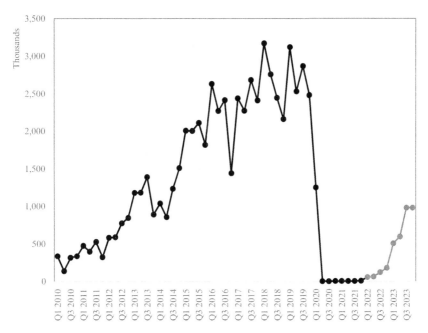

FIGURE 11.5 Quarterly forecasts of tourist arrivals from mainland China, 2022Q1–2023Q4

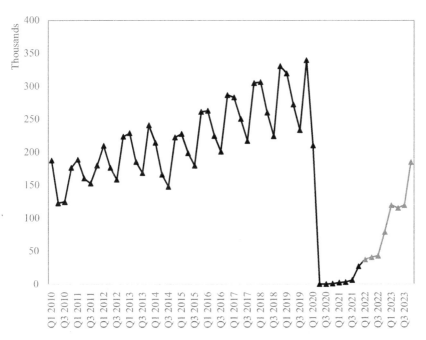

FIGURE 11.6 Quarterly forecasts of tourist arrivals from the USA, 2022Q1–2023Q4

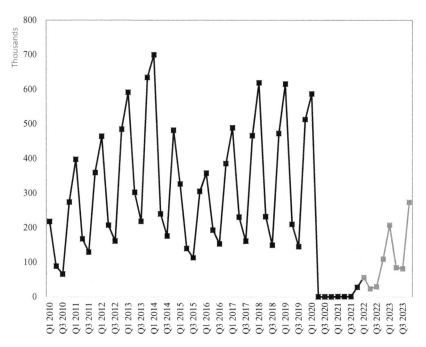

FIGURE 11.7 Quarterly forecasts of tourist arrivals from Russia, 2022Q1–2023Q4

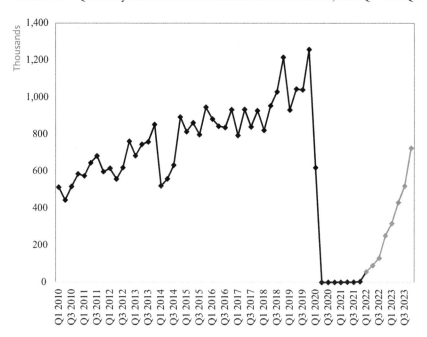

FIGURE 11.8 Quarterly forecasts of tourist arrivals from Malaysia, 2022Q1–2023Q4

used to further improve statistical estimates and produce more accurate forecasts.

The Delphi method's cognitive value has long been acknowledged as a framework for incorporating and integrating opinions from experts in a variety of areas to attain a proper group judgement through consensus. In general, the Delphi technique has not been strictly ordered with specific conditions set for implementation. However, when selecting experts, researchers must keep the panel's balance and size in mind. Furthermore, researchers should define a clear Delphi approach before attempting to develop survey questionnaires. A precise definition of the research problem, as well as a background statement and any necessary data, must be included in the questionnaire.

The Delphi initiator should supervise the entire research process, keeping a close eye on when a consensus has been reached based on statistical data collected from at least two rounds of surveys. Following the resolution of the divergence disagreement, the research team should collect and aggregate the expert responses using a variety of descriptive statistics, then analyse and present the findings in a final report using tables and figures.

Most Delphi forecasting studies in tourism have relied on descriptive statistics (e.g., mean, median, interquartile range, and standard deviation) and statistical tests to reach consensus, with the former strategy being more popular. More research is needed into the use of advanced statistical tools to assess consensus. The Delphi technique has been extensively applied in long-range forecasting, most notably for qualitative forecasting. Statistical approaches have thus been restricted to the analysis of Delphi data. Although few studies have used these data to predict tourism demand, tourism scholars have adopted the Delphi method to generate quantitative forecasts and to facilitate integrative forecasting. The actual performance of Delphi projections should be better emphasised, particularly for panel-produced quantitative estimates. Subsequent research is also suggested to examine the Delphi procedure from a Bayesian perspective—particularly in circumstances where data are inaccurate, thus rendering the conventional Delphi method ineffective. Another area for investigation concerns the roles of situational variables (e.g., time horizons, data variability, contextual knowledge, and technical knowledge) and other factors in the relative forecasting performance of judgemental forecasts (or Delphi forecasts). Topics of interest could include feedback, data presentation, and task structure.

Self-study questions

1   When is it appropriate to use judgemental forecasting?
2   Briefly outline the Delphi-based judgemental forecasting procedure.
3   In a Delphi survey, how many experts are required?
4   How should expert opinions be aggregated?

References

Austin, D. R., Lee, Y., & Getzb, D. A. (2008). A Delphi study of trends in special and inclusive recreation. *Leisure/Loisir, 32*(1), 163–182. https://doi.org/10.1080/14927713.2008.9651404

Briedenhann, J., & Butts, S. (2006). Application of the Delphi technique to rural tourism project evaluation. *Current Issues in Tourism, 9*(2), 171–190. https://doi.org/10.1080/13683500608668246

Cunliffe, S. (2002). Forecasting risks in the tourism industry using the Delphi technique. Retrieved from: http://citeseerx.ist.psu.edu/viewdoc/download?doi=10.1.1.131.5350&rep=rep1&type=pdf

Dyck, H. J., & Emery, G. J. (1970). *Social futures: Alberta, 1970–2005*. Edmonton: Human Resources Research Council of Alberta. OCLC Number: 1151 277867

Frechtling, D. C. (2001). *Forecasting tourism demand: Methods and strategies.* Oxford: Butterworth-Heinemann. ISBN: 9780750651707

Green, H., & Hunter, C. (1992). The environmental impact assessment of tourism development. In P. Johnson & B. Thomas (Eds.), *Perspectives on tourism policy* (pp. 29–48). London: Mansell. ISBN: 9780720121216

Heiko, A., & Darkow, I. L. (2010). Scenarios for the logistics services industry: A Delphi-based analysis for 2025. *International Journal of Production Economics, 127*(1), 46–59. https://doi.org/10.1016/j.ijpe.2010.04.013

Hyndman, R. J., & Athanasopoulos, G. (2018). *Forecasting: Principles and practice* (2nd ed.). OTexts: Melbourne, Australia. https://otexts.com/fpp2. Accessed on March 16, 2022.

Kauko, K., & Palmroos, P. (2014). The Delphi method in forecasting financial markets—An experimental study. *International Journal of Forecasting, 30*(2), 313–327. https://doi.org/10.1016/j.ijforecast.2013.09.007

Kollwitz, H. (2011). Evaluating cruise demand forecasting practices: A Delphi approach. In P. Gibson, A. Papathanassis, & P. Milde (Eds.), *Cruise sector challenges: Making progress in an uncertain world* (pp. 39–55). Wiesbaden: Gabler. https://doi.org/10.1007/978-3-8349-6871-5

Li, J., Xu, L., Tang, L., Wang, S., & Li, L. (2018). Big data in tourism research: A literature review. *Tourism Management, 68*, 301–323. https://doi.org/10.1016/j.tourman.2018.03.009

Lin, V. S., Goodwin, P., & Song, H. (2014). Accuracy and bias of experts' adjusted forecasts. *Annals of Tourism Research, 48*, 156–174. https://doi.org/10.1016/j.annals.2014.06.005

Lin, V. S., & Song, H. (2015a). A review of Delphi forecasting research in tourism. *Current Issues in Tourism, 18*(12), 1099–1131. https://doi.org/10.1080/13683500.2014.967187

Lin, V. S., & Song, H. (2015b). Judgmental forecasting in tourism. In C. Cooper (Ed.), *Contemporary tourism reviews: Volume 1* (pp. 300–333). Oxford: Goodfellow. ISBN: 9781910158050

Liu, A., Vici, L., Ramos, V., Giannoni, S., & Blake, A. (2021). Visitor arrivals forecasts amid COVID-19: A perspective from the Europe team. *Annals of Tourism Research, 88*. https://doi.org/10.1016/j.annals.2021.103182

McCleary, K. W., & Whitney, D. L. (1994). Projecting western consumer attitudes toward travel to six eastern European countries. In M. Uysal (Ed.), *Global tourist behavior* (pp. 239–256). New York: International Business Press. ISBN: 9780789000965

Önkal-Atay, D., Thomson, M. E., & Pollock, A. C. (2004). Judgmental forecasting. In M. P. Clements & D. F. Hendry (Eds.), *A companion to economic forecasting* (pp. 133–151). Oxford: Blackwell. ISBN: 9781405126236

Rowe, G., & Wright, G. (1999). The Delphi technique as a forecasting tool: Issues and analysis. *International Journal of Forecasting, 15*(4), 353–375. https://doi.org/10.1016/S0169-2070(99)00018-7

Sadi, M. A., & Henderson, J. C. (2005). Tourism in Saudi Arabia and its future development. *Journal of Business and Economics, 11*, 94–111. http://hdl.handle.net/10576/8105

Singh, S., Nicely, A., Day, J., & Cai, L. A. (2022). Marketing messages for post-pandemic destination recovery-A Delphi study. *Journal of Destination Marketing & Management, 23*. https://doi.org/10.1016/j.jdmm.2021.100676

Song, H., Gao, B. Z., & Lin, V. S. (2013). Combining statistical and judgmental forecasts via a web-based tourism demand forecasting system. *International Journal of Forecasting, 29*(2), 295–310. https://doi.org/10.1016/j.ijforecast.2011.12.003

Song, H., Qiu, R. T., & Park, J. (2019). A review of research on tourism demand forecasting: Launching the Annals of Tourism Research Curated Collection on tourism demand forecasting. *Annals of Tourism Research, 75*, 338–362. https://doi.org/10.1016/j.annals.2018.12.001

von Bergner, N. M., & Lohmann, M. (2014). Future challenges for global tourism: A Delphi survey. *Journal of Travel Research, 53*(4), 420–432. https://doi.org/10.1177/0047287513506292

Wheeller, B., Hart, T., & Whysall, P. (1990). Application of the Delphi technique: A reply to Green, Hunter and Moore. *Tourism Management, 11*(2), 121–122. https://doi.org/10.1016/0261-5177(90)90027-7

Wright, G., & Goodwin, P. (1998). *Forecasting with judgment.* Chichester: Wiley. ISBN: 9780471970149

Zhang, G. P. (2003). Time series forecasting using a hybrid ARIMA and neural network model. *Neurocomputing, 50*, 159–175. https://doi.org/10.1016/S0925-2312(01)00702-0

Zhang, H., Song, H., Wen, L., & Liu, C. (2021). Forecasting tourism recovery amid COVID-19. *Annals of Tourism Research, 87*. https://doi.org/10.1016/j.annals.2021.103149

Ziglio, E. (1996). The Delphi method and its contribution to decision-making. In M. Adler & E. Ziglio (Eds.), *Gazing into the oracle: The Delphi method and its application to social policy and public health* (pp. 3–33). London: Kingsley. ISBN: 9781853021046

12

SCENARIO FORECASTING DURING CRISES

Richard T. R. Qiu

12.1 Introduction

Scenario forecasting is fundamentally different from the approaches discussed in the previous chapters. While most forecasting approaches intend to provide the most likely outcome as their result, the scenario forecasting approach generates several forecasts based on multiple plausible scenarios, which may have different probabilities of occurring. This feature of multiple forecasts under diverse scenarios constitutes the essence of scenario forecasting. Generating multiple forecast scenarios can be important to forecast practice for several reasons. Forecasts generated under different scenarios allow the forecasters to cover a wider range of possibilities, providing a holistic and comprehensive view of future tourism demand trends. In addition, establishing forecast scenarios allows forecasters to analyse 'what if' questions and comprehend the consequences of potential or hypothetical plans or policies.

Tourism is a complex industry that interrelates with many other industries. While service is at the centre of tourism experiences, the consumption of tourism goods and services also relies on intermediate products from other industries. Consequently, shocks to many industries may lead to fluctuations in tourism. For example, economic recessions may influence both tourist income in the origin and prices in the destination, and therefore have an impact on the demand for tourism. Terrorism, political instability, and natural disasters may change the perceived safety of a destination in the eyes of tourists and lead to hesitation. Health crises, such as the ongoing COVID-19 pandemic, may cause strict border control policies and limit travel. In these scenarios, international tourism demand not only relates to the factors discussed in the previous chapters but also heavily

DOI: 10.4324/9781003269366-12

depends on the future trends of these external shocks. Due to extensive uncertainty during these crises, it may not be ideal to provide one most likely forecast of the market to facilitate business planning and strategy. Scenario forecasting is more desirable so that more possibilities can be considered and discussed.

Compared with other forecasting techniques, scenario forecasting has two main advantages, which are the coverage of diverse scenarios and the provision of 'what if' analyses. Covering multiple scenarios is especially useful when the future trend of the market is uncertain. Stakeholders can gain a holistic and comprehensive understanding of the future demand in the market and prepare for fluctuations accordingly. Reintinger, Berghammer, and Schmude (2016) utilised an agent-based model to investigate the travel destination preference of German tourists and to simulate the dynamics of Germany's outbound market in the European region between 2016 and 2030. To reveal the possible development paths, three potential scenarios were developed, namely, the baseline scenario, in which tourist behaviour was assumed to resume as it was between 2011 and 2015; the mobility scenario, in which the world was assumed to develop into a flexible and mobile society with a 'significant level of resource consumption'; and the vicinity scenario, in which society was assumed to consume fewer resources and focus on the environment (Reintinger et al., 2016: 243). Instead of merely being three separate predictions, the forecasts in the three scenarios described different storylines of societal development. In particular, the forecasts for the two extreme cases (i.e., the mobility and vicinity scenarios) provided a funnel within which the future path of market development could lie.

The COVID-19 pandemic has had a profound impact on our society. As of the end of 2021, over 288.19 million cases were confirmed worldwide with 5.44 million deaths (Our World in Data, 2022). Border control policies and the risk of infection have severely reduced the market demand for tourism, putting the industry at stake. Various studies have been conducted during this time to forecast the trend of the international tourism market during the pandemic and the recovery pattern of the industry after the pandemic. Among others, scenario forecasting has been frequently adopted. In a tourism demand forecasting competition organised by the International Association of Tourism Economics (IATE), three teams made forecasts of international visitor arrivals to 20 destinations in 2021 under three scenarios (mild, medium, and severe) describing different pandemic severity levels (Kourentzes et al., 2021; Liu, Vici, Ramos, Giannoni, & Blake, 2021; Qiu et al., 2021; Song & Li, 2021). In these studies, the mild scenario corresponded to a low persistence of the pandemic and a fast recovery of the tourism industry; the severe scenario corresponded to minor improvements in the pandemic situation and a slow recovery of the industry; and the medium scenario was between the two extremes. The competition was organised around October 2020, a time when all three scenarios seemed plausible. Stakeholders in the tourism industry should consider their own beliefs about the pandemic situation and utilise the forecasts in the corresponding scenario. Nevertheless, as the COVID-19 pandemic evolves, with three waves of infections occurring around November 2020, April 2021, and August 2021, stakeholders should realise that the severe scenario is more likely to happen in most destinations, and they should prepare accordingly.

The two cases above describe situations in which forecasts are generated for multiple scenarios due to uncertainty in the market trend. The results provide stakeholders with a wide range of plausible forecasts so that they can adopt one or several forecasts according to their beliefs and information about the market conditions. Nonetheless, generating forecasts for plausible scenarios may not always be the goal. Quite often, stakeholders seek the answer to a 'what if' analysis. For example, Mai and Smith (2018) investigated the potential of the tourism industry in Cat Ba Island, Vietnam, under different economic and tourism planning scenarios. Utilising a system dynamic model, they asserted the unsustainable condition of tourism development on Cat Ba Island due to some environmental issues. They applied five scenarios, corresponding to different levels of sustainable development policies, to the tourism economic model of Cat Ba Island. Therefore, their forecasting results revealed the potential benefits and costs of different levels of environmental preservation on tourism and economic development. This information could be used by local authorities as a foundation for designing and implementing sustainable tourism development policies.

A 'what if' analysis can also provide answers to investigations on the impact of events and crises. Page, Song, and Wu (2012) adopted a time-varying parameter (TVP) model to investigate the impacts of the swine flu (H1N1 influenza virus) pandemic and the 2008 global economic crisis on the UK's inbound tourism market. Their analysis established two hypothetical scenarios: a 'no-impact scenario' that assumed the absence of both the pandemic and the economic crisis and an 'economic impact scenario' that only assumed the absence of the pandemic. By comparing the forecasting results of the two scenarios and the actual data, Page et al. (2012) estimated the impact of both crises on the international tourism demand of the UK. Similarly, Zhang, Song, Wen, and Liu (2021) examined the impact of the COVID-19 pandemic on the international tourism market of Hong Kong. They used the autoregressive distributed lag-error correction model to generate a baseline forecast of tourism demand assuming the absence of the COVID-19 pandemic and carried out two rounds of Delphi adjustments to generate three scenario forecasts corresponding to different levels of severity of the pandemic (mild, medium, and severe). The differences between the baseline forecast and the COVID-19-adjusted forecasts revealed the potential loss of visitor arrivals in different scenarios. Analyses such as these allow the relevant authorities and practitioners to estimate the impact of crises on their inbound tourism markets. This information can be used as a basis for contingency plans, crisis bailout packages, and recovery-stimulating schemes before or after a crisis.

Unlike other forecasting methods, which have specific statistical models or analytical processes, the scenario forecasting approach is a framework rather than a technique. After determining the scenarios to be analysed, researchers have to generate predictions under each scenario using relevant forecasting techniques, such as the quantitative and qualitative methods introduced in the previous chapters. The remaining part of this chapter elaborates on the key elements of scenario forecasting in tourism demand forecasting practice.

12.2 Scenario setup

One of the most important elements of the scenario forecasting is the setup of the scenarios. The validity and significance of the scenarios directly determine the significance of the investigation. The scenarios can have different bases that are in line with the purpose of the investigation. Two questions can be asked while setting up the scenarios: (1) What can happen in the market in the future? and (2) What do we want to know about the future? If researchers want to know the future trend of the market, the setup of the scenarios should cover the most plausible (and/or important) situations. This type of setup can be referred to as *future-oriented scenarios*, which often require an understanding of the market and information about relevant factors. Alternatively, if researchers want to know the trajectory of the market under a specific condition, the setup of the scenarios should coincide with this need and describe the specific condition. This type of setup can be named *need-oriented scenarios*. This subsection elaborates on these two types of scenario setups.

Future-oriented scenarios. During a crisis, it is common to ask what will happen next. Unlike times when the market and global economy are stable, the future trend of the market during a crisis can be very uncertain. In such uncertain times, researchers need to come up with a list of plausible and important scenarios under which the forecasts can be generated. Essentially, the future-oriented scenario forecasting approach requires researchers to predict future scenarios. The prediction of these future scenarios can be quantitative and data driven. For example, Fotiadis, Polyzos, and Huan (2021) estimated the decrease in international tourist arrivals due to the COVID-19 pandemic. Their analysis applied historical tourism demand data during previous crises (health crises such as severe acute respiratory syndrome [SARS] and Middle East respiratory syndrome, and the global financial crisis) to statistical models. The scenario setup in Fotiadis et al. (2021) assumed that the trend of tourism demand during and after the COVID-19 pandemic would repeat the pattern during other crises. This method draws on the logic of time series analysis and predicts future scenarios with historical patterns. It is relatively simple – it requires only tourism demand information during other crises – and is usually effective for both academia and industry. However, when the target crisis is unique, such as the ongoing COVID-19 pandemic, the method may provide less informative scenarios. Due to the long persistence of the COVID-19 pandemic, which is unexpected and different from previous crises, even the worst scenario forecast in Fotiadis et al. (2021) considerably exceeded the actual trend of worldwide tourism demand.

In addition to information about previous crises, researchers can use data on other influential factors to set up their scenarios. This type of scenario setup emphasises the interrelationship between the tourism industry and other industries in the economy. Ricardo (2015) adopted artificial intelligence-based forecasting techniques to investigate the tourism demand for the Lisbon region in 2016. The model was trained with independent variables covering economic factors such as gross domestic product (GDP), consumer price index (CPI), exchange rate, and interest rates, and a leading indicator from Google Trends. To capture the possibility of the rise and fall of the economy, Ricardo (2015) generated three scenario forecasts by feeding the model with different sets of independent variables. A set of variables describing an economic downturn led to the 'unfavourable' scenario; a set of variables describing an economic boom led to the 'favourable' scenario; and a set of variables with moderate values led to the 'moderate' scenario. This type of scenario setup is common in econometric analysis and captures the interlock between the tourism industry and other sectors of the economy. It has the advantage of a solid theoretical foundation, but has the disadvantage of a high demand for relevant data. In addition to tourism demand data, this type of scenario setup requires information on major drivers of tourism demand, such as tourist income, relative tourism price of the destination to that of the origin, and tourism price of the substitute destinations. Furthermore, the econometric scenario setup assumes a stable long-run relationship between tourism demand and its influential factors, which may be unrealistic during a crisis.

The above two quantitative scenario setup methods establish scenarios with numerical data. While these setups are objective, they may exhibit fallacies. The foundation of these scenarios is the link between the past and the future, which can be weak during crises. In this case, subjective adjustments are needed to establish meaningful scenarios. Researchers can utilise their own experiences or include experts' opinions to set scenarios qualitatively. Reintinger et al. (2016) developed their scenarios with a two-round Delphi survey. In the first round, 40 experts were surveyed to elicit future challenges of the tourism industry. Another 34 experts were then asked to evaluate the relevance and likelihood of these challenges in the second round. The result of the Delphi survey was summarised into the three scenarios in the study. Qiu et al. (2021) defined their scenarios according to different assumptions on the evolution of the COVID-19 pandemic, vaccination coverage, and border control policies. By assuming important dates for these significant events, they came up with three recovery patterns of tourism demand: a V-shaped recovery pattern corresponding to the mild scenario; a deep V-/U-shaped recovery pattern corresponding to the medium scenario; and an L-shaped recovery pattern corresponding to the severe scenario. A qualitative scenario setup method can embed the experiences of researchers or experts in the scenarios, but it is also subject to criticism due to its subjectivity. Neither quantitative nor qualitative scenario setup methods can be considered the best methods of scenario setting. Researchers should consider the goal of their study as well as the availability of data to choose the most appropriate method. A combination of quantitative and qualitative scenario setup methods can also be considered to consolidate the setting.

Need-oriented scenarios. Compared with *future-oriented* scenarios, *need-oriented* scenarios are easier to set up. In this case, researchers should emphasise justifying the validity and significance of the need rather than the scenario. For example, Page et al. (2012) investigated the impacts of two simultaneous crises, the global financial crisis in 2008 and swine flu in 2009 – the effects of which overlapped in 2009, on the tourism industry of the UK. A scenario in which both crises were absent was needed to facilitate this counterfactual analysis. Therefore, the authors extrapolated the trends of economic variables in the absence of the economic crisis, fed these variables into a statistical model, and established the 'no-impact scenario'. In the 'no-impact scenario', the tourism demand forecast described the expected trend if none of the crises occurred. Comparing this forecast to the actual data provided an estimation of the impact of the crises on the UK's inbound tourism market. To isolate the impact of one crisis from the other, Page et al. (2012) further established an economic impact scenario that reflected the expected volume of tourism demand under only the global economic crisis.

Mai and Smith (2018) evaluated the potential of various sustainable tourism development strategies in Cat Ba Island, Vietnam. Their scenario setup therefore described different sustainable tourism strategies for five scenarios with different levels of development on protected land, waste treatment, and water usage, which were closely related to the sustainable development of the tourism industry in Cat Ba Island. Comparing the forecasts from these scenarios illustrated the costs and benefits of different sustainable strategies and pointed out the direction of future development for Cat Ba Island.

Figure 12.1 summarises the types of scenario setup in scenario forecasting.

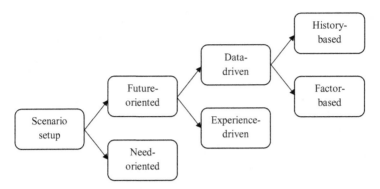

FIGURE 12.1 Types of Scenario Setups in a Scenario Forecasting Approach

The name of a scenario should reflect its condition, but some terms should be used with caution. For example, the name 'most likely scenario' gives the audience an explicit indication of the likelihood of the scenario, which may sometimes mislead them. Similarly, the 'best or worst scenario' conveys the sense that the scenario is extreme, which may lead the audience to focus on less extreme scenarios. In many cases, neuters are better choices for the names of scenarios.

12.3 Forecasts under each scenario

Once the scenarios have been set, researchers can use appropriate forecasting techniques under each scenario. The two main types of forecasting practices at this stage are (1) independently generating the forecast for each scenario, and (2) generating a baseline forecast and adjusting it according to the scenarios.

In Mai and Smith (2018), the tourism demand forecasts in the different scenarios were generated through feeding different sustainable policy parameters into a system dynamic model. In Reintinger et al. (2016), the forecasts in the different scenarios were generated through the agent-based model using parameters that depicted different societal framework conditions. The forecasting process of each scenario was independent in these studies. One advantage of an *independent forecasting* approach is the clear causal relationship between influential factors and tourism demand. The model used in a study should be empirically justified based on data prior to the forecasting period. However, in some cases, this assumption of a causal relationship may become a limitation. The long-run relationship established using data prior to the forecast period might fail to hold true during a crisis. For example, travel was limited by border control policies during the COVID-19 pandemic, leading to a low volume of international tourist arrivals regardless of GDP (the common proxy for tourist income),

CPI, and exchange rate (the common proxy for tourism prices in a destination). The approach of generating a forecast for each scenario separately from the causal model can only be used when the fluctuation in the tourism market is purely channelled from other parts of the economy. The change in the causal relationships between tourism demand and its influencing factors during a crisis makes this approach less likely to be accurate.

Alternatively, researchers can generate a baseline forecast and adjust each scenario accordingly. This approach is frequently adopted in scenario forecasting investigations during crises. Zhang et al. (2021) produced a baseline forecast of international visitor arrivals to Hong Kong from 2020 to 2024 using data prior to the COVID-19 pandemic. This forecast described the expected market trajectory without the pandemic. Based on the baseline forecast, a panel of 17 experts – 7 scholars and 10 practitioners – were asked to identify two sets of important figures in the recovery of the tourism market: the quarter in which the international visitor arrivals would be the lowest and the quarter in which the arrivals would recover back to the baseline forecast. A linear recovery path between the bottom and the fully recovered date was assumed, and seasonal adjustments were applied to this linear recovery path. These adjustments were followed by a second round of Delphi survey, in which the experts were asked to adjust their initial predictions. Statistical convergence between expert opinions was achieved before the authors concluded the survey. Different from those in Mai and Smith (2018) and Reintinger et al. (2016), the scenario forecasts in Zhang et al. (2021) used the subjective judgements of the panel. This approach utilised the conventional wisdom of the experts, but the adjustments did not exhibit a clear causal relationship. The mechanism through which the experts reached their subjective adjustments could not be fully explained.

Some objectivity can be achieved by incorporate statistical data into experts' judgements. In addition to subjective judgements, Qiu et al. (2021) drew insights from industrial reports and national statistics to assist their adjustments. The reports from the United Nations World Tourism Organization (UNWTO, 2020a), the World Health Organization (WHO, 2020), and the Oxford Coronavirus Government Response Tracker (Our World in Data, 2020) were cross-referenced to determine the percentage declines of tourism demand in the target destinations. Liu et al. (2021) further regularised their adjustment process by developing a COVID-19 risk exposure (CORE) index. The CORE index describes a destination in terms of accessibility and pandemic protective measures. These two aspects jointly measure the risk exposure of the destination to the COVID-19 pandemic. The developed CORE index was combined with the authors' knowledge of the destinations to finalise the forecasts under each scenario. The *adjustment on baseline* approach trades off the clear causal relationship in the *independent forecasting* approach with contextual expert opinions.

This is extremely helpful when fluctuations in the tourism market are caused (partially) internally. For example, the travel bans during a pandemic limit the volume of international travel. This shock invalidates the long-run relationship between tourism demand and its influential factors, and significantly limits the accuracy of statistical models.

12.4 Interpreting the results from scenario forecasts

Unlike the forecasting methods introduced in the previous chapters, scenario forecasting is a framework rather than a technique. Instead of being considered as a competing method, scenario forecasting complements other methods when uncertainty is a challenge to forecasting practice. It is mainly used to generate ex ante forecasts, with the results reflecting either the future condition of the market or some states of the world that will never be realised (in the case of a 'what if' analysis). Therefore, in general, no accuracy evaluation can be conducted on the results from scenario forecasting. Nonetheless, researchers can always evaluate, compare, and select the best forecasting technique for each scenario or for the baseline forecast. The accuracy of the forecasting technique under each scenario directly determines the validity and significance of the scenario forecasting results.

Another practical issue with the scenario forecasting approach is the forecast frequency. Although the forecast can be generated at all frequencies if the data allow, scenario forecasts at a high frequency may be less reliable due to the impact of uncertainty. For example, during the recovery of the international tourism market after a pandemic, a change in border control policy in June or July would have a significant impact on the realised volume of tourist arrivals at a monthly or quarterly frequency, but not at an annual frequency. Therefore, when a scenario forecasting approach is used during times of crisis, while forecasting practice can still utilise high-frequency data, researchers and the audience are recommended to pay more attention to the forecasting results at an aggregate level (e.g., annual frequency).

The audience should keep in mind that the scenarios are established due to significant uncertainty in the market. It is the audience's responsibility to collect and comprehend relevant information so that they can estimate the likelihood of each scenario. The audience should bear in mind that, in most cases, the scenario with the highest (lowest) forecast does not correspond to the upper (lower) extreme of the market, and that the scenario that lies in the middle of the two extremes does not have a higher probability of occurring. The probability of occurrence is likely to be unclear for all of the scenarios.

Due to high uncertainty, forecasts with long horizons are relatively less reliable than those with shorter horizons. Researchers are encouraged to consider longitudinal updates of their scenario forecasts. Although this may not be an easily fulfilled proposition in academic papers due to the time needed for the publication cycle, industrial and consultancy reports can easily be updated. The Pacific Asia Travel Association (PATA) used to publish annual forecast reports since 2012. To account for the uncertainty in the tourism industry during the COVID-19 pandemic, their forecasting unit adopted scenario forecasts for the 2020 report (PATA, 2020) and released several updates on the scenarios and forecasts (PATA, 2021a; 2021b). Such scenario forecasts and updates can help industry practitioners and local authorities to understand their tourism market and to prepare for recovery.

12.5 Applications

We continue to use the inbound tourism market of Thailand as an example. Two specific examples are provided for the scenario forecasting of tourist arrivals from mainland China to Thailand during the 2008 economic crisis and the ongoing COVID-19 pandemic.

12.5.1 Tourism demand forecasting during the 2008 financial crisis

The global financial crisis in 2008 had a devastating impact on economies worldwide. Annual GDP growth in the world dropped from 4.4% in 2007 to 2.0% in 2008. China's five years of double-digit growth was terminated, and the country only achieved a GDP growth of 9.7% in 2008 (compared with 14.2% in 2007), and Thailand's three years of accelerating GDP growth was interrupted (2005: 4.2%; 2006: 5.0%; 2007: 5.4%; 2008: 1.7%). In such a situation, with tourism being one of the major industries in Thailand, and mainland China being one of the major source markets of Thailand's inbound tourism market, forecasting tourist arrivals from mainland China to Thailand during the financial crisis is in the interest of many people.

Assuming a time point at the end of 2008 and foreseeing uncertainty in the following years, a set of scenario forecasts can be generated to provide a comprehensive understanding of the market trend. The purpose of this forecasting practice is to predict the future trend; hence, a *future-oriented* scenario setup should be considered. Furthermore, because the main uncertainty in the tourism market comes from fluctuations in economic factors (e.g., tourist income and tourism prices), a *factor-based data-driven* approach should be adopted.

Three scenarios, corresponding to three sets of possible economic situations, are developed by summarising the projections of some international non-governmental organisations (such as the World Bank and International Monetary Fund) and governments. These scenarios mainly describe the GDP trends in mainland China (as the proxy for tourist income) and the relative price trends in Thailand over mainland China (as the proxy for tourism prices in the destination):

1 *Recovery scenario.* The economy in mainland China recovers quickly in 2009, and GDP growth is restored to the average pre-crisis level. The relative prices in Thailand versus mainland China increase considerably due to the better recovering condition in mainland China than in Thailand.
2 *Sustainable scenario.* The impact of the crisis sustains in mainland China in 2009 with a low level of GDP growth and stable relative prices between Thailand and mainland China.
3 *Recession scenario.* The recession continues in mainland China with decreased GDP and a decrease in relative prices in Thailand compared with mainland China in 2009.

With the *factor-based data-driven* approach scenario setup, the tourism demand in each scenario is independently forecasted. The factors assumed in each scenario are applied in the forecasting model to reflect the dynamics of the situation. This example adopts the autoregressive distributed lag model (ADLM) discussed in Chapter 3. Quarterly GDP index data for mainland China and the exchange rate-adjusted relative prices of Thailand relative to mainland China between 2000 and 2008 are used to train the model. The projections of the GDP index and relative prices in 2009 and 2010 in the three scenarios (Figure 12.2) are used as explanatory variables for the forecasts.

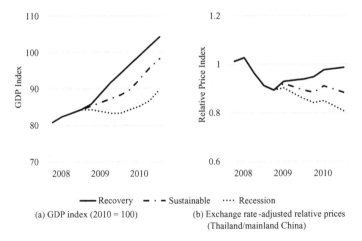

FIGURE 12.2   The Setup of Three Scenarios under the 2008 Financial Crisis.

Figure 12.3 represents the scenario forecasting results for tourist arrivals from mainland China to Thailand in 2009 and 2010. The figure shows that the volume of tourist arrivals in 2009 can be as high as 0.8 million in the *recovery scenario* or as low as 0.4 million in the *recession scenario*. The researcher and the audience may realise that the actual paths of mainland China's GDP index and Thailand's relative prices to mainland China follow the grey line in Figure 12.4. The reality is relatively close to the setup in the *recovery scenario*. Therefore, more attention should be paid to the forecasts of the *recovery scenario*.

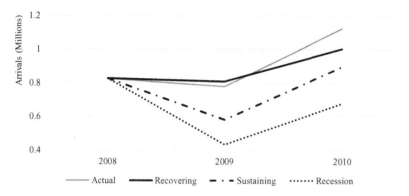

FIGURE 12.3 Scenario Forecasts during the 2008 Financial Crisis

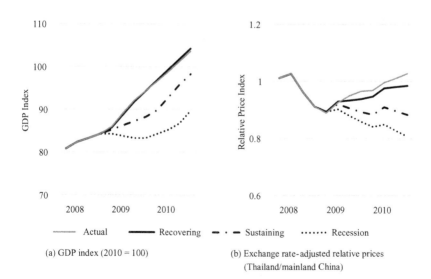

(a) GDP index (2010 = 100)

(b) Exchange rate-adjusted relative prices (Thailand/mainland China)

FIGURE 12.4 Comparison between Scenario Setups and Actual Observations.

12.5.2 Tourism demand forecasting during the COVID-19 pandemic

The COVID-19 pandemic has had a disastrous impact on the global economy and the tourism industry. In particular, border control policies and travel restrictions have limited international travel fundamentally. In May 2020, around 80% of the destinations were under complete closure, with other destinations under partial closure or other border control measures (UNWTO, 2020b). The travel/non-travel decision of a potential tourist is not only driven by those influential factors but also constrained by the regulations in force at the destination. In this situation, an *experience-driven* scenario setup approach can be used if the researcher would like to foresee the possible future trends. Alternatively, if the researcher wants to understand the market trends under different degrees of severity of the pandemic, a *need-oriented* approach can be adopted.

Assuming a mid-year time point in 2020, while seeing the damage that the pandemic has done to the tourism industry, predicting the future trends of international tourist flows would be in the interest of the government and industry practitioners. In this example, we explore the trend of tourist arrivals from mainland China to Thailand under different degrees of severity of the pandemic. Specifically, we follow the three scenarios of Qiu et al. (2021) in this exploration:

1   *Mild scenario.* The pandemic ends at the end of 2020. The travel restrictions and border controls are all lifted soon afterwards.
2   *Medium scenario.* The pandemic ends in the summer of 2021. Most travel restrictions and border controls are (partially) lifted by then.
3   *Severe scenario.* The pandemic persists through 2021. Most travel restrictions and border controls are still in effect.

As the potential tourist's travel/non-travel decision is limited by the regulations in force at the destination and the availability of flights, a statistical model with regular explanatory variables loses its effectiveness, and the *adjustment on baseline* scenario forecasting approach is used in this example. The method described in Chapter 11 is used, where the quarterly volumes of tourist arrivals in 2019 are adopted as baseline values. The impact of the pandemic is then determined by judgementally adjusting the baseline values in each scenario (Table 12.1).

According to the estimates in Figure 12.5, tourist arrivals from mainland China to Thailand in 2021 can be as high as 4.63 million (42% of the 2019 level) in the *mild scenario* or as low as 5,500 (0.05% of the 2019 level) in the *severe scenario.*

The likelihood of the scenarios is strongly related to the pandemic situation in Thailand. The *mild scenario* represented a good wish but soon became unrealistic after a wave of newly confirmed cases in Thailand in December 2020. The *medium scenario* became unrealistic after the spread of the Alpha variant of concern (VoC) in Thailand in April 2021. With the

TABLE 12.1 Judgemental adjustments for tourism demand forecasts during the COVID-19 pandemic

	2020Q3	2020Q4	2021Q1	2021Q2	2021Q3	2021Q4
Mild scenario	5.00%	20.00%	35.00%	40.00%	45.00%	50.00%
Medium scenario	0.00%	0.00%	1.00%	5.00%	25.00%	40.00%
Severe scenario	0.00%	0.00%	0.05%	0.05%	0.05%	0.05%

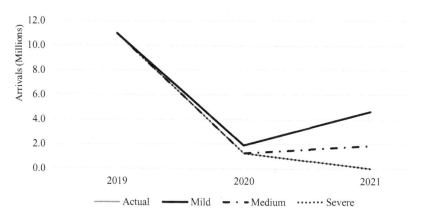

FIGURE 12.5 Scenario Forecasts during the COVID-19 Pandemic

depressing spread of the Delta VoC in Thailand in the latter half of 2021, the *severe scenario* is the most likely scenario in the case of tourist arrivals from mainland China to Thailand. As of November 2021, there were 8,528 tourist arrivals recorded from mainland China to Thailand (Thailand Ministry of Tourism & Sports, 2022), which made the estimated annual tourist arrivals from mainland China to Thailand around 10,000 – a number very close to the forecast in the *severe scenario*.

12.6 Conclusion and future directions

This chapter starts with the rationale for scenario forecasting and a brief review of the relevant literature. A scenario forecasting approach is usually adopted by researchers and practitioners when market uncertainty poses a significant challenge to forecasting practice. The forecasting results using this approach not only enrich the coverage of different scenarios during a crisis but also allow 'what if' analyses under different conditions. More specifically, the scenario forecasting approach provides multiple forecasts under different scenarios. The audience of the forecasting results can choose one or several forecasts according to their beliefs on the market trend and situation. Furthermore, the scenario forecasting approach allows the generation of forecasts under hypothetical scenarios, which is necessary in the evaluation of current or future policies and events.

The chapter then discusses different types of scenario setups in the scenario forecasting approach. According to the purpose of the investigation, the scenarios can be set to manifest plausible future trends (*future-oriented scenarios*) or to reflect the target conditions (*need-oriented scenarios*). To predict the plausible future scenarios, a *data-driven* approach can be adopted in which researchers either use data on previous crises and events (*history-based*) or feed a statistical model with the plausible trends of the major influencing factors of tourism demand (*factor-based*). These scenario setups have solid theoretical foundations, but may suffer from statistical fallacy during a crisis. Alternatively, an *experience-driven* approach can be used in which researchers determine the future scenarios by surveying experts for their opinion. The establishment of a *need-oriented* scenario purely depends on the purpose of the investigation. The chosen scenarios should reflect the conditions of the need, and researchers may need to justify the appropriateness and significance of their need. An *experience-driven* approach may be criticised for its subjectivity, but its flexibility and information richness can be useful in forecasting practice during a crisis. Researchers need to consider the purpose of the investigation, the availability of data, and the condition in the market to decide the scenario setup approach in scenario forecasting practices.

After setting up their scenarios, researchers can choose to conduct scenario forecasting through two approaches. In the *independent forecasting* approach, the tourism demand forecasts in each scenario should be generated separately. The benefit of this practice is that the causal relationship is preserved in all scenarios. The statistical estimates of the model can help researchers and the audience understand the link between tourism demand and its influential factors, as well as the dynamics of this link in different scenarios. Nevertheless, the causal relationship in such a model is usually established from historical data, which may fail to hold true during a crisis. Therefore, the *independent forecasting* approach is a better choice when the researcher is sure that the causal relationship remains relatively stable during the crisis (e.g., a financial crisis). Alternatively, in the *adjustment on baseline* approach, researchers generate a baseline forecast and develop scenario forecasts by adjusting the baseline forecast. This approach allows researchers to apply subjective adjustments to scenario forecasts. When the statistical model fails to capture market dynamics during a crisis (e.g., a pandemic), such judgemental adjustments can help researchers to include contextual information in their forecasts.

Although the different scenario setups and scenario forecasting approaches are introduced separately in this chapter, they can be combined. For example, researchers can further apply subjective adjustments on the forecasts from an *independent forecasting* approach to capture additional market fluctuations on top of statistical results. Researchers should always consider the needs and conditions of forecasting practice to determine the best approach.

The scenario forecasting approach also have limitations. One significant drawback of this approach is the probability of the scenarios. While all of the scenarios are considered plausible, their probabilities of occurrence are usually unclear. The audience often has to use their own information and beliefs to guess the most likely scenario. Wu, Cao, Wen, and Song (2021) adopted a TVP panel vector autoregressive model to estimate the probabilities of certain tourism demand scenarios. To the author's knowledge, their attempt was the first investigation on the probability of scenarios in the tourism demand forecasting literature. Further investigation is encouraged to explore the probability of more diverse scenarios.

Self-study questions

The outbreak of SARS in 2003 was a major global health crisis. First identified in Guangdong, China, the viral disease soon spread to Hong Kong and some regions/countries in Southeast Asia, such as Vietnam and Singapore. In the six months that the epidemic lasted (November 2002 to July 2003), the virus caused over 8,000 infections and more than 800 deaths globally. This epidemic also caused a significant drop in international travel, especially in Asia. The number of international tourist arrivals to Asia and the Pacific region declined by 9% to around 119 million in 2003 (UNWTO, 2004).

If you were appointed as the minister to oversee the tourism industry after the epidemic and were asked to produce scenario forecasts of international tourist arrivals to Thailand,

1   which scenario setup approach would you take and why?
2   which scenario forecasting approach would you use and why?
3   what advices would you give to the audience who reads your forecasts?

References

Fotiadis, A., Polyzos, S., & Huan, T. C. (2021). The good, the bad and the ugly on COVID-19 tourism recovery. *Annals of Tourism Research, 87,* 103117. https://doi.org/10.1016/j.annals.2020.103117.

Kourentzes, N., Saayman, A., Jean-Pierre, P., Provenzano, D., Sahli, M., Seetaram, N., & Volo, S. (2021). Visitor arrivals forecasts amid COVID-19: A perspective from the Africa team. *Annals of Tourism Research, 88,* 103197. https://doi.org/10.1016/j.annals.2021.103197.

Liu, A., Vici, L., Ramos, V., Giannoni, S., & Blake, A. (2021). Visitor arrivals forecasts amid COVID-19: A perspective from the Europe team. *Annals of Tourism Research, 88,* 103182. https://doi.org/10.1016/j.annals.2021.103182.

Mai, T., & Smith, C. (2018). Scenario-based planning for tourism development using system dynamic modelling: A case study of Cat Ba Island, Vietnam. *Tourism Management, 68,* 336–354. https://doi.org/10.1016/j.tourman.2018.04.005.

Our World in Data. (2020). *Policy responses to the coronavirus pandemic: International travel controls.* Retrieved August 31, 2020, from https://ourworldindata. org/policy-responsescovid#international-travel-controls.

Our World in Data. (2022). *COVID-19 data explorer.* Retrieved January 1, 2022, from https://ourworldindata.org/explorers/coronavirus-data-explorer.

Page, S., Song, H., & Wu, D. C. (2012). Assessing the impacts of the global economic crisis and swine flu on inbound tourism demand in the United Kingdom. *Journal of Travel Research, 51*(2), 142–153. https://doi.org/10.1177/0047287511400754.

PATA. (2019). *Asia Pacific visitor forecasts 2020–2024.* Pacific Asia Travel Association.

PATA. (2020). *Asia Pacific visitor forecasts 2021–2023.* Pacific Asia Travel Association. https://www.pata.org/research-qlv63g6n2dw/p/asia-pacific-visitor-forecasts-2021-2023-6s4ek-pfjzt.

PATA. (2021a). *Asia Pacific visitor forecasts 2021–2023 updates.* Pacific Asia Travel Association. https://www.pata.org/research-qlv63g6n2dw/p/asia-pacific-visitor-forecasts-2021-2023-updates.

PATA. (2021b). *Asia Pacific visitor forecasts 2021–2023 September 2021 updates.* Pacific Asia Travel Association. https://www.pata.org/research-qlv63g6n2dw/p/asia-pacific-visitor-forecasts-2021-2023-september-2021-updates.

Qiu, R. T. R., Wu, D. C., Dropsy, V., Petit, S., Pratt, S., & Ohe, Y. (2021). Visitor arrivals forecasts amid COVID-19: A perspective from the Asia and Pacific team. *Annals of Tourism Research, 88,* 103155. https://doi.org/10.1016/j.annals.2021.103155.

Reintinger, C., Berghammer, A., & Schmude, J. (2016). Simulating changes in tourism demand: A case study of two German regions. *Tourism Geographies, 18*(3), 233–257. https://doi.org/10.1080/14616688.2016.1169312.

Ricardo, H. D. R. B. (2015). *Forecasting tourism demand for Lisbon's region – A data mining approach,* MEGI paper, NOVA Information Management School, Universidade Nova de Lisboa.

Song, H., & Li, G. (2021). Editorial: Tourism forecasting competition in the time of COVID-19. *Annals of Tourism Research, 88,* 103198. https://doi.org/10.1016/j.annals.2021.103198.

Thailand Ministry of Tourism & Sports. (2022). *International tourist arrivals.* Retrieved February 18, 2022, from https://www.mots.go.th/mots_en/more_news_new.php?cid=330&page=2.

UN World Tourism Organization. (2004). *Tourism market trends, Asia and the Pacific. 2004 edition.* Retrieved April 6, 2022, from https://www.e-unwto.org/doi/epdf/10.18111/9789284407996.

UN World Tourism Organization. (2020a). *UNWTO world tourism barometer and statistical annex, August/September 2020.* Retrieved from https://doi.org/10.18111/wtobarometereng.

UN World Tourism Organization. (2020b). *UNWTO World Tourism Barometer, December 2020, 18*(7). Retrieved from https://doi.org/10.18111/wtobarometereng.

World Health Organization. (2020). *WHO coronavirus disease (COVID-19) dashboard.* Retrieved from https://covid19.who.int/table.

Wu, D. C., Cao, Z., Wen, L., & Song, H. (2021). Scenario forecasting for global tourism. *Journal of Hospitality & Tourism Research, 45*(1), 28–51. https://doi.org/10.1177/1096348020919990.

Zhang, H., Song, H., Wen, L., & Liu, C. (2021). Forecasting tourism recovery amid COVID-19. *Annals of Tourism Research, 87,* 103149. https://doi.org/10.1016/j.annals.2021.103149.

13

A WEB-BASED TOURISM FORECASTING SYSTEM

Xinyan Zhang

13.1 Introduction

Business organisations view forecasting as a semi-structured decision-making process. Typically, decision-makers and analysts combine judgement and quantitative analyses within a forecasting system. As a type of decision support system, a forecasting system is 'a set of procedures (typically computer based) that supports forecasting' (Armstrong, 2001: 784). Such systems increase forecasting performance through technology-facilitated human-system interactions (Fildes & Goodwin, 2013; Zellner, Abbas, Budescu, & Galstyan 2021). The growing use of forecasting applications in organisations indicates that forecasting systems are viable and important managerial tools (Fildes, Schaer, Svetunkov, & Yusupova, 2020).

Accurate forecasting is a crucial element of tourism planning and decision-making. When uncertainties and unpredictable factors increase, it becomes difficult for tourism organisations to predict demand. Over the past several decades, a wide range of advanced quantitative forecasting techniques, including time-series, econometric and artificial intelligence approaches, have been applied in tourism research. However, many tourism organisations are not familiar with or do not have the time to learn modern forecasting methods. Some large tourism practitioners achieve more accurate forecasts by using commercial forecasting systems or software; however, most commercial forecasting systems require significant investment and many do not use up-to-date forecasting methods (Fildes et al., 2020).

Although there is a large body of research on developing forecasting systems (Arvan, Fahimnia, Reisi, & Siemsen, 2019), relatively little effort has been devoted to examining whether forecasting systems meet the needs of

DOI: 10.4324/9781003269366-13

the tourism sector. Ghalia and Wang (2000) proposed an intelligent system to support judgemental forecasting and the knowledge of hotel managers (IS-JFK). Petropoulos, Patelis, Metaxiotis, Nikolopoulos and Assimako-poulos (2003) established a statistical and forecasting tourism information system (SFTIS) that analysed tourism data and supported inbound tourism demand forecasting. Judgemental interventions were not considered in their system design. In contrast, Croce and Wöber (2011) proposed an online judgemental forecasting platform that supported collaboration between tourism managers. The platform was not supported by quantitative methods. To improve forecasting accuracy, Song, Witt and Zhang (2008) and Song, Gao and Lin (2013) developed a web-based tourism demand forecasting system (TDFS). In that system, modern quantitative forecasting techniques were combined with judgemental inputs from academics and tourism industry stakeholders collected through Delphi surveys. Thus, this system bridged the gap between academics and industry practitioners in tourism forecasting (Wu, Song, & Shen, 2017).

The rest of this chapter describes the development process of the TDFS together with an introduction to the recent developments in information and communication technologies and their implications for the further development of a more advanced and self-adaptive TDFS.

13.2 Development of the web-based TDFS

The development of internet and web technologies in the early 2000s resulted in the transformation of many information systems from server-based systems to web-based systems. Many web-based applications have been developed for a range of decision-making problems. However, web-based forecasting systems in the tourism industry have received limited attention from researchers (Wu, Liu, Song, Liu, & Fu, 2019). One notable exception was a study by Song et al. (2008), who developed the web-based TDFS to generate more accurate tourism demand forecasts for Hong Kong. A web-based distributed computing platform was selected because this structure is convenient and allows contributions from a wide range of tourism forecasters and forecasting data, and thus promotes collaboration in tourism demand forecasting.

13.2.1 Forecasting process

The web-based TDFS adopted a two-stage rigorous forecasting process that combined advanced quantitative tourism forecasting techniques with judgemental interventions from a panel of experts and industry decision-makers. In the first stage, quantitative methods were applied to historical data to produce statistical forecasts that formed the initial input for the next stage. The second stage consisted of Delphi-type judgemental adjustments to the statistical forecasts made by a panel of tourism experts based on their experience and practical knowledge. The Delphi method was used because it allows a forecasting system to consider the contributions of a panel of geographically dispersed experts and to integrate these judgements with quantitative methods, achieving more accurate forecasting results (Song, Qiu, & Park, 2019).

The Delphi experts were chosen from three major categories – academia, industry (e.g., hotels, travel services, attractions, entertainment, transportation, catering, etc.) and the public sector (e.g., the Hong Kong Tourism Board). The Delphi surveys were regularly initiated by the system administrator, and each implementation consisted of multiple rounds until a consensus was reached among the panel of experts. The panel members were provided with the statistical forecasts produced by the quantitative models and asked to give their own estimates of the future values of tourism demand and the reasons for their answers. They provided this information independently through the system's web pages. To facilitate the judgemental adjustments, the system allowed the Delphi panel of experts to make their own 'what-if' scenario forecasts. At the end of each round, the administrator developed the adjusted forecasts and summarised them in the next round.

13.2.2 System design and development

Development of the TDFS began in 2006. When launched in 2008, TDFS (version 1) was written in ASP and hosted on a Microsoft IIS server. The architecture of the system is presented in Figure 13.1. The system used a

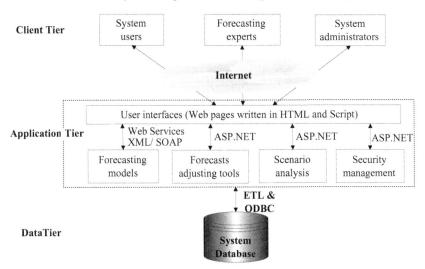

FIGURE 13.1 TDFS (version 1) architecture

three-tier architecture. The first/client tier contained the user interface in the form of a 'thin client' web browser. System clients including registered users, the Delphi panel of experts and system administrators could simultaneously access the web-based system independently through this tier. The clients' machines were not part of the web-based system, but interacted with the system when they visited the web server to input data or to conduct forecasting, analysing and decision-making.

The second/application tier consisted of the core of the architecture, called the system engine. This tier was the centre of the system. It conducted the procedures used by the forecasting panel members and controlled the information communication between various tiers. Specifically, the system engine contained a collection of software procedures written in ASP.NET on the Microsoft IIS server. The communication between the user interface and the engine was accomplished through HTTP. There were five main components to the procedures conducted by the system engine: security management, user interfaces, forecasting models, scenario analysis and forecast adjusting tools.

Although the TDFS (version 1) was successful, there was room for improvement. The quantitative models were estimated using third-party software (i.e., Eviews), and the system could not independently produce statistical forecasts. In 2009, the system was updated to the TDFS (version 2), which was an automatic and autonomous forecasting system. In the improved system, shown in Figure 13.2, the integration of the quantitative models was achieved using R, which is a free software package that can perform statistical analysis and produce graphics. Based on a formal computer language, R has tremendous flexibility. Other software packages,

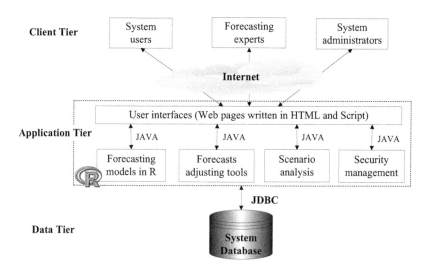

FIGURE 13.2 TDFS (version 2) architecture

such as Eviews, have simpler interfaces in terms of menus and forms, but often lack flexibility and cannot be customised and integrated into forecasting systems. The independent forecasting components that were integrated into TDFS version 2 were implemented using R. Then, the web-based TDFS accessed these components using Java server pages (JSP) and the Java programming language. The system server was transferred to an Apache Tomcat Server to allow communication between the web platform and the R environment.

13.2.3 System implementation and feedback

The TDFS was launched on 4 March 2008 and was used over the next decade to forecast tourism demand in Hong Kong. It remains the only web-based TDFS. Demand was measured by tourist arrivals, tourist expenditure and hotel room nights. The system attracted noticeable attention from tourism practitioners and organisations and was awarded the Dr Hai Sik Sohn Award by the Asia Pacific Tourism Association.

Experimental studies were carried out to evaluate the forecasting performance of the system. Lin (2013) evaluated the forecast accuracy of the system by comparing the forecasts with the actual tourist arrivals over the 2008Q1–2011Q4 period and found that the judgementally adjusted forecasts were more accurate than the statistical forecasts, with error reductions in the mean absolute percentage error (MAPE) for total arrival forecasts ranging from 11.1% to 45.7%. Even larger reductions in errors were found for the mainland market arrival forecasts (from 23.9% to 52.4%). Song et al. (2013) examined the forecast accuracy of the system for the 2010Q1–2011Q2 period. They found that the accuracy of the judgementally adjusted forecasts was higher than that of the statistical forecasts, with a reduction in MAPE from 8.86% to 8.02%, and thus concluded that forecasting performance significantly improved with the use of the Delphi technique. Similarly, Lin, Goodwin and Song (2014) found that the judgemental adjustments to the statistical forecasts improved forecast accuracy over the 2011Q2–2012Q2 period, and the mean MAPE decreased from 8.6% to 6.5% with the Delphi survey rounds.

In July and August 2012, semi-structured in-depth interviews were conducted with industry users and experts to collect feedback on the web-based TDFS and data on the industry's needs. Six industry users and experts who worked in tourist attractions, hotel chains, airlines and travel services in Hong Kong participated. The interview questions asked how they used the forecasts from the TDFS, how they viewed its judgemental forecasting adjustment process and what improvements they would like to see in the TDFS. The experts from the tourist attractions, hotel chains and travel services sectors reported that the forecasts generated by the TDFS were very helpful. One respondent said, 'Tourist arrivals is a very important piece of information for our hotel because it tells us about the trend'. Another respondent stated that the TDFS 'helps because I can use it as a reference for my own budgeting'. All of the experts agreed that judgementally adjusting the statistical forecasts was necessary. One respondent said, 'Judgemental forecasts and expert opinions are more important than the models themselves and the number the system is forecasting'. The respondents suggested the Delphi panel should be more open and diverse to expand the pool of experts, and they wanted to know who the panel experts are and to hear their detailed opinions.

13.3 Design of the cloud-based TDFS

Recent developments in information and communication technologies have increased the amount of available tourism-related data, with databases reaching the PB or even ZB size. Cloud computing has become a dominant platform for small businesses as well as major enterprises. In response to the opportunities created by this big data phenomenon, the web-based TDFS will be moved to a cloud-based platform that supports the adoption of more advanced forecasting approaches.

13.3.1 Cloud computing

Many tourism and hospitality systems are migrating to cloud platforms (Law, Sun, & Chan, 2020). Cloud-based computing architecture has the following strengths.

- Convenience
  System developers do not need trained personnel to maintain the hardware and the software. Equipment maintenance and software updates are done by the cloud service provider. Thus, the cloud services enable the system developers to focus on developing and improving the system.

- Cost
  Cost saving is one of the biggest benefits of cloud computing, as it does not require any investment in hardware. Furthermore, it is not necessary to purchase, install or update expensive software in-house, as these services are managed by the cloud service provider.

- Scalability
  System developers can scale up or scale down the computing/operation and storage needs quickly to suit dynamic situations.

- Simplicity and efficiency in terms of collaboration
Cloud services offer advanced online security. System developers can use cloud computing to give various clients (e.g., users, experts and administrators) access to the same files. Collaboration and information sharing are simpler and more efficient in a cloud environment than in a traditional web-based environment.

With its cost savings, scalability and collaborative benefits, cloud-based computing architecture will make TDFS more sustainable. System users and forecasting experts will be more willing to adopt a system that is sustainable, which will generate additional applications in tourism practices.

13.3.2 System architecture

The proposed system architecture is illustrated in Figure 13.3. In the system design, a browser/server architecture will be adopted to enhance the system's usability. The back-end layer will be developed in a Java

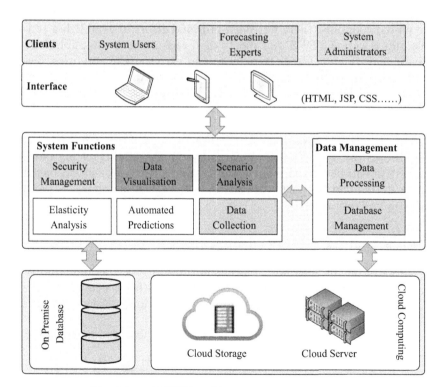

FIGURE 13.3 Cloud-based TDFS architecture

environment using the Spring framework to process data with Apache Spark, which is an open-source computing architecture for real-time processing of big data. Spark supports an extensive range of languages, including R, SQL, Python and Java. Spring is the world's most popular Java web framework.

The forecasting system will interact with the end-users through a dashboard and user interfaces at the front end. The React.js framework will be used to develop the front-end layer, together with HTML, JavaScript and CSS. Bootstrapping will be integrated to enable the user interfaces and the dashboard to adjust automatically.

Large internet-based datasets drawn from search engines and social media platforms will be automatically collected by Python crawler tools. These data will be processed and stored on the cloud. Data produced by the forecasting models and users' and experts' inputs will be saved in an on-site database.

13.4 Conclusion and future directions

Although tourism has become an increasingly important industry in the global economy, there has been minimal effort to establish a reliable and effective TDFS that meets the needs of both the public and private sectors as they seek to manage and plan tourism activities. Developed by the Hong Kong Polytechnic University's Public Policy Research Institute and School of Hotel and Tourism Management, the TDFS forecasting system elaborated in the chapter is the only web-based system in the world. After reviewing the development of the system, this chapter examines some of the proposed enhancements. In response to the opportunities created by the availability of big data, the system will be moved from a web-based platform to a cloud-based platform that can support more advanced forecasting approaches and industry collaborations.

Self-study questions

1 Discuss the reasons why judgement adjustments and quantitative analyses should be used jointly within a forecasting system.
2 List and elaborate the main components of a tourism demand forecasting system.
3 Discuss why many tourism and hospitality systems are migrating to cloud platforms.
4 What would be potential problems if the web-based TDFS described in this chapter were moved to a cloud-based platform?

References

Armstrong, J. S. (2001). *Principles of Forecasting: A Handbook for Researchers and Practitioners.* Boston, MA: Kluwer Academic Publishers. https://doi.org/10.1007/978-0-306-47630-3

Arvan, M., Fahimnia, B., Reisi, M., & Siemsen, E. (2019). Integrating human judgement into quantitative forecasting methods: A review. *Omega, 86*, 237–252. https://doi.org/10.1016/j.omega.2018.07.012

Croce, V., & Wöber, K. (2011). Judgemental forecasting support systems in tourism. *Tourism Economics, 17*(4), 709–724. https://doi.org/10.5367/te.2011.0062

Fildes, R., & Goodwin, P. (2013). Forecasting support systems: What we know, what we need to know. *International Journal of Forecasting, 2*(29), 290–294. https://doi.org/10.1016/j.ijforecast.2013.01.001

Fildes, R., Schaer, O., Svetunkov, I., & Yusupova, A. (2020). Survey: What's new in forecasting software? *Operations Research Management Science Today, 47*(4), 54–58. https://doi.org/10.1287/orms.2020.04.05

Ghalia, M. B., & Wang, P. P. (2000). Intelligent system to support judgmental business forecasting: The case of estimating hotel room demand. *IEEE Transactions on Fuzzy Systems, 8*(4), 380–397. https://doi.org/10.1109/91.868945

Law, R., Sun, S., & Chan, I. C. C. (2020). Hotel technology: A perspective article. *Tourism Review, 75*(1), 286–289. https://doi.org/10.1108/TR-05-2019-0150

Lin, V. S. (2013). Improving forecasting accuracy by combining statistical and judgmental forecasts in tourism. *Journal of China Tourism Research, 9*(3), 325–352. https://doi.org/10.1080/19388160.2013.812901

Lin, V. S., Goodwin, P., & Song, H. (2014). Accuracy and bias of experts' adjusted forecasts. *Annals of Tourism Research, 48*, 156–174. https://doi.org/10.1016/j.annals.2014.06.005

Petropoulos, C., Patelis, A., Metaxiotis, K., Nikolopoulos, K., & Assimakopoulos, V. (2003). SFTIS: A decision support system for tourism demand analysis and forecasting. *Journal of Computer Information Systems, 44*(1), 21–32. https://doi.org/10.1080/08874417.2003.11647548

Song, H., Gao, B. Z., & Lin, V. S. (2013). Combining statistical and judgmental forecasts via a web-based tourism demand forecasting system. *International Journal of Forecasting, 29*(2), 295–310. https://doi.org/10.1016/j.ijforecast.2011.12.003

Song, H., Qiu, R. T., & Park, J. (2019). A review of research on tourism demand forecasting: Launching the Annals of Tourism Research Curated Collection on tourism demand forecasting. *Annals of Tourism Research, 75*, 338–362. https://doi.org/10.1016/j.annals.2018.12.001

Song, H., Witt, S. F., & Zhang, X. (2008). Developing a web-based tourism demand forecasting system. *Tourism Economics, 14*(3), 445–468. https://doi.org/10.5367/000000008785633578

Wu, D. C., Song, H., & Shen, S. (2017). New developments in tourism and hotel demand modeling and forecasting. *International Journal of Contemporary Hospitality Management, 29*(1), 507–529. https://doi.org/10.1108/IJCHM-05-2015-0249

Wu, D. C., Liu, J., Song, H., Liu, A., & Fu, H. (2019). Developing a web-based regional tourism satellite account (TSA) information system. *Tourism Economics, 25*(1), 67–84. https://doi.org/10.1177/1354816618792446

Zellner, M., Abbas, A. E., Budescu, D. V., & Galstyan, A. (2021). A survey of human judgement and quantitative forecasting methods. *Royal Society Open Science, 8*(2), 201187. https://doi.org/10.1098/rsos.201187

EPILOGUE

This book comes following the profound impact of the COVID-19 pandemic on global tourism. Facing the challenges imposed by the pandemic, tourism practitioners are eagerly searching for suitable methods of forecasting future tourism demand, with the goal of planning for tourism recovery. The purpose of this book, therefore, is to introduce advanced econometric methods of tourism demand forecasting (Chapters 3–10). Particular attention is paid to the application of these methods in combination with qualitative approaches, such as the Delphi method (Chapter 11) and scenario analysis (Chapter 12), which are particularly useful for forecasting in times of crisis. Although this book mainly focuses on modern econometric models, tourism demand theory is the foundation of these models, which depict the relationships between tourism demand and its determinants.

The empirical results presented throughout this book suggest that different models have their own distinctive merits in explaining and forecasting tourism demand and that no single model performs best in all situations. These results align with the consensus in the literature. The autoregressive distributed lag model discussed in Chapter 3 is one of the most widely used econometric methods, in which demand relationships are dynamically modelled and demand elasticities are systematically estimated. The time-varying parameter model presented in Chapter 4 is a nonlinear model that relaxes the assumption of constant relationships between the dependent variable and the explanatory variables. Therefore, the time-varying parameter model has been shown to have superior forecasting performance when demand relationships vary over time due to gradual behavioural change in demand.

The global vector autoregressive models and spatiotemporal econometric models introduced in Chapters 5 and 6, respectively, are system models in which tourism demands at different destinations are assumed to be interrelated, with possible spillover effects. The global vector autoregressive models are well suited to modelling large-scale intraregional tourism demand with external shocks. Spatiotemporal econometric models consider both spatial and temporal dependencies in tourism demand across destinations. Because of these characteristics, the global vector autoregressive and spatiotemporal econometric models have been successfully used in tourism demand forecasting when the interdependency of tourist destinations is of concern to policymakers.

The rapid development of internet technologies has generated considerable amount of tourism-related search engine and online review data. As a result, tourism forecasters have started to use these data to forecast tourism demand. Such data contain timely information about tourists' behaviour or behavioural intentions, which helps improve forecasting accuracy. Online data are high-frequency (e.g., daily or hourly) data, whereas tourism demand variables tend to be low-frequency (e.g., monthly, quarterly or annual) data. Thus, mixed-frequency models (Chapter 7) are effective tools for combining variables with different frequencies in forecasting tourism demand without losing any valuable information provided by the online data.

Both hybrid modelling and forecast combinations (Chapters 8 and 10) aim to integrate the strengths of different models to obtain more accurate forecasts. The hybrid modelling approach integrates different models at different stages of the forecasting process, whereas forecast combination merges forecasts from different models with certain weighting strategies to reduce forecast error. The empirical results presented in Chapter 10 indicate that combined forecasts tend to be superior to individual model forecasts.

The majority of tourism demand forecasting studies have adopted point forecasts, which do not provide information on the associated uncertainties in the forecasts. Interval forecasts and density forecasts address this concern. In particular, the density forecasting method (Chapter 9) takes account of forecast uncertainties by providing a complete predictive distribution of forecasts, which facilitates confident decision-making.

Rather than combining forecasts from different quantitative models, judgemental forecasting (Chapter 11) innovatively integrates experts' judgements into quantitative forecasts to achieve more accurate forecasts when future uncertainties cannot be accounted for in quantitative models. Judgemental forecasting is particularly effective in the context of structural changes in tourism demand caused by major crises, such as the COVID-19 pandemic.

Scenario forecasting (Chapter 12) can also be viewed as probabilistic forecasting, in which different sets of forecasts, either point or interval forecasts, are generated separately according to different scenarios of interest. Scenario forecasting is particularly useful when an unexpected crisis occurs, such as the COVID-19 pandemic. In such circumstances, it is very difficult to predict tourism demand using econometric models alone, as the factors that affect tourism demand are obsolete during the crisis. The scenarios are normally formulated according to the evolution of the crisis in light of the need for policy formulation and business decision-making.

To facilitate public access to tourism demand forecasts, it is important to develop online forecasting systems using internet technologies. The web-based tourism demand forecasting system introduced in Chapter 13 is an early attempt in this area.

In addition to demonstrating the applications of various forecasting techniques, this book discusses possible future research directions, which are broadly summarised as follows. The first is the use of tourism big data in future studies. Four types of big data have been applied in tourism demand forecasting, web search and website traffic data, social media statistics, online textual data and online photo data. Both textual and photo data contain a wide variety of useful information for both modelling and forecasting, but research on how to extract the information needed to improve forecasting accuracy remains scant, and the issue deserves further exploration. Second, tourism demand forecasting under uncertainty/ crisis is gaining increasing attention. Probabilistic forecasts, such as density forecasts, interval forecasts, event probability forecasts and scenario forecasts, are well suited to this situation, as they provide comprehensive information for evidence-based decision-making under different levels of uncertainty and risk. Meanwhile, risk forecasting may also be a future research direction in which the volatility of tourism demand is the focus of prediction. Third, integrating forecasts from different models is an important future research direction. Hybrid models that integrate forecasts from different models during different forecasting stages, and across different components of tourism demand, are worth exploring. In terms of combination forecasts, various weighting strategies and interval or density combinations are possible avenues of exploration. It would also be valuable to examine whether different ensemble techniques can lead to forecasting performance improvement. Finally, from a practical perspective, the development of automated and self-adaptive forecasting systems using Web 4.0 technologies is a desirable pursuit. Such systems would provide convenient and user-friendly platforms not only for forecasting information consumption but also for government policy and business decision-making.

With the COVID-19 pandemic evolving into an epidemic and the metaphorical light at the end of the tunnel emerging, we, as enthusiastic travellers and forecasters, predict that international travel will resume and grow in the very near future!

Doris Chenguang Wu
Gang Li
Haiyan Song

INDEX

Note: **Bold** page numbers refer to tables and *Italic* page numbers refer to figures.

Printed in the United States
by Baker & Taylor Publisher Services